Promoting

Promoting Democracy in the Americas

Edited by
Thomas Legler
Sharon F. Lean
Dexter S. Boniface

The Johns Hopkins University Press
Baltimore

© 2007 The Johns Hopkins University Press
All rights reserved. Published 2007
Printed in the United States of America on acid-free paper
9 8 7 6 5 4 3 2 1

The Johns Hopkins University Press
2715 North Charles Street
Baltimore, Maryland 21218-4363
www.press.jhu.edu

Library of Congress Cataloging-in-Publication Data
Promoting democracy in the Americas / edited by Thomas Legler,
Sharon F. Lean, and Dexter S. Boniface.
    p.   cm.
Includes bibliographical references and index.
ISBN-13: 978-0-8018-8675-1 (alk. paper)
ISBN-13: 978-0-8018-8676-8 (pbk. : alk. paper)
ISBN-10: 0-8018-8675-9 (alk. paper)
ISBN-10: 0-8018-8676-7 (pbk. : alk. paper)
1. Democracy—Latin America. 2. Latin America—Politics and
government—1980— I. Legler, Thomas F., 1967—   II. Lean, Sharon Frances,
1967—   III. Boniface, Dexter S., 1973—
JL966.P753 2007
320.98—dc22
2006103128

A catalog record for this book is available from the British Library.

Special discounts are available for bulk purchases of this book. For more information, please contact Special Sales at 410-516-6936 or specialsales@press.jhu.edu.

Contents

Foreword

In 1993 the Inter-American Dialogue asked me to lead an inquiry into the role external actors could play in consolidating, deepening, and defending democracy in the Western Hemisphere. As the animator of this inquiry, the Dialogue seemed particularly appropriate, because it is an institution inspired by liberal democratic values. A think tank and a formal network of influential North and Latin Americans stretching ideologically from the center-left to center-right, the Dialogue works to identify and promote policy initiatives its members see as advancing both state (some might use the word "national") interests and human welfare throughout the hemisphere. Democracy in turn is presumed to serve both interests and welfare.

The timing also seemed appropriate. After experiencing more than two decades of military-dominated governments, many of which did not even pretend to be democratic, much less liberal, by 1993 Latin America together with Eastern Europe appeared in the forefront of a move to democratic government famously named by Harvard professor Samuel Huntington as "the third wave." Why was it washing over the hemisphere at that moment? Like many other observers, I saw a number of factors at work. The Cold War was over. On the Latin right, while fascists remained fascists, the merely conservative no longer feared the loss of power and privilege through Marxist revolutions, just as their collaborators in Washington, D.C., had ceased to fear what they had previously perceived as a southern flanking movement encouraged, if not directed by Moscow, to advance its broad strategic interests. Moreover, having waged the Cold War in the name of liberty while often colluding in its suppression, right-wing tyranny being deemed the lesser evil to leftist governments, Washington seemed intent on bringing its policies more in line with its rhetoric and, one might argue, the natural ideological inclinations of the United States polity. As it had once reinforced the natural appeal to conservatives of authoritarian solutions to the perennial problem of order in societies marked by chronic injustice, Washington now lent its influence to democratic ones.

The terrain on which its influence fell was auspicious, not only because the middle and upper classes no longer feared revolution but also because, during the era of state terror, their normal insulation from hyperviolence by state agents had been removed. With the risk of revolution ended, the restoration of legal restraints on executive authority and, more generally, of a stable democratic system for the maintenance of order again served their class interests.

On the Latin left, meanwhile, the experience of state terrorism in the service of the right had sharpened appreciation of bourgeois political values like free speech and due process (and the institutions of democracy with which they are associated), while the ruthless efficiency of repression by military establishments backed by the power of the United States had dissolved utopian dreams.

Another force driving the democratic wave, I suspected, was the heightened prestige of market-based solutions to the reduction of poverty, a defining concern of the left whether in Latin America or anywhere else, stemming from the East Asian experience: first Japan, then Taiwan, Singapore, and South Korea, then Thailand, Malaysia, and Indonesia and, finally, China, once the iconic statist development model. Of course, as China was demonstrating, a regime did not have to be democratic in order to employ market mechanisms. Still, while there was precedent for the use of such mechanisms by undemocratic regimes, there was no precedent for a democracy not using them. The East Asian experience at least demonstrated that democracies and their invariable concomitant—an economic model fueled by the individual desire to consume and employing market-set prices to coordinate with relative efficiency the supply and demand for goods, services, and capital—could generate growth while reducing poverty.

Whatever its ultimate explanation (the origins of shifts in the zeitgeist being invariably speculative), the convergence of Latin elites and counterelites toward democratic institutional solutions to social conflict and human needs (and a parallel convergence of popular opinion), along with the prospect for a measure of success in mitigating the social deficits Latin societies had been accumulating over most of their respective histories, provided some grounds for optimism about the sustainability of the democratic renewal. Liberal scholars in the United States who studied Latin America were constitutionally committed to such a renewal not only because participation in political decision making is itself a human right but primarily because other liberal values like free speech, association, and freedom from arbitrary and cruel punishment have never had much traction in any institutional environment other than democracy.

They were not, however, constitutionally committed to optimism about democracy's sustainability south of the Rio Grande. For they were sensible of the size of the social deficit in relation to the resource-raising capacity of most Latin states, of the inefficiency of Latin state bureaucracies, of the enduring resistance of the Latin upper classes even to minor reallocations of income much less wealth, of the historically accumulated weaknesses of systems of justice, of weak party structures, and of the military establishment's enduring sense of itself rather than constitutional courts as the ultimate arbiters of the acceptable limits of socioeconomic and constitutional change and the ultimate guarantors of social peace. They were sensible as well of the problematical impact of global economic integration on employment and welfare among the less privileged social groups.

If a democratic politics could not clarify, normalize, and implement rational policy responses to the majority's demands for enhanced welfare and opportunity or if in trying to do so it alienated the upper classes, how long could a democratic politics survive? And who would care about its survival in form if its substance were so hollowed out that it could not contribute substantially to quotidian human welfare? Without such a contribution, nondemocratic competitors for popular mandates would again emerge. Among the casualties of the resulting attenuation of restraints on the means for waging social conflict would be core civil and political rights.

Being sensitive to the fragility of the new democratic project and committed to its success, scholars of the liberal persuasion were drawn naturally to an inquiry into the ways in which external actors of all kinds—affluent states, intergovernmental organizations, nongovernmental organizations, and civil society organizations—could contribute to that project's success. So I had no difficulty in recruiting a team of distinguished collaborators. The result of our collaboration was published in 1996 under the arguably melodramatic title *Beyond Sovereignty.*

The title implied one of the inquiry's conclusions, namely that large gaps had opened in the traditional resistance of Latin American elites to any effort by external agents to assess, much less to influence, their national political institutions and processes. For decades the generality of Latin states, realistically alert to the threat of U.S. dictation, had sought to limit the thrust of

U.S. power by constructing a hemispheric norm of nonintervention in part by embedding it in the Charter of the Organization of American States (OAS). Yet by rhetorically grounding hemispheric solidarity in a shared commitment to democracy and human rights (the American Declaration on the Rights and Duties of Man [*sic*] actually preceded the UN General Assembly's Universal Declaration of Human Rights), the OAS member states were laying the normative foundation for challenges to absolutist interpretations of the doctrine of nonintervention. The UN Charter contains the same tension between the post-Westphalian notion that sovereignty implies a state's absolute discretion in its choice of means for maintaining social order and allocating political power, on the one hand, and the post–World War II claim, heralded a century and a half earlier by the declarations accompanying the American and French revolutions, that all human beings held rights that the state could not trump.

In the early going after World War II, many states, probably a majority, continued to talk as if sovereignty remained trumps. Whenever their treatment of their citizens was challenged, they would decry "intervention in internal affairs." And yet, at the same time, they endorsed or at least grudgingly acquiesced in the development of institutions for monitoring state compliance with human rights norms, albeit trying, in some cases, to emasculate those institutions at birth. By the time I became a member of the Inter-American Commission on Human Rights (CIDH) of the Organization of American States in 1976, the balance of normative power between human rights and absolutist interpretations of nonintervention was already beginning to shift, a fact evidenced by the very existence of a commission with a mandate to consider not only individual complaints of human rights violations but also the general situation of human rights in a member state and to submit reports on these matters to the OAS's highest political body. While the advocates for unreviewable national discretion were then on the defensive, they were not yet in headlong retreat. Some states continued, in the name of national sovereignty, to resist requests from the commission for permission to conduct on-site investigations.

By the end of my second term in 1983, however, one could see retreat, albeit a fighting one. Invocations of sovereignty as a defense against charges of human rights violations seemed less frequent both at the OAS and the UN. Instead states challenged the facts or claimed to be responding to transient states of emergency or declared themselves victims of double standards and political bias. This effort to evade rather than confront challenges to state behavior came to predominate in cases where the violations charged concerned core rights of personal security: the rights not to be tortured, summarily executed, or arbitrarily punished or to be discriminated against on the basis of ascriptive traits like race and ethnicity. Where it came to political rights, however, some consequential states continued to choose confrontation —that is, resistance on principle, not facts. Mexico, a champion of the CIDH in its exposure of terror campaigns (thereby burnishing the ideological legitimacy of a one-party regime with revolutionary roots), led this resistance. (It was also a haven for refugees from terror regimes like those in the Southern Cone of South America.) Both within and outside the commission, the Mexican regime claimed immunity from external scrutiny of its internal political arrangements and went on so claiming until it too decided to risk riding rather than resisting the global democratic wave. Today, all OAS members subscribe to the position that democracy is a sine qua non for recognition of a government's legitimacy, and external monitoring of election procedures has become commonplace.

In noting this ongoing movement of ideas and practices, *Beyond Sovereignty* was on target in its substance and an exaggeration in form only if the title were read to imply the coming collapse of sovereignty. All of the authors believed that borders would continue to matter and that states would retain a considerable measure of substantive autonomy in the organization of their political, economic, and social structures.

The conclusion of a decade since the publication of *Beyond Sovereignty* seems a natural point at which to take a new snapshot of the continuing effort to defend and to deepen democracy in the hemisphere. And so I welcome the project of which this book is the happy culmination. Its many excellent essays speak well for themselves, and the authors and editors provide an excellent synthesis. Collectively they draw on the past decade's events to illuminate, more clearly than our 1996 volume did, the complexity of projects for the defense and deepening of democracy in countries marked by all of the features that had qualified my optimism when I was writing my synthesizing chapter for the earlier volume.

The present volume documents the proliferation of national, intergovernmental, and nongovernmental actors in the defense-of-democracy project and their apparent success in a number of cases in averting a downward spiral of social conflict into massive violence. What they also demonstrate, however, is the still limited role of outside actors in fostering revision of the basic national bargain over the allocation of power, wealth, social status, and economic opportunity that is required for democracies to function. As a number of the authors note, at least implicitly, despite the progressive strengthening in the hemisphere of a norm of democratic legitimacy and of agents with a remit to defend it, the obstacles for doing so effectively may also have multiplied. One of the largest ones, ironically, is the consciousness of rights and of some potential for vindicating them that has grown among masses of the population in many countries long excluded from effective citizenship. This transformation of consciousness has been strongest in the Andean countries of South America with their relatively large indigenous populations, but the phenomenon is a more general one.

Anyone concerned with human rights must applaud when long-repressed people lift their heads and find voice. But in 2007 as in 1996 the question remains whether political institutions in weak states with huge social deficits can handle the surge of new demands being made on them. After all, even when the poor were more easily excluded from the political game, most Latin states experienced crises of democracy because of their inability to satisfy sufficiently the competitive claims of those who could participate. Do the ideational, institutional, normative, and material conditions of the post–Cold War era constitute an environment sufficiently more propitious than the one that led to the breakdown of democracies or aborted efforts to establish them in many hemispheric states during the Cold War? The answer to that question remains hidden in the mists of the decade that lies ahead.

Tom Farer

Preface

Our collaboration on this volume began at the International Congress of the Latin American Studies Association in Las Vegas, Nevada, in October 2004, for which Sharon Lean, with the help of David Goldberg, had organized a set of panels entitled "International and Civic Influences Shaping Democracy in the Americas." At these panels the editors recognized a common interest in finding new, more encompassing ways to look at a phenomenon that has been a fixture of the Latin American and Caribbean political landscape for nearly three decades now: the region's ongoing, often problematic, internationalized processes of democratization. Our respective research interests (democracy defense and promotion by the Organization of American States, international election monitoring, and emerging regional democracy norms) underscored for us the importance of international and transnational agents in contemporary processes of political change in the Americas. We resolved to explore possibilities for future collaboration.

The next formative step was the organization of a workshop called "The Transnational Dimensions of Democracy in the Americas," hosted by Tom Legler at Mount Allison University in June 2005. Twenty-one scholars from Canada, Mexico, and the United States participated, representing subfields of comparative politics and international relations. From this event, eleven papers ultimately found their way into this volume along with two additional requested papers. At Mount Allison, we identified a significant gap in the existing literature regarding our teaching needs. While many of us continued to use Tom Farer's seminal volume *Beyond Sovereignty* (1996) in the classroom to teach about the international dimensions of Latin American democratization processes, we all agreed there was a need for an up-to-date treatment of the subject.

The initial optimism surrounding international democracy promotion in the 1990s had been replaced by skepticism in the new millennium. New types of democratic crises were emerging at the same time that the range of international mechanisms and actors engaged in democracy promotion was expanding. We were convinced that there was a need not only to document achievements but also to pose critical questions about the democracy promotion record. How effective have international and transnational actors been in their democracy promotion efforts in the Americas? What type of democracy are they promoting? How transnational are recent democratization processes? These are the questions that underpin the chapters in this volume.

As in any undertaking of this size and ambition, we have incurred a number of debts of gratitude along the way. A Standard Research Grant and an Aid to Occasional Scholarly Conferences Grant from the Social Sciences and Humanities Research Council of Canada as well as generous support from Mount Allison University financed the June 2005 workshop. Sharon Lean's and Dexter Boniface's home institutions of Colgate University (Sharon's institutional home for the 2004-5 academic year), Wayne State University, and Rollins College extended their hospitality for necessary editorial meetings as we worked collectively to conceptualize the project and eventually put the volume together.

We are indebted to a series of colleagues and friends whose ideas, feedback, and encouragement helped shape the volume: Bruce Bagley, Lesley Burns, Max Cameron, Aroa El Horani, Antonio Franceschet, Susan Franceschet, Yvon Grenier, Annette Hester, Aida Hozic, Pamela Martin, Shelley McConnell, Gerry Munck, Ken Ozmon, Anne Pitcher, Pablo Policzer, John Read, Hans Peter Schmitz, Munir Squires, Lavinia Stan, and Robert Summerby-Murray. In addition to contributing a chapter, Arturo Santa-Cruz joined us for some early editorial meetings and provided important formative suggestions. Tom Farer was wonderfully encouraging of our project. We are grateful to an anonymous reviewer for endorsing the book and for most useful feedback. Several students and staff also helped to shape this project. Raine Phythian and Emily Shepard were the logistical backbone of the Mount Allison workshop. Ivonne Soler and Anthony Talarico provided candid feedback to help make our text accessible to a student audience. Claire Gilchrist provided invaluable assistance in producing the final manuscript.

The opportunity to collaborate on this volume has been both demanding and rewarding and was made all the more enjoyable by the surprisingly seamless collaboration among the three editors, each of whom shouldered an equal share of the work in this project. We are grateful for the spontaneous discovery of each other's complementary strengths and for friendships now cemented.

We extend our sincere thanks to Henry Tom, Claire McCabe Tamberino, Brian R. MacDonald, and the Johns Hopkins University Press. Lastly, thanks to our spouses and family members who supported us throughout this entire endeavor. Thank you, Ann, Roanne, Jane and David, Greg and little Gillian.

Acronyms and Abbreviations

AD	Democratic Action party (Venezuela)
AHPEL	Association Haitienne pour des Elections Libres
ALADI	Latin American Integration Association
CAFTA	Central American Free Trade Agreement
CARICOM	Caribbean Community
CEP	Provisional Electoral Council (Haiti)
CIDA	Canadian International Development Agency
CIDH	Comisión Interamericana de Derechos Humanos
CIIR	Catholic Institute for International Relations
CNE	National Electoral Council (Venezuela)
COHA	Council on Hemispheric Affairs
COPEI	Committee for Independent Political Electoral Organization (Venezuela)
DFAIT	Department of Foreign Affairs and International Trade (Canada)
DMO	domestic monitoring organization
DPD	Department for the Promotion of Democracy
DR-CAFTA	Dominican Republic–Central American Free Trade Agreement
EDI	Electoral Democracy Index
EERP	Emergency Economic Recovery Plan (Haiti)
FAC	Foreign Affairs Canada
FTAA	Free Trade Area of the Americas
IADC	Inter-American Democratic Charter
ICIO	International Coalition of Independent Observers (Haiti)
IDB	Inter-American Development Bank
IFES	International Foundation for Election Systems
IFI	international financial institution

IGO	intergovernmental organization
IHRLG	International Human Rights Law Group
IMF	International Monetary Fund
INGO	international nongovernmental organization
IRI	International Republican Institute
LASA	Latin American Studies Association
MERCOSUR	Southern Common Market
MINUGUA	United Nations Verification Mission in Guatamala
MINUSTAH	United Nations Stabilization Mission in Haiti
NAFTA	North American Free Trade Agreement
NDI	National Democratic Institute for International Affairs
NED	National Endowment for Democracy
NGO	nongovernmental organization
OAS	Organization of American States
PDVSA	Petróleos de Venezuela, Sociedad Anónima
PVT	parallel vote tabulation
TAN	transnational advocacy network
TCC	The Carter Center
UN	United Nations
UNDP	United Nations Development Program
UN-EAD	United Nations Electoral Assistance Division
UPD	Unit for the Promotion of Democracy
USAID	United States Agency for International Development
WOLA	Washington Office on Latin America

Promoting Democracy in the Americas

CHAPTER ONE

The International and Transnational Dimensions of Democracy in the Americas

Thomas Legler, Sharon F. Lean, and Dexter S. Boniface

Since the onset of the so-called third wave of democratic transitions and the end of the Cold War, Latin America has experienced a proliferation of international and transnational pro-democracy activity by state, intergovernmental, and nonstate actors. This has given rise to a situation where the outcomes of "domestic" processes of political change are increasingly shaped by a host of transnational and international actors.

For example, in Haiti, on February 29, 2004, President Jean-Bertrand Aristide was ousted after months of growing rebel activity. This act occurred with the alleged complicity of the Bush administration. A loose transnational network of advocates in favor of restoring Aristide to power formed quickly. It included supporters of Aristide's party Fanmi Lavalas in Haiti, African American members of the U.S. Congress, members of the overseas Haitian diaspora, and leftist groups in North America and Europe. It could also potentially be understood to include sympathetic governments like those of Jamaica and South Africa and the multilateral organization of the Caribbean Community (CARICOM). This loose network faced another powerful transnational network opposed to Aristide that included local economic elites in Haiti, other members of the Haitian diaspora abroad, significant elements within the U.S. government and the Republican Party, and the governments of France and Canada. Between these actors, the Organization of American States (OAS), the United Nations Security Council and the United Nations Stabilization Mission in Haiti (MINUSTAH), and a peace-keeping force led by Brazil participated actively to restore order and to organize elections after Aristide's departure. Ultimately, Aristide did not return, and after several postponements, elections were held in early 2006.

In Venezuela after an aborted coup attempt against Hugo Chávez in April 2002, a tripartite mission comprised of the Organization of American States, the Carter Center, and the United Nations Development Program (UNDP) convened to facilitate a democratic dialogue between the Chávez government and the opposition umbrella organization Coordinadora Democrática. Both pro-government and pro-opposition factions in Venezuela rallied a range of other supporters from outside the country in their efforts to overcome the political crisis. These outside actors included the international media, the U.S. government, the Cuban government, a binational, multipartisan group of Venezuelan and U.S. congressional members called the Boston Group, and a group of representatives of interested states (Brazil, the United States, Chile, Mexico, Portugal, and Spain) convened by the OAS secretary-general under the moniker "The Group of Friends." The transnationalized debate about how to move the Venezuelan political situation forward stretched out over a two-year period. After a long and bumpy mediation process, the tripartite OAS–Carter Center–UNDP mission furnished technical assistance and monitored the August 2004 presidential recall referendum, which confirmed Chávez's mandate.

In Nicaragua in 2005 embattled President Enrique Bolaños turned to the U.S. government and the OAS for assistance in countering the efforts of an unexpected alliance between political figures from opposite sides of the political spectrum: former Liberal president Arnoldo Alemán and former Sandinista president Daniel Ortega. These two influential actors had conspired in an attempt to curb executive powers, reinterpret the Constitution, and end Bolaños's presidency before he had completed a full term in office. With the consent of the Bolaños government, in June 2005 the OAS invoked the Inter-American Democratic Charter (IADC; see appendix B). As a first step, it authorized a special diplomatic mission led by the OAS secretary-general José Miguel Insulza to promote dialogue between the rival elites. Insulza subsequently appointed Dante Caputo, former Argentinean foreign minister, to facilitate the process. Concurrently, a new transnational nonstate actor comprised of former presidents, prime ministers, senior government officials, and their advisers called the Friends of the Democratic Charter undertook several behind-the-scenes fact-finding visits in support of an internationally mediated solution to the crisis. By October 2005 a political compromise was forged that defused the crisis and allowed Bolaños to serve out the remainder of his term.

The lesson of cases like Haiti, Venezuela, and Nicaragua is that we cannot rightly characterize such moments of political crisis and change in the Americas as purely domestic processes. As we argue in this volume, however, even in extreme cases of outside influence such as Haiti, neither are these processes wholly internationally driven. The contributions in this volume stress that international and transnational phenomena are integral to understanding democratization in places undergoing transition, the preservation of democracy in places that have already adopted democratic institutions, and the persistence of democratic deficits in some arenas.

Understanding the Dimensions of Democratization

A tradition of comparative politics scholarship on democratization accords a marginal role to international factors in the analysis of transitions to democracy (O'Donnell, Schmitter, and Whitehead 1986; Linz and Stepan 1996). In the concluding volume of *Transitions from Authoritarian Rule,* Guillermo O'Donnell and Philippe Schmitter (1986, 19) state that "domestic factors play a predominant role in the transition." Yet scholars now notice a qualitative shift in international relations and the regional democratization problematic, particularly since the end of the Cold War. This shift is noticeable in terms of both overall international engagement in democratization processes and the degree of influence that international actors appear to have over outcomes (Pridham 1991; Lutz and Sikkink 2001, 296). Karen Remmer (1996, 288), comparing democracy promotion in Haiti, El Salvador, Chile, and Peru in the early 1990s, writes: "From a historical perspective, what stands out about the contemporary situation is less the conditioning impact of domestic forces than the extraordinary capacity of outside actors to shift the political momentum in the direction of democratic options and to maintain that momentum through time in the face of apparently insuperable obstacles and repeated setbacks."

The increase in international engagement in and influence over domestic democratization processes, now widely documented (Goldman and Douglas 1998; Carothers 1999; Cox, Ikenberry, and Inoguchi 2000a; Halperin and Galic 2005; Pevehouse 2005; Cooper and Legler 2006) demands a new set of analytical tools for understanding the mechanics of democratization. To begin, we must recognize that the debate has moved beyond assertions about the relative weight and primacy of domestic versus international variables in democratization. Grugel (1999a, 157) has proposed that just as the boundaries between "internal" and "external" are increasingly blurred, it is no longer useful to separate domestic from international factors in our explanations of democratization. In Remmer's words (1996, 289), "the key theoretical issue is not the relative importance of domestic as opposed to international variables but, rather, varying patterns of interaction across time and space." Whitehead, once practically a "nativist" himself,[1] concurs: "it may be artificial to dichotomize the analysis into domestic and international elements. Although there will always be some purely domestic and some exclusively international factors involved, most of the analysis will contain a tangle of both elements. In the contemporary world there is no such thing as democratization in one country, and perhaps there never was" (Whitehead 1996, 24).

We propose that the traditional dichotomy between "domestic" and "international" factors, reinforced by the artificial separation between comparative politics and international relations, is often analytically inaccurate and misleading, particularly when applied to contemporary democratization processes in the Americas. Contemporary scholarship that blends comparative politics and international relations scholarship pushes our study in the direction of a trichotomy with overlapping categories: domestic, international, and transnational. A key insight has to do with the problematization of the international. Whereas "international" once served as a catchall category for all actors and influences emanating from beyond a country's borders, it is now increasingly confined in meaning to the realm of states and their foreign affairs, as in a traditional realist conception. Meanwhile, the idea of transnational politics as distinct from the domestic or international has become an increasingly important area of inquiry (Risse-Kappen 1995; O'Brien et al. 2000; Tarrow 2001, 2005; Khagram, Riker, and Sikkink 2002; H. P. Schmitz 2004).

What do we mean by transnational? In the simplest sense, Keohane and Nye (1971, xii–xvi) define transnational relations as "regular interactions across boundaries when at least one actor is non-state." This definition helps differentiate transnational from interstate relations; however, it is so broad as to include virtually all other kinds of cross-border human activity (Risse 2002, 255).

For our purposes, the term transnational requires greater specification. It emphasizes the role of nonstate actors in international relations, but in our view it does not diminish the importance of states (Tarrow 2001, 2–3). States engage in transnational politics just as nonstate actors do; they are enmeshed in transnational politics just as nonstate actors are.

Our transnational approach pays particular attention to the role of norms and ideas in politics. It recognizes that regional norms of democracy are socially constructed, and their construction is not contained within the borders of individual states. They are defined through formal, relatively bounded processes, such as the periodic Summits of the Americas in which the thirty-four heads of state and government from the hemisphere meet to discuss issues of mutual interest, and also through relatively unbounded practices, such as the transnational cybercommunications and support network that grew up around the Zapatista movement in Chiapas in Mexico from 1994 onward (Olesen 2005).

Furthermore, we consider democratization to be transnational in that it plays out in a spatial context that is not confined within the boundaries of the democratizing state in question. Political change is fueled by what occurs in key political centers such as Washington, D.C., at regional multilateral meetings, and even within the quasi-spatial dimension of the Internet. Following the path-breaking work of Keck and Sikkink (1998) on transnational advocacy, there is increasing recognition that political change can often be generated by domestic opponents of intransigent governments when they extend their struggle for democracy and human rights abroad.

In summary, the contributors to this volume view democracy in the Americas as a process that is best characterized as transnational, and not dichotomized as domestic or international. When we speak of the transnational dimensions of democracy in the Americas, we are referring to the cross-border actions of networks of state, multilateral, and nonstate actors, the transnational development of regional democracy norms, and the transnational spatial context in which democratic practices are established.

Beyond Sovereignty? Emerging Democratization Issues in the New Millennium

In 1996 Tom Farer published a pioneering edited volume entitled *Beyond Sovereignty: Collectively Defending Democracy in the Americas*. In this text, Farer and a collection of notable authors considered the dynamics of the democratic wave that swept Latin America between 1978 and the mid-1990s. It was the first systematic attempt to examine the interplay between domestic and international actors in processes of democratization in the Americas.[2] The authors concluded that external actors played a significant role in the regional shift from authoritarian government to electoral democracy and that tolerance for the participation of international actors in domestic political processes increased markedly during this time (Farer 1996b, 4). Farer's contention is that these dual phenomena—the increased international role in fostering democratic transitions and increased acceptance of such a role—resulted in the shrinking of state sovereignty.

Now, a decade since the publication of the Farer volume, two important sets of changes have occurred that warrant a new, updated treatment of the subject. First, the empirical record has changed. While there are some continuities, the current regional democratization problematic is markedly different from the situation that prevailed in the mid-1990s. During the 1990s, the threat of coups d'etat was a prime concern for still young democracies as evidenced by the illegal seizure of power in Haiti in 1991 and attempted coups in Venezuela in 1992 and Paraguay in 1996. The OAS was prompted to sign the Santiago Commitment to Democracy in 1991 and create Resolution 1080 (see appendix A) to respond to coups. The advent of the self-coup or *autogolpe,* evidenced in Peru (1992) and Guatemala (1993), created a new worry for governments and multilateral organizations in the region.[3] Analysis in the Farer volume reflected a general optimism regarding the prospects for global democracy in the period following the Cold War, highlighting innovation in international responses to the coups and self-coups of the early 1990s.

By the end of the decade, however, authoritarian backsliding by democratically elected leaders had joined coups and self-coups as a widespread threat to democracy. The dismantling of Peruvian democracy under the twice democratically elected president Alberto Fujimori (1990–2000) and his security chief Vladimiro Montesinos stands out as a particularly illustrative case of authoritarian regression. Guillermo O'Donnell (1994) calls this phenomenon "delegative democracy," wherein incumbent, elected presidents maintain their popular legitimacy through vertical accountability (elections), while simultaneously eroding horizontal accountability by circumventing legislatures, ruling instead through presidential decrees and compromising the autonomy of the judiciary by stacking courts with hand-picked appointees. In a similar vein, various authors point to the emergence in the Americas of "electoral authoritarianism" (Levitsky and Way 2002; Schedler 2006). The problem of authoritarian backsliding catalyzed the OAS to create the Inter-American Democratic Charter in 2001 and forced scholars to question early evaluations of the efficacy of regional democracy promotion.

Popular discontent with the quality of third-wave democracy in the region surfaced in the 1990s. Scholars began to employ the term "low-intensity democracy" to describe situations in which elections occurred with regularity and relative fairness, but popular citizenship was limited (Gills, Rocamora, and Wilson 1993; Robinson 1996). By the end of the decade, surveys across the region confirmed that Latin American citizens perceived that democracy (as it had taken hold in their countries) and democratically elected political elites had consistently failed to deliver desired benefits to their constituents. Marta Lagos (2003, 167), examining data from Latinobarometer public opinion surveys for the period from 1998 to 2002, found that, although a majority expressed support for democracy in theory, around 60 percent of Latin American citizens were "dissatisfied with the way their democracies work." In 2004 a comprehensive United Nations Development Program study again found startlingly low levels of citizen satisfaction with existing democracy throughout the region (UNDP 2004).[4]

This popular discontent has found expression in the form of yet another potential threat to stable democratic rule, that of mass citizen protests called "civil society coups" (Encarnación 2002) or "impeachment coups" (Boniface in this volume). These mass outpourings of popular dissatisfaction with the performance of democratic institutions have helped topple elected leaders in Argentina (2001), Bolivia (2003, 2005), Ecuador (2000, 2005), and Venezuela (2002). On one level, these are potentially unconstitutional and therefore antidemocratic means to advance democracy. They often present real threats for democratic governance when they are connected with the antidemocratic machinations of military officers or legislatures or when they are accompanied by political violence. On another level, however, they are distinct from classic military coups in that they often express popular efforts to exercise effective citizenship in countries where profound crises of representation and ineffective, corrupt, and often racist political institutions exist. As we take pains to qualify in various chapters in this volume (Boniface, Levitt, McCoy), these actions are not wholly undemocratic, especially because they are important expressions of citizenship and citizens' political rights. Not surprisingly, the paradoxical nature of uncivil civil society, potentially both democratic and undemocratic, presents a real dilemma for efforts by the international community to defend democracy.

Another new threat to democracy is exemplified by events in Ecuador (2004–5) and Nicaragua (2005). In each of these cases, under conditions of divided government with severe executive-legislative gridlock, powerful legislative alliances intentionally sought to weaken presidents for questionable ends, contributing to a governability crisis. International actors interested in promoting democracy have found the task of developing mechanisms to address the problems of authoritarian backsliding, impeachment coups, and antidemocratic presidential-legislative conflict to be complex and challenging.

The second important change since the publication of the Farer text has to do with theoretical developments that facilitate a greater understanding of the phenomena studied in *Beyond Sovereignty*. The constructivist project in international relations has given us a new appreciation for the role of ideas in processes of political change.[5] A constructivist perspective recognizes that democratization struggles occur on two interconnected planes, the political and the ideational. Accordingly, the limits of the possible for international and transnational actors in democratization are shaped not only by resource availability, strategic self-interests, and other political motivations. They are also conditioned by ideas about democracy and democracy promotion, such as the normative constructs of sovereignty, multilateralism, and democracy.[6] The constructivist project, also called normativist by some authors in the volume, highlights the ways in which actors resolve apparent differences or tensions among established norms of nonintervention, human rights, and citizenship, as well as the interests that these norms underpin. Norms, understood here as standards of appropriate behavior for actors of a given identity (Katzenstein 1996; Finnemore and Sikkink 1998), have an important role in shaping the behavior of the full spectrum of actors in the transnational democracy promotion field.

The chapters in this volume all reflect the idea that transnational democratization politics takes place on two interconnected levels. Actors advance tangible, immediate political agendas in their struggles while engaging simultaneously in normative, symbolic, and identity politics. Not all purposive action, though, is best categorized as normative. Sometimes the relevant players in transnational democracy activism act as "norm entrepreneurs" (Finnemore and Sikkink 1998) by struggling to convince other actors of the high moral purpose of their cause; at other times the players act in a self-interested, power-maximizing way. Put differently, there is a dialectic between strategic constraints and motivations and norm-based action and advocacy on the part of these actors. The interplay between actions that are normatively grounded and those that are self-interested and strategic is touched on in every chapter.

To understand contemporary political change in the Americas, we have adopted a two-pronged approach that draws on the constructivist tradition. First, our analysis is *agency driven*. Each chapter asks which domestic, international, and transnational actors are acting, when and how they act, and what outcomes their actions produce. It is a conscious effort to move beyond earlier comparative democratization studies that attributed agency to domestic actors and treated international variables, including international and transnational actors, largely as background conditions (as structure or environment). By contrast, we see networks of states, multilateral organizations, and nonstate actors, often transnational in their expanse, as a crucial part of the democratization picture. A prime terrain for transnational agency resides in the definition and evolution of regional norms in the areas of democracy, human rights, multilateralism, and sovereignty.

Second, we seek to be conscious of what Wimmer and Glick Schiller (2002, 302), call *methodological nationalism,* that is, "the assumption that the nation/state/society is a natural social and political form of the modern world." Similarly, Agnew (1994, 92) calls this the "territorial trap." In a manner that parallels the consolidation of nation-states historically, social scientists have tended to encapsulate their analysis in nation-states. This leads to an artificial dichotomization between domestic and international and, accordingly, the invisibility of influences that span or permeate borders.

At the same time, our analysis does not assume that transnationalization necessarily diminishes the importance of states. Although recent transnational analysis has focused heavily on nonstate actors, we also want to acknowledge *the state as a transnational actor.* It is not just nonstate actors that transnationalize their struggles. The state is not a passive target of transnational activism or norm entrepreneurship; it can and does engage in transnational politics. As the chapters in this volume show, states and state agencies "work" the international community as skillfully as transnational activists, sometimes more so. States can also be norm entrepreneurs, projecting their new democratic values through their foreign policy positions. Thus, while we seek to avoid methodological nationalism, our analysis does not negate the continued importance of the national political domain or of interstate relations; rather, we attempt to trace how these political forms intersect with transnational ones.

Transnational Democracy Promotion: Core Questions

Evaluating the role of international and transnational actors in contemporary democratization processes in the Americas raises a set of core questions. First, *how effective have international and transnational actors been at promoting and defending democracy in the Americas?* Against the optimism that seemed to pervade research on the democratizing influence of international (and transnational) actors during the 1990s, impasse has been one of the principal themes emerging in the new millennium. The international community has so far found it very difficult to prevent political crises from occurring, to intervene in a timely and effective manner in defense of democracy, and to stay on the ground in the aftermath of crises long enough to help strengthen democratic institutions and processes. Nor have transnational democracy promoters significantly narrowed the sovereign prerogatives of governments between elections. This observation, of course, contrasts with Farer's (1996a) assertion that the Americas were moving "beyond sovereignty." The international community has had great difficulty in converting the noble principles contained in the Inter-American Democratic Charter into practice. The impasse is borne out by the series of governance crises in Argentina, Bolivia, Ecuador, Haiti, Nicaragua, and Venezuela.

Second, *what type of democracy is being promoted by international and transnational actors?* In the 1990s, the democracy project was aimed at constructing political institutions and achieving elite support for democratic procedures. The international community as well as many scholars focused on the problematic of democratic consolidation, which was, quoting Linz and Stepan (1996, 5), when democracy became "the only game in town" (particularly as regards elites). In contrast, an important theme in the new millennium is the struggle for the extension of citizenship beyond its existing narrow elitist confines (Grugel 1999b). Yet, as the contributions to this volume underline, international and transnational actors have had a disappointing track record in terms of promoting expanded citizenship and democracy that is more meaningful to its citizens. The chapters assembled here highlight how geopolitical, normative, and political economy constraints limit the very type of democracy that can be promoted on the ground by these actors. A key challenge for would-be democracy promoters is the growing disconnect between the more narrow and elitist conception of procedural democracy or "electoralism" (Schmitter and Karl 1996) that the OAS and the inter-American system is able to promote and defend under the rubric of "representative democracy" and what citizens mean by democracy, which often embodies broader substantive notions of equality and effective representation.

There is a profound sense of dissatisfaction with the quality of democracy across much of the Americas. Citizens are frustrated with the disappointing performance of their elected officials and with public institutions in general. Their frustration often extends to international actors such as the United States or the OAS, as evidenced recently in Haiti and Ecuador. As they take to the streets in "civil society" or "impeachment" coups, or vote for antiestablishment candidates such as Hugo Chávez of Venezuela or Evo Morales of Bolivia, they in effect seek to redefine democracy along lines that have more meaning for them. Their actions highlight a tension between both procedural and substantive definitions of democracy and elitist and popular understandings of democracy. The ideal of representative democracy also faces a potential challenge on a regional scale as evidenced by the active international diplomacy of Hugo Chávez. The Venezuelan president has repeatedly attacked representative democracy for its alleged elitist bent and organic links with capitalism, holding up the ideal of direct or participatory democracy as the desired alternative. The discursive struggle between Chávez and his allies in the region and the proponents of representative democracy in the Inter-American system highlights the social construction of the meaning of democratization and the contested nature of the term.

Thus, in this volume we studiously avoid imposing a single definition of democracy and instead emphasize the socially constructed and disputed nature of the term. In asking what type of democracy is being promoted, we seek to determine how the interactions of real domestic, international, and transnational actors shape both debates about democracy and practices on the ground.

Finally, *how transnational are contemporary democratization processes in Latin America?* In terms of agency, there has certainly been no dearth of transnational activism in the Americas over the past decade, from the Zapatista rebellion in Mexico, to the downfall of Fujimori in Peru, to the struggles of the indigenous poor in Ecuador and Bolivia. Nonstate actors from across the region actively participated in the elaboration of the IADC in 2001. The

Friends of the Democratic Charter, a network of former high-ranking elected officials, bureaucrats, and academics from across the region, continues to press OAS member states to strengthen the IADC. Nongovernmental organizations from the North such as the Carter Center and the National Democratic Institute have cooperated with the OAS in observing multiple elections. South-South cooperation has also expanded on the electoral front through a growing regional network of civic organizations including Peru's Transparencia, Chile's Participa, and Mexico's Alianza Cívica (Lean in this volume).

We must recognize, however, that increased transnational pro-democracy activity in current politics does not necessarily translate into lasting or powerful influence on political change. While nonstate actors have rightly been acknowledged for their important roles as norm entrepreneurs or whistle-blowers, they tend to be resource poor and therefore must rely on states and multilateral organizations for crucial symbolic and material support. Accordingly, the impact of transnational actors may be uneven, diffuse, or episodic. By extension, the current cachet of transnational analysis, with its emphasis on cross-border civil society networks, should not distract us from the very real, continued importance of more conventional state and intergovernmental actors and their influence on democratization. This position is illustrated in our examination of the role of the United States, Canada, and Brazil, as well as in the analysis of the 2004–5 crisis in Ecuador (Shaw, Major, Burges and Daudelin, and Levitt in this volume). Certainly we must explore the interdependence, albeit asymmetrical, among nonstate, state, and intergovernmental actors engaged in transnational politics.

Does democratization become truly a transnational phenomenon in a spatial sense? The multiple transnational linkages among agents of political change have clouded the distinction between domestic and international. Yet at the same time a paradox exists: we generally observe transnational means being used for what are fundamentally parochial, idiosyncratic, and national ends: *Haitian* democracy, *Bolivian* democracy, *Mexican* democracy. Transnationalism may blur borders but it does not erase them.

Organization of the Volume

Our volume is divided into four parts. The first part examines the role of the OAS and regional powers in the promotion of democracy in the Americas. In chapter 2, Darren Hawkins and Carolyn Shaw describe an ongoing trend of legalization of democratic principles within the OAS, as captured in such instruments of international law as Resolution 1080, the Washington Protocol, the Declaration of Québec City, and the Inter-American Democratic Charter. They ask why states legalize measures that compromise state sovereignty. They consider four hypotheses and conclude that "U.S. hegemony and the self-interests of new democracies are necessary but not sufficient conditions" as they "must be accompanied by low fears of unilateral intervention and strong background democracy norms in order to produce results." Furthermore, they argue that the OAS is less transnationalized than it may appear—"the OAS still remains relatively difficult for nonstate actors to reach or to influence."

Building on the theoretical analysis of Hawkins and Shaw, chapter 3, by Dexter Boniface, takes a look at how the increased legalization of democracy norms has translated into on-the-ground activity. Boniface's chapter details the OAS's ongoing challenge of converting its democracy-related principles into practice. In a survey of nineteen democratic crises in the region, Boniface finds that the OAS has been fairly consistent in utilizing its legal instruments to condemn severe democratic ruptures such as coups and *autogolpes*. However, the OAS has been more hesitant to act in less severe democratic breaches, such as irregular presidential resignations, electoral controversies, and constitutional crises, which are often defended by member states as being sovereign practices outside the scope of international intervention.

In chapter 4, Carolyn Shaw traces the historical evolution of U.S. efforts to promote democracy from 1820 to the present. She argues that democratic principles and norms have competed with (and generally lost out to) other strategic priorities in the making of U.S. foreign policy, with the reality of the U.S. commitment to democracy often falling far short of the rhetoric. She demonstrates the ways in which U.S. democracy promotion policy has been inconsistent, "selective," or contradictory and concludes, ultimately, that "U.S. influence in the region was largely detrimental to the democratization process." Shaw suggests that the United States could improve upon its historical record by adopting the role of "enabler," abandoning unilateral strategies in favor of cooperation with like-minded actors at both the domestic and international levels.

In contrast, Flavie Major in chapter 5 highlights the way Canada has assumed a principled, activist agenda in Inter-American affairs since it joined the OAS in 1990. Notably, Canada has succeeded in developing an "autonomous foreign policy" distinct from that of the United States, projecting a role for itself as democracy's new champion. Furthermore, she makes the implicit case that Canada is one source of expanding transnationalism in the democracy promotion arena, in that it engages both states and civil society actors in its actions. At the same time, Major notes that Canada's actions have sometimes fallen short of its ideals. For example, Canada has not formally endorsed a series of international human rights mechanisms and has resisted attempts to strengthen the IADC. Canada has also been criticized for promoting a narrow, procedural definition of democracy with limited attention to human rights and socioeconomic issues. In particular, Major considers the question of whether Canada's response to the Haitian crisis of 2004 was adequate. Major attributes some of Canada's shortcomings to its political culture and to lack of coordination among agencies of the state.

Brazil's somewhat ambivalent role in regional democracy dynamics is considered by Sean Burges and Jean Daudelin. In chapter 6, they seek to determine if Brazil's foreign policy regarding democratization is predominantly norm driven (fitting a constructivist hypothesis) or based on self-interest (fitting a realist hypothesis). Using an innovative survey of Brazilian responses to crises in the Americas, they observe that Brazil has intervened on behalf of democracy most actively only where strong Brazilian interests were at stake. In contrast to recent writing on the spread of democratic norms in the Americas (Boniface 2002), their findings suggest that sovereignty and narrowly defined strategic interests continue to trump any democratic norm as determinants of Brazil's reactions to democratic crises.

The second part of the book provides two distinctly focused evaluations of a key mainstay of democracy promotion, international election monitoring. In chapter 7 Arturo Santa-Cruz examines the impact of election monitoring on the shared normative understanding of sovereignty in the Americas, while in chapter 8 Sharon Lean takes on the more pragmatic question of whether international election monitoring has improved electoral accountability. Santa-Cruz seeks to explain the emergence of a new global norm in the form of international election monitoring, a practice that originated in the Western Hemisphere. To explain this new practice (and its attendant modification of the existing sovereignty norm of nonintervention), he argues that conventional interest-based theories are inadequate and that a constructivist and transnational approach is required. More specifically, he asserts that the emergence of international election monitoring cannot be explained without reference to the unique *normative structure* of the Americas, the so-called

Western Hemisphere Idea, which was conducive to the emergence of this new practice and norm.

Lean maps the evolution of election monitoring activities in the region with attention to the role of different types of actors. She argues that election monitoring has evolved from a largely symbolic exercise into an institutionalized and meaningful mechanism that can validate or even invalidate elections. This occurred because of the participation of a range of state and nonstate actors (transnationalization) and because of their use of information politics, such as public reporting of election practices by grass-roots election observers. Lean also outlines some inherent limitations to the monitoring exercise. Specifically, Lean notes that while domestic election monitoring organizations can gain prestige and resources though their international ties, they can also sacrifice credibility, sometimes simultaneously. Similarly, international organizations may lose credibility depending on the domestic company they keep.

The third part of the book provides detailed analyses of three "crisis cases" that exemplify the new threats to democracy and the ways in which international and transnational actors involved in the collective defense of democracy have responded. The first case is that of the Haitian crisis that culminated in 2004 with the ouster of President Jean-Bertrand Aristide. In chapter 9, David Goldberg provides a much-needed look at the role of subregional organizations in democracy assistance through a study of the Caribbean Community's (CARICOM) involvement in Haiti. He documents how in the Haitian case, where the UN and OAS have struggled to support democracy, CARICOM has tried to carve out a separate space for subregional multilateral influence. His main argument is that CARICOM's reaction to the Haitian crisis, particularly following Aristide's departure, was decidedly more assertive than that of the OAS and considers whether this case can be taken as an example of effective subregional defense of democracy.

Thomas Legler takes on the case of Venezuela's President Hugo Chávez in chapter 10. He argues that the international community's efforts to defend democracy during Venezuela's political crisis of 2002–4 had decidedly mixed results. On the one hand, the OAS and its partners, the Carter Center and the UNDP, helped prevent political violence or civil war and facilitated the 2004 recall referendum that decisively renewed Chávez's popular mandate. On the other hand, as so often in the past, the OAS was unable to help prevent the crisis or to stay engaged on the ground to strengthen Venezuelan democracy in the longer run. Legler also identifies some worrisome unintended consequences of international pro-democracy efforts. Following international mediation efforts to support representative democracy in Venezuela, Chávez emerged in a stronger position to advocate his own brand of direct or participatory democracy. In short, Chávez not only represents a potential threat to democracy in Venezuela but by 2006 had also solidified a reputation as the region's most vocal opponent of representative democracy. Legler attributes the OAS's uneven performance to the inherent limits of its preferred mode of soft intervention.

In chapter 11, Barry Levitt focuses on the OAS's efforts to defend democracy in Ecuador, a country marred by persistent democratic instability. Levitt's chapter provides a detailed analysis of Ecuador's recent chain of political crises that toppled three elected presidents. In analyzing the Ecuadorian case, he also examines the more general difficulty of marshaling an international response to the problem of impeachment coups. He finds the OAS's performance to be rather lackluster. Echoing the analysis of Burges and Daudelin on Brazil, Levitt argues that the Ecuadorian case illustrates that OAS efforts are hampered because the national interests and domestic politics of member states determine their foreign policies much more than any collective, principled commitment to uphold democracy.

The volume concludes with two critical assessments of the practice of democracy promotion in the Americas. In chapter 12, Yasmine Shamsie questions whether the international community's democracy promotion efforts in the Americas can succeed when combined with a consistent emphasis on neoliberal market reforms. Using Haiti and Guatemala as illustrative cases, Shamsie argues that both market reforms mandated by international financial institutions and free-trade agreements produce economic winners and losers in a way that exacerbates income inequality and poverty, fostering uneven citizenship. Moreover, she argues, the constraints of the new global economy often proscribe the range of policy options available to elected leaders, thus diminishing the notion of choice implied by democracy. In other words, neoliberal economic reforms such as trade and investment liberalization create dual, competing constituencies for governments: the national electorate and international investors. Where the state is more beholden to capital than to its citizens, the result is a "low intensity" democracy that does little to address the deeper structural economic problems that often plague developing countries. The simultaneous promotion of representative democracy and market reforms in places like Haiti and Guatemala has therefore led to low voter turnout and even to the collapse of democratic institutions.

Jennifer McCoy's contribution in chapter 13 closes the volume with a critical look at the track record of international and transnational efforts to protect and promote democracy in the Americas from 1990 to 2005. Consistent with the emphasis on agency found in this volume, she documents how international and transnational responses to political crises have varied according to five different domestic originators of those crises: military actors, incumbent elected leaders, intragovernmental conflict, armed nonstate actors, and unarmed nonstate actors. She finds patterns of strong and effective defense of democracy in responding to more traditional types of crisis but persistent dilemmas in responding to the newest types of crises: "civil society" or "impeachment" coups and constitutional crises born of intragovernmental clashes. McCoy offers some reflections on the tasks ahead if international and transnational actors are to be effective in promoting and preserving democracy. She advocates an important role for transnational actors, in the form of international nongovernmental organizations, to strengthen the efforts of states and intergovernmental organizations to defend democracy.

Our collective examination reveals the complexity of democracy promotion in the Americas, involving the power and clash of ideas as well as the actions and interests of multiple domestic, international, and transnational actors. If we cannot accurately characterize contemporary political transitions as purely, or even predominantly, domestic processes, we also find abundant evidence that reports of the demise of sovereignty have been greatly exaggerated. The authors of this volume are engaged in an ongoing debate on this score. On one side, Hawkins and Shaw, Major, Santa-Cruz, Lean, Shamsie, and McCoy demonstrate clear elements of the transnationalization of political change in the Americas. On the opposite side, Shaw, Burges and Daudelin, and Levitt assert the continued primacy of the domestic determinants of democratization and the self-interests of states, despite the semblance of transnational activity. Between the two extremes, authors such as Boniface, Legler, and Goldberg acknowledge both the transnational character of democratization as well as the limits of promoting democracy from outside. Certainly our chapters underline the merits of considering the specifics of each individual democratization case. Just as the authors in this volume come from diverse scholarly traditions, in the end we hope our contributions and the debate among them constitute a modest step toward a necessary integration of the fields of comparative politics and international relations in the study of promoting democracy in the Americas.

NOTES

1. A "nativist" asserts the primacy of domestic over international causality in explaining democratization. The nativist notion was coined by Philippe C. Schmitter (2001, 27).

2. Prior to the Farer volume, Abraham F. Lowenthal (1991) edited a comprehensive treatment of U.S. efforts to "export" democracy to Latin America. Kevin Middlebrook (1998) edited an important contribution on one type of democracy promotion in Latin America, election observation.

3. On self-coups, see Cameron (1998), and on the multilateral response, see Cooper and Legler (2001a) and Legler (2003).

4. See also P. Smith (2005) and O'Donnell, Vargas Cullell, and Iazzetta (2004).

5. For a review of the key assumptions motivating constructivist theories, see Checkel (1998).

6. For important pioneering normative analyses in the Latin American context, see Hawkins (2002) and Kacowicz (2005).

Part I / The Role of the OAS and Regional Powers

CHAPTER TWO

The OAS and Legalizing Norms of Democracy

Darren Hawkins and Carolyn M. Shaw

On September 11, 2001, the Organization of American States (OAS) unanimously adopted the Inter-American Democratic Charter, declaring that "the peoples of the Americas have a right to democracy and their governments have an obligation to promote and defend it."[1] The charter specified numerous elements of representative democracy, including citizen participation, the rule of law, free and fair elections, separation of powers, a pluralistic system of political parties, government transparency, responsible public administration, the supremacy of civilian authority, and even a balanced and fair system for election campaign finance (see appendix B). Moreover, the charter endowed the OAS with the authority to suspend member states experiencing an "unconstitutional interruption of the democratic order."

Twenty, or even ten, years previously, such a charter had been unimaginable. In 1985, as enthusiasm for democracy spread through the region, American states amended the OAS Charter to declare that one of the organization's essential purposes was "to promote and consolidate representative democracy, with due respect for the principle of nonintervention."[2] The language left democracy undefined (and thus largely empty of meaning) and paradoxically insisted on nonintervention. Even earlier, in the late 1950s, an effort to create something like the charter was opposed by an unlikely coalition: the Dominican Republic, Guatemala, the United States, Mexico, Brazil, Chile, and Argentina, all of whom supported the 2001 charter (OAS 1965).

What accounts for the strengthening of multilateral democracy commitments in the OAS? Who are the key actors propelling the process and under what conditions has it occurred? This change poses a difficult puzzle because states who value their sovereignty are unlikely to empower others to judge their domestic political institutions. While most international rules govern relations between states, international agreements on democracy, such as the Democratic Charter, seek to regulate relations between a state and its citizens. States have been reluctant to create strong international rules on most issues; they should be even more reticent when it comes to issues that so directly concern leaders' political power. Moreover, the OAS seems an especially unlikely place for multilateral democracy commitments to develop. The organization has been marked historically by mistrust between the United States and many Latin American states. Latin American countries have been wary of international rules that would facilitate U.S. intervention, and the United States has been concerned about rules that would bind its own hands unnecessarily.

We begin this chapter by arguing that the charter and other developments to advance democracy in the OAS are examples of a broader global phenomenon known as legalization (Goldstein et al. 2000). The term refers to increasing the level of obligation, precision, and third-party delegation in international rules. We argue that since 1990 the OAS has legalized democracy to moderate levels. We then evaluate a series of four explanations for this phenomenon: U.S. hegemonic power, the self-interests of new democracies, threats posed by U.S. interventionist behavior, and the strength of regional democracy norms. Throughout, we examine the most significant events in the legalization of democracy in the 1990s and discuss them in relation to earlier periods in inter-American history, recent events in 2005, and other regions of the world where states have not engaged in legalization.

We find that legalization of democracy is quite difficult to achieve and occurred in the Americas due to a confluence of strong state interests and important regional conditions. In particular, we find that U.S. hegemony and the self-interests of new democracies are necessary but not sufficient conditions. These means and motives must be accompanied by low fears of unilateral intervention and strong background democracy norms in order to produce results. These findings largely support the overall theoretical framework advanced in this volume, though with one cautionary note. In particular, the findings suggest that a variety of state actors are essential to explain democratic change, thus affirming an actor-oriented approach that goes well beyond explanations focusing on U.S. hegemony. In fact, rather than aiding the legalization of democracy, U.S. behavior can easily undermine it through interventionist tendencies. At the same time, as the editors point out, these actors interact within an important normative structure supportive of democracy. This normative structure constitutes an important condition for successful democratic change. The cautionary note is that transnational and nonstate actors are not as relevant in this case as in some of the others in this volume, suggesting, perhaps, that the OAS still remains relatively difficult for nonstate actors to reach or to influence.

Legalization in Theory and Practice

Conceptualizing Legalization

Legalization constitutes one form of institutional change and can be defined as a process in which institutional rules become more obligatory and precise and in which institutional actors receive more delegated authority to interpret, monitor, and implement those rules (Goldstein et al. 2000, 387). In the spirit of theoretical clarity, we define obligation, precision, and delegation in substantially the same way as the *International Organization* special issue on legalization. "*Obligation* means that states or other actors are bound by a rule or commitment or by a set of rules or commitments. Specifically, it means that they are *legally* bound by a rule or commitment in the sense that their behavior thereunder is subject to scrutiny under the general rules, procedures, and discourse of international law, and often of domestic law as well" (Abbott et al. 2000, 401). The notion of an obligatory international institution runs directly counter to the common assumption that states jealously guard their sovereignty and that the international arena is characterized by anarchy. The desirability of such obligatory rules is a theoretical debate at least as old as Grotius and Westphalia. The apparent increase in the number of obligatory institutions in recent years (the European Union broadly, the European Central Bank, the World Trade Organization, the International Criminal Court) has renewed scholarly interest in the concept. As usual, however, theories have lagged behind real-world developments.

Precision "means that rules unambiguously define the conduct they require, authorize, or proscribe" (Abbott et al. 2000, 401). In turn, *delegation* "means that third parties have been granted authority to implement, interpret, and apply the rules; to resolve disputes; and (possibly) to make further rules." In the international arena, individual states often delegate to a collective body of states. In the European Union, for example, states allow a number of policy issues to be decided by qualified majority votes in collective deliberations in the Council of Ministers. While the council is not a "third party," states have still yielded their sovereign authority to a collective of other states that can determine domestic policies. Such a step constitutes partial delegation. Stronger acts of delegation would include independent third parties like the European Court of Justice or the International Criminal Court. Despite a long-standing scholarly interest, there have been few explanations of international organization autonomy. Rather than consider particular characteristics such as obligation and delegation, scholars have focused on the existence of institutions themselves. More broadly, they have moved past the debate on whether institutions matter to explain variation in the nature of those institutions and the conditions in which they matter. This chapter forms part of that broader effort.

Legalization of Democracy in the OAS

Analysis of OAS documents suggests that legalization of the democracy norm has increased across each of the three analytical components of the concept in the past sixty years, although it has proceeded in fits and starts and has sometimes stalled.[3] Democracy has been a principle of the inter-American system for many years, but legalization did not begin until 1990. During the 1990s, legalization of democracy moved from low to moderate levels through amendment of the OAS Charter and by the creation of new mechanisms to promote and protect democracy. Since the late 1990s, however, further legalization has slowed considerably despite the efforts of some states.

The original OAS Charter (1948) broke new ground internationally by declaring that American solidarity was based on "the effective exercise of representative democracy" (Article 5). This principle, however, lacked precision and delegation, with no authority given to any OAS organ for oversight. While the charter was legally binding, the democratic norm was simply "reaffirmed" as a "principle," and thus was not strongly obligatory—an observation confirmed by long experience with brutal authoritarian rule in multiple countries in subsequent years.

One of the first steps to increase the legalization of democratic principles in the hemisphere was the creation of the Unit for the Promotion of Democracy (UPD).[4] In 1990 the OAS General Assembly established the UPD to provide advisory services and technical assistance to member states in order to modernize and strengthen their political institutions and democratic processes. Renamed the Department for the Promotion of Democracy (DPD), in recent years the DPD has become a key source of support for the efforts made by member states to defend, consolidate, and advance democracy. It has monitored more than seventy elections since its establishment and regularly provides support to the OAS bodies in their deliberations on strengthening and preserving democracy. Although the creation of the UPD did not affect levels of obligation by states, the UPD's generation, dissemination, and exchange of information on democratic political systems has made the concept of democracy in the region more precise. The creation of the UPD also signaled a slight increase in delegation even though the unit does not engage in electoral observations except by invitation from a member state. OAS organs often rely on the technical expertise of the UPD/DPD when they consider measures to strengthen and preserve democracy.

A second step to legalize democracy came shortly after the creation of the UPD. In June 1991 in Santiago, Chile, the General Assembly passed Resolution 1080 creating automatic procedures for convening the Permanent Council in the event of a democratic crisis.[5] The council would examine the situation and then convene either a meeting of the ministers of foreign affairs or a special session of the General Assembly. The resolution authorized states to "adopt any decisions deemed appropriate, in accordance with the Charter and international law," in response to the threat to democracy. Resolution 1080 slightly increased levels of obligation, precision, and delegation within the OAS by instructing the secretary-general to call for immediate convocation of the Permanent Council to address a democratic crisis and by vaguely identifying the scope of such a crisis. The resolution specified that the Permanent Council should be convened in the event of a "sudden or irregular interruption of the democratic political institutional process or the legitimate exercise of power by the democratically elected government." These were conditions that resulted in the resolution being invoked four times in the 1990s in response to events in

Haiti, Peru, Guatemala, and Paraguay (Acevedo and Grossman 1996, 140–45; Valenzuela 1997; Boniface 2002; Parish and Peceny 2002, 237–43).

At the same meeting in Santiago in 1991, the General Assembly also approved the "Santiago Commitment to Democracy and the Renewal of the Inter-American System," which reiterated states' commitment to democracy. The commitment noted that the "effective exercise, consolidation, and improvement" of democratic government is a "shared priority" of member states. States declared their determination to strengthen "representative democracy," recognizing it as "an expression of the legitimate and free manifestation of the will of the people." Members were determined to "adopt efficacious, timely, and expeditious procedures to ensure the promotion and defense of representative democracy, in keeping with the Charter."

In December 1992 member states took their most dramatic step to legalize democracy by amending the OAS Charter through the Washington Protocol, which went into effect in September 1997. The protocol added a provision authorizing suspension from the OAS of any government that had seized power by force. Such a suspension would require a two-thirds vote of member states in the General Assembly. The amendment was widely supported, with only Mexico voting against it. As an amendment to the charter, the measure imposes the highest possible level of obligation on ratifying states. The protocol also increased the level of precision, especially by laying out clear and specific procedures to be followed when democratic governments are overthrown by force. States did not delegate to an autonomous third party but rather to a subset of states by empowering two-thirds of them with the ability to suspend member states from participation in the OAS. Many states clearly saw this as increasing the powers of the OAS to intervene in domestic politics; in fact, this was the basis of Mexico's opposition to the amendment. In a formal declaration, Mexico insisted that "it is unacceptable to give to regional organizations supranational powers and instruments for intervening in the internal affairs of our states" (OAS 1992a, 53).

Since the enactment of the Washington Protocol states have made less progress on legalizing the democracy norm. In September 2001 the General Assembly approved the Inter-American Democratic Charter, which mostly reinforced existing OAS instruments for the active defense of representative democracy. While the charter substantially advanced the specificity of the democracy norm, it increased the level of delegation and obligation only minimally. In addition to granting the peoples of the Americas a right to democracy and specifying what democracy means the charter broadens the conditions under which a member state can be suspended from the OAS by a two-thirds vote: whereas the Washington Protocol authorizes suspension only if a democratic government is overthrown by force, the charter includes an "unconstitutional interruption of the democratic order" (Article 21). Despite its name, the Democratic Charter is not a treaty and thus has a lesser level of obligation than the OAS Charter and Protocols. At the same time, its repeated invocation in OAS resolutions and documents since it was adopted implies that it has a fairly high level of obligation despite its status as a resolution. States have invoked the charter in responding to problems in Haiti, Venezuela, Ecuador, and Nicaragua.

Since then, states have not further advanced legalization. In early June 2005 the OAS considered a proposal to create a new committee to receive civil society input on the quality of democracy and make recommendations for action. Rather than substantially increasing state obligations and the level of delegation, however, the Declaration of Florida (OAS 2005a), adopted at the end of the thirty-fifth session of the OAS General Assembly, instructed the secretary-general to present proposals to the Permanent Council, after joint consultation, that would promote initiatives for gradual and balanced cooperation on democracy promotion. The council, in turn, was instructed to consider initiatives in the area of representative democracy. At the same time, states also emphasized respect for the principle of nonintervention and the right of self-determination, principles largely absent from the Democratic Charter. Although the secretary-general may revisit the issue of legalization, the document specifies no obligations and little if any delegation of authority. It is mostly a reaffirmation of the Democratic Charter and other preexisting pro-democracy measures.

Explaining Legalization: Four Possibilities

U.S. Power

To account for increasing legalization, one hypothesis is perhaps the most common in inter-American studies: U.S. preferences and hegemony, defined as a preponderance of power, shape the behavior of the OAS and member states (P. H. Smith 2000). This argument ties into a realist view of the world in which powerful states create international institutions to serve their purposes

(Mearsheimer 1994–95). While the extent of U.S. hegemony in Latin America is often a matter of heated debate, most measures suggest that the variation is less noticeable than the consistency. The U.S. share of GDP in the Western Hemisphere from 1960 to 2004 has varied from a high of 85.46 percent in 1960 to a low of 80.24 percent in 1980. During those years, the United States experienced a steady if very gradual decline in its share of GDP. After 1980, it experienced a fairly steady ascent until 2003, when it stood at 83.93 percent. We conclude that U.S. hegemony has not changed much in the past fifty years.

U.S. preferences, in contrast, appear to have changed dramatically. In the 1950s the United States opposed efforts to legalize democracy, declaring that "because of the structure of its Federal Government, [it] does not find it possible to enter into multilateral conventions with respect to the effective exercise of representative democracy" (OAS 1965, 16–18). The logical connection between federalism and multilateral conventions is unclear; what is self-evident is that the United States sought to avoid any international agreements on democracy that might affect it. That attitude changed in the early 1990s when the United States pushed hard for the Washington Protocol, even lending its name to the accord. The United States was also a primary supporter of the Democratic Charter.

But U.S. power is not always a useful explanation of legalization. In May and June 2005, when the United States pressed for further legalization in the Declaration of Florida,[6] it was opposed by nearly every other country in the Western Hemisphere. The draft U.S. proposal called on the Permanent Council to routinely assess any situation that might affect a state's democratic process, a significant broadening of the Democratic Charter (2005b). It also called for establishing a new committee that would ensure "that civil society organizations can present their views and advice to the OAS on a systematic and regular basis," again a significant step forward from the vague rhetoric welcoming civil society views. The final draft, however, authorized the secretary-general only to consult with the Permanent Council and then to devise proposals for "gradual initiatives for cooperation, as appropriate" and barely mentioned civil society's input. Even these measures were weakened by a phrase calling for respect for the principle of nonintervention and the right of self-determination, two concepts that were absent from the operative part of the draft resolution.

The proposal failed despite President Bush's appearance at the General Assembly to exhort states to cooperate to preserve the gains from democracy[7] and Secretary of State Condoleezza Rice's call for the OAS to act on the pledge of the Democratic Charter and for governments that fail to meet democratic standards to "be accountable to the OAS."[8] Rice insisted that the democracy norm must be enforced by the Permanent Council and "repeatedly called on the organization to allow citizens groups with concerns about their country to testify."[9]

In the case of the Florida Declaration, U.S. power may have discouraged support among the Latin American states. As one senior OAS official put it, U.S. officials "don't realize that they are like an elephant entering a bazaar—the minute they come in, everybody runs for cover."[10] The United States failed to sway anyone except Panama and Colombia on this issue. Nearly every other country in the region opposed the proposal, including Chile—generally a good U.S. ally and home state of the secretary-general of the OAS, who supported the measure.

Lock-In: Newly Established Democracies

The wave of democratization that swept Latin America in the 1980s and into the early 1990s offers an intuitively promising explanation for legalizing democracy in the OAS (Parish and Peceny 2002, 236). This hypothesis, closely related to a liberal theoretical perspective, suggests that the leaders of new and unstable democracies will seek to shore up their authority against domestic challengers by creating commitments to international institutions that can help protect their fragile democracies (Moravcsik 2000). At first glance, this "lock-in" explanation helps make sense of Resolution 1080, the Washington Protocol, and subsequent OAS actions resulting from these mechanisms. A wide variety of Latin American countries, including some of the largest and most influential, such as Brazil, Argentina, Chile, and Peru, made transitions to democracy in the 1980s and early 1990s. Almost all faced serious threats from domestic actors with more authoritarian preferences.

Evidence for the lock-in argument, though generally positive, is mixed. News reports suggest that a group of Andean countries—Bolivia, Colombia, Ecuador, Peru, Venezuela—led the effort to approve Resolution 1080 in 1991.[11] Although three of these were relatively recent democracies, Venezuela and Colombia were established democracies. The following year, Argentina, a new democracy, took the lead in proposing the Washington Protocol (OAS 1992b).[12] Interviews with diplomats confirm the impression that new democracies were especially interested in international protection. "Look, I am part of an entire generation that came into adulthood under a military regime," said Heraldo Muñoz, Chile's delegate to the OAS. "We have established democracies out of our own traumatic experiences. We are tired of internal war. So you've got to try to set up some kind of mechanism to protect these democracies."[13] By the same token, Mexico was the only country to vote against the Washington Protocol when the OAS adopted it, and Mexico was one of the most notably nondemocratic countries in Latin America in 1992 (OAS 1992a).

Furthermore, a widely used measure for democracy—known as Polity2— provides firm evidence for the lock-in argument by demonstrating that a wave of new democracies appeared in Latin America in the late 1980s and early 1990s.[14] Using the Polity2 data, there were four new or newly strengthened democracies in 1980, nine in 1985, eleven in 1990, and nine in 1995. This measure is somewhat conservative because some democracies undoubtedly remained under threat from authoritarian sectors for longer than ten years, but the data only count the first ten years. Even more impressive is the correlation between the low number of new democracies in 2005 and the failure to legalize democracy further, thus helping explain Latin America's lack of interest in the U.S. proposal in Florida. By our measure, there were only four new democracies left in the Americas in 2002, the last year for which data are available, and probably none in 2005. These results suggest that states lacked any interest in legalizing democracy further.

Evidence drawn from earlier time periods in the Americas suggests, however, important limitations on the lock-in argument. A key group of new or newly strengthened democracies emerged in Latin America in the late 1950s, including (using Polity2 data) Uruguay, Panama, Chile, Colombia, and Venezuela. The undercounting of new democracies here is undoubtedly more severe than in the early 1990s because the threats to democracy were so much greater. For example, Ecuador and Brazil, both new democracies in the late 1940s, lost their democracies in the early 1960s and were under threat in the late 1950s, yet they are not counted by our standards. Argentina did not quite make it out of the negative, authoritarian, range in the late 1950s according to Polity2, yet most observers of the period classify it as relatively democratic. Certainly the subjective perspective of the time—when the bar was lower for being considered a democracy—was that Argentina was a struggling democracy in the late 1950s.

As lock-in theory would predict, some of these new democracies attempted to legalize democracy. Contrary to expectations, they failed to make much progress, and some new or threatened democracies strongly opposed the efforts. At a meeting of foreign ministers in August 1959, the OAS adopted the "Declaration of Santiago," which declared that the existence of antidemocratic regimes constitutes a violation of OAS principles and a danger to peace (OAS 1965, 4). Yet this nonbinding resolution was not obligatory. At the urging of Venezuela, a new democracy, the OAS also appointed a committee at that same meeting to draft a procedure that would determine whether states were complying with their democratic obligations (OAS 1965). The resulting draft convention, from December 15, 1959, laid out the characteristics of democracy and required individual governments and the OAS to take a variety of actions against nondemocratic governments, principally the nonrecognition of governments seizing power from democracies (OAS 1965). Argentina, Brazil, Chile, the Dominican Republic, Mexico, and the United States all issued strong written objections, claiming that the draft convention violated the OAS Charter and the United Nations Charter (OAS 1965). Of these, Argentina, Brazil, and Chile were all new, newly improved, or struggling democracies at the time, yet they saw little value in an international agreement. We explore their opposition in greater detail in the next section.

Proponents did not give up, repeatedly placing the issue on the OAS's agenda over the next few years. Significantly, those proponents were not always new democracies. For example, the Dominican Republic and Honduras (both authoritarian regimes), Venezuela (new democracy), and Costa Rica (established democracy) requested a meeting in August 1962 to discuss how states should react to coups (Muñoz 1998, 5–6). It is difficult to understand the motivation for this failed effort, unless it is seen as an effort to head off U.S. intervention in the region. In November 1965 the Second Special Inter-American Conference in Rio finally adopted a weak resolution, whose general irrelevance is partially revealed by its title, "Informal Procedure on Recognition of De Facto Governments." The resolution recommended that governments consult with one another after the overthrow of democracy in one state and that individual governments decide for themselves whether to recognize a new government that has taken power by force (Muñoz 1998, 6).

Sovereignty Costs

Our third hypothesis suggests that the stronger the interventionist threats from the United States are, the less the opportunity for legalization will be because states will see too many costs to sovereignty. Historically, fear of multilateral mechanisms and institutions that would give the United States a pretext to intervene runs extremely deep in Latin America (P. H. Smith 2000). Since their independence in the 1820s Latin American states have attempted to fashion international rules that would constrain U.S. interventionism and have opposed international rules that might facilitate it. During the Cold War, unilateral U.S. intervention in Latin America produced substantial fear and resentment from countries in the region. The 1954 U.S.-sponsored coup against a relatively democratic government in Guatemala emphasized that no one was exempt from U.S. efforts (Parish and Peceny 2002, 235).

A close reading of the documentary evidence from the effort to legalize democracy in the late 1950s and early 1960s confirms that Latin American states frequently cited sovereignty concerns when expressing their opposition. Although no state invoked the fear of U.S. intervention publicly, it was not far below the surface in state comments. The Dominican Republic, for example, objected to legalization by arguing that the proposal would permit "direct intervention in both the internal and external affairs" of states, in direct contradiction to the OAS Charter (OAS 1965, 13–14). Even more significantly, the three new democracies to oppose legalization also cited sovereignty concerns. Brazil, less than four years away from a coup that would dismantle its struggling democracy, claimed that "recognition is an act of sovereignty that permits of no limitations." As a result, the draft convention "breaches principles of international law that are fundamental to the American system" (OAS 1965, 21). Chile refused even to review a draft text proposing legalization, arguing that such an analysis would be "superfluous" because the draft contravened the OAS Charter (OAS 1965, 24). Argentina simply cited a decision by the Inter-American Juridical Council, which concluded that collective action in the defense of democracy violated nonintervention principles in the charter (OAS 1965, 25).

Soon after the end of the Cold War, however, the United States signaled radically different intentions by cooperating with multilateral institutions before using military force, the most dramatic example being U.S. cooperation with the UN Security Council prior to the first Gulf War. No less striking, especially for a Latin American audience, were the patient U.S. efforts to work with first the OAS and then the Security Council to resolve the crisis in Haiti from 1991 to 1994. The amount of time that passed before the United States finally utilized force was itself a strong indication of its preferences and intentions. Over the course of nearly four years, the United States sought and received the OAS's blessing for diplomatic and economic sanctions on Haiti.

When it looked like force would be necessary, the OAS passed a resolution deferring to the UN Security Council, which then authorized the use of force. Although Latin American states could not bring themselves to authorize military intervention, the fact that they failed to oppose it and in fact immediately welcomed the change when it occurred constitutes strong evidence that they did not feel threatened by U.S. actions.

As a result, states rarely cited sovereignty concerns in the 1990s when dealing with the same issues and even with the same types of penalties: diplomatic isolation and suspension from the OAS. The United States even sought to "find ways of increasing the leverage" of the OAS and to advance law as the basis of action (OAS 1992b, 340), and Latin American states still responded positively. Argentina proposed the Washington Protocol, and its delegate could now state "categorically" that international decisions on democracy are "perfectly consistent" with the principle of nonintervention (OAS 1992c, 192). Brazil, the most skeptical of the old foes to legalization, declared its willingness to entertain proposals that maintained the balance between nonintervention and the promotion of democracy (OAS 1992b, 339). Despite consistently promoting a single-state veto throughout the negotiations, Brazil ultimately accepted the protocol.

Either states valued sovereignty less in the 1990s or they felt their sovereignty was less threatened in the 1990s. The first is possible, but the second is more likely. In fact, several states explicitly invoked the end of the Cold War as a reason to endorse legalization because they had been freed from traditional security concerns. Chile's ambassador, who was one of the most important proponents, opened his lengthy seventeen-page defense of the Washington Protocol by citing the opportunities provided by the historical moment. "The end of the Cold War has furthered the promotion and defense of democracy in the region by removing the ideological and strategic connotations attached to it for many years. In other words, the perception today is that representative democracy can be defended here in the hemisphere without running the risk of being trapped in the logic of the East-West confrontation" (OAS 1992c, 285). The Argentine delegate argued the point more succinctly: "For years the impact of the east-west conflict significantly undermined the regional Organization's commitment to democracy by subjecting democratic institutions to the fight against communism" (OAS 1992c, 187).

After 2001 the United States once again changed course and signaled new intentions.[15] In 2002 the United States was widely perceived as tacitly backing a coup that toppled the president of Venezuela before other countries acted to help return him to power. Then in early 2004 the OAS brokered a political compromise in Haiti that would have retained its president in office amid mounting political and social crises, but a few days later the United States acted, unilaterally in the view of many Latin American countries, to help push him out of office and install the opposition in power. By acting in these ways, the United States signaled preferences for unilateral intervention in Latin America.

It is little wonder, then, that Venezuela and Haiti were so often mentioned by diplomats and analysts as the discussion unfolded on the U.S. proposal. Most Latin American states care little for the governments of these countries, who are officially democratic but in practice quite authoritarian, yet they fear U.S. meddling more. During the Florida negotiations, Venezuela argued that it was the target of the United States, which wanted to turn the OAS into its policeman. As a result, other Latin American diplomats emphasized the language of nonintervention and self-determination in their comments. The ambassador from Argentina argued that "no one can be sure that in the future they would not be seated and judged by this committee in one year, two years, three years. Every country has its problems. But I can tell you one thing: the most powerful countries will never be there."[16] Mexico echoed these concerns by declaring that, "in principle, we are not in agreement with any tutelage from anybody."[17] Likewise, foreign ministers from the fourteen Caribbean island members expressed their opposition by claiming that a combination of the U.S. government and civil society groups helped oust the Haitian president in 2004, an action that they have repeatedly condemned.

Norms

Our final hypothesis suggests that the normative structures within which states interact account for their behavior by informing their interests and creating behavioral possibilities where none would otherwise exist (Santa-Cruz 2005). In other words, before states can act to protect democracy, they must first understand the concept of democracy in similar ways and value it abstractly—a theoretical perspective known as constructivism (Finnemore 1996). Consistent with this view is the OAS's legalization of democracy in the 1990s: it did not create an entirely new norm but rather built on a strong tradition of multilateral democratic discourse and norms stretching back to the early 1900s (Muñoz 1998). The first multilateral agreement to promote democracy in the Americas dates to the 1907 Conference in Washington, whose participants consisted of the United States and Central American states (Drake 1991, 11–12). Their commitment not to recognize any Central American government that did not arise from free elections was designed to serve U.S. interests, but it nevertheless marked the advent of a multilateral discourse endorsing democracy. This discourse gained more widespread support in 1936 at the Inter-American Conference for the Maintenance of Peace. In the light of trouble brewing in Europe, Latin American states made reference to "the existence of a common democracy throughout America" as the basis for the "political defense" of the hemisphere (Atkins 1997, 122). For the first time, Latin American states endorsed democracy as a "common cause" (Muñoz 1998, 3).

After World War II, American states expanded and systematized their commitments to representative democracy, thereby creating a clear, specific regional norm (Atkins 1997, 123; Muñoz 1998, 3–5). A variety of states picked up the rhetoric of freedom and liberty that resonated during the war and enshrined those values in postwar international documents. A Mexico City conference on war and peace in 1945 declared that American states could not conceive of "life without freedom" (Muñoz 1998, 4). Significantly, states then endorsed a democratic norm in the central security treaty for the Americas, the 1947 Inter-American Reciprocal Assistance Treaty, which states that peace is "founded on justice and moral order and, consequently, on the international recognition and protection of human rights and freedoms . . . and on the effectiveness of democracy."[18] This democracy norm obviously suffered from repeated violations throughout the Cold War, but norm violations do not necessarily mean that the norm ceases to exist. In fact, American states reiterated their commitment to the democracy norm in a number of OAS declarations in 1959, 1962, 1965, and 1980. Behavior consistent with the democracy norm was irregular until 1959, when the average Polity2 score climbed into the positive (nonauthoritarian) range for the first time, remaining there until 1967. It then climbed to positive levels again in 1982, gained strength in 1989 when it hit an average of 5 (moderately democratic), and strengthened still more in 1994 when it leveled off at 7 (fully democratic, though with a few restrictions), where it has since remained.

The strength of the democracy norm in the Americas is thrown into sharp relief when contrasted with the absence of democracy norms in other regions of the world. The Charter for the Organization of African Unity, adopted in

1965, does not mention the concept of democracy, emphasizing instead principles of sovereignty, nonintervention, self-determination, and nonalignment. The 1980 African Charter on Human and Peoples' Rights guarantees a right to participate in the government, but this is hardly an endorsement of a systematic set of institutions that constitute democracy. The Constitutive Act of the African Union, adopted in 2000, finally endorsed "democratic principles and institutions," which put African states in the same normative position that American states occupied in 1948. Democracy norms are even less developed in Asia. The Association of Southeast Asian Nations, for example, came into existence in 1967 but did not mention the word democracy in key regional agreements until the Bali Concord II of 2003, when it called on countries to cooperate in an international democratic environment but still said nothing of domestic democratic institutions. The states composing the Asian Pacific Economic Cooperation group have yet to mention democracy in their annual leaders' statements, despite the leadership of several prominent democracies among those states. When examining democracy-consistent behavior, no region outside of Europe comes close to Latin America. Africa, for example, did not achieve an average positive Polity2 score until 2002, when it finally became a 1. South Asia does the best, hovering in the low positive range for much of the 1990s before falling back to zero in 2002.

In short, Latin America did not legalize democracy norms until several decades after states first endorsed those norms. Other regions of the world (outside of Europe) lack strong democracy norms and have made no effort to legalize democracy. Process tracing supports this correlation by demonstrating that American states consciously invoked long-standing values and norms as reasons to support legalization during their debates over the Washington Protocol. The Argentine delegate began his speech by arguing that the democracy norm among American states stretched back to the time when Simon Bolivar convened an international congress (OAS 1992c, 187). The Chilean delegate was so inspired by the history of the norm that he traced its evolution in a carefully researched text that he submitted to his fellow delegates as a key argument for action (OAS 1992c, 287–97). Even though Mexico opposed the Washington Protocol, it nevertheless felt compelled to argue that the promotion of democracy was unquestionably a priority for the OAS and one that was widely valued (OAS 1992c, 279–81). Where opponents feel constrained to endorse the same norms that proponents use to advance their cause, we have evidence of the importance of norms in shaping the debate and affecting its outcome.

Summary and Analysis

The most important finding to emerge from our analysis is that neither strong state interests in locking in democracy nor hegemonic U.S. power has been sufficient to legalize democracy in the Americas. An important set of new democracies attempted legalization in the 1950s yet failed. The United States, as strong a regional hegemon as ever, attempted further legalization in 2005, yet failed.

In both cases, process-tracing evidence suggests that the factor most closely correlated with opposition is fear of intervention. In the 1950s the United States opposed legalization, but so did many Latin American countries, whose representatives expressed concerns about undermining sovereignty. In 2005 Latin American states may have seen diminished benefits from legalization of democracy, but their opposition was driven more clearly by their concerns about undermining sovereignty. The United States adopted unilateralist stances toward intervention during the Cold War and after September 11, and Latin American states responded by strongly citing sovereignty concerns during those two periods.

What then produces legalization? The evidence suggests it is a relatively rare event that requires a confluence of factors. Diminished fear of intervention is not itself sufficient to drive legalization forward. States must also be motivated by some positive gain from legalization. Both hegemonic pressure and the desire to lock in democratic gains were present in the 1990s, and so it is impossible to decide which was more important.

Cross-regional comparison suggests that democracy norms also seem to play a role. As with many kinds of norms, that role is not noticed until analysts examine a part of the world where the norm does not exist. Other regions in the world enjoyed a surge of new democracies after the Cold War, but none legalized democracy in international institutions. Why not? None of them faced a strong regional hegemon with unilateralist interventionist tendencies. Instead, the absence of a well-established norm of democracy seems the most likely stumbling block preventing legalization in other regions, whereas the presence of the norm appears to have facilitated legalization in the Americas.

Why do states legalize issues like democracy in international institutions, thereby yielding some of their sovereignty? Many analysts have viewed the OAS and its associated rules through the lens of U.S. power. As Peter H. Smith

(2000, 8) argues, in view of U.S. regional hegemony, "the study of US-Latin American relations becomes a meditation on the character and conduct of the United States." While we do not dispute the pervasive reality of U.S. power, such power clearly has limits, as illustrated by U.S. efforts in Florida in 2005. Alternatively, the most obvious answer is that new democratic states wanted to protect their gains by legalizing democracy internationally. Yet this explanation too is incomplete, as illustrated by the difficulties faced when new democracies pushed legalization in the 1950s.

In both cases, the benefits to be derived from legalization foundered on the costs of handing the United States new legal tools with which it might justify unilateral interventionism. While international rules do not determine U.S. behavior, Latin American states clearly felt compelled to support the concept of sovereignty during the Cold War but also more recently during the War on Terror.

These results suggest that stronger international protection for democracy is a rare result and one that is difficult to achieve. States still guard their sovereignty in this issue area. Both power and strong motive are insufficient to produce legalization. Either or both of these factors must coexist with low fears of unilateral intervention and robust norms of democracy. These conditions suggest that further legalization of democracy is unlikely anywhere in the world. While the United States clearly desires to establish stronger international norms of domestic democracy, it may paradoxically be undermining this effort by its willingness to intervene in unilateral ways to accomplish this goal.

NOTES

1. Available at www.oas.org/OASpage/eng/Documents/Democractic_Charter.htm.
2. Protocol of Cartagena de las Indias, available at www.oas.org/juridico/english/treaties/a-50.htm.
3. To operationalize obligation, precision, and delegation, we adopted the rules and guidelines laid out in detail by Abbott et al. (2000, 408–18).
4. Historical information and documents about the UPD, now part of the Department of Democratic and Political Affairs, are available at www.ddpa.oas.org/main.htm.
5. Resolution 1080 is reprinted in appendix A. This and all other OAS documents related to democracy cited here are available at www.ddpa.oas.org/about/documents_related.htm.

6. The United States also made an attempt at legalization in 1999—though it had much lower visibility and apparently lower levels of effort—but likewise failed. See Associated Press, "U.S. shelves proposal aimed at helping democracies in the hemisphere," June 8, 1999.

7. "Opening of the Organization of American States General Assembly," June 6, 2005, www.oas.org/speeches/speech.asp?sCodigo=05–0113.

8. "Remarks by Secretary of State Condoleezza Rice," June 5, 2005, www.oas.org/speech/speech.asp?sCodigo=05–0110.

9. "Latin States Shun US Plan to Watch over Democracy," *New York Times*, June 9, 2005.

10. Quoted in Oppenheimer Report, "US Proposal: Great Idea, Bad Strategy," *Miami Herald*, June 6, 2005.

11. Inter Press Service, "OAS seeks 'collective defense' of democracy," June 1, 1991.

12. See also Agence France-Presse, "Peruvian president receives limited support for democracy plans," May 19, 1992; Inter Press Service, "Latin America: OAS committed to democracy and human rights," May 20, 1992.

13. "Latin nations get a firmer grip on their destiny," *New York Times*, June 9, 1991.

14. Marshall and Jaggers (2002). Using the measure's range of −10 to 10, we classify a state as a new democracy for ten years after it attains a positive score or for ten years after its positive score jumps by 3 points or more in a single year.

15. The analysis in this paragraph draws on news reports and conversations with senior OAS officials.

16. Quoted in "US proposal in the OAS draws fire as an attack on Venezuela," *New York Times*, May 22, 2005.

17. "Mexico rejects 'tutelage' on democracy," *El Universal*, June 7, 2005.

18. Available at www.oas.org/juridico/english/Treaties/b-29.html.

CHAPTER THREE

The OAS's Mixed Record

Dexter S. Boniface

The international defense of democracy in the Americas has become an urgent issue. On June 6, 2005, Bolivian president Carlos Mesa, besieged by massive street protests, became the eighth Latin American president since 2000 to resign or be ousted before finishing his term.[1] Mesa's resignation occurred just as the Organization of American States (OAS) General Assembly was meeting in Fort Lauderdale, Florida, to discuss how the organization could best promote and defend democracy. The meeting itself was generally viewed as a setback for the extension of the organization's democracy promotion efforts— an ambitious proposal from the United States to create a new, permanent committee to monitor the state of democracy in the region was rejected by most of the Latin American states.[2] What, then, can the OAS contribute to sustaining or possibly deepening democracy in the region?

The preamble of the Charter of the OAS is explicit about a commitment to representative democracy as "an indispensable condition for the stability, peace and development of the [Western Hemispheric] region" (OAS 1997). Yet during the Cold War the OAS failed to develop a consistent policy regarding the promotion of democracy in the hemisphere. For example, the organization excluded Cuba but not the authoritarian military regimes of South America. At a meeting in Santiago, Chile, in June 1991, however, the OAS renewed its pledge to protect democracy in the region and, through the adoption of Resolution 1080 (and a variety of complementary measures), established the institutional mechanisms for doing so. These measures have proved to be more than rhetorical gestures; Resolution 1080 (see appendix A) was invoked in relation to the 1991 coup in Haiti, *autogolpes* (or "self-coups") in Peru and Guatemala in 1992 and 1993, and the civil-military crisis in Paraguay in 1996. In each of these four cases, OAS action proved to be an important (if not sufficient) instrument in the maintenance and/or restoration of democracy. In short, OAS action in the early 1990s offered confirmation of the existence of a vigorous international regime for the defense of democratic rule in the hemisphere.[3]

Following a successful experience in the first half of the 1990s, however, the OAS has since been faced with more pernicious obstacles to democratic stability in the region, whether among the smaller countries of the region (e.g., the Dominican Republic, Ecuador, and—again—Haiti and Paraguay) or the intermediate powers (e.g., Argentina, Colombia, Peru, and Venezuela). To discern how deep and consequential the organization's normative commitment to democracy is, this chapter examines OAS action (and inaction) in response to democratic crises in Latin America from 1991 to the present. Utilizing both qualitative and quantitative data, the chapter seeks to answer three key questions. First, when (and how) is the OAS most likely to intervene on behalf of democracy? For example, has the OAS consistently responded to clear democratic interruptions such as coups and *autogolpes*? Second, what explains why the OAS takes action in some cases and not others? And, finally, what impact has intervention had on democratic quality and sustainability in the region?

Ascertaining the depth of the OAS's commitment to democracy is important for a variety of reasons. In the first place, the defense of democracy by the OAS challenges the fundamental principle of state sovereignty, implying that governments are not free to act as they please in terms of their internal affairs.[4] Second, a consensually adopted commitment to democracy begs the question of whether the OAS continues to be dominated by the United States (as it was during the Cold War) or whether its actions now reflect a true multilateral consensus among member states. Last but not least, an analysis of the OAS is important in a very practical sense; within the past several years, not only has Latin America witnessed coups or coup attempts in Paraguay (2000), Ecuador

(2000), Venezuela (2002), and Haiti (2004), but some of Latin America's more established democracies (such as Argentina, Colombia, and Trinidad and Tobago) have also come under strain. An analysis of the OAS, thus, helps to answer the practical question of what international organizations can do to prevent the breakdown of democracy.[5]

In what follows, I advance a number of interrelated arguments. I argue, in brief, that the OAS's response to recent democratic crises in the region suggests an ambiguous and potentially weakening commitment on the part of the OAS to utilize its formal legal instruments for the collective defense of democracy. The OAS has tended to use these instruments only for the most extreme cases of democratic interruption, such as coups and *autogolpes,* and never directly in relation to violations of electoral or constitutional procedures, which are often privileged as sovereign state practices. At the same time, however, the OAS has successfully developed an array of informal and ad hoc procedures—such as public condemnation, diplomatic pressure, and high-level missions—that permit a flexible if inconsistent response to electoral irregularities, constitutional challenges, and other threats to democracy. In short, the defense of democracy regime in the Americas remains uneven.

The reasons for the OAS's ambiguous and inconsistent behavior are complex and require a nuanced investigation of global-, organizational-, and domestic-level factors. First, at a geopolitical level, the organization's attempts to promote democracy have been hampered by a growing divergence in the strategic priorities of the organization's most important member states. This divergence has been driven, on the one hand, by the increasingly unilateral and security-focused foreign policy posture of the United States following 9/11 and, on the other hand, by the rise of left-wing and populist governments in South America, above all that of Hugo Chávez in Venezuela. The increased distance between the United States and the Latin American states as regards what constitutes democracy and what appropriate diplomatic measures should be taken to defend it has stymied the organization's attempts to promote a consistent doctrine.[6]

Second, at an organizational level, the extremely limited resources and budget of the OAS have hindered the organization's ability to develop longer-term programs to deepen democratic practices in the region.[7] Consequently, the organization remains ill equipped to address issues such as the quality of democracy itself. It has tended to focus more narrowly on easily observable democratic procedures, such as elections and egregious violations of the constitutional order (namely coups and *autogolpes*).[8]

Finally, and perhaps most importantly, the ability of the OAS to promote democracy has been challenged by the changing nature (and frequency) of domestic threats to democracy themselves. One particularly disturbing on-the-ground trend is a rash of what I term *impeachment coups*: illegal (and often violent) acts by a disloyal opposition that unseat elected presidents and effect a quasi-legal transfer of power to a constitutionally designated successor.[9] Examples can be found in countries as diverse as Argentina, Bolivia, and Ecuador. The blending of illegality and constitutionality in these crises is a particular challenge for the OAS because they combine both democratic and anti-democratic practices. This challenge is made all the more daunting by the very real possibility that those who seek to undermine democratic governments in the region (whether from within or from without) have increasingly learned to "cloak" their undemocratic activities under constitutional banners in order to shield themselves from international criticism.[10] This possibility, in turn, highlights the necessity of examining the interaction among global-, organizational-, and domestic-level processes in studying the behavior of the OAS.

Lastly, as regards the impact that intervention has had on democratic quality and sustainability in the region, I conclude that OAS actions have had an immediate but short-lived positive impact. In short, a dispassionate summary of OAS practice might be as follows: it is a relatively weak organization doing an imperfect job of promoting a rather limited notion of representative democracy. Yet, in spite of all its weaknesses, the OAS still makes a contribution to the promotion of democracy that would be impossible without it.

This chapter is organized into three sections. First, I briefly review the main mechanisms developed by the OAS to promote democracy in the Western Hemisphere and review the literature addressing the defense of democracy regime since 1991. Second, I outline a set of systematic criteria for assessing when the OAS is most likely to intervene in response to democratic crises. Third, I analyze the behavior of the OAS in response to democratic crises since 1991 and assess the impact intervention has had on democratic quality and sustainability in the region.

The Evolution of the Inter-American Defense of Democracy Regime since 1990

Beginning in 1990, the OAS created a number of mechanisms designed to institutionalize more firmly the organization's commitment to democracy (see table 3.1).[11] In 1990 it first created a new administrative arm, the Unit for the

Table 3.1. Summary of OAS Mechanisms for the Promotion of Democracy, 1991

Mechanisms	Description of What Constitutes a Democratic Crisis	Nature of OAS Response
DPD and Electoral Observations	Electoral irregularities	No mandate is specified beyond reporting the results of electoral observation.
OAS Resolution 1080 (the Santiago Commitment), 1991–	A "sudden or irregular interruption of the democratic political institutional process"	The response is (theoretically) automatic: the Permanent Council must examine the situation and recommend whether a special meeting of the Ministers of Foreign Affairs or of the General Assembly is warranted within ten days of the crisis.
Washington Protocol, 1992–	A "democratically constituted government has been overthrown by force"	The response *may* entail suspension from the OAS *with a two-thirds vote in the General Assembly.*
Inter-American Democratic Charter (IADC), 9/11/2001–	An "unconstitutional interruption of the democratic order or an unconstitutional alteration of the constitutional regime that seriously impairs the democratic order in a member state" (Article 19)	Convocation of the Permanent Council can be called at the request of *any* state or the secretary-general to undertake a collective assessment and appropriate "diplomatic initiatives" (Article 20). The Permanent Council can recommend an immediate meeting of the General Assembly (GA); and, with a two-thirds vote, the GA can suspend the member state in question (Article 21).

Promotion of Democracy (UPD), to develop programs reinforcing the hemispheric trend toward democracy (since renamed the Department for the Promotion of Democracy or DPD).[12]

Second, in June 1991, following on the heels of the sudden collapse of the Soviet Union, the OAS issued a landmark declaration in support of democracy and, through the adoption of Resolution 1080, created an automatic mechanism to respond to democratic crises in the region, especially illegal seizures of power. In particular, Resolution 1080 pledges the OAS secretary-general to convene an immediate emergency meeting of the OAS Permanent Council following any "sudden or irregular interruption of the democratic political institutional process," a phrase meant to apply, in particular, to coups (OAS 1991). The Permanent Council then examines the situation and recommends whether a special meeting of the ministers of foreign affairs or of the General Assembly is warranted, all within ten days of the democratic interruption.

Third, in amending the charter through the adoption of the Washington Protocol (1992), the organization furthermore established that the General Assembly could, with a two-thirds vote, suspend any member state from the OAS in the event that "its democratically constituted government has been overthrown by force" (OAS 1992d).[13]

Fourth and finally, with the adoption of the Inter-American Democratic Charter (IADC; see appendix B) on September 11, 2001, the OAS broadened its conception of what constitutes a democratic crisis to include any "unconstitutional alteration of the constitutional regime," a phrase meant to apply specifically to the undemocratic actions of elected officials (OAS 2001b). Beyond this, the IADC outlined a broad definition of what constitutes representative democracy (Articles 3 and 4) and provided new provisions (found in Articles 17 and 18) that enable member states to invite OAS mediation when a democratic crisis appears to be developing. The new IADC, thus, can be considered an extension of Resolution 1080, superseding its mandate and potentially widening its scope.[14]

Scholarly assessments of the Inter-American defense of democracy regime have varied considerably. Reflecting on the OAS's response to democratic crises in Haiti (1991), Peru (1992), and Guatemala (1993), Heraldo Muñoz (1998, 1–2) found evidence to support the claim that the "right to democracy" in the Americas had evolved "from a moral prescription to an international legal obligation."[15] Yet, on the other hand, Richard Bloomfield concluded that "the cases of Haiti and Peru demonstrate [that] the Santiago mechanism is *no guarantee* that an elected constitutional government, once overthrown, will be restored" (1994, 167, emphasis added). Debates regarding the salience of the democracy regime have continued since 1993, as the OAS has confronted a continuation of, and arguably an increase in, democratic crises in the region—from among the smaller countries of the Caribbean, Central America, and the Andes to the larger, intermediate powers. This chapter seeks to make a further contribution to the debate by analyzing the OAS's response to every major democratic crisis in Latin America since 1991.

An Assessment of Democratic Crises: Determining the Relevant Cases

In order to assess the OAS's commitment to democracy, we must identify what qualifies—under the OAS rubric—as a democratic crisis and then evaluate whether the OAS has taken action commensurate with its legal, procedural commitments as specified in OAS doctrine (see table 3.1). First, we can briefly review both the qualitative and quantitative assessments of democracy in Latin America since 1991.[16]

Larry Diamond (1996, 61) concluded in 1996 that, "since 1987, despite commonplace North American conceptions to the contrary, Latin America has not made significant net progress toward greater democracy." A look at more recent data available from Freedom House would not alter this assessment; democracy in Latin America is alive but not well. As of 2004, only a handful of countries in the region—Chile, Uruguay, Costa Rica, Panama, Argentina, and Mexico—fit Diamond's criteria for "liberal democracy" or "democracy," that is, a combined Freedom House score of between 2 and 4.[17] Today, most of the countries of Latin America match Diamond's labels of "partially illiberal democracy," or "near democracy," including the most populous, Brazil. Moreover, these limited democracies (which have a combined freedom score of 5 or 6) appear to be entirely stable regime types.[18] Finally, a significant minority of countries persists in the least democratic categories of "semidemocracy" (Venezuela), "semicompetitive authoritarian" (Guatemala and Colombia), and varying degrees of authoritarian rule (Haiti and Cuba).[19]

Despite their utility, existing datasets do not necessarily tell us anything about the nature of democratic crises in Latin America, and much less of course about the nature of the OAS response pursuant to its formal-legal obligations. What, then, characterizes a democratic crisis as defined by OAS protocols? Certainly a military coup unseating a democratically elected leader constitutes a "sudden or irregular interruption of the democratic political institutional process" (Resolution 1080)—but what else? One useful starting point is OAS practice itself.[20] Since the Santiago Declaration in June 1991, the OAS has invoked Resolution 1080 in response to four cases: the 1991 coup in Haiti, *autogolpes* (or "self-coups") in Peru (1992) and Guatemala (1993), and the civil-military crisis in Paraguay in 1996, which entailed a credible threat of a military coup.[21] In addition, Article 20 of the Democratic Charter was invoked—although not without controversy—in response to the brief coup against President Hugo Chávez in Venezuela in April 2002.[22] OAS practice, in short, makes plain that, at a minimum, examples of democratic crises ("interruptions" or "alterations") would include successful coups that unseat elected presidents, self-coups by elected presidents that nullify legislative and judicial checks and balances, and civil-military crises in which there is a credible threat of a military coup. Indeed, the OAS mandate following the Cold War clearly envisioned coups as the primary threat to democracy in Latin America.

Failed coup attempts, on the other hand, do not appear (by OAS practice) to constitute a "sudden or irregular interruption of the democratic political institutional process," because the OAS did not invoke Resolution 1080 (or the IADC) in response to such attempts in Venezuela (twice in 1992), Paraguay (2000), and Haiti (2001). This does not mean that such episodes should be excluded from an empirical analysis of OAS behavior (in fact, each case provoked some declaratory response by the OAS) but rather that they do not appear to be part of the OAS's envisioned mandate of Resolution 1080 and the IADC.

An additional consideration is whether major election failures or constitutional crises constitute an "interruption" or "alteration" of a democratic regime. These urgent situations do not appear to have been contemplated by the Santiago Declaration of 1991. However, in adopting the Democratic Charter in 2001, which broadened the scope of crises (beyond the narrow definition of Resolution 1080) to include any "unconstitutional alteration of the constitutional regime," the OAS seemed to be opening itself to this possibility—while also giving itself the flexibility to determine on a case-by-case basis when such action "seriously impairs the democratic order."[23] In summary, we can conclude that OAS practice prioritizes coups as the primary threat to democracy and treats coup attempts, major election failures, and constitutional crises as second-order threats, to be handled largely on a case-by-case basis—contingent on how gravely they threaten the democratic order.

Beyond looking at OAS practice, can we develop a set of reasonably objective empirical standards to determine whether a given event qualifies as a "sudden or irregular interruption of the democratic political institutional process" (Resolution 1080) or an "unconstitutional alteration of the constitutional regime that seriously impairs the democratic order in a member state" (IADC, Articles 19 and 20)? Ultimately, given the limitations of current datasets (i.e., the inexistence of any comprehensive and up-to-date datasets on democratic crises), the assessment will have to be largely qualitative. Nevertheless, a few tentative insights might be gleaned from a survey of the available quantitative data.

As a starting point, it is useful to examine the Electoral Democracy Index (EDI) of the United Nations Development Program (UNDP 2004). The EDI disaggregates the concept of democracy into four components, allowing for precise and rank-ordered comparisons of democracy along several dimensions and in language that can be easily paired to OAS protocols. For the immediate post–Cold War period (1990–2002), the EDI reveals ten instances (in a sample of eighteen countries) in which Latin American countries experienced a decline in their EDI score from one year to the next: Argentina (2001), Ecuador (1997 and 2000), Guatemala (1993), Nicaragua (2001), Paraguay (1999), Peru (1992 and 2000), the Dominican Republic (1994), and Venezuela (2002). Of course, these cases differed in both substance and severity. Two cases, the Dominican Republic (1994) and Peru (2000), correspond to major election irregularities that had a determinative impact on the outcome of the election results.[24] One other case, Nicaragua (2001), was downgraded by virtue of an observed decline in the freeness of elections, namely efforts by the two leading parties to exclude smaller parties.[25] The remaining cases of democratic decline represent examples of irregularities with respect to displacement and replacement of elected officeholders. Significantly, the UNDP dataset ranks these cases in terms of their relative severity: the *autogolpe* in Peru (1992) is considered the most significant deviation, followed by the crises in Paraguay (1999), Venezuela (2002), Ecuador (2000), Guatemala (1993), and, less severely perhaps, Ecuador (1997) and Argentina (2001).[26] In summary, although the UNDP dataset is somewhat limited in terms of spatial and geographical coverage, it nevertheless provides an excellent foundation for an inventory of the major democratic crises since 1990.[27]

Examining the Freedom House data is also useful.[28] For example, it is reasonable to insist that any instance of a country in the Americas passing from a "free" or "partly free" rating into the "not free" category of the Freedom House dataset would constitute a democratic crisis. This ignominious distinction would include Haiti in 1991–93 (the military junta) and Haiti in 2000–2004 (democratic breakdown under Aristide).[29] In addition to these clear-cut cases, we might also propose (as a simple and tentative heuristic) that any sharp decline in political freedom (a 2-point drop in the Freedom House data over a one-year period) would constitute a democratic crisis. This would include Venezuela (1992 and 1999), Chile (1998), and Argentina (2001).[30] Allowing for a two-year period of decline (admittedly a less robust measure for a "sudden" crisis) would additionally qualify Colombia (1994–95); the Dominican Republic (1993–94), Trinidad and Tobago (2000–2001), and Bolivia (2002–3)— corresponding, respectively, to the corruption scandal under President Samper in Colombia, failed elections under President Balaguer in the Dominican Republic, the constitutional crisis in Trinidad and Tobago, and the fall of Bolivia's government under Gonzalo "Goni" Sánchez de Lozada in October 2003.

Beyond looking at the available quantitative data, a qualitative assessment should likewise inform our discussion. To begin, if we were to accept that major election failures or constitutional crises fit the language of either Resolution 1080 or particularly the IADC, are there other potential examples of democratic crisis in Latin America since 1991? Two experts on the subject of electoral observation, Jonathan Hartlyn and Jennifer McCoy, identify three major election "failures" in the period 1991–2000: the Dominican Republic in 1994, Peru in 2000, and Venezuela in 2000.[31] Apart from the cases already mentioned, Latin America has also recently been beset by constitutional crises (of varying degrees of severity) in Venezuela (2003–4), Ecuador (2004–5), Bolivia (2005), and Nicaragua (2005). A very broad and comprehensive account of democratic crises, then, would include the following nineteen cases: Haiti (1991–94), Peru (1992), Guatemala (1993), Dominican Republic (1994), Paraguay (1996), Ecuador (1997), Paraguay (1999–2000), Venezuela (1999–2004), Ecuador (2000), Peru (2000), Haiti (2000–2003), Trinidad and Tobago (2000–2001), Argentina (2001), Nicaragua (2001–5), Venezuela (2002), Bolivia (2003), Haiti (2004), Ecuador (2004–5), and Bolivia (2005).[32]

This preliminary exercise of identifying democratic crises in Latin America errs on the side of inclusiveness. For purposes of analyzing the OAS's response, however, it will be useful to make a further and necessarily contentious distinction between those crisis cases that represent a direct threat to the defense of democracy regime (for instance, coups and *autogolpes*) and those that are arguably of a second-order nature (electoral crises, constitutional crises, and other noncoup emergencies). The former category includes five critical cases in which force was used to unseat elected officials: Haiti (1991), Peru (1992), Guatemala (1993), Ecuador (2000), and Venezuela (2002), and one case, Paraguay (1996), where an army general threatened to use force to unseat a sitting president. These are all cases in which we would expect the OAS to invoke its primary instruments for the defense of democracy (see table 3.2). A second group of cases—Paraguay (1999–2000), Bolivia (2003), Haiti (2004), and Ecuador (2004–5)—is ambiguous and difficult to classify as either an "interruption" or a serious "alteration" of democracy: each crisis involved significant violence, the resignation (and eventual exile) of a sitting president, and allegations of a coup (or, in the case of Paraguay in 2000, a subsequent coup attempt).[33] In short, these cases occupy a gray area in relation to coups, alleged coups, and what might be termed "near-coup crises." How the OAS ought to respond to these crises is likely to be contentious (see table 3.3). Finally, the remaining nine cases can largely be considered "second-order" threats to

Table 3.2. Democratic Crises in Latin America: Coups and Autogolpes

Crises	Did the OAS Invoke Its Primary Democratic Instruments?	OAS and Regional Response (and Relevant Documents)
Haiti, 1991–94 (coup in 1991 followed by authoritarian rule)	Yes: Resolution 1080	Condemnation (CP/RES. 567/91); multilateral sanctions (MRE/RES. 2/91, 3/92); establishment of a joint OAS-UN mission to monitor the regime's human rights practices; eventual UN military intervention in 1994 (S/RES/940/94)
Peru, 1992 (*autogolpe*)	Yes: Resolution 1080	Condemnation (CP/RES. 579/92); high-level mission; some bilateral sanctions imposed and/or threatened (no collective sanctions imposed by the OAS)
Guatemala, 1993 (*autogolpe*)	Yes: Resolution 1080	Condemnation (CP/RES. 605/93); bilateral sanctions threatened
Paraguay, 1996 (civil-military crisis with credible threat of a coup)	Yes: Resolution 1080	Condemnation (CP/RES. 681/96); bilateral and regional sanctions threatened
Ecuador, 2000 (coup)	No (Resolution 1080 would likely have been invoked had the junta not quickly stepped down from power)	Support for the Mahuad government (CP/RES. 763/00); sanctions threatened against the junta; condemnation of the threat to democracy and support of succession to the vice president (CP/RES. 764/00)
Venezuela, 2002 (coup)	Yes: IADC Article 20	Condemnation of the coup (CP/RES. 811/02); high-level tripartite mission to support dialogue (CP/RES. 821/02, 833/02)

Note: OAS documents are abbreviated by their common three- or four-digit descriptors and followed by their date of publication in two digits. CP = Permanent Council; MRE = ministers of foreign affairs; RES = resolutions; S = Security Council of the United Nations.

democratic regimes in the region, though a few cases are admittedly difficult to classify. These are all crises that we would expect the OAS to evaluate on a case-by-case basis.

We can thus ask two related but distinct questions about OAS behavior: (1) has the OAS consistently intervened in response to coup crises (particularly by invoking its main legal protocols), and (2) how has the OAS responded to near-coup and noncoup crises? These questions are addressed in the next section. Tables 3.2–3.4 provide a summary of each crisis and an indication of the OAS's response.[34]

Table 3.3. Democratic Crises in Latin America: Coups and Near-Coup Crises

Crises	Did the OAS Invoke Its Primary Democratic Instruments?	OAS and Regional Response (and Relevant Documents)
Paraguay, 1999–2000 (assassination of vice president and civil-military crisis)	No	Condemnation of assassination in 1999 (AG/DEC. 20/99); condemnation of coup attempt in 2000 and support for President González Macchi (CP/RES. 770/00)
Bolivia, 2003 (civil disorder and presidential resignation; allegations of a coup)	No	Condemnation of violence and support for the Sánchez de Lozada government (CP/RES. 838/00, 849/00); OAS support for succession of power to the vice president (CP/RES. 852/00)
Haiti, 2004 (civil disorder and presidential resignation; allegations of a coup)	No (Article 20 of the IADC was referenced only retroactively; use of the IADC was contemplated by some policy makers before the crisis, particularly by CARICOM members)	Condemnation of violence and support for constitutional government and existing missions (CP/RES. 861/04); appeal to UN to resolve crisis (CP/RES. 862/04); OAS acknowledgment that an alteration of the constitutional regime took place (prior to Aristide's resignation) and support for the provisional government to hold new elections (AG/RES. 2058/04)
Ecuador, 2004–5 (constitutional crisis; civil disorder and presidential resignation; allegations of a coup)	Yes/No: IADC Article 18 (invoked in 2005 by Ecuadorian government but only *after* the president's resignation)	High-level mission sent after the president resigns (CP/RES. 880/05); mission raises questions regarding the legality of constitutional succession (CP/DOC. 4028/05); eventual support and recognition of the new government (CP/RES. 883/05)

Note: OAS documents are abbreviated by their common three- or four-digit descriptors and followed by their date of publication in two digits. AG = General Assembly; CP = Permanent Council; DEC = declarations; DOC = documents; RES = resolutions.

Before turning to the response of the OAS to post–Cold War democratic crises in Latin America, it is useful to reflect on the pattern of crisis itself. On the one hand, the temporal aspect of the crises reveals that they have actually increased in frequency following a period of relative calm between the time of the United Nations military intervention in Haiti in 1994 and the election of Hugo Chávez in December 1998. However coincidentally, the inauguration of Chávez in 1999 presaged a new wave of democratic crises (of varying severity) in Latin America. On the other hand, the geographical aspect of the crises reveals that, for the entire post–Cold War period, the Andean countries (Venezuela,

Table 3.4. *"Second-Order" Democratic Crises:*
Flawed Elections and Unconstitutional Alterations of Power

Crises	Did the OAS Invoke Its Primary Democratic Instruments?	OAS and Regional Response (and Relevant Documents)
Dominican Republic, 1994 (failed elections)	No (Resolution 1080 contemplated by some U.S. policy makers)	Report by OAS electoral observers of serious electoral irregularities (CP/INF.3682/94); offer by OAS observation mission to mediate postelection Democracy Pact
Ecuador, 1997 (removal of president by constitutionally dubious procedure)	No	No significant response
Venezuela, 1999–2004 (failed elections and constitutional crisis)	No (on 2002 crisis, see table 3.3)	Observation and endorsement of elections in 1999 and 2000; high-level tripartite mission to support dialogue and an eventual recall referendum after the coup (CP/RES. 821/02, 833/02); observation and endorsement of the recall referendum in August 2004 (CP/RES. 869/04)
Haiti, 2000–2003 (flawed elections and democratic breakdown)	No (in 2000, Resolution 1080 contemplated by some U.S. policy makers; on 2004 crisis, see table 3.3)	Report by OAS electoral observers of electoral irregularities in 2000; a high-level mission sent to mediate the electoral and growing social-political crisis (CP/RES. 772/00, 786/01, 806/02, 822/02, AG/RES. 1959/03)
Peru, 2000 (failed elections)	No (Resolution 1080 contemplated by some OAS member states)	Report by OAS electoral observers of serious electoral irregularities (AG/DOC. 3936/00); high-level mission sent to Peru to facilitate national dialogue (AG/RES. 1753)
Argentina, 2001 (civil disorder and presidential resignations)	No	No significant response
Trinidad and Tobago, 2000–2001 (constitutional crisis)	No	No significant response
Bolivia, 2005 (civil disorder and presidential resignation)	No	Expression of regret regarding the political crisis which resulted in Carlos Mesa's resignation, offer of OAS mediation to the government of Bolivia (AG/DEC. 42/05)

Table 3.4. Continued

Crises	Did the OAS Invoke Its Primary Democratic Instruments?	OAS and Regional Response (and Relevant Documents)
Nicaragua, 2001–5 (constitutional crisis)	Yes: IADC (Article 18) invoked in 2005 by Nicaraguan government	High-level mission sent to establish dialogue and support democratic institutions (AG/DEC. 43/05); report issued to the Permanent Council; resolution issued in support of Nicaraguan democracy and President Enrique Bolaños (CP/RES. 892/05)

Note: OAS documents are abbreviated by their common three- or four-digit descriptors and followed by their date of publication in two digits. AG = General Assembly; CP = Permanent Council; DEC = declarations; DOC = documents; INF = informative document; RES = resolutions.

Colombia, Ecuador, Peru, and Bolivia) appear to be the most prone to democratic crisis (representing nearly half of the total of the crisis cases), followed by the Caribbean states and, finally, the countries of the Southern Cone.[35]

Of course, the fact that the chronically weak democracies of Central America have not recently experienced democratic crises should not obscure the fact that many of them appear to be in what I would term a semipermanent state of semicrisis. By Freedom House standards, for example, many of the crisis-ridden cases in the Andes are quantitatively indistinguishable from, say, Honduras and Guatemala. This highlights an important and little-discussed limitation of OAS doctrine, namely that it addresses interruptions and alterations of democracy but not the quality of democracy itself. Thus, a constitutional framework with patently undemocratic features, such as Chile's (from 1980 until the recent reforms), would be immune from criticism by the OAS as long as the constitutional framework was upheld.

Finally, with respect to income, no clear pattern emerges. In the 1990s democratic crises were mostly a phenomenon plaguing the relatively poor "low" and "lower-middle" income countries of Latin America—particularly those with a per capita gross national income of less than US$2,350—namely Haiti, Paraguay, Ecuador, Guatemala, Peru, and the Dominican Republic.[36] In the past five years, however, many of the richest "middle" income countries of the region—Argentina, Trinidad and Tobago, and Venezuela—have also experienced crises of varying degrees of severity.[37]

Evaluating the Pattern of Crisis and Intervention

Having determined the relevant cases of unconstitutional interruptions and alterations since 1991, we can now turn to our primary task: analyzing the OAS response. Has the OAS consistently invoked its primary democracy instruments, Resolution 1080 and the IADC, in response to democratic crises in the post–Cold War era? The evidence is decidedly mixed: some threats to democracy, such as military coups and *autogolpes,* have elicited a strong response from the OAS, whereas others, such as electoral and constitutional irregularities, have educed a more passive reaction. The defense of democracy regime in the Americas remains uneven.

The OAS response has been fairly (though not entirely) consistent with respect to condemning the most egregious cases of democratic interruption in the region, such as coups and *autogolpes* (see table 3.2). The invocation of Resolution 1080 and the IADC in Haiti, Peru, Guatemala, Paraguay, and Venezuela, in turn, became the basis for sustained diplomatic pressure by the OAS against illegal seizures of power. In the case of Haiti in 1991, for example, the use of Resolution 1080 set in motion a process that led to a series of escalating sanctions that ended with a U.S.-led military intervention to restore the elected president, Jean-Bertrand Aristide, to power in 1994. Indeed, in marked contrast with the Cold War period, classic coups d'etat have now become effectively proscribed as a legitimate means of domestic political change. Even in the narrow realm of opposing coups and *autogolpes,* however, some qualifications are in order, particularly with respect to the cases of Venezuela (2002) and, equally significant, Ecuador (2000).

In the case of Venezuela, where a coup in April 2002 temporarily unseated elected president Hugo Chávez, what stands out about the OAS response is not the (appropriate) invocation of the IADC but rather the delayed response of the United States—which, in its failure to immediately condemn the coup, appeared to endorse it.[38] The muted response by the United States, in turn, lends itself to at least two possible interpretations. On a positive note, the process revealed the independence of the regional powers of Latin America as well as Canada to take principled action—even against the interests of the United States, which harbored a pronounced hostility toward the left-wing Chávez government. Far more negatively, however, the episode revealed that the United States, particularly under George W. Bush's administration, had become unreliable in its defense of democracy against illegal seizures of power in the region. To be sure, the response of the Bush administration quickly damaged the hard-fought credibility that had been earned by the United States in its consistent support for democracy in the region during the preceding decade, specifically under the George H. W. Bush and Clinton administrations (Valenzuela 2002).

The response of the OAS to the coup in Ecuador in January 2000 also demands further explication. Indeed, the failure of the OAS to invoke Resolution 1080 in response to the coup is a conspicuous case of OAS nonintervention because it involved a *successful* coup against a democratically elected government, that of Jamil Mahuad, who was ousted from power by a coalition of the military and indigenous groups.[39] It is all the more surprising as a case of nonintervention because of Ecuador's seemingly trivial strategic import; few countries had much to lose by invoking Resolution 1080 against Ecuador. Nevertheless, in practical terms, the mere threat of invoking sanctions in Ecuador proved sufficient in bringing about an end to the short-lived junta that seized power on January 21. The United States, for example, warned the Ecuadorian military that it would confront international isolation if the junta stayed in power (*Economist* 2002). Similarly, the OAS Permanent Council issued Resolution 763 (1220/00), making explicit reference to Resolution 1080 and giving "decisive support" to President Mahuad. With the threat of sanctions looming, the junta opted for an interesting compromise: in an attempt to restore some semblance of constitutionality, power was handed over to Mahuad's successor as vice president, Gustavo Noboa. In seeming contradiction of Resolution 1080, the OAS accepted this practical compromise—lending its support to Noboa's government in Permanent Council Resolution 764 (1221/00) in spite of the fact that his (albeit unpopular) predecessor had been ousted illegally. Although a semblance of constitutional order had been preserved in Ecuador, the "unfortunate events of January 21" represented a potentially dangerous precedent.[40]

Ultimately, I argue, the crisis in Ecuador in 2000 presaged a series of what I term impeachment coups, or illegal (and often violent) acts by a disloyal opposition that unseat elected presidents and effect a quasi-legal transfer of power to a constitutionally designated successor. In different manifestations (and often with quite different implications for democracy), this new form of crisis spread quickly from Ecuador in 2000 to Argentina in 2001 and Bolivia in 2003, and it revisited both Ecuador and Bolivia in 2005.

The case of Haiti in February 2004 represents yet another type of challenge.

In failing to invoke the IADC in response to an armed rebellion and the gathering coup threat in early 2004, the OAS (again) appeared to condone the illegal overthrow of an elected (though unpopular and at times autocratic) president; without questioning the nature of Aristide's departure from power, the organization moved to try to ensure that a legal (or quasi-legal?) constitutional successor be appointed to take his place.[41] In ambiguous near-coup crises such as these, the OAS must be sure not to confuse legal ends with illegal means; the use of street violence to unseat elected presidents is a disastrous substitute for the constitutional process of impeachment. Indeed, the tendency of the OAS to recognize and grant legitimacy to the successors of such crises is likely to encourage future conspirators.

Having examined the fairly consistent (though problematic) response of the OAS to the relatively clear-cut cases of coups and *autogolpes* in the region, we now turn to how the OAS has responded to the more ambiguous or, in some cases, less severe cases of authoritarian regression in the region. In vivid contrast to its response to coups and *autogolpes,* the OAS response with respect to near-coup crises (table 3.3) and electoral and constitutional irregularities (table 3.4) has been fairly (though not entirely) consistent in *not* invoking its primary legal instruments—in spite of the fact that the adoption of the IADC in September 2001 provided increasing scope for such intervention in the more recent cases.[42] Nevertheless, the failure of the OAS to invoke Resolution 1080 or the IADC in these crises should not be equated with complete inaction. For example, with respect to the most glaring cases of electoral irregularities in the region—the Dominican Republic in 1994, Peru in 2000, and Haiti in 2000—the OAS adopted a critical posture in its electoral observation reports and, in each case, played a critical role in attempting to mediate social conflict after the election, in particular through the deployment of high-level missions, a technique that has been used in responding to several other crisis cases as well.[43] In the case of Nicaragua, moreover, the OAS has even registered its capacity for taking preventative measures to safeguard democracy, in this case following President Enrique Bolaños's rather exceptional request for OAS mediation under the auspices of Article 18 of the IADC—the only time other than the case of Paraguay in 1996 that either Resolution 1080 or the IADC has been invoked *before* a coup occurred.

The reluctance of the OAS to invoke its primary democratic instruments directly in response to electoral and constitutional irregularities (table 3.4) is perhaps not that surprising. On the one hand, it is only since September 2001 that the IADC has established a formal mandate for the OAS to intervene in "alterations" of a constitutional regime. Moreover, the IADC stipulates in Articles 19 and 20 that, in order to merit application of the charter, an alteration must be one "that seriously impairs the democratic order in a member state," a phrase infused with ambiguity, because it is not clear what types of alterations might be considered serious threats to democracy. No doubt this ambiguity is intentional because, perhaps more than any other aspect of the IADC, it directly challenges the sovereign right of individual governments to rule as they see fit. And whereas the elected presidents of Latin America may see coups as a realistic threat to their rule, they may also view alterations such as ballot-stuffing or court-stacking as a convenient expedient to maintain their rule. Indeed, the application of the IADC to "unconstitutional alterations" in Haiti (2004) and Ecuador (2005) occurred only retroactively—that is, after the elected president was overthrown. And in Nicaragua its application occurred only at the request of a besieged government. In short, the IADC has never been invoked by the OAS against a sitting president. Thus, the OAS's response to democratic crises in Latin America has varied according to the nature of the crisis itself and the challenges particular crises pose for issues of state sovereignty.

Finally, let me respond to the question of whether the OAS has had any constructive impact where it has intervened. The Freedom House data reveal, ultimately, that in the few cases where the OAS has taken some form of action, it has generally had an immediate and positive but short-lived impact.[44] In its initial impact, for example, the Haitian case (post-1994) could be counted as a successful intervention (democracy was, after all, restored); however, any gains in democratic consolidation were lost by 2000 and continued to deteriorate thereafter. In Peru, OAS action appears to have curbed the worst excesses of Fujimori but had no subsequent impact on the quality of democracy in Peru (until a corruption scandal forced the three-term president out of power). Still, the OAS (which had monitored six Peruvian elections in nine years) likely contributed to Fujimori's ouster, which, after it was over, enabled Peru to become "free" by Freedom House standards; however limited, Peru is perhaps the closest thing to a successful case of OAS intervention.[45] On the other hand, Haiti, Guatemala, Paraguay, and Venezuela have followed paths of negligible and/or zero improvement (all were partly free before the OAS interventions and remained so afterward). Then again, these results are not particularly surprising when considered in light of the OAS's extremely limited resources and the rather restricted scope of its interventions.

In summary, the OAS response to democratic crises in the region suggests an ambiguous commitment on the part of the OAS to utilize its formal instruments for the collective defense of democracy. The OAS has tended to use these instruments only for the most extreme cases of democratic interruption, such as coups and *autogolpes*, and never directly in relation to violations of electoral or constitutional procedures. The reasons for the OAS's ambiguous and inconsistent behavior are complex and can be explained, in part, by important long-term organizational weaknesses, the shifting strategic priorities of the organization's most important members (particularly the United States), as well as by the changing nature (and frequency) of threats to democracy themselves. Pessimistically, we might conclude that the OAS is a relatively weak organization doing an imperfect and inconsistent job of promoting a rather limited notion of representative democracy. For all its weaknesses, however, the OAS has made a positive contribution to democracy promotion efforts in the Americas, particularly in its (generally) unified condemnation of coups, *autogolpes*, and egregious election failures.

NOTES

1. The other seven examples are Jamil Mahuad (Ecuador, 2000), Alberto Fujimori (Peru, 2000), Fernando de la Rúa (Argentina, 2001), Hugo Chávez—temporarily (Venezuela, 2002), Gonzalo Sánchez de Lozada (Bolivia, 2003), Jean-Bertrand Aristide (Haiti, 2004), and (less than two months earlier) Lucio Gutiérrez (Ecuador, 2005). On the phenomenon of Latin America's interrupted presidencies, see Valenzuela (2004).

2. See, for example, *Miami Herald* (2005a); *New York Times* (2005a); *Economist* (2005b); and *San Francisco Chronicle* (1999).

3. For assessments (both optimistic and pessimistic) of the "Defense-of-Democracy Regime" (Bloomfield 1994) in the Western Hemisphere, see especially Franck (1992); Hakim (1993); Muñoz (1993; 1996; 1998); Bloomfield (1994); Acevedo and Grosman (1996); Farer (1996a); Valenzuela (1997); Cooper and Legler (2001a; 2001b; 2005; 2006); McClintock (2001); Boniface (2002); Cameron (2003); Pastor (2003); Cooper and Thérien (2004); and Legler (2007).

4. The OAS is one of a growing number of international organizations to have institutionalized a commitment to democracy within its regional institutions. The European Union is obviously the most important example of this practice. The British-led

Commonwealth, which recently suspended Zimbabwe from participation, affords another example, perhaps more comparable to the OAS in terms of its membership composition. See *Economist* (2003). On the Commonwealth, see also Klotz (1995, 55–72).

5. For an extended analysis of the issue of whether membership in international organizations promotes democracy, see especially Pevehouse (2002a; 2002b; 2005). See also Halperin and Lomasney (1998).

6. On deteriorating United States–Latin American relations, see, among others, Hakim (2006).

7. On the inability of the OAS budget to keep up with its expanding mandates, see especially Graham (2005).

8. On the notion of the quality of democracy, see Diamond and Morlino (2004).

9. As used here, impeachment coups are similar but not equivalent to what Omar Encarnación (2002, 38–39) describes (in reference to Venezuela's coup in 2002) as a "civil society coup" or "the handling of governing crises by extraconstitutional, undemocratic means by such actors as the business community, organized labor, religious institutions, and the media." In contrast to the case of Venezuela in 2002, impeachment coups do not imply a significant regime change; rather they entail continuity in terms of the underlying constitutional structure. The overthrow of Chávez in April 2002 was more like a traditional military coup than what I am describing here.

10. Similar arguments motivate work on semi-authoritarianism by scholars such as Carothers (2002), Ottaway (2003), and Levitsky and Way (2005).

11. Explanations for the increasing legalization of democratic principles in the OAS in the 1990s are examined by Hawkins and Shaw (in this volume).

12. The organization is best known for the role it has played in monitoring elections in the hemisphere; for example, the UPD played a critical role in denouncing electoral irregularities during Peru's 2000 presidential elections, dubiously won by Alberto Fujimori. See Cooper and Legler (2001b) and McClintock (2001), as well as Lean (in this volume) and Santa-Cruz (in this volume).

13. The Washington Protocol was adopted by the Sixteenth Special Session of the OAS General Assembly on December 14, 1992, and went into force in 1997; it applies only to signatories.

14. The Democratic Charter was an outgrowth of the Third Summit of the Americas held in Québec in April 2001, during which democracy was contemplated as a conditional prerequisite to a state's participation in the summit process and in the proposed Free Trade Area of the Americas (FTAA). On the charter and the summit process, see especially Cooper (2001; 2004) and Lagos and Rudy (2002).

15. See also the contributions in the Farer volume (1996a) and Boniface (2002).

16. The quantitative reflections are based on data available from Freedom House (2003a; 2003b; 2004) for 1972–2004, assembled by Mainwaring, Brinks, and Pérez-Liñán (2001) for 1945–99, and released by the UNDP for 1990–2002. Following Larry Diamond (1996, 57), and in the interest of manageability and comparability, I limit my analysis to countries with populations of 1 million people or more (this excludes, among others, the countries of Belize and Guyana).

17. According to Diamond's regime typology, countries are ranked by adding their Freedom House scores for "political rights" and "civil liberties"; the lower the score, the more "democratic" the country. Those countries with a combined score of 2 are

classified as "liberal democracies" while those with a score of 3–4 are "democracies." See Diamond (1996, 55–58). My classifications are based on these same criteria using data from Freedom House (2003a; 2003b; 2004). These data, it must be stressed, are used primarily for heuristic or illustrative purposes; for a methodological critique of the Freedom House data, see Mainwaring, Brinks, and Pérez-Liñán (2001) and Munck and Verkuilen (2002). For an alternative assessment, see UNDP (2004).

18. Guillermo O'Donnell in his writings on "Delegative Democracy" (1994) and the "Illusions about Consolidation" (1996) was among the first scholars to draw attention to the remarkable institutionalization and stability of Latin America's semidemocratic regimes; see also the discussion by Carothers (2002) and the ensuing debate in the *Journal of Democracy* 13, no. 3 (2002).

19. Data from the UNDP, discussed in greater detail later, paints a decidedly more optimistic picture of Latin American democracy since the end of the Cold War.

20. By this standard, a democratic crisis has taken place when the OAS invokes its formal-legal instruments, Resolution 1080 and the IADC. Of course, an analysis of such interventions may leave out democratic crises to which the OAS did not respond, a form of selection bias. For this reason, OAS practice is used here merely as a point of departure. Furthermore, there are many informal practices available to the OAS for responding to democratic crises that do not entail invoking Resolution 1080 or the IADC.

21. For a precise definition of the term *autogolpe,* and a summary of the Peruvian and Guatemalan cases, see Cameron (1998). On the Paraguayan crisis, see Valenzuela (1997).

22. Article 20 was also referenced (retroactively) in an OAS resolution criticizing Aristide's less-than-democratic rule in Haiti, though it was never invoked while he was in power. In May and June 2005, one of the so-called preventative clauses of the charter (Article 18) was invoked by the OAS at the request of the governments of Ecuador and Nicaragua in response to democratic crises in each country. In contrast to Articles 19 and 20, Article 18 is designed to lend OAS support to member states before a crisis threatens the democratic order.

23. The qualification in Articles 19 and 20 of the charter that an "unconstitutional alteration of the constitutional regime" must "seriously" impair the democratic order introduces tremendous ambiguity into the application of the charter. On this and other ambiguities, see especially Cameron (2003). Furthermore, the lack of explicit descriptions of serious alterations of the constitution is compounded by the practical problem of the OAS determining what is and is not constitutional in a given member state.

24. According to the UN data, and specifically component II of the EDI (clean elections), these are the only two cases for the 1990–2002 period in which significant electoral irregularities occurred that had a determinative impact on the outcome. They differ, then, from irregularities (in terms of cleanness) observed in countries such as Colombia, Guatemala, and Paraguay (the UNDP dataset does not register any irregularities in Venezuela, though some observers rejected the results of the May 2000 elections there). The dataset excludes Haiti, where 2000 elections were certainly flawed.

25. Other irregularities were registered by the UNDP in component III of the EDI (free elections), but no other case registers a decline from one year to the next for the period 1990–2002 except Peru (1992 and 2000).

26. The scores for component IV (elected public offices) range from a low of 0 and a

high of 4 (and allow a plus/minus adjustment). The exact scores are as follows: Peru, 1992 (2); Paraguay, 1999 (2+); Venezuela, 2002 (3−); Ecuador, 2000 (3); Guatemala, 1993 (3); Ecuador, 1997 (3+); and Argentina, 2001 (4−).

27. At the time of writing, data were unavailable for 2003 to 2006. Furthermore, the UNDP dataset excludes the key cases of Haiti and Trinidad and Tobago, among others.

28. This heuristic exercise serves, in part, to check the consistency of the multiple datasets available and also to expand coverage to countries not included in the UNDP study, such as Haiti and Trinidad and Tobago.

29. Peru in 1992 is on the borderline between "not free" and "partly free," receiving Freedom House's second lowest score possible in terms of political rights. In data gathered by Mainwaring, Brinks, and Pérez-Liñán (2001), Haiti and Peru are similarly the only two cases in the dataset (1945–99) that are classified as "authoritarian" during the post-1991 period, yet for Mainwaring, Brinks, and Pérez-Liñán (2001), Haiti was authoritarian for all of the 1990s.

30. The multiple coup attempts in Venezuela in 1992 did elicit condemnation from the OAS and support for the elected government (see OAS resolutions AG/RES. 1189 and CP/RES. 576). The Chilean case corresponds to the attendant polarization brought on by Augusto Pinochet's detention in London in 1998. The Argentine and Venezuelan (1999) crises are described in more detail later.

31. Election failures are those that are rejected by both observers and major parties. The authors also identify many "flawed" elections besides, most notably in Haiti (2000). See Hartlyn and McCoy (2001).

32. Some cases were excluded based on my own professional judgment. For example, because the Freedom House data on Venezuela (1992), Chile (1998), and Colombia (1994–95) are inconsistent with the UNDP data and other expert assessments, they are excluded from this analysis. Countries with fewer than 1 million inhabitants, such as Belize, were also excluded.

33. The case of Ecuador in 2004–5 encompasses two separate but related democratic crises. The first crisis occurred in late 2004 when President Lucio Gutiérrez and his congressional allies took aggressive measures to stack the country's judiciary with their political followers. The second crisis occurred in April 2005 when Gutiérrez was removed from the presidency by a controversial congressional vote (see Levitt in this volume).

34. The data in tables 3.2–3.4 are based on an exhaustive review of primary and secondary materials on the OAS and, in particular, archival materials available online at the OAS Web page, www.oas.org.

35. On the democratic crises in the Andes, see Shifter (2003) and Mainwaring (2006).

36. Data and income classifications are from the World Bank (2002; 2004).

37. On the relationship between per capita wealth levels and democratic sustainability, see Przeworski et al. (1996) and Przeworski and Limongi (1997).

38. On Venezuela, see Conaway (2002); Cameron (2003); and Legler (in this volume).

39. On the Ecuadorian coup, see Lucero (2001); McConnell (2001); and Walsh (2001).

40. After the junta stepped down from power, Ecuadorians curiously began referring to Mahuad's overthrow not as a coup but rather the "unfortunate events of January 21" (quoted in McConnell 2001, 76).

41. On the Haitian crisis, see especially O'Neill (2004); Shamsie (2004); Wucker (2004); Erikson (2005); and Goldberg (in this volume). Regarding accusations that the events of February 2004 amounted to a coup, see Marquis (2004) and *Economist* (2004).

42. It is worth reiterating that under Articles 19 and 20 of the IADC, such crises would have to "seriously" impair "the democratic order in a member state" for the OAS to take action. Under Articles 17 and 18 of the Democratic Charter, the OAS may also take action to prevent a minor or potential crisis from getting worse—but only with the prior consent of the host government. This is a potential obstacle to OAS action because elected leaders who find themselves under threat may be reluctant (for reasons of political survival) to acknowledge that their rule is in jeopardy.

43. The deployment of high-level missions and political mediation is a particularly novel (and arguably quite effective) form of "intervention" in the OAS repertoire of action, and has been employed, in addition to the cases indicated already, in the aftermath of the coup against Chávez in Venezuela in 2002 and the collapse of the Gutiérrez government in Ecuador in 2005. For a detailed analysis of this new form of OAS intervention, see Cooper and Legler (2005; 2006).

44. My findings are thus consistent with previous analyses of the limited ability of international organizations to effect positive democratic change. See, for example, Isaacs (1996); Remmer (1996); and Levitsky and Way (2005).

45. The OAS contribution to democratization in Peru is discussed in detail in Legler (2003).

CHAPTER FOUR

The United States

Rhetoric and Reality

Carolyn M. Shaw

> During its occupation of [the country], the United States did attempt to develop the semblance of constitutional government and made numerous improvements in the areas of health, public works, and bureaucratic administration. But these efforts did little to satisfy the [people], who grew increasingly rebellious and contemptuous of the U.S. presence in their country. Contrary to [the president's] ideals, the [people] did not see the United States as providing them with an opportunity to develop democracy, but rather as a powerful neighbor instituting a new form of colonialism
>
> KRYZANEK 1996

Given events in Iraq following the U.S. invasion in 2003, this excerpt could be a description of conditions in Iraq. The quotation, however, describes conditions dating back to the U.S. occupation of Haiti in 1915 ordered by President Woodrow Wilson and could accurately be applied to other cases during the past century. The United States has had a tradition of "promoting democracy" in Latin America and around the world for many years and still uses this rhetoric today to justify actions being taken in the war on terrorism. Although promoting democratic institutions in both Afghanistan and Iraq has followed the overthrow of the existing authoritarian regimes, militarized intervention is just one of a variety of strategies that the United States has adopted historically to promote democracy.[1] Justifications for U.S. involvement in the Western Hemisphere have always been controversial and Latin American states have often struggled to prevent unwanted U.S. interference in the region.

A lack of consistency has marked U.S. democracy promotion policy in the Western Hemisphere in recent years. The United States served as a key sponsor of the Washington Protocol (1992), an advocate of the restoration of President Aristide to power in 1994, as well as an important supporter of the Inter-American Democratic Charter (2001; see appendix B). Yet the United States also stands accused of questionable conduct concerning the failed coup against Venezuelan president Hugo Chávez in April 2002 as well as the ouster of President Aristide of Haiti in February 2004. These actions illustrate some of the contradictions in U.S. foreign policy when it comes to the promotion of democracy. Historically, U.S. strategies to promote democracy in Latin America have been inconsistent as well, based more on rhetoric than reality, and have often been counterproductive.

The decade following the end of the Cold War served as an exceptional time when U.S. and Latin American efforts to promote democracy coincided, supporting multilateral efforts through the Organization of American States (Shaw 2004). Democratic norms were strengthened with the passage of Resolution 1080 (1991; see appendix A), the Santiago Declaration (1991), and the Washington Protocol (1992). Although the initial euphoria of the 1990s for promoting and strengthening democracy throughout Latin America has subsided, the democratization process continues to move forward in the Western Hemisphere. Some have even suggested that the 1990s began a new era in which the norms of sovereignty and nonintervention evolved to allow greater intervention to protect democracy in the region (Farer 1996b). This certainly appears to be the case with OAS member states agreeing in the Washington Protocol to give the General Assembly authority to suspend a member state where a democratically constituted government has been overthrown by force. In addition to apparent normative changes, there are a variety of factors that affect the democratization process, including domestic, transnational, and international/external actors, not the least of which is the United States. Although the United States was significantly involved in the multilateral efforts of the OAS to promote democracy in the 1990s (see Boniface in this volume), U.S. engagement in the region has diminished with the rise of the war on terrorism. Despite this shift in focus away from Latin America, the United States, as the regional hegemon, will continue to be an influential actor affecting the democratization process in the region, although this possible evolution of norms may affect both its behavior and the democratization processes in the region.

This chapter begins by examining the contradictions in and the driving forces behind U.S. foreign policy making. A second section explores historical relations when economic and trade considerations, not democracy, were the

prominent issues on the U.S. foreign policy agenda. The third section examines relations during the Cold War when anticommunist ideology predominated U.S.-Latin American relations but the norm of democracy gradually
grew. The fourth section explores the "era of democratization" in the 1990s
and the changes in U.S.-Latin American relations following September 11,
2001. Finally, I conclude by making several policy recommendations for the
United States based on an assessment of different strategic models and evolving norms in the region. Although the United States still faces many of the
same policy constraints that it has in the past, it does have a variety of policy
options to consider, which include serving as an Instructor, Enforcer, Role
Model, Observer, or Enabler. Each of these roles has its own advantages and
disadvantages, but I argue that the Enabler role appears to have the most
positive potential.

Contradictions in U.S. Foreign Policy

The United States has a mixed record of promoting democracy in the
Western Hemisphere. The factors that drive U.S. foreign policy making particularly as it relates to democracy promotion are not simply normative ones,
strengthening democracy based on principle, but also include consideration of
system-level factors such as the balance of power between states. Peter Smith
(2000, 357) argues that four variables shape U.S. foreign policy toward Latin
America: the relative importance of Latin America vis-à-vis other world regions, perceptions of extrahemispheric rivalry, definitions of U.S. national
interest, and the relationship between state actors and social groups in policy
formation. Historically, Latin America was a very significant region with regard to U.S. imperial interests, as evidenced by the Monroe Doctrine of 1823.
This importance has waxed and waned over the years, as the United States has
alternately viewed Europeans and later the Soviets as rivals in the region,
threatening U.S. commercial and security interests. Although U.S. national
interests have shifted from territorial expansion and commercial influence in
the 1800s and early 1900s, to ideological competition during the Cold War, to
economic and social concerns today, the core element of accumulating power
as an international bargaining tool has remained (P. Smith 2000, 358). Whereas
policy makers were essentially unchallenged in their geostrategic manipulations during the Cold War, other pressure groups have begun to make increasing demands concerning the nature of U.S. foreign policy in Latin America.

Smith (2000, 359) adds that "throughout this sweep of history the United States steadfastly professed its intention of fostering democracy throughout the Americas, often invoking notions of hemispheric solidarity and the existence of a 'Western Hemisphere idea.' The promotion of democracy supplied a useful, sometimes crucial, rationalization for the application of American power." In other words, the rhetoric of promoting democracy has been present for many years. The question remains whether the United States will move beyond rhetoric to fully support the growth of democracy in the region based on a redefinition of its national interests.

Because of its strength within the Western Hemisphere, the United States has the potential power to move beyond rhetoric to reality, to formulate policies that actually facilitate democratization, not just advocate it. It does not always take this path, however. The United States faces other constraints that sometimes produce contradictory policies. U.S. principles and interests such as security and trade do not always dovetail. Democracy has been a core principle since the founding of the United States but has only gradually become a reality in the country over time as the franchise has been extended to minorities and women and additional efforts have been made to secure these rights. We see a similar evolutionary pattern in U.S. foreign relations with its Latin American neighbors. Although the United States was founded on democratic principles, these were not a driving force in its foreign policy in the 1800s. Economic and trade issues dominated U.S. foreign affairs. With the rise of empire in the late 1800s and early 1900s, security interests also became an important feature in U.S. foreign policy. Security concerns, framed in terms of anticommunism, predominated in the Cold War era.

Not until the administration of President Jimmy Carter did such principles gain significant standing in the formation of U.S. foreign policy. Even then, however, Carter was forced to make choices for the sake of security that contradicted democratic principles. Lars Schoultz (2002) argues that democracy first became a priority only in the 1980s. Prior to this the United States had other concerns and only paid lip service to democracy. The end of Cold War tensions and security concerns presented an opportunity to strengthen democracy in the hemisphere and the United States took advantage of this opportunity to cooperate with Latin American states through the OAS.

U.S. policy makers today face the same challenges that previous administrations have in terms of trying to reconcile power, prosperity, and principles as the driving forces of foreign policy (Jentleson 2004). Will U.S. leaders continue to invoke the rhetoric of promoting democracy? Will the United States move beyond rhetoric to action? What form will these actions take and what impact will they have? Before answering these questions, it is important to look back at relations between the United States and Latin America to see what role the United States has played in promoting democracy historically.

Historical U.S.–Latin American Relations

Early U.S. relations with Latin American states placed very little emphasis on the principle of democracy. U.S. engagement in the region waxed and waned, and economic and security concerns tended to take precedence. Early interactions among the United States and Latin American states can be divided into four eras dating from the 1820s to 1948 that reflect these shifting relations and priorities. The first era, which began in the 1820s and lasted until 1889, was one of U.S. isolationism. Throughout this period, the United States watched the growing number of interactions and agreements in Latin America and the nascent Pan-American movement but did not actively participate. The main focus of U.S. policy in the region was on fostering trade and avoiding political commitments. Despite U.S. commitment to the region stemming from the Monroe Doctrine (1823) that defended the hemisphere against external (i.e., European) intervention, the United States remained largely disengaged. The "political" focus (i.e., security concerns between states) of the early inter-American congresses did not appeal to U.S. administrations.

The second era, which was characterized by U.S. dominance, lasted from 1889 to 1923. This era began with the First International Conference of American States held in Washington in 1889. At this conference, the focus of the inter-American system shifted away from the security matters predominant among Latin American states in earlier conferences toward economic concerns that were the priority of the United States. Unlike the first era in which the United States remained uninvolved, the United States took the lead in bringing Latin American states together to discuss how to keep peace among themselves, to avoid European intervention, and, most importantly, to promote trade.

This era of U.S. dominance is best characterized by President Theodore Roosevelt's Corollary to the Monroe Doctrine. On December 6, 1904, in an address to Congress, Roosevelt stated that, "Chronic wrongdoing, or an impotence which results in a general loosening of the ties of civilized society, may in

America, as elsewhere, ultimately require intervention by some civilized nation, and in the Western hemisphere the adherence of the United States, however reluctantly . . . to the exercise of an international police power." Michael Kryzanek (1996, 44) argues that "under Roosevelt the United States began to view the Caribbean and Central America as an area that this country ha[d] an absolute right to control, whether through financial management, business investment, governmental reorganization, or outright military presence." Under President Taft (1909–13) the goals of economic penetration and the maintenance of political stability remained the same (Kryzanek 1996, 51; LaFeber 1999, 123). Taft intervened militarily in both Nicaragua and Honduras to restore order and stability (following coups). Latin American states had a slightly different experience with President Woodrow Wilson (1913–21). He continued to intervene in the region but argued that his actions stemmed from "his firm belief that the United States must take the initiative to ensure that constitutional democracies be established and protected in Latin America" (Kryzanek 1996, 51). The democratic rhetoric, however, was largely a cover for continued U.S. efforts to expand markets and enhance its security, and it ultimately caused considerable resentment toward the United States (Wood 1999, 109; Scheman 2003, 38).

The United States worked to establish de facto protectorates in several countries under Wilson. In Haiti, for example, when President Sam's government collapsed in 1915, Wilson quickly ordered U.S. troops into the country to restore order and prevent the French, Germans, or British from attempting to intervene. When the Haitian Congress selected Philippe Dartiguenave as the new president, the United States pressured him to sign a treaty authorizing it to take action to maintain "a government adequate for the protection of life, property and individual liberty" (Kryzanek 1996, 52). This treaty prohibited Haiti from increasing public debt without U.S. approval and placed a U.S. officer in charge of the constabulary force. In 1918 it was amended to require U.S. approval of all proposed legislation. Despite good intentions to promote stability in Haiti, Haitians grew increasingly resentful of the U.S. presence. After nineteen years of occupation, U.S. forces finally returned full sovereignty to the Haitians.

The situation was similar in the case of the Dominican Republic, where the assassination of President Ramón Cáceres in 1911 led to unrest and ultimately to U.S. occupation when an anti-American faction came to power. The U.S. forces promoted well-intentioned reforms in the areas of health care, sanitation, infrastructure, and finances, but Dominicans remained opposed to the U.S. presence and engaged in sporadic guerrilla attacks on U.S. forces throughout the eight-year occupation (Kryzanek 1996, 53). Despite these efforts at reform, a few years later Rafael Trujillo came to power as a harsh dictator and remained in power for thirty years.

Cuba and Nicaragua also experienced extended periods of direct U.S. intervention. U.S. forces were in Cuba from 1917 to 1923 with the U.S. commander actually taking an active hand in managing Cuban national finances. Marines remained in Nicaragua from the time of the Taft administration until 1933 during ongoing diplomatic wrangling about acquiring rights to construct a trans-isthmus canal. Ironically, in places where the U.S. actively intervened, some of the most enduring dictators came to power (such as Somoza in Nicaragua, Duvalier in Haiti, Batista in Cuba, and Trujillo in the Dominican Republic). In Costa Rica, Chile, and Venezuela, where the United States exercised only limited influence, democracies flourished.

The third era in early U.S.–Latin American relations was a brief transition period from 1923 to 1933. It began with the Fifth Inter-American Conference in 1923 where Latin American states became more assertive and brought more political topics to the agenda. Presidents Calvin Coolidge (1923–29) and Herbert Hoover (1929–33) gradually loosened U.S. political control over its "protectorates" (while still maintaining fiscal control). Hoover quietly repudiated the Roosevelt Corollary as a justification for military intervention with the Clark memorandum (1928). During a tour of South America, Hoover declared, "true democracy is not and cannot be imperialistic" (quoted in Shifter 2002b). U.S. policy gradually evolved from aggressive involvement to restraint, but relations remained quite contentious between Latin American countries and the United States. Latin Americans sought U.S. endorsement of the principle of nonintervention, but the United States refused to accept it as a basis for inter-American relations.

The fourth era from 1933 to 1948 was a cooperative, unifying period in which the foundations for the creation of the OAS were laid. During this time, relations between the United States and Latin American states gradually improved beginning with the Good Neighbor Policy of President Franklin D. Roosevelt (1933–45). At the Seventh Inter-American Conference held in Montevideo in 1933, the United States reversed its long-held position and declared that it was open to discuss any topic of general interest to the hemisphere including the principle of nonintervention. This reversal was the culmination of a number of changes in U.S. policy. The hostility of the previous era provided a clear indication that the tensions between the United States and Latin America could not be resolved except by reorienting U.S. policy. Five themes became evident in FDR's foreign policy as he sought better relations with Latin America: a deep concern for securing goodwill in Latin America, the idea that goodwill would increase trade, a favorable attitude toward working in association with Latin American states, hostility to "arbitrary intervention" in the domestic affairs of Latin American countries, and emphasis on "the spirit" of U.S. policy (Wood 1999, 110). Even when Mexico nationalized some U.S. oil facilities in 1938, Franklin Roosevelt chose to accept the ruling of the World Court, which called for monetary compensation, rather than intervening as American businessmen requested.

Although U.S. relations with Latin America improved under Franklin Roosevelt, this improvement did not translate into greater success in promoting democracy. Under Coolidge, Hoover, and Roosevelt, the United States struggled to stabilize Nicaragua by holding elections and ending U.S. occupation. After a decade of efforts and an election held in March 1947, however, Anastasio Somoza overthrew the newly established government. Lars Schoultz notes that this was a setback for U.S. democracy promotion efforts in the region (2002, 37). Schoultz further notes that the frustration over Nicaragua led to the abandonment of democracy as a policy goal based on the assessment by senior foreign policy officials that Latin American culture was lacking democratic characteristics and was thus too "immature" to embrace democracy (2002, 38).

Regardless of the "maturity" of Latin American society, the nature of early U.S. relations with Latin American states did little to establish strong foundations for the development of democracy in the region. The U.S. deliberately chose to remain disengaged early on, but when it finally did become active in the region, the interventions that occurred and the rancor that was aroused made Latin America unreceptive to many American ideals and policy preferences. Although Woodrow Wilson deliberately employed democratic rhetoric, calling for constitutional governments, the self-interested interventions that perpetuated economic inequalities and injustices did nothing to convince Latin Americans to embrace democratic practices. Even when Franklin Roosevelt ended military interventions and encouraged democratic practices, the results were discouraging. Despite occasional references to democracy, it was not until the creation of the OAS in 1948 and further norm development that democratic principles became a regular rhetorical feature in the region. Even then the realization of democratic Latin American regimes was a long way off.

Relations after World War II and during the Cold War

Following the end of World War II, inter-American relations evolved to the point of creating the OAS. The United States remained engaged in the region and worked with its neighbors to promote hemispheric solidarity and foster democratic governance and economic cooperation through the OAS.[2] Democratic principles were included within the OAS Charter with the preamble declaring that "the true significance of American solidarity and good neighborliness can only mean the consolidation on this continent, within the framework of democratic institutions, of a system of individual liberty and social justice based on respect for the essential rights of man." Article 3(d) further added that "the solidarity of the American States and the high aims which are sought through it require the political organization of those States on the basis of the effective exercise of representative democracy." References to these democratic norms was sporadic, however, and often self-serving. For example, at the Eighth Meeting of Consultation of foreign ministers in January 1962, Cuba was suspended from participation in the OAS because of the incompatibility of its Marxist-Leninist form of government with the principles of the inter-American system. The foreign ministers resolved that governments "whose structure or acts are incompatible with the effective exercise of representative democracy [should] hold free elections in their respective countries, as the most effective means of consulting the sovereign will of their peoples, to guarantee the restoration of a legal order based on the authority of the law and respect for the rights of the individual" (quoted in Atkins 1997, 333). This meeting and the resolutions that came out of it were largely in response to Cuban intervention in the affairs of other Caribbean states. The United States opposed the Castro regime and wanted to limit its revolutionary influence in the region. Other states such as Venezuela simply wanted to end Cuban interference in their domestic politics.[3] This apparent support for democratic government, however, was quite selective. As the Cold War deepened, security concerns and anticommunist ideology overshadowed all efforts at democratization. U.S. involvement in Latin America from the 1950s to the 1980s did little to help the democratic rhetoric become a reality. In fact, U.S. policies in the region served to threaten democracy in several instances.

By the 1950s U.S.–Latin American relations were based almost exclusively on anticommunism, not promoting democracy. It is ironic that these goals were not linked within foreign policy circles since promoting democracy would ideally also serve to thwart communist insurrections. U.S. officials, however, believed that "wherever a dictator was replaced, communists gained" (quoted in Schoultz 2002, 38). George Kennan (1999, 178), head of the State Department's Policy Planning Staff, visited the region in 1950 and reported that the "political culture [was] too weak and selfish to support a democracy strong enough to resist the superior determination and skill of the Communist enemy." Anticommunism became the guiding force for U.S. policy, and both security and economic issues were framed in terms of a struggle between communism and capitalism. The United States sought to protect against communist encroachment and support governments that were seeking to quell revolutionary movements deemed to be communist inspired (Kryzanek 1996, 62). Kennan (1999, 178) argued that the United States "must concede that harsh governmental measures of repression may be the only answer; that these measures may have to proceed from regimes whose origins and methods would not stand the test of American concepts of democratic procedures." This view led to a policy that supported dictatorships and in some instances even acted against democratic institutions.

The case of Guatemala in 1954 is a classic example of the United States acting to undermine democracy. Forces covertly supported by the United States overthrew President Jacobo Arbenz Guzmán, elected in 1950. When he had first come to power, he had undertaken a number of reforms including land redistribution, expansion of labor rights, and the nationalization of the United Fruit Company. U.S. secretary of state John Foster Dulles viewed these actions as a sign of Arbenz's communist connections. Evidence of diplomatic or military connections to the Soviet Union, however, was limited to a one-time cash payment for arms from Czechoslovakia.

A more significant threat involved U.S. economic interests in the region. United Fruit Company was the largest employer and largest landowner in the country, controlling both the railroads and the ports in Guatemala. The Guatemalan labor minister stated that "all the achievements of the Company were made at the expense of the impoverishment of the country and by acquisitive practices. To protect its authority it had recourse to every method: Political intervention, economic compulsion, contractual imposition, bribery . . . as suited its purposes of domination" (quoted in Schlesinger and Kinzer 1999,

150).The company risked considerable financial losses, when the government expropriated its holdings. The U.S. government publicly pressured President Arbenz to return the land and distance himself from his supposed communist ties. Arbenz refused to be swayed. Guatemalan foreign minister Toriello and U.S. ambassador Peurifoy negotiated for eight months to determine an appropriate compensation for the expropriation of United Fruit Company lands. United Fruit wanted $16 million, Guatemala offered United Fruits' own declared valuation for tax purposes—$627,000 (Schlesinger and Kinzer 1999, 147). According to Schlesinger and Kinzer (1999, 147), Ambassador Peurifoy had been sent to Guatemala with one mission: "to change the direction of the reformist government, no matter how." When it was clear Toriello and the United States would not reach an agreement, the U.S. ambassador put in motion the plans to oust President Arbenz. The United States covertly aided a deposed Guatemalan military leader, Carlos Castillo Armas, who led 1,000 men with U.S. weapons to overthrow the Arbenz government. Arbenz attempted to get help from both the United Nations and the OAS without success and eventually chose to go into exile rather than fight a battle he knew he could not win.

During the earliest years of the Cold War, the U.S. view of Latin America was very narrow, with revolutionary movements being blamed strictly on communism. The United States often failed to address the unequal economic conditions that led to much of the social unrest, and Latin American complaints about trade and aid had little impact on U.S. anticommunist policies (Kryzanek 1996, 63). Recognizing that development issues needed to be addressed, President Dwight Eisenhower (1953–61) helped create the Inter-American Development Bank in 1959. When Castro came to power in 1959 and drew increasingly close to the USSR, U.S. policy adapted further to include military aid and additional economic aid. U.S. policy became more complex. It included three broad strategies: economic aid, military assistance, and both direct and indirect intervention.

The new emphasis on economic assistance was evident under President Kennedy when he proposed the Alliance for Progress in 1961. He recognized that the United States could no longer ignore the relationship between revolution and poverty in Latin America. In order to avoid future revolutions, the United States would have to use its economic power and democratic principles to challenge communism. At a conference in Punta del Este, Kennedy proposed a plan that included funding for a Social Progress Fund, support for

Latin American economic integration, technical training programs, technology sharing and cooperation, and educational and cultural exchange programs. Member states laid out a number of goals, which included improving and strengthening democratic institutions, accelerating economic and social development, and attaining comprehensive land reforms, as well as additional social and political reforms (Kryzanek 1996, 70). The Alliance for Progress represented a new, more subtle mechanism to influence Latin American behavior, a shift away from the unilateral military interventions of the past (Schoultz 2002). Although many Latin American leaders welcomed the economic assistance, they were not blind to the reality of this "economic imperialism," as Che Guevara described it. Kennedy was not the only president to emphasize economic assistance. Reagan undertook the Caribbean Basin Initiative during the 1980s as a way to respond to the communist-inspired revolutions in the Caribbean and Central America. George H. W. Bush similarly pursued the Enterprise for the Americas Initiative that linked debt reduction and economic aid.

Following Kennedy's assassination, President Johnson chose to put less energy into the Alliance for Progress and economic assistance. He emphasized instead providing military aid to anticommunist allies such as Somoza in Nicaragua and Stroessner in Paraguay. Johnson supported the "Mann Doctrine" articulated by Assistant Secretary of State for Latin American Affairs Thomas Mann, who argued that military or rightist regimes should be tolerated as long as they were strongly anticommunist. The resulting U.S. policy was tacit acceptance of harsh military rule. Not only did the United States tolerate these regimes, it provided them with military aid and training to suppress social unrest in their countries. President Reagan, a strong cold warrior when he first came to office in 1981, embraced this strategy by supporting the right-wing government in El Salvador as it battled leftist guerrillas. Reagan provided $700 million in military and economic assistance to El Salvador from 1981 to 1983 (Kryzanek 1996, 92).

Although the United States did not militarily intervene in Latin America to the same degree as it had in the early 1900s, it did not entirely reject intervention as an option. This was particularly evident in the case of the Dominican Republic in 1965. Following a coup in 1963 and a countercoup in 1965, the United States chose to intervene when it appeared that the "Constitutionalist" faction with supposed communist connections might gain power. President

Johnson sent in more than 15,000 U.S. marines, fearing "another Cuba." Although the United States sought to legitimize this action by gaining OAS approval of the force as a multilateral peace-keeping force to restore order to the country, the United States was clearly involved in the operation to protect against the spread of communism. The United States remained in the country until the U.S.-backed candidate, Joaquín Balaguer, won the election held in June 1966. Ironically, the Constitutionalists had been attempting to restore democratically elected Juan Bosch to office after he had been overthrown in 1963. Clearly U.S. intervention was not directed at protecting or restoring democracy but at preventing the spread of communism. President Reagan also chose military intervention in 1983 when an orthodox socialist faction replaced the moderate prime minister of Grenada and pledged closer ties to Cuba and the USSR. Just as Johnson sought to legitimize U.S. actions in the Dominican Republic through the OAS, Reagan justified his actions based on a request to intervene received from the Organization of Eastern Caribbean States. This intervention signaled that Reagan was serious about containing communism and willing to use military force to do so.[4]

The cases of the Dominican Republic and Grenada were the most blatant military interventions of the United States during the Cold War, but the United States was also involved more covertly in a number of intervention efforts. President Nixon was engaged in toppling the regime of Salvador Allende in Chile in 1973. Nixon deliberately chose a strategy of internal destabilization to protect U.S. business interests and contain communism. His tactics were designed to limit Allende's ability to govern. Nixon denied Chile multilateral loans through international financial institutions, which weakened the Chilean economy; then he encouraged right-wing conspirators to overthrow Allende. The coup is particularly notable considering the long democratic history of Chile prior to U.S. intervention in the country. President Reagan similarly took covert action in the civil war in Nicaragua. The United States provided aid to the Contras who were fighting the leftist Sandinista government. This support was controversial in Congress and aid was eventually cut despite Reagan's strong calls for continued assistance. After Congress cut aid to the Contras, Reagan issued an executive order that ended all U.S. trade relations with Nicaragua.[5] This resembled the actions taken by Nixon against Chile. It weakened the Nicaraguan economy but failed, however, to topple the regime.

These strategies to contain communism were largely rejected by President Jimmy Carter. U.S. relations with Latin America took a decidedly new direction under the Carter administration from 1976 to 1980. Carter was critical of his predecessors' support for authoritarian regimes. His criticisms went beyond rhetoric. He chose to link U.S. assistance to the protection of human rights. He actually cut back or eliminated military assistance to Argentina, Brazil, Chile, Guatemala, Paraguay, and Uruguay (Kryzanek 1996, 82). These efforts to promote human rights and democracy, however, were quickly reversed by Ronald Reagan when he came into office in 1981. He made new overtures to Brazil, Chile, and Guatemala and ended efforts that Gerald Ford had begun to normalize relations with Cuba. Aside from Carter's actions, U.S.-led efforts toward democratization were largely unsuccessful during the Cold War. Reagan struggled to convince dictators such as Jean Claude Duvalier of Haiti to accept the transition to democracy but had little success. Duvalier held elections in Haiti in 1987, but following violence by the secret police, the polls were shut down and Duvalier remained in power.

Scholars of the "third wave" of democratic transitions have observed that Latin America democratized despite an unfavorable external environment that included U.S. foreign policy under Reagan in the closing days of the Cold War (Karl 1990). Contrary to U.S. assessments at midcentury that Latin Americans did not possess the characteristics necessary to successfully democratize, some Latin American leaders did make efforts to promote democracy. The Contadora Peace Process (1987), led by Oscar Arias, serves as an example. One of the conditions of the peace plan was an agreement by the parties to "begin the process of democratization based on complete freedom of the press and electronic media, complete pluralism, and the termination of any state of siege and reestablishment of constitutional guarantees" (quoted in Kryzanek 1996, 100). The parties also agreed to establish a framework leading to free and open elections throughout Central America. Although this agreement eventually crumbled in 1989, the parties were finally able to establish peace and hold democratic elections with the additional assistance of the UN.

In addition to the provisions in the Central American peace process, democratic norms were also developing within the inter-American system as a whole. The American Convention on Human Rights entered into force in 1978 and created the Inter-American Commission on Human Rights and the Inter-American Court. The Convention laid out a wide range of civil, political, economic, and social rights, including Article 23, which specified that,

Every citizen shall enjoy the following rights and opportunities: a) to take part in the conduct of public affairs, directly or through freely chosen representatives; b) to vote and to be elected in genuine periodic elections, which shall be by universal and equal suffrage and by secret ballot that guarantees the free expression of the will of the voters; and c) to have access, under general conditions of equality, to the public service of his country. (OAS 1969)

Although U.S.-Latin American relations were not ideal for promoting democracy at this time given the American preoccupation with containing communism at all costs, democratic norms continued to evolve. After being a regular rhetorical feature in the region for more than half a century, the practice of democracy finally began to blossom in the 1990s with the end of the ideological struggles of the Cold War.

U.S.–Latin American Relations in the 1990s and the New Millennium

The end of the Cold War provided a historic opportunity for the United States to place greater emphasis on the promotion of democracy that had been sacrificed regularly throughout the Cold War for the support of anticommunist dictators. The new opportunity manifested itself in the renewal of the OAS and the creation of new mechanisms to promote and strengthen democracy in the hemisphere. A number of Latin American states had recently transitioned to democracy and were determined to strengthen their institutions to prevent reversals. As discussed in Dexter Boniface's contribution to this volume, the OAS created the Unit for the Promotion of Democracy in 1990, passed Resolution 1080 and the Santiago Commitment in 1991, adopted the Washington Protocol in 1992, and the Inter-American Democratic Charter in 2001.

During the 1990s the United States played an active and positive role in Latin America, contributing to democratization efforts in the region. The U.S. government emphasized multilateralism not only in promoting democracy as the United States joined with its Latin American neighbors in the Santiago Commitment and the Washington Protocol, but also in U.S. trade policies such as NAFTA and negotiations for a Free Trade Area of the Americas (FTAA) launched at the inaugural Summit of the Americas in Miami in 1994. President Clinton (1993–2001) was particularly interested in developing policies that advanced U.S. standing in the global economy and in linking economic partnership with democratic consolidation. Clinton's preference was to act multi-laterally through the OAS and avoid military commitments. This reluctance to use unilateral military force was evident in his policies toward Bosnia as well as Haiti.

After September 11, 2001, however, attention shifted away from multilateral cooperation with the United States's Latin American neighbors. Although OAS members did issue a resolution supporting the United States after the attacks and have pursued antiterrorism efforts through the Inter-American Committee against Terrorism, the level of cooperation and multilateral engagement has dropped considerably in recent years. This lack of unity was evident in April 2002 when Venezuelan President Hugo Chávez was temporarily removed from office and then restored to power (see Legler in this volume). The United States hesitated before joining Latin American and Caribbean members of the OAS in condemning the coup. Rather, the U.S. government appeared more concerned with Chávez's leftist orientation and his growing relations with Castro in Cuba than with defending Venezuelan democracy. The United States's attitudes and actions had tarnished its reputation for supporting democracy.

U.S. actions in Haiti in 2004 further weakened its claim as a force for democracy in the region. When a rebel group began to capture territory in the north of the country in early 2004, President Jean-Bertrand Aristide was under increasing pressure from his political opponents and the international community to reach a negotiated settlement that would end the growing violence. Aristide finally left the country on February 29 to go into exile in the Central African Republic. Despite the threat posed to Haiti's constitutional order by an armed insurrection, the U.S. government did not push for invoking the Inter-American Democratic Charter. It also waited until after Aristide had been ousted to call for United Nations Security Council intervention in Haiti. Aristide himself claimed that he had been pressured to relinquish power because of fears that violence would erupt if he did not comply with the demands of U.S. agents (BBC 2004). The United States categorically denied stories that Aristide had been abducted, insisting that he "went onto the airplane willingly and that's the truth" (Colin Powell, as quoted by CNN.com 2004). Following his departure, Secretary of State Colin Powell noted that Aristide was "a man who was democratically elected, but he did not democratically govern, or govern well. Now we are there to give the Haitian people another chance" (CNN.com 2004). The chairman of the Caribbean Community (CARICOM), Jamaican Prime Minister Patterson, argued that "The removal of President Aristide in these circumstances sets a dangerous precedent for democratically elected governments anywhere and everywhere, as it promotes the removal of duly elected persons from office by the power of rebel forces" (CNN.com 2004).

Future Democracy Promotion: What Role for the United States?

The U.S. response to events in Venezuela (2002) and Haiti (2004) raises important questions about the role the United States will play in supporting democracy in Latin America. Despite positive normative changes in the region in support of democracy, the United States still faces many of the same policy priority dilemmas that it has in the past. Although the United States has become much more committed to the reality, not just the rhetoric, of support-ing democracy and has even supported greater legalization efforts (see Haw-kins and Shaw in this volume), there are still times when its economic or security interests override its principles. One change that is evident for U.S. foreign policy making, however, is that democratization, regional security, and economic stability are becoming increasingly intertwined, so that pursuit of security need not necessarily conflict with promotion of democracy as it has in the past. This linkage is evident in the George W. Bush administration, which has defined the promotion of democracy as being in the strategic interest of the United States in its war on terrorism.

It is likely the United States will continue to encourage democratization efforts abroad. But what form will these efforts take in Latin America and how will they be received? The United States has long argued that promoting de-mocracy is good not only in terms of principles but also in terms of its self-interest in regional stability and national security. A hemispheric community of democratic states is likely to be more peaceful and prosperous than non-democratic states. Securing democracy in neighboring states, however, is not a simple task. The imposition of democracy may not ultimately improve U.S. security if it creates tension and resentment or incurs a long-term military commitment, as some historical efforts have.

Thus the means by which democracy is promoted becomes an important consideration. As a powerful regional actor with many resources and multiple interests, the United States has a number of options from which to choose. Some models for U.S. action include serving as an Instructor, Enforcer, Role Model, Observer, and/or Enabler of democracy in the region. It is evident by looking at historical cases that some of these models have had a more positive impact on democratization in the past than others.

Under President Woodrow Wilson, the United States served as an Instructor, essentially telling states to "Do what I say (but not what I do)." This democratic rhetoric, however, was largely a cover for continued U.S. efforts to expand markets and enhance its security, and ultimately caused considerable resentment toward the United States (Wood 1999, 109; Scheman 2003, 38). The Good Neighbor policies of Franklin Delano Roosevelt might also be characterized in this fashion. There was little progress in democratization because there was only rhetoric from the United States and interventionist actions that were actually contrary to the rhetoric. The United States called for democratic norms, but its own behavior did not uphold those principles.

In a number of instances the United States has played the role of an Enforcer, demanding "Do what I say, or else." When states have chosen not to act according to U.S. preferences, the military has intervened to achieve a more agreeable "democratic" outcome. U.S. forces remained in the Dominican Republic for more than a year in 1965–66 to oversee an election that placed a U.S.-friendly leader in office. Panamanian strong man Manuel Noriega was forcefully removed from office in 1989 when he ignored the electoral outcomes that were not in his favor. Jean-Bertrand Aristide was returned to the Haitian presidency in 1994 only after the imminent use of military force by the United States brought down the Cédras junta. In each of these instances, it can be argued that democracy was upheld, but the militarized means for achieving this had some negative consequences as well. The Dominican case was seen as blatant intervention for ideological reasons and left Latin American states reluctant to support "multilateral peacekeeping" efforts led by the United States.[6] The Panamanian action was also viewed as a violation of state sovereignty and was condemned by OAS member states in the Permanent Council. Democracy was "restored" to Haiti in 1994 but subsequently withered. Clearly the forceful restoration or imposition of democracy is not necessarily the optimal action that must be taken in order for democracy to thrive.

There are times when the United States has not been very engaged in Latin America and has chosen to pursue more of a Role Model policy, in which the U.S. message is to "Do as I do." This strategy resembles that of the Instructor, but with less rhetoric. Rather than making demands on Latin American states to change their behaviors, the United States is largely disengaged. This disengagement also extends to avoiding intervention as an option. Perhaps the period that most closely resembles this model of behavior is the era prior to 1889 when the United States expressed only limited interest in Latin American affairs. One consequence of this particular model is that the United States has only limited influence on the democratization processes in the region and thus does not play a major role. This could be seen as either a drawback or a benefit. The United States might avoid accusations of interference and provocation of resentment in the region, but it might also inspire criticism about hypocrisy, by not putting any effort into strengthening the principles for which the United States stands.

If the United States chose to adopt the role of an Observer, it would have even less of an impact than as a Role Model because it chooses deliberately to disengage. The Observer model would allow the United States not only to avoid interventionism and rhetorical demands but also to free itself from the constraints of serving as a role model. Its own actions need not necessarily be based fully on democratic principles. The United States has never distanced itself this much from Latin America, recognizing that the region deserves some measure of attention even when other regions demand more.

Each of these roles describes the United States as a largely unilateral force as it promotes democracy in Latin America. The final role that the United States might take is a less unilateral one. The United States might choose to serve as an Enabler. This could be pursued *externally* by working with others in the international community to promote democracy or *internally* by working with domestic actors. This strategy of serving as an Enabler, cooperating with other actors who have similar interests to promote democracy, may not produce results quickly, but it does offer a potentially more positive outcome than militarized intervention as an Enforcer or weak or hypocritical influence as an Instructor or Role Model.

Although the United States is a powerful actor in Latin America, its power alone cannot establish democracy. It must seek other strategies that will produce the desired outcome of a strong community of democracies in the Western Hemisphere. Anita Isaacs (1996, 277) reiterates the limited influence of the United States (and other external actors) by noting that the contribution of outside actors toward promoting democracy is relatively minor and that the international community can only make a difference at the margins by nurturing a domestically rooted process of regime change.

Even when pursuing a strategy of enabling domestic actors to promote democracy, however, there are potential drawbacks. Lars Schoultz (2002, 41) argues that U.S. efforts to promote democracy in the case of Nicaragua are more likely to retard democratic development than encourage it. When a major power intervenes in the democratic negotiation process by giving money or other forms of support to some actors and not others, it alters the political balance of power in a country. Groups may adjust their behavior to fit the pattern that the United States wants to see to gain U.S. support (e.g., learning English, adopting anticommunist or antiterrorist stances). The United States currently favors supporting "civil society" organizations in the region. Schoultz argues that Nicaraguans need to develop their own consensus on democratic policies and procedures and to negotiate for themselves the context of civilian-military relations and police and judicial reforms without the United States dictating terms by supporting certain civil society groups. The Department for the Promotion of Democracy in the OAS takes these concerns into account. By supporting domestic efforts through multilateral channels, there is less opportunity to "skew" political development according to the desires of a neighboring state, or the most powerful state in the region.

Each of these different models has its potential flaws as can be seen with some of the historical examples. The Instructor model is often perceived as condescending and largely ineffective. Enforcement provokes resentment and has high costs involved without any guarantee of success. The Role Model and Observer models do not allow the United States to take a proactive stance in promoting democracy. The Enabler model has the most positive potential but also must be adopted with care. Each of these options reveals that the United States has always been faced with a number of less than ideal options in its policies toward Latin America and still faces many of the same dilemmas. Some of the choices the United States must consider as it formulates its policies include taking a lead in the region or adopting a lower profile; focusing more on Latin America or maintaining a more global focus; being more concerned with prevention or simply reacting to events; acting unilaterally or multilaterally. In the past, when the United States has chosen one option, it has often faced criticism for not choosing the other.

The United States must take several additional factors into account as it considers what role to play in the democratization process. The United States needs to consider whether it believes "one size fits all" in terms of democratization processes, and if not, whether it has the ability or desire to tailor its responses to each country. Furthermore, there are notable subregional distinctions in the Western Hemisphere, and it is an oversimplification to discuss "Latin American" policies without considering these important differences.

The United States must also consider two "environmental" factors. First, the actions and attitudes of the United States in the past have shaped its current relations with states in Latin America. Although some policy makers argue that the United States should be more principled and less pragmatic in terms of promoting democracy and security, it is unlikely that the United States can greatly change its image with its neighbors overnight. Even if the United States were completely sincere about helping in every way to transform states to democracies, it is likely that Latin American states would still be hesitant about U.S. help because of previous unwanted interventions. A second (and related) environmental factor to consider is the purported normative changes affecting attitudes about intervention. Farer (1996b) suggests that there is a new normative environment concerning sovereignty, intervention, and democracy. Multilateral intervention in support of democratic government is being increasingly tolerated. Even if this is an accurate characterization of the normative climate, it seems unlikely that such a change would favor active U.S. intervention in the future. Attitudes may support an OAS intervention to support threatened democracy but not unilateral action by the United States.

Taking all of the different models for policy and the other factors into consideration, there are several actions that the United States can take as an external actor that can have a positive effect on democratization in the region. If the United States is committed to democracy in reality, not just rhetorically, it will not intervene against democratically elected governments, consistently oppose all threats to the democratic order, and support multilateral mechanisms that are in place to guarantee democracy in the region. These policy recommendations do not require the United States to focus exclusively on Latin America or to take an exclusive leadership role in the region. The United States can maintain its focus on other regions of the world and follow the lead of other regional actors supporting democracy through the OAS. This careful strategy would avoid provoking resentment in the region and avoid accusations of having double standards. If democracy and security are truly connected and part of the United States's strategic goals, then these actions should only serve to strengthen democracy as well as serve the U.S. national interest.

Although domestic and transnational actors play a significant role in the democratization process, the actions of the United States and their impact cannot be overlooked. The United States is a powerful regional actor that can positively or negatively affect democratization efforts in Latin America. Historically, U.S. influence in the region was largely detrimental to the democratization process. Other issues deemed to be in the national interest prevented genuine democracy promotion, although democratic rhetoric was still often employed. Trade issues were preeminent prior to World War II. During the Cold War, the preoccupation with communism dictated U.S. foreign policy. Although arguably by employing the rhetoric of democracy the United States helped the norm of democratic government develop in the region, in reality the United States has not served as a model for democracy. The 1990s saw the closest link between rhetoric and reality with U.S. commitment to the multilateral mechanisms of the OAS to strengthen democracy through new declarations and mechanisms. A collective response to disruptions to democracy helped restore constitutional order in Haiti (1994), Peru (1992), Guatemala (1993), and Paraguay (1996) (although democracy is much weaker in some of these states than in others).

Following the attacks of September 11, 2001, however, the United States has reverted to its previous pattern of behavior, giving less attention to issues in the region generally and acting unilaterally to protect its perceived national security interests, even to the detriment of democratic principles. Although the new war on terrorism has shifted the focus of the United States farther abroad, there is still room for the United States to promote democracy in Latin America by upholding the work of the OAS and maintaining its democratic principles when they are challenged by unconstitutional actors and events.

NOTES

1. President Woodrow Wilson used the rhetoric of promoting constitutional governments in Latin America as he engaged in various interventions, but most agree that democracy was not the primary force driving U.S. policy at the time.

2. Collective security was pursued through the signing of the Inter-American Treaty of Reciprocal Assistance (Rio Treaty) in 1947.

3. These actions by the foreign ministers, however, were quite controversial and sparked much debate. The final resolution barely received the two-thirds votes necessary to pass.

4. George H. W. Bush also militarily intervened in Panama in 1989 to remove Manuel Noriega from power. This operation, however, was to remove a corrupt drug kingpin rather than to contain communism.

5. The Iran-Contra scandal broke in 1986, revealing that the administration was also engaged in the illegal funding of the Contras through the sale of arms to Iran in exchange for releasing hostages in Lebanon.

6. The OAS rejected a U.S. proposal to send a peace-keeping force into Nicaragua in 1978–79.

CHAPTER FIVE

Canada

Democracy's New Champion?

Flavie Major

Shortly after Canada joined the Organization of American States (OAS) in 1990, one of its first initiatives as a permanent member was to propose the creation of a new unit that would work to support democratic development in its member states. Among the reasons invoked by Canada for joining the OAS was precisely the fact that most countries in the region had undergone a transition to democracy by the end of the 1980s and Canada felt that it could now work with other democratic countries toward achieving common goals. Canada's proposal resulted in the Unit for the Promotion of Democracy (UPD), whose aim is to contribute to the strengthening of democratic institutions in various countries of the region.[1] Throughout the 1990s, Canada continued to speak firmly in favor of democracy. In 2000, in the midst of the political scandal that struck the Fujimori government in Peru, Canada opposed any further backsliding to authoritarianism and was closely involved in the diplomatic measures deployed to ensure the holding of new elections and the restoration of democratic rule in the country. In the following months, while preparing to host the Third Summit of the Americas in Québec City in April 2001, Canadian diplomats worked to make this presidential meeting a "democracy summit," where tangible steps would be taken to further strengthen the inter-American regime for the collective defense of democracy. One achievement of the Québec summit was a mandate for OAS member states to negotiate the Inter-American Democratic Charter (IADC; see appendix B), subsequently adopted in September 2001.

Since it joined the OAS in 1990 and increased its presence in the region, Canada has been recognized as an important pro-democracy actor in the Western Hemisphere. Yet democratization is a complex task, and it is pertinent to reflect on the impact that a state actor such as Canada can have when it engages in the process of promoting and strengthening democracy in other sovereign countries, as well as on the limits that it faces along the road. The central argument developed in this chapter is that while Canada tends to be perceived as a principled actor in matters of democracy promotion, its policy of democracy promotion in the Americas has not been sustained or consistent. Canada has internalized the democratic norm and has worked to promote this norm in the region and elsewhere in the world, yet the question of national interest is also at play when it decides to pursue bilateral or multilateral efforts to promote and strengthen democracy.

This chapter analyzes Canada's role in promoting democracy in the Americas, from 1990 to 2006. It addresses the manner in which Canada has encouraged democratic development and the question of how effective Canada has been at promoting and strengthening democracy in the region. The first section of the chapter outlines Canada's foreign policy toward the promotion and protection of democracy in general. In a second section, I highlight Canada's experience in the Americas and review three particular cases: Haiti, Cuba, and Peru. These selected examples provide a better understanding of the different ways in which a regional power such as Canada can promote democratization in bilateral and multilateral settings and have a tangible impact on the ground. A third section examines contradictions in Canada's pro-democracy efforts and considers the reasons for this apparent inconsistent performance. The chapter concludes with a broad policy-oriented discussion of Canada's future role vis-à-vis democratic development in the Americas.

Democracy Promotion in Canada's Foreign Policy

Students of Canadian foreign policy and inter-American affairs know that Canada is a relatively new player in the Western Hemisphere. For much of the twentieth century, decision makers in Ottawa had their heads turned toward Europe and had little interest in developing extensive ties with their neighbors to the south. During the 1970s and 1980s, Canada developed bilateral ties with some Central American and Southern Cone countries, yet it did not seek to position itself as a strategic player at the regional level. It was not until 1990 that in a rather sudden policy shift, Canada decided to join the OAS as a permanent member. For strategic and symbolic reasons, Canada had decided to become more seriously involved in inter-American affairs.[2] Canadian officials acknowledged that many problems affecting countries in the region, such as environmental and security issues, were transnational in nature and required concerted actions among all countries on the continent. Moreover, with Europe consolidating its regional integration process, Canada recognized that its long-term political and commercial interests were directly engaged with the interests of other countries in the hemisphere.

Another important motivation was the fact that most countries in the region had undertaken transitions to democracy. For many years, Canada had perceived the OAS to be a malfunctioning organization, dominated by the United States, both incapable of maintaining peace and security on the continent—its raison d'être—and faced with internal shortcomings. With the end of the Cold War and because the Americas had become a community of democracies, there were positive signs of reform of the inter-American system, and Canada wanted to contribute to those hemispheric developments.

Canada is also a relatively new player in the complex world of promoting and defending democracy abroad on a global scale. As Gerald Schmitz (2004, 9) puts it, "Canada's experience with the complicated enterprise of assisting democratic development is less than two decades old, and still very much a work in progress." Only at the end of the 1980s did Canada start to develop a foreign policy and development strategy that explicitly took into consideration the intricate interrelations between economic aid, human rights promotion, and democratic development. The traditional approach until that time had been to condemn regimes that did not respect human rights. With the end of the Cold War, Canadian policy makers started to consider that Canada could play a role in the strengthening of democratic institutions abroad, with the understanding that democratic regimes, in turn, would ensure a more transparent and responsible use of Canadian aid money. In 1987 parliamentarians recommended the creation of an "innovative Canadian organization" that could increase Canadian initiatives in support of human rights and democratic development abroad. The result was the International Centre for Human Rights and Democratic Development (now called Rights and Democracy), based in Montreal.

Democratization became more prominent when the Liberals came to power in 1993, both as a means of elaboration and an objective of Canadian foreign policy.[3] In the first years of its mandate, the Chrétien government undertook a foreign policy review. The Canadian government conducted its review in a novel way, reaching out to civil society organizations, journalists, academics, and business leaders in order to encourage debate around Canada's foreign policy goals and priorities. Results of the review were published in February 1995.

"Canada in the World" identified three compatible and mutually reinforcing foreign policy objectives: "the promotion of prosperity and employment; the protection of [Canadian] security within a stable global framework; and the projection of Canadian values and culture" (DFAIT 1995). As part of the latter goal (projection of Canadian values and culture), the document stated that "Canada [was going to] give priority to supporting democracy in the world over the coming years." The formulation was vague but nonetheless echoed the recommendation made by parliamentarians that human rights, good governance, and democratic development needed to be central to Canada's foreign policy (Thede 2005). "Canada in the World" also demonstrated the will of the Canadian government to link its democratization efforts with its development assistance programs, and the promotion of democracy became one of the six priorities of the overall official development assistance initiative.

There have been mixed perceptions and opinions in Canada over the years about the role that the country could and should play in democracy promotion overseas. On the one hand, it has frequently been suggested by policy makers and analysts that Canada has something "distinct" to offer to international democratic development, in comparison, for example, with the United States, a country that has a more extensive, but more controversial, experience in the field (Sundstrom 2005). Because Canadians share values of tolerance and respect for diversity and human rights, and because of the federalist, multicultural, and bilingual nature of the country, it is commonly argued that Canada has valuable experience in good governance that can be useful to other countries engaged in the process of developing and strengthening their democratic institutions. On the other hand, Canada's stance on international democratic development is also described as "timid" and "too hesitant," mainly because Canadians do not want to be perceived as imposing a Western or Canadian "model" of democracy in other countries.

When the Liberal government undertook a second, much-awaited foreign policy review in the early 2000s, it again organized consultations and forums of discussion with diverse sectors of Canadian society. Commentators such as journalist Jeffrey Simpson (2004a, 2004b, cited in G. Schmitz 2004, 37–38) argued that Canada needed to devote greater resources and develop a more coherent policy drive for its democracy promotion initiatives. Other analysts proposed the creation of a "Democracy Canada Institute," an independent institution that could ensure a better coordination of objectives and programs among the numerous Canadian actors already contributing to democracy promotion in various regions of the world (Axworthy and Campbell 2005; Axworthy, Campbell, and Donovan 2005a, 2005b). Despite the country's expertise in democracy promotion, these analysts note that "Canadian efforts [remained] disparate, underfunded, and often anonymous" (Campbell, cited in G. Schmitz 2004, 38).[4]

Canada's "International Policy Statement," released in early 2005, signaled democracy promotion as an important component of the country's foreign policy and international development strategies. An official document titled "Diplomacy" presented democracy promotion as a strategy that Canada could use to tackle important global issues and promote a "new multilateralism," focused on results (FAC 2005, 15). To some extent, the new policy addressed the problem of a lack of a centralized point of coordination for Canadian democracy promotion initiatives. As a remedy, it announced greater collaboration between the Department of Foreign Affairs, the Canadian International Development Agency (CIDA), and its newly created Canada Corps. Canada Corps was established in 2004 as "a new vehicle to strengthen Canada's contribution to human rights, democracy and good governance internationally" (FAC 2005, 28). The initiative aimed at mobilizing Canadians from different backgrounds and deploying their governance expertise in various situations abroad. Canada Corps was meant to coordinate the actions of various other governmental and nongovernmental actors that had in the past played a role in democracy promotion, such as Rights and Democracy, the Parliamentary Centre and Elections Canada.

Critics were quick to argue that initiatives laid down in the new foreign policy review were not sufficient. In particular, Axworthy and Campbell (2005) feared that Canada Corps, as a program within CIDA with a limited budget, would not be enough to provide the needed focal point in the various existing democratization-related initiatives. Sundstrom (2005) argued that the promotion of democracy overseas should have been more specifically addressed in the new foreign policy document, highlighting the fact that it did not appear in the criteria used to select recipients of Canada's development aid.

The 2005 foreign policy review document was short-lived, however, and lost much of its relevance when a Conservative government took office in early 2006. As of September 2006 the Harper government was primarily focused on domestic issues and had not yet launched a foreign policy review, although it had signaled a clear intent to pursue and consolidate Canada's traditional policy of promoting democracy abroad. The April 2006 Speech from the Throne announced that the Canadian government was "committed to supporting Canada's core values of freedom, democracy, the rule of law and human rights around the world" (Canada 2006, 12). The Parliament's Standing Committee on Foreign Affairs and International Development started a Study on Democratic Development in the fall of 2006 to examine Canada's role in promoting and strengthening democracy. Both the prime minister and the minister of foreign affairs made frequent reference to values of "freedom, human rights, democracy and rule of law" in the first months of their mandate. For example, in a speech preceding his appearance at the meeting of the United Nations General Assembly in New York in the fall of 2006, Prime Minister Harper stated: "We are determined that Canada's role in the world will extend beyond this continent. Our needs for prosperity and security, our values of freedom, democracy, human rights and the rule of law, [are] also the common destiny of all humanity."[5]

Hemispheric Democracy Promotion

Democracy promotion became central to Canada's engagement in the Americas dating from the early 1990s. Canada's actions and initiatives in the region include financial contributions to democracy promotion initiatives; the monitoring of elections, both within the multilateral framework of the OAS and through bilateral programs established in selected countries; and public as well as behind-the-scenes diplomacy to solve particular democratic crises. Canada's three principal general contributions are its support for regional democracy instruments, its provision of technical and financial assistance for democracy initiatives, and its efforts to open regional institutions to input from civic society actors. It has also played a special role in states such as Haiti, Cuba, and Peru.

First and foremost, Canada has been a strong supporter of the development of an inter-American regime for the collective defense of democracy, backing all key OAS resolutions and declarations that serve as the normative basis of that regime. At the 1991 General Assembly held in Santiago, Chile, Canada supported the adoption of Resolution 1080 (see appendix A) in which OAS member states resolve to "instruct the Secretary General to call for the immediate convocation of a meeting of the Permanent Council in the event of any occurrences giving rise to the sudden or irregular interruption of the democratic political institutional process or of the legitimate exercise of power by the democratically elected government in any of the Organization's member states." Canada subsequently supported the application of Resolution 1080 in Haiti in 1991, in Peru in 1992, in Guatemala in 1993, and in Paraguay in 1996 (Thérien et al. 2004). Canada also supported the 1992 Washington Protocol, which altered the OAS Charter to make democracy an official condition for participation in OAS activities.[6]

As host of the Québec City Summit of the Americas, Canada led the effort to include the so-called Democracy Clause in the final Political Declaration. The Democracy Clause made democracy an essential condition for a state's participation in the Summits of the Americas process, stating that "any unconstitutional alteration or interruption of the democratic order in a state of the Hemisphere constitutes an insurmountable obstacle to the participation of that state's government in the Summits of the Americas process." Canada also forcefully endorsed the proposal put forward by Peru to develop a democratic charter for countries of the region (Graham 2002). During the preparatory meetings leading to the Québec City Summit, there was an increasing awareness of the need to strengthen existing inter-American instruments for the collective defense of democracy in order for the inter-American system to be able to respond not only to coups d'etat but also to more subtle threats to democracy. Moreover, as protesters were gearing up and getting their signs ready, Canada wanted to avoid the criticism that the summit would be a mere "symbolic photo opportunity" (Cooper 2001). Canada was thus proud of the Democracy Clause and the subsequent IADC as "tangible results" of the Québec City Summit. In the first "test" of the IADC, Canada supported its application following Venezuela's April 2002 coup, although it maintained a secondary role in the Venezuela crisis.

A second way in which Canada has worked to promote democracy in the region is by providing technical and financial assistance to countries engaged in the strengthening of their democratic institutions. One of Canada's first initiatives after joining the OAS was to propose the creation of the Unit for the Promotion of Democracy (UPD) as a specialized unit within the regional organization.[7] The UPD was created in 1990 with the mandate "to provide a program of support for democratic development that can respond promptly and effectively to member states which, in the full exercise of their sovereignty, request advice or assistance to preserve or strengthen their political institutions and democratic procedures" (OAS 1990). Since its creation, the UPD, now called the Department for the Promotion of Democracy (DPD), has been active in electoral technical assistance and democratic institution-building programs and has organized more than ninety-five electoral observations missions.[8] Significantly, directors of the UPD/DPD have always been Canadian citizens.

Through its bilateral aid program, Canada also supports a series of initiatives in Latin America, notably in Andean, Central American, and Caribbean countries. These initiatives are mainly managed by the Canadian International Development Agency and range from programs for the protection of human rights, to technical training for election monitoring and the development of judicial institutions, to special democratic development funds aimed at building a democratic culture, strengthening citizen participation, and reforming public institutions.

Third, the Canadian government has promoted democracy by actively working to "democratize" regional institutions and make room for national and transnational nongovernmental actors interested in having a voice in inter-American affairs. Civil society participation in international fora became a growing concern worldwide toward the end of the 1990s. It became common to see protesters gathering on the margins of various high-level summits to denounce the democratic deficit of these meetings and to criticize their opaque agenda. The inter-American institutions, such as the OAS General Assembly and the Summits of the Americas Process, were not spared from demands for greater transparency. For Canada, increasing civil society participation in multilateral organizations became a general concern in the second half of the 1990s, as the Liberal government sought to democratize foreign policy.[9] The Canadian government believed that civil society organizations could provide information, expertise, and a critical perspective on numerous issues traditionally discussed solely by government representatives (McKenna 1995).

At the OAS, Canada was among the few countries that actively campaigned to see the organization adopt guidelines for the accreditation of civil society organizations and allow their participation in various meetings, such as the annual General Assembly.[10] Initial efforts were unproductive as member states of the organization were unable to reach consensus on the role that was to be given to civil society organizations. Following the 1998 Santiago Summit, however, where leaders agreed on the principles of greater transparency and inclusion within the OAS and hemispheric institutions, some initiatives started to be more successful.[11] During the 1998 OAS General Assembly held in Caracas, Venezuela, the organization adopted Resolution 1539, strongly supported by Canada and the United States. Resolution 1539 called for the modernization and formalization of the relationship between the OAS and civil society organizations in all member states. At the General Assembly held in Guatemala City the following year, in June 1999, the OAS adopted a "Resolution for the Establishment of a Committee of the Permanent Council of the OAS on the Participation of Civil Society," another Canadian initiative. The "Guidelines for the Participation by Civil Society Organizations in OAS Activities" were subsequently approved by all member states in December 1999, and to date, according to the OAS Civil Society website, the Committee on the Participation of Civil Society has accredited more than 170 civil society organizations. Accredited organizations may attend public meetings of the Permanent Council, receive and distribute documents to the various bodies of the organization, and attend annual and extraordinary sessions of the General Assembly. When it hosted the 2000 OAS General Assembly in Windsor, Ontario, Canada took pride in the fact that the meeting was a model of institutional transparency and openness, with the largest civil society contingent ever to participate in an OAS General Assembly.

Canada, along with the United States and others, pushed for greater inclusion of civil society in the Summits of the Americas Process. In October 1999, under the chairmanship of the Canadian ambassador to the OAS, meetings of the Special Committee on Inter-American Summits Management were both broadcast live on the Internet and made open to representatives of civil society organizations wishing to attend. This enabled civil society organizations to comment on the agenda and priorities of future summits, as well as follow the implementation of mandates passed by previous summits. Following the Québec City Summit in 2001, the Special Committee became the Committee on Inter-American Summits Management and Civil Society Participation in OAS Activities, establishing a more direct link between the work of the OAS, the summits' agenda, and civil society participation. While efforts to increase civil society participation in the OAS and the summits' process were not always successful (Shamsie 2000), over time the desirability of consultation and discussion with civil society actors became commonly accepted.[12]

In the remainder of this section I turn to three country cases where Canada was particularly active in promoting democracy, using both multilateral settings but also bilateral programs to encourage political reforms and democratic development. These three cases reveal a wide array of means that a state actor such as Canada has used to defend, promote, and strengthen democracy in the region.

Haiti

Canada has maintained a commitment toward the democratization process in Haiti, having both material and symbolic interests for contributing to the stabilization and the reconstruction of Haiti. The province of Québec is home to a large Haitian community, and because of its relative proximity to the Caribbean island, Canada is affected by its instability, in terms of immigration flows and security-related problems, and will ultimately benefit from a stable Haiti. Canada, moreover, has multilateral connections with Haiti not only through inter-American institutions but also as a member of La Francophonie.

Canada was involved in the organization of the first free and fair elections in the country, in 1990, which brought Jean-Bertrand Aristide to power (Thérien et al. 2004, 23). Nine months later, following the coup d'etat perpetrated by General Cédras, Canada reacted strongly by cutting its trade links and bilateral aid programs with Haiti. Canada participated in all four United Nations missions deployed throughout the 1990s in Haiti. Over the years, Canada has provided considerable development aid, electoral support, peace-keeping and peace-building expertise, and support for police and judicial reforms. Haiti is Canada's most important aid partner in the Americas. The Canadian government has used multilateral gatherings such as the Québec City Summit of the Americas to achieve collective support for the democratic process in Haiti and press Haitian leaders to adhere to democratic norms and principles. Canada also joined the "Friends of Haiti" group, along with other OAS member states and a few European states, in a collective effort to find an acceptable solution for all parties in the aftermath of the contested 2000 elections (Thérien et al. 2004).

Analysts of the situation in Haiti insist that rebuilding democratic institutions in that country will require a serious and sustained engagement on the part of the international community. Canada is perceived as having a comparative advantage to make a difference and show leadership in that process (Dade 2004). Canada's behavior in the 2004 ousting of President Aristide has been criticized, something that is addressed in the next section. Yet Canada's role in Haiti since 2004 indicates readiness to accompany Haiti in the long road ahead. Canada contributed $190 million between 2004 and 2006 in reconstruction and development projects. In the framework of the 2006 elections, Elections Canada led the International Mission for Monitoring Haitian Elections that was deployed for both the first and second round of voting, in February and April, respectively. In terms of future commitment, Canada planned an overall contribution of $520 million for the first five years of the new government of Haiti to support governance, national reconstruction, and reform of security and justice systems.[13]

Cuba

Canada's policy approach toward Cuba dates from the 1960s (Thérien et al. 2004). Some analysts have argued that Canada's unique relation with Cuba serves Canadian interests mostly by showing Americans, Latin Americans, and the rest of the world that Canada is capable of having an autonomous foreign policy and maintaining its distance from the United States (McKenna and Kirk 2002; Warren 2003). Canada always opposed the U.S. embargo on Cuba and is one of the two countries of the Americas (the other being Mexico) that has maintained diplomatic relations with Havana since the beginning of the Castro regime in 1959.

When the Liberal government came to power in 1993, Canada developed a "constructive engagement" policy toward Cuba, which included increased senior-level contacts, development assistance and aid programs, and support to Canadian companies active in Cuba (Warren 2003). Lloyd Axworthy, who served as minister of foreign affairs from 1996 to 2000, the main architect of the constructive engagement policy, believed that by maintaining diplomatic contacts and contributing to the development of the island through assistance programs, Canada could stabilize the region and moderate the Castro regime, as well as facilitate the eventual transition to democracy in Cuba.[14] At the multilateral level, since joining the OAS Canada has also petitioned for Cuba's reintegration into the regional body (McKenna 1995).

In 1999, however, in light of increased political oppression and human rights violations by Cuban authorities, Prime Minister Chrétien ordered a review of Canadian foreign policy vis-à-vis Cuba. Canada hardened its position and insisted it would support Cuba's reintegration in the OAS only under the condition that the Castro government undertake political and economic reforms. This shift in Canada's policy led Castro to verbally attack Canada on many occasions, especially as Canada was hosting the Summit of the Americas in April 2001. By 2002, however, senior-level contacts between the two countries had resumed, and a "cordial" relation was back on track.

The success of Canada's constructive engagement in Cuba is debatable (Randall 2002). Warren (2003) notes that policy makers and officials themselves were not certain that Canada's approach had been the right one, given the lack of tangible democratization results in Cuba and the apparent hardening of Castro's position over the years. He also suggests that following the departure of Axworthy from Foreign Affairs in 2000, the "constructive engagement" approach continued in large part because of "bureaucratic momentum" rather than concerted commitment. McKenna and Kirk (2002), for their part, argue that Canada was unrealistic in its expectations for changes in Cuba and did not understand the reality of the Castro regime. Yet Canada's long-standing policy of engagement endures. In the 2005 "International Policy Statement," Cuba still stood out as a priority for Canada in the Latin American and Caribbean region. The document stressed that "Cuba remains an exception to [progress toward democracy in the region] and Canada will continue its policy of engagement with Cuba across the full range of bilateral issues, including on human rights" (FAC 2005, 25–26).

Bilateral relations between Canada and Cuba have generally been "cooler" when Conservative governments were in power in Ottawa and more "cordial" under the Liberals (McKenna and Kirk 2002). In any case, its unique and sustained engagement vis-à-vis Cuba may give Canada a privileged position to work with Cuban authorities when they consider that the time is ripe for political reforms and democratization on the island.

Peru

Canada became a key actor in the multilateral efforts deployed to protect and strengthen democracy in Peru mostly because of the circumstances surrounding the 2000 political crisis in the Andean country.[15] Unlike the cases of Cuba and Haiti, where Canada has been involved for numerous years, the Peruvian episode demonstrates that a combination of timely public diplomacy and sustained, behind-the-scene mediation efforts can result in concrete positive change. The democratic crisis arose as Peruvian president Alberto Fujimori was seeking a controversial third mandate in the 2000 presidential elections after ten years in power, during which he had significantly weakened democratic institutions. On the basis of irregularities and fraud observed during the April 2000 first-round election, the OAS Electoral Observation Mission withdrew from the electoral process, and opposition candidate Alejandro Toledo decided to boycott the May runoff. Fujimori went ahead, nonetheless; facing no opposition, he was elected for a controversial third mandate.

A few days after the runoff election, the annual OAS General Assembly took place in Windsor, Canada, on June 4–6. While protesters shouted antitrade slogans on the margins of the meeting, ministers of foreign affairs from countries of the Americas were inside addressing the democratic crisis in Peru. On June 6, OAS member states adopted Resolution 1753, which sent a high-level mission to Peru to promote the democratic process and explore the possibility of institutional reforms (OAS 2000c). Because Canada was the host of the OAS General Assembly, Minister of Foreign Affairs Lloyd Axworthy was serving as chair of the meeting. In this capacity he played a key role in reaching a compromise on Resolution 1753. With OAS secretary-general César Gaviria, Axworthy later served as head of the high-level mission to Peru.

The Canadian Mission to the OAS and the Canadian Embassy in Lima were also closely involved as the events unfolded in Peru. Visits to Peru were conducted by the Canadian permanent representative to the OAS, Ambassador Peter Boehm, and the OAS secretary-general and his chief of staff, both before and after the official OAS high-level mission. The Canadian and OAS mediation efforts facilitated the organization of a roundtable (*mesa de diálogo*) that brought together political actors from government and opposition as well as civil society actors. This dialogue process encouraged important democratic reforms and facilitated the transition to an interim government and the eventual holding of new, free, and fair elections in the spring of 2001 (Cooper and Legler 2001b).

The return to democracy in Peru after ten years of backsliding under Fujimori was, as of 2006, a work in progress. Despite high expectations that the Toledo government (2001–6) would rebuild confidence in democratic institutions, results were somewhat mitigated. Yet Canadian efforts in 2000 and 2001, especially the mediation role played by Ambassador Boehm and Minister Axworthy, are credited by Peruvians as having been key in convincing officials from the Fujimori government to accept a dialogue with nongovernmental actors and in forging a national consensus around a democratic reconstruction process (Randall 2002). In the 2006 elections, Lloyd Axworthy was back in the country serving as head of the OAS Electoral Observation Mission, thus demonstrating Canada's continued support to strengthening democratic institutions and processes in Peru.

Contradictions in Canada's Democracy Promotion Policy

Despite Canada's positive track record, some observers remain critical and draw attention to various contradictions in Canada's foreign policy toward democracy promotion in the Western Hemisphere. A first criticism is that Canada maintains a contradictory image by presenting itself as a strong supporter of democracy promotion in the region while refusing to adhere to inter-American instruments for the defense of human rights. Canada has not ratified the Inter-American Convention on Human Rights and does not recognize the jurisdiction of the Inter-American Court of Human Rights, on the basis that some provisions of the convention are in conflict with federal and provincial legislation. Thede (2005) argues that the problem instead is a "clear lack of political leadership," as numerous Canadian human rights advocates have shown Canada could ratify the convention without contradicting its own domestic jurisdiction. As long as Canada remains on the margins of the inter-American system of human rights, its capacity to encourage the protection of human rights in the region, as well as its capacity to promote democracy under a rights-based approach, are seriously undermined (Thérien et al. 2004; Thede 2005).

Another criticism frequently addressed to Canada is related to the narrow definition of democracy that it promotes through various multilateral initiatives in the region (Thérien et al. 2004; G. Schmitz 2004; Thede 2005). Canada adheres to a procedural definition of democracy, or "representative democracy" in the inter-American context, while many countries in the region have demanded that regional efforts for democracy promotion also address the difficult but necessary task of combating poverty. Poverty is recognized by many Latin American and Caribbean countries as a real threat to democracy, whereas Canada, according to Thérien et al. (2004), maintains a polite and symbolic position on this issue and has not dealt with it in any meaningful way. Schmitz (2004) argues that Canada's procedural vision of democracy is reflected in the UPD mandate, which focused on elements such as institution building and election monitoring. Without a comprehensive approach to societal development that involves human rights, good governance, and economic progress, critics argue, regional democracy promoters such as Canada will be repeatedly confronted by the same problems.

A third criticism is related to Canada's ambiguous position during the negotiation of the design of the IADC. There is no doubt that Canada was a strong supporter of the Peruvian initiative to develop a Democratic Charter for the Americas (Graham 2002). Because the charter was a mandate from the Québec City Summit and because Canada had been involved in mediation efforts during the democratic crisis in Peru, Canada worked closely with the Peruvians and a small group of states from the beginning of the negotiation process, within the framework of the OAS, to make the charter a reality. Yet a close look at the negotiations process reveals that when the time came to negotiate the actual wording of the document, Canada was hesitant to give the charter what many observers lament it now lacks: an effective means of enforcement.

Canada, on the one hand, objected to the inclusion of a reference to the "right to democracy" in the first article of the charter. Canadian judicial advisers feared that using "juridical language" would establish a precedent and create a new international obligation for Canada, because such a "right to democracy" did not exist in Canadian or international law. Canada instead proposed the weaker wording that "Democracy is essential for the social, political and economic development of the people of the Americas" (OAS 2001a). Because the "right to democracy" was in the end included in the text of the charter, Canada asked to add a "Statement of Understanding" as an annex to the document, in which it reaffirmed that the Democratic Charter was political in nature and that such a "right to democracy" corresponded to the "right of individuals to the elements of democracy as set out in relevant international instruments."

On the other hand, Canada remained discreet when other countries discussed a proposal, submitted by Peru in its initial draft, to give the Inter-American Commission of Human Rights the authority to issue "appreciation reports" regarding the status of civil and political rights in countries undergoing a democratic crisis. Such an independent, monitoring mechanism, had it been included in the final design, would have allowed greater neutrality in the application of the charter. But Canada, not having ratified the Inter-American Convention on Human Rights, did not press to include such a proposal in the final version of the Democratic Charter.[16]

Canada's preference for low levels of obligation and delegation in the design of the IADC may seem counterintuitive if we conceive it as a principled actor in matters of democracy and human rights promotion. From a rationalist perspective, however, Canada's position corresponds to an explanation put forward by Moravcsik (2000) that stable and established democracies may support the adoption of international agreements aimed at the collective defense of democracy but may be more hesitant to accept high sovereignty costs if these agreements are self-binding. Independent surveillance mechanisms to monitor the behavior of states, or language establishing new obligations for governments, are design features that can be costly for sovereign states. Rather, argues Moravcsik, it is unstable democracies whose governments are faced with domestic democratic uncertainty (such as Peru, in the case of the IADC) that are most likely to benefit from "locking-in" democratic institutions at the international level and are thus most interested in adopting clear and binding international obligations.

A final criticism is that, in a number of key circumstances, Canada has sided with the United States instead of reacting forcefully to use inter-American instruments for the collective defense of democracy. Indeed, Thérien et al. (2004) argue that in the Venezuelan coup in 2002 Canada maintained a low profile, probably because it was sensitive to the United States's ambivalence toward Venezuelan president Hugo Chávez. Canada was not part of the "Friends of Venezuela" group of countries that, along with the OAS and the Carter Center, worked to find a democratic solution to the political crisis in the country. In a similar fashion, during the ousting of President Aristide of Haiti in 2004, Cameron (2004) criticized the U.S. resolution of the overall political crisis and suggested that Canada "failed [an] elected leader" by not insisting on solving the Haitian crisis within the framework of the Inter-American Charter. As much as Chávez's and Aristide's own democratic records can be criticized, if multilateral instruments created to solve such political crises are not publicly and forcefully applied by Canada and other parties, this can only undermine the credibility of those instruments.

Explaining Canada's Uneven Performance

Canada is generally perceived as a serious and committed actor in the inter-American collective defense of democracy. Yet its democracy promotion efforts in the Americas are not as consistent as Canadians might think, and while there are successes, there are also situations when Canada has not lived up to expectations.

A first possible explanation for Canada's uneven performance lies in Thede's (2005) observation that since human rights and democracy promotion became explicit elements of Canadian foreign policy in the 1980s, there has existed a systematic bias against social and economic rights and against "emerging transversal rights," such as the right to democracy or the right to development. Such a bias, argues Thede, has negatively affected Canada's international human rights commitments and undermined its efforts to promote democratic development. By hesitating to recognize collective rights such as the right to democracy, as was the case during the negotiation of the IADC in 2001, Canada presents the contradictory image of an actor interested in promoting human rights and democracy but unwilling to adopt binding international treaties that would allow the further institutionalization of those rights in developing countries.

A second potential explanation lies in Canada's relation with the United States, its neighbor and closest ally and commercial partner. Canada is sensitive to the United States's interests and foreign policy objectives. Because of the importance of the bilateral relationship between the two countries, Canadian interests vis-à-vis the United States often take precedence over other foreign policy objectives. While the two countries' interests in the region have often converged, the means employed to achieve them are often quite different, which adds to the complexity of managing this important bilateral relationship for Canadian policy makers. Canada has generally been determined to preserve its distinct and independent voice in international affairs. As reviewed previously, Canada is usually seen as a credible and respected actor in the Americas, in part because, contrary to the United States, it does not carry a history of frequent and unilateral interventions in other countries' domestic affairs. Canada has always accorded much importance to that distinction. When Canadian officials first started to think about formally developing democracy promotion as a foreign policy objective in the 1980s, they certainly did not want to be perceived as "ideological imperialists overriding the sensibilities of others," as Gerald Schmitz (2004, 14) puts it. This attitude remains a defining trait of Canada's foreign policy today.

But to a certain extent, could this restraint, coupled with sensitivity for U.S. interests, have led to situations where Canada was not assertive enough in playing a front role in situations where it could make a difference? Observers note that one of Canada's "successes" in democracy promotion in the Americas, the Peruvian episode of 2000, was rather "circumstantial" (Cooper and Legler 2001a; 2001b). Had Canada not been chair of the OAS General Assembly taking place in Windsor in 2000 just days following the fraudulent presidential elections, perhaps it would not have taken a lead in the subsequent events. As previously mentioned, Canada did not act with the same vigor it had shown in Peru following the 2002 Venezuelan coup and the 2004 ousting of Aristide in Haiti, two episodes where the United States clearly did not feel sympathy for the incumbents. In such democratic crises, Canada might have introduced a balanced perspective, yet hesitated to be at the forefront of collective efforts to protect and strengthen democracy through established multilateral instruments.

A third potential explanation lies in what could be described as an "Americas fatigue" in Canada's foreign policy. From 1990 until 2001, we can observe a crescendo of Canadian interest in hemispheric affairs. It began with Canada joining the OAS in 1990, continued throughout the 1990s while Canada proved to be a serious actor in inter-American affairs, and was reinforced with Canada hosting a series of inter-American meetings, notably the Summit of the Americas in Québec City in 2001. Following 2001, however, many factors contributed to a sense of Canadian disengagement from the region.

On the one hand, the September 11, 2001, events led to important policy changes not only in the United States but also in Canada. Issues that were presented as priorities during the April 2001 Summit of the Americas, such as the creation of a Free Trade Area of the Americas (FTAA) and the collective protection and promotion of democracy in the hemisphere, lost political attention as homeland security and the fight against terrorism became White House priorities. Because of the important flow of peoples and goods between Canada and the United States, and because so many of its domestic policy issues are directly affected by its proximity to the United States, Canada had a clear interest in also turning its attention to security issues, which created a "distraction" from Latin America (Randall 2002).

On the other hand, analysts and politicians were also becoming less optimistic about the future of the inter-American integration process. Many doubted that the FTAA would ever become a reality, while political crises in Bolivia and Ecuador, persistent violence and political tension in Haiti, and polarization of politics in Venezuela represented discouraging news for the state of democracy in the region. Moreover, the OAS went through an internal leadership and credibility crisis in the aftermath of the sudden resignation of Secretary-General Miguel Angel Rodríguez in September 2004 following allegations of corruption in his native Costa Rica. A long and divisive campaign to elect his successor followed his resignation.

In Canada, an internal reorganization of senior management at the Department of Foreign Affairs in January 2005 resulted in the creation of a new assistant deputy minister position for "North America" (United States and Mexico), the elimination of the assistant deputy minister position that previously existed for the "Americas," and the attribution of responsibility for Latin America and the Caribbean to the assistant deputy minister for "bilateral relations," also responsible for the rest of the world. To outside observers, these actions created the perception that the Americas as a region was being downgraded in Canada's foreign policy priorities.

A final possible explanation lies in the observation that after years of increased interest in the issue of democracy promotion in various governmental and nongovernmental milieus, Canada had still not developed a coherent or unified front to pursue democracy promotion abroad. In 1988 when two special rapporteurs, law professor Gisèle Côté-Harper and political scientist John Courtney, were appointed by the Mulroney government to establish a new Canadian organization that could serve as a "needed focal point" for Canada's international activities in promoting human rights and democratic development (eventually Rights and Democracy), they first assessed the work already being done in Canada, both by governmental and nongovernmental actors. They realized, writes Gerald Schmitz (2004, 14), that "a surprising amount of activity [was] already taking place at home" by various government departments including Justice and Labour, CIDA, Elections Canada, the International Development Research Center, the Royal Canadian Mounted Police, human rights organizations, university-based institutes, nongovernmental organizations, churches, and trade unions, to name but a few. Seventeen years later, in their 2005 Blueprint for a "Democracy Canada Institute," Axworthy, Campbell, and Donovan (2005b, 1) also started by assessing Canadian expertise and experience in the field of democracy promotion and came to the same conclusion: "Canada does not possess an all-encompassing, single organization, such as the National Democratic Institute in the United States or the Centre for Democratic Institutions in Australia, [but Canada] maintains a series of smaller associations devoted to the international promotion of democracy."[17] Numerous Canadian organizations thus pursue activities related to democracy promotion in many parts of the world, yet the "needed focal point" proposed in 1988 is still being discussed today. Could the persistent lack of coordination among the various Canadian actors involved in democracy promotion activities be a part of the explanation for Canada's uneven performance in the Americas and elsewhere? As Axworthy, Campbell, and Donovan (2005b, 6) put it, "policy coherence requires a driver of coherence," and such a concern certainly deserves further thought.

I have argued in this chapter that Canada has not always been a principled actor when it comes to promoting democracy in the Americas, and that national interests (domestic, regional, and bilateral, notably vis-à-vis the U.S.) are also at play when Canada chooses to take a front role in bilateral or multilateral initiatives to defend, restore, or strengthen democracy in the region. While there have been contradictions in Canada's policy and behavior, the country remains well positioned to continue playing a leading role in democracy promotion efforts in the hemisphere. Canada maintains its reputation of a credible and balanced actor, which affords its officials the opportunity to play a constructive role in sensitive circumstances, a role that other regional powers, notably the United States, simply cannot play. And Canada's leadership in this sector is central to its relevance and credibility, not only in inter-American affairs but also in the eyes of the U.S. administration, something that is important for successive Canadian governments (Cohen 2002). On the multilateral front, after an intense leadership race, Chilean José Miguel Insulza was elected OAS secretary-general in May 2005. Insulza's expressed commitment to democracy promotion provides an opportunity for Canada to continue to position itself as a leader in multilateral efforts to promote and strengthen democracy in the Americas.

Canada's disengagement from the region that observers sensed after 2001 is likely to be temporary. Certainly, resources are scarce and the Western Hemisphere will always be one of many areas of the world where Canada tries to, and should, maintain an "activist" role (Cooper and Legler 2001a; Thérien et al. 2004). Yet Canada is part of the Americas, and for that reason has a genuine interest in working toward the sustainable economic and political development of the region. Speaking at the June 2006 OAS General Assembly, Canada's minister of foreign affairs, Peter MacKay, told his OAS counterparts that they could "count on [his] personal support and commitment to expand Canadian relations throughout [the] hemisphere" (DFAIT 2006b). Statements like this indicate an honest intent on the part of the Canadian government to strengthen its engagement in the Americas.

On the democracy front, there are many ways in which Canada can expand and consolidate its presence in the region. By working to improve existing inter-American instruments for the collective defense of democracy such as the IADC, by continuing to work closely with countries in transition or countries faced with the challenge of strengthening their democratic institutions, by being at the forefront of collective efforts deployed to protect democracy when a governance crisis erupts in a member state of the OAS, and by working with democratic governments of the region to ensure that democracy "delivers the goods" and responds to citizens' expectations for free and more equal societies, Canada can continue to make a positive difference in the Americas.

NOTES

At the time this piece was written, Flavie Major was a Ph.D. candidate in political science at Université Laval in Québec City. She has since started to work as a policy analyst in the Department of Foreign Affairs and International Trade (DFAIT) in Canada. The opinions expressed in her chapter are the author's alone and do not reflect the views of DFAIT or the Government of Canada.

1. In September 2004, following a restructuring initiative led by then secretary-general Miguel Angel Rodríguez, the UPD was renamed the Office for the Promotion of Democracy (OPD), under the newly created Department for Democratic and Political Affairs (DDPA). In 2006, following a restructuring led by current secretary-general José Miguel Insulza, the OPD became the Department for the Promotion of Democracy, under the Subsecretariat for Political Affairs.

2. For a detailed account of Canada's historical position toward the region in general and the OAS in particular, see Rochlin (1994); McKenna (1995); and Stevenson (2000).

3. Cameron and Appel Molot (1995) recall that, while in opposition, the Liberal Party had frequently criticized the previous Conservative government on the need to "democratize" Canada's foreign policy and give a greater say to both citizens and parliamentarians in determining Canada's role in the world.

4. Leslie Campbell cited in G. Schmitz (2004). Thomas Axworthy is former adviser to Prime Minister Trudeau and chairman of the Center for the Study of Democracy at

Queens' University; Leslie Campbell is senior associate at the National Democratic Institute for International Affairs (NDI) based in Washington, D.C.

5. As reported in the *Globe and Mail* (2006).

6. Resolution 1080 and the 1992 Washington Protocol are discussed in greater detail in Dexter Boniface's chapter in this volume.

7. The UPD is now the Department for the Promotion of Democracy (see note 1).

8. A complete list of all electoral observation missions undertaken by the OAS since 1990 is available on the organization's Web site, www.sap.oas.org.

9. As is briefly discussed in the first section of this chapter. On the "democratization" of Canada's foreign policy, see Cameron and Appel Molot (1995).

10. See OAS (1999) and Shamsie (2000) for a detailed history of OAS–civil society relations.

11. The Santiago Plan of Action devotes one subsection to civil society participation in inter-American affairs, in which leaders encourage "public sector–civil society dialogue and partnerships in the areas considered pertinent of [the Santiago Summit] Plan of Action." See Office of Summit Follow-Up (2002), 284.

12. Whether civil society organizations participating in such meetings succeed in changing government policies is another discussion; the fact that governmental representatives now meet to listen to their observations and proposals is a sign of opening and democratization that was not foreseeable only a few years ago.

13. Canadian funding will include an annual contribution of $95 million from CIDA to support political governance, national reconstruction, and economic recovery and facilitate access to basic services; $15 million from DFAIT's Global Peace and Security Fund to strengthen security and justice sectors; and $20 million to allow Canadian police officers to remain in Haiti as part of the United Nations Stabilization Mission in Haiti. See the "Americas" page of the Canadian International Development Agency Web site, as well as press releases by DFAIT (2006a) and from CIDA (2006). All documents are available on DFAIT's and CIDA's web sites, www.dfait-maeci.gc.ca and www.acdi-cida.gc.ca.

14. Warren (2003) recalls that Axworthy devoted a significant amount of time to the Cuba file both because of his personal interest in the role that Canada could play in Cuba and because of the rapid escalation of the United States–Cuba tensions during his time as foreign affairs minister, following the adoption in 1996 of the Helms-Burton Act.

15. The following discussion of the Peruvian episode is mainly inspired by McClintock (2001), Cooper and Legler (2001b), and Randall (2002).

16. These observations are based on numerous interviews conducted in September 2004 and March 2005 with Canadian, Peruvian, American, Chilean, and Costa Rican diplomats involved in the negotiation of the Inter-American Democratic Charter in 2001.

17. Many of the institutions these authors listed in 2005 were already mentioned in the 1988 survey: CIDA, Foreign Affairs Canada, Elections Canada, Rights and Democracy, the International Development Research Center. Others are new: Institute on Governance, Parliamentary Center, Forum of Federations, Canadian Institute of Public Administration, Canada World Youth, CANADEM.

CHAPTER SIX

Brazil

How Realists Defend Democracy

Sean Burges and Jean Daudelin

In April 2002 Venezuela was again in crisis. A few years before, bucking what was then a continental trend, the country had elected a classic populist *caudillo* as its president. Former army colonel Hugo Chávez had organized a coup attempt in 1992 for which he had spent two years in prison. The man was fond of street politics, mass meetings, inflammatory rhetoric, and inflationary economic policies. As president, he was betting on continuing high prices for oil to finance a fast-expanding edifice of social programs, all the while deepening the country's vulnerability to cyclical crises and economic volatility.

Nothing in Chávez's persona, his troubled past, current politics, or economic policies could be reassuring to his neighbors. This was particularly true for Brazil, whose government was presided over by Fernando Henrique Cardoso, a liberal critic of populism and himself a victim of military authoritarianism. His government was committed to taking his country down the path of long-term, sustainable, low-inflation growth and was doing its best to encourage and help its neighbors to do the same thing, promoting regional integration and policy convergence for that purpose. Cardoso himself was foreign minister in 1992, when Brazil had joined the region in denouncing

Chávez's attempted coup against President Carlos Andrés Pérez. And yet when Chávez's liberal opposition, with some support from the military, tried to push him out in April 2002, Cardoso and the other South American heads of state were quick and uncompromising: the Venezuelan president had been elected democratically, and only through open and clean elections could he be removed from office. In the end, the coup plotters failed, just like Chávez himself ten years before, and Brazil had proved to be superbly consistent. Cardoso thus seems entitled to claim, as he does in his memoirs, that "Brazil always defends the maintenance of the democratic order."[1] But does Cardoso's assertion stand up to greater scrutiny?

Barely two years later, on February 29, 2004, and in an atmosphere of growing social and political unrest, Haiti's President Jean-Bertrand Aristide resigned and fled the country. The United States and France, both of which were increasingly worried about the governability of the country and whose soldiers had been with Aristide during his last hours on the island, argued that he had taken those decisions on his own. Aristide himself and most independent analysts, however, have suggested that he had been forced to resign by the United States and France (Fatton 2006; Goldberg in this volume; Shamsie in this volume). Caribbean countries, through the Caribbean Community (CARICOM), as well as Venezuela and even South Africa, where Aristide eventually took refuge, strongly objected to the way in which Aristide's departure had taken place. While Aristide had few fans in the region or in the world, nobody at the time could convincingly present the change of government as legitimate. Western powers had their hands full and could have faced a public relations disaster. But an unlikely ally showed up as Brazil, headed by Luis Inácio Lula da Silva, immediately volunteered to help, announcing it would take the lead in the United Nations stabilizing force that was to be sent to Haiti. A former union leader who had fought the military dictatorship and then the old elites to reach the presidency, Lula was a symbol for progressive democrats the world over. Brazil's left-wing government, in other words, gave a varnish of legitimacy to an intervention that had more to do with political expediency than with the protection of democracy.

How can one reconcile Brazil's actions in Haiti with a principled commitment to the defense of democracy? Is this the exception that proves Cardoso's rule or is Brazil's commitment to democracy less absolute than the former president would have us believe?

This is the puzzle we try to unravel. Can we explain Brazil's behavior toward political crises in the Western Hemisphere since 1989 by assuming that it is primarily driven by a preoccupation with the defense and promotion of democracy? To answer this question, we first review Brazil's efforts at formalizing a commitment to democracy in the Americas, mostly by supporting the introduction of democratic clauses in the constitutive documents of the regional and subregional organizations of which it is a member, and by introducing references to democracy in their public pronouncements. This section examines Brazil's contribution to the formal transformation of democracy into a regional norm, or a principle that commands respect from all the states of the region. We then examine the country's policy toward the whole universe of democratic crises and quasi-crises that befell the Americas since 1990. We find that the country's positions and actions have been generally consistent with the defense and promotion of democracy during this period. However, we also identify a number of ambiguities and inconsistencies that cast doubt on the primacy of that norm in the design and practice of Brazilian foreign policy. We contend, in fact, that a realist agenda privileging Brazil's economic and political interests in the region (and in the world) still dominates the country's foreign policy. Although the defense and promotion of democracy are often consistent with that agenda, economic and political interests retain primacy and ultimately dictate Brazilian foreign policy. When the principled defense of democracy clashes with broader political and economic objectives, it is the latter that win the day.

Brazil and the Hemispheric Commitment to the Defense of Democracy

Ever since the 1989 presidential election, the first direct election for president in twenty-nine years, Brazil has contributed heavily to the construction of the web of declarations, commitments, and charters that Latin American governments have devised to keep dictators at bay. Brazil's diplomacy has also been vocally committed to the protection of the region's democracies and has played a prominent role in defusing a number of democratic crises.[2] Successive governments have been keen to entrench references to democracy in the international agreements and declarations to which the country is a party, particularly at the hemispheric level. In fact, even under indirectly elected President José Sarney (1985–89), Brazil had already supported the inclusion of a reference to democracy in a new preamble to the Organization of American

States (OAS) Charter. The significance of that gesture, however, should not be exaggerated, given Sarney's long and fruitful association with the military regime. Moreover, at the time of Brazil's 1985 transition to civilian rule, the OAS's commitments to democracy had a long but essentially irrelevant history (Muñoz 1998, 3–8). Thus, one should probably see the Collor de Mello government (1989–92) as the first under which Brazil really becomes an active promoter and defender of democracy in the hemisphere.

The record is impressive. Brazil supported the adoption by the OAS of an increasingly clear and compelling series of measures that were meant to protect democracy, beginning in 1985 with the changes to the preamble of the charter, continuing through 1991 and 1992 with the Santiago Declaration and the Washington Protocol, and culminating in 2001 with the adoption of the Inter-American Democratic Charter (see appendix B). Perhaps more tellingly, Brazil's diplomacy systematically built democratic clauses and references into the charters, protocols, and declarations of the subregional institutions of which it is a member. The importance of democracy in the constitution and activities of the Rio Group, MERCOSUR, and the more recent South American Community of Nations can to a large extent be traced back to Brazil's activism (Santiso 2003; Gardini 2005).

Such a multiplication of multilateral fora where the defense and promotion of democracy may be invoked can be seen as an important contribution to the consolidation of a flexible and comprehensive defense-of-democracy regime in the region. It makes available a wider range of channels and pressure points that can be used to compel a given government to respect democratic principles. The adoption of democratic clauses or membership requirements by basically all of the subregional fora also promises to more fully isolate potential violators of the democratic norm. And, in contrast to the OAS, these subregional fora also open a space for Brazil and the other members of the various groups to act together without having to court the approval of the United States. This insulates to some extent the regional democratic regime from U.S. strategic interests and from the compromises that typically come with them. It opens up the possibility of acting decisively but without any involvement from the United States, which can lessen traditional (and understandable) preoccupations with violations of national sovereignty. Finally, each of the hemispheric fora and institutions has its own advantages and constraints, and in each the most influential players have a different weight. Brazil is by far the largest player in MERCOSUR, but decisive action also depends on Argentina's cooperation. MERCOSUR's reach does not really extend beyond its membership—Argentina, Brazil, Paraguay, Uruguay, and, most recently, Venezuela. Mexico adds weight to the Rio Group, while lessening Brazil's and Argentina's relative influence. But if Mexico's cooperation proves hard to get, the South American Community of Nations, from which Mexico is by definition excluded, holds at least the promise of an alternative multilateral forum.

A most interesting dimension of Brazil's democratic activism is that the various instruments that were established since 1990 have actually been put to use by its diplomacy in the management of real crises. Many of those instruments, such as the June 1996 Commitment to Democracy that was adopted by MERCOSUR countries in response to an attempted coup in Paraguay (Valenzuela 1997), were in fact developed in reaction to concrete situations and to expand the range of options available for dealing with similar democratic challenges in the future. The tools, in sum, are numerous and varied. Let us now examine the specific ways and circumstances in which they were or were not used by Brazil, beginning with a brief outline of the methodology we have devised to make sense of the country's "democratic" foreign policy.

Assessing Brazil's Enforcement of the Democratic Norm in the Americas since 1990

Our analysis is based on an overview of all the disruptions of democratic regimes in the Americas between 1990 and 2005 for which we could find reliable information on Brazil's attitude and action. We start in 1990 because this is the year when democratically elected Fernando Collor de Mello became president of the country, putting a final point to more than twenty years of authoritarianism. For the identification of the democratic crises, we used an extremely low threshold of what constitutes a crisis in order to generate as large a sample as possible of "occasions" for Brazil to react to. Accordingly, we were able to identify twenty-seven cases. The sample includes several cases of what the OAS, under Resolution 1080 (see appendix A), terms a "sudden or irregular interruption of the democratic political institutional process, or of the elected government," even if these cases have not been defined as such by the OAS. It also includes a number of less clear-cut cases, including for instance significant electoral irregularities or clear manipulations of constitutional provisions.

We are trying to see if, and to what extent, Brazil's behavior in these twenty-seven cases can be explained by a principled commitment to the defense and promotion of democracy. To that end, we ask four key questions. First, is Brazil a consistent advocate of a principled, pro-democracy foreign policy (norm consistency)? Second, has the consolidation of democracy within Brazil since 1990 made it a more consistent advocate of a principled, pro-democracy foreign policy (domestic-international continuity)? Third, were Brazil's preferred methods of intervention in each case really the ones to protect democracy most effectively (adequacy of the preferred type of action)? Finally, were the bilateral or multilateral institutional arrangements chosen to deal with the crisis best able, in the circumstances, to protect democracy (suitability of the institutional arrangements)? We begin by outlining the way in which we plan to answer these four questions.

Norm consistency: Is Brazil a consistent advocate of a principled, pro-democracy foreign policy?

Because the issue of consistency over time and in a variety of circumstances is the most important test of a country's commitment to a given principle, much of our discussion of Brazil's policy focuses on it. In order to assess the consistency of Brazil's foreign policy, we have coded Brazil's reaction to a variety of democratic crises using a six-level scale whereby higher numbers represent a greater commitment to democracy on behalf of Brazil:

0: support for (undemocratic) challenges to the norm;
1: opposition to any initiative meant to actively enforce the norm and defend the democratic regime;
2: indifference or ambivalence toward norm enforcement;
3: passive support to measures taken to enforce the norm;
4: secondary enforcement, that is, active support for enforcement initiatives taken by others;
5: primary enforcement, that is, initiation, alone or as part of a coalition, of actions to defend and enforce the democratic norm.

The rationale behind this scale is straightforward, except perhaps for the distinction we introduce between levels 4 and 5. We have considered that support for another actor's enforcement initiative regarding a given violation of the norm expresses a lesser commitment than direct involvement in the launching of the initiative because the political implications are typically lower. This is particularly the case when the measures adopted involve a violation of sovereignty, something that is most likely to happen in major crises, because the impact and consequences of those measures are typically attributed primarily to the initiating countries.[3]

Domestic-international continuity: As Brazil has become more democratic since 1990, has it become a more consistent advocate of a principled, pro-democracy foreign policy?

This question focuses on the degree of continuity between domestic democratic consolidation and the defense and promotion of the democratic norm at the international level. The assumption here is that if a given state's international commitment to the democratic norm derives from a principled commitment of the country's population and/or elites to that norm, it should be roughly consistent with the degree of internal democratic consolidation. One should find, in other words, continuity between the country's commitment to democracy in the domestic and international arena. That is, as a democracy consolidates, so should its commitment to defending the democratic norm abroad. By contrast, a realist would predict that Brazil's foreign policy would not be influenced by the state of democracy at the domestic level. To answer this question, we have identified on the basis of the secondary literature a number of markers of domestic democratic consolidation. We examine if Brazil's democratization resulted in a growing or lesser commitment to the protection of democracy, as measured by the consistency scale we have just discussed.

Adequacy of the preferred type of action: Were Brazil's preferred modalities of intervention in each case really the ones to protect democracy most effectively?

The adequacy of the measures adopted to the circumstances of democratic norm violation is another window into a state's commitment to that norm. A strong commitment to democracy will be expressed through the adoption of measures that are likely to have a real impact on the crisis. Conversely, measures that are unlikely to counter a serious challenge to democracy effectively imply a more limited commitment. We have tried to approach this by looking at four types of action, which can be understood as expressing growing levels of pressure: a simple declaration, the sending of an envoy explicitly tasked with putting pressure on the violator, the imposition of sanctions, and finally, military intervention. To correlate these responses to the severity of the crises, we first divide the crises in two broad categories, those where Resolution 1080 could have reasonably been invoked (even if it was not), and those where it clearly could not. The "severe crises" category includes twelve instances where presidents were toppled, forced out, or compelled to resign by illegal or highly irregular means, or where legislative assemblies were closed or their activities suspended, also by illegal or highly irregular means. For those cases, we then look at the type of measures that Brazil supported or advocated, thereby getting an idea of the strength of the country's commitment to the effective defense of democracy in the cases where it was most clearly under attack.

Suitability of the institutional arrangements: Were the institutional arrangements chosen to deal with the crisis best able, in the circumstances, to protect democracy?

A similar rationale underlies our fourth question, which looks at the adequacy of the institution that Brazil chose to use to deal with given democratic crises. We distinguish here between bilateral and multilateral interventions and, among the latter, between the various organizations of which Brazil is a member and whose involvement in the various crises it supported or advocated. Once again, credible support for the democratic norm would imply that the chosen or preferred institution would at least have the political weight needed to deal with the violation.

Before presenting the data, two caveats are in order. The first one regards coding. Our assessment of the norm consistency and domestic-international continuity of Brazil's behavior, of the adequacy of the measures Brazil has advocated, and of the suitability of the institution it privileged is clearly subjective and subject to further verification. Given the absence of scholarly consensus or even partial agreement on the severity of many of the crises examined and on Brazil's reaction to them, we used our best professional judgment. The second caveat regards the quality of the data on which the characterization of both the situations and Brazil's reaction was based. We have used a variety of sources, including interviews with members of Brazil's foreign policy establishment, press reports, primary documentation, and secondary analyses. However, the most reliable primary material—internal memos and diplomatic correspondence, for instance—is in most cases unavailable. Additionally, the secondary literature on Brazil's policy in those cases is extremely sparse. That being said, we think that the richness of our sample enables us to reach reasonably valid conclusions.

Brazil's Record

Using this basic framework we now examine Brazil's record. Our discussion is organized around the four questions presented in the previous section and makes use of tables that summarize the information we have gathered about Brazil's reaction to democratic crises.

Question 1: Is Brazil's foreign policy consistent with a principled defense of democracy?
Table 6.1 presents the whole universe of cases for which we could document the Brazilian government's reaction. The crises are presented in chronological order, which makes it easier to identify the possible evolution of that reaction through the four administrations that have governed Brazil since 1989.

As a rule, one can say that Brazil has been quite supportive of efforts to protect democracy in the Americas since 1990. The Brazilian government was actively involved in democratic norm enforcement in eight of the twenty-seven cases considered and expressed passive support for the defense of democracy in eleven cases; we found only six instances where it showed indifference or opposition to enforcement. The case of Haiti in 2004 is the lone example of de facto support for the toppling of a democratically elected government. The case is admittedly not straightforward, as Jean-Bertrand Aristide's own democratic credentials were far from beyond reproach. Nevertheless, his challengers' credentials, which in several cases included documented association with death squads as well as the previous military regime (Fatton 2006; Shamsie in this volume), were probably worse. The victory of René Préval, the candidate most closely associated with Aristide, in the February 2006 presidential elections, also suggests that Aristide, who at the time of this writing remains in exile, continues to enjoy strong support in the country. Nothing suggests that Aristide's return would contribute much to ending the developmental and humanitarian emergency that has plagued Haiti for generations, but such pragmatic considerations cannot make his toppling and exile, or Brazil's support for both, consistent with the defense and promotion of democracy.

As we noted in the introduction, Haiti could be the exception. But this is not the impression that Table 6.1 conveys. Support for norm enforcement is often tepid, and in the few cases where forceful collective actions were on the table, Brazil typically opposed them. Peru's two major crises during this time

Table 6.1. Democratic Crises and Brazil's Reaction (N = 27)

Country	Date	Event	Brazil's Reaction[a]	Type of Action[b]
Argentina	December 1990	Military uprising	3	D
Suriname	December 1990	Military coup	1	D
Haiti	January 1991	Coup attempt	4	D
Haiti	September 1991	Coup	2	SD
Venezuela	February 1992	Coup attempt	3	D
Peru	April 1992	*Autogolpe*	2.5	D
Venezuela	November 1992	Coup attempt	4	D
Nicaragua	December 1992	Congress closure	2	D
Guatemala	May 1993	*Autogolpe* attempt	3	D
Venezuela	May 1993	Presidential impeachment	3	
Mexico	March 1994	Political assassination	3.5	SD
Haiti	April 1994	Democratic invasion	3	D
Dominican Republic	May 1994	Electoral fraud	3	D
Paraguay	April 1996	Coup attempt	5	ID
Ecuador	February 1997	President fired	1	
Paraguay	March 1999	Political assassination	5	ID
Ecuador	January 2000	President forced out	2.5	D
Paraguay	May 2000	Coup attempt	5	ID
Peru	June 2000	Disputed electoral results	1	
Peru	November 2000	Presidential resignation	3	D
Guatemala	February 2001	Disputed electoral results	5	D
Argentina	December 2001	President forced out	3	D
Venezuela	April 2002	Coup attempt	5	D
Bolivia	October 2003	President forced out	4.5	ED
Haiti	February 2004	President forced out	0	I
Ecuador	April 2005	President forced out	2	ED
Bolivia	June 2005	President forced out	3	ED

[a]0: Challenges to the norm; 1: Opposition to enforcement; 2: Indifference or ambivalence; 3: Passive support for enforcement; 4: Secondary enforcement; 5: Primary enforcement. Data given only where reliable coding possible.

[b]I: Intervention (4); S: Sanction (3); E: Envoy (2); D: Declaration (1).

period illustrate this starkly. In the first instance, that of Fujimori's *autogolpe* in 1992, Brazil refused to go beyond a broad declaration in which it expressed hope that Peru would overcome its difficulties, return to constitutional order, and recognize that there was no space for authoritarian regimes. More decisive action was not supported. Then in 2000, when Fujimori, in the face of a strong opposition challenge, clearly manipulated electoral results, Brazil showed a similar reluctance to move decisively, settling instead for a declaration indirectly defending the probity of the polls—Cardoso noted simply that Peruvians

Table 6.2. Brazil's Reaction to Severe Crises

Country	Date	Event	Support Strong Action	Brazil's Reaction[a]	Type of Action[b]
Suriname	December 1990	Military coup	N	1	D
Haiti	September 1991	Coup	Y	2	SD
Venezuela	February 1992	Coup attempt	N	3	D
Peru	April 1992	*Autogolpe*	N	2.5	D
Nicaragua	December 1992	Congress closure	N	2	D
Guatemala	May 1993	*Autogolpe* attempt	Y	3	D
Haiti	April 1994	Democratic invasion	N	3.5	SD
Paraguay	April 1996	Coup attempt	Y	5	ID
Ecuador	January 2000	President forced out	N	2.5	D
Venezuela	April 2002	Coup attempt	N	5	D
Haiti	February 2004	President forced out	N	0	I
Ecuador	April 2005	President forced out	N	2	ED

[a]0: Challenges to the norm; 1: Opposition to enforcement; 2: Indifference or ambivalence; 3: Passive support for enforcement; 4: Secondary enforcement; 5: Primary enforcement.
[b]I: Intervention (4); S: Sanction (3); E: Envoy (2); D: Declaration (1).

had participated in it—and becoming the decisive obstacle to U.S. and Canadian efforts to formally censure, condemn, and cancel the poll result at the OAS General Assembly in Windsor.

This lack of enthusiasm shows starkly when one limits the analysis to the much smaller number of serious threats to or breaches of democratic rule (table 6.2). Support for norm enforcement, even leaving aside the case of Haiti in 2004, is again tepid. Out of eleven cases, we found only two instances of strong support (Paraguay in 1996 and Venezuela in 2002); three cases of a more passive attitude, where the norm is affirmed but no specific action advocated; and four instances (five with Haiti in 2004) of indifference, opposition to norm enforcement, or outright support for norm violation. Let us review the latter cases briefly.

Suriname, December 1990. The bloodless military coup deposing President Ramsewak Shankar was met by a communiqué from Brazil expressing a desire to see a return to constitutionality and the end of a state of emergency. Venezuelan suggestions that there be an international intervention to restore democracy were firmly blocked. There was little substantive disruption to bilateral relations between Suriname and Brazil, with efforts focused on reviving large infrastructure contracts for Brazilian firms such as the Kabalebo hydroelectric program, narcotrafficking problems, and the potential to draw Suriname into the Brazilian political orbit by acting as a counterweight to U.S. and Dutch pressures (Ministério das Relações Exteriores do Brasil 1990; Associated Press 1990; Guimarães Reis 1991).

Haiti, September 1991. The September 30 military coup overthrowing the Aristide presidency prompted a call for action by and within the OAS, which debated two possible responses. One group of countries, drawing on the Haitian representative's waiving of the principle of nonintervention, pressed for direct intervention to restore democracy. Brazil's response, however, prevented the adoption by the OAS of a resolution calling for active intervention. With Bolivia and Chile, Brazil worked instead on a resolution calling for the coup plotters to step aside and allow Aristide's return. Direct responses were confined to a hemispheric embargo on Haiti, whose impact on the new regime, if not on the population, was negligible. In the end, the coup plotters were thrown out three years later by a UN-sanctioned military operation that was led by the United States but never actively supported by Brazil.

Nicaragua, December 1992. President Violeta Chamorro closed Congress and ordered the military to occupy its facilities after members of her own party attempted to force her to break the agreements she had reached with the opposition Sandinistas, particularly about their continued control of the army. A provisional administration was named that governed until a new assembly directorate was elected at the beginning of 1993. Brazilian and hemispheric reaction was very subdued, with calls for adherence to constitutional norms, but no attempts were made to pressure the government into compromising with what was the legally constituted directorate of the Congress (Agence France-Presse 1992; BBC 1993; Merrill 1994).

Ecuador, April 2005. Responding to protests and the firing of the Supreme Court, Ecuador's Congress voted for a motion declaring that president Lucio Gutiérrez had abandoned his post and named Vice President Alfredo Palacio as his successor. Although many Ecuadorians demanded that Gutiérrez stay and face corruption charges, Brazil insisted on giving him political asylum and eventually arranged his transit from Quito to Brasília. Brazil then helped forestall discussions of sanctions within the OAS and President Lula pushed for the Community of South American Nations, not the OAS, to broker a dialogue between contending political factions in Ecuador, even sending his foreign minister to Quito to mediate (*Valor Econômico* 2005; Agence France-Presse 2005a, 2005b).

In summary, these cases confirm the impression conveyed by the larger universe of democratic norm violations. Brazil's foreign policy since 1990, quite simply, is not always consistent with a principled defense of democratic rule.

Question 2: As Brazil has become more democratic since 1990, has it become a more consistent advocate of a principled, pro-democracy foreign policy?

By any measure, democracy matters profoundly to Brazilians and to their leaders. Their country's experience with authoritarianism in the twentieth century was uncomfortably long and grueling, and a very large number of its current political leaders, intellectuals, and social activists have personally experienced exile, torture, prison, harassment, and the death and suffering of friends, as well as fear for themselves, their families, and their colleagues (Stepan 1989). For them, there is nothing abstract and disembodied in expressions like "transition to democracy" or the protection of human rights (Cardoso 2001; 2006a; 2006b). They know what democracy and its protection mean, and what its demise entails. Since 1990, moreover, almost every indicator points to the progressive consolidation of democracy in the country (Font 2003; 2004). Brazil, in fact, provides us with a remarkably regular progression of democratic consolidation, from the accession to power of Collor de Mello in 1989, following an election that, while formally clean, was profoundly influenced by the mass media's and the economic elites' opposition to the candidacy of Lula, to the election of Lula himself to the presidency thirteen years later, in a poll universally considered clean and honest. Collor's impeachment, his peaceful replacement by Itamar Franco (1992–95), and the two mandates of Fernando Henrique Cardoso (1995–99; 1999–2003) saw the institutionalization of democratic practices, the consolidation of democratic bargaining in Congress (Armijo, Faucher, and Dembinska 2006), and the progressive if still incomplete marginalization of clientelistic practices in the functioning of the government. Recent scandals have shown that corruption is still rife, but few would suggest that Brazil's democratic institutions themselves are at risk. Moreover, the consistent digging up of irregularities by the press, government prosecutors, and congressional commissions testifies to the existence of democratic political institutions that are very effective at regulating themselves (Daudelin 2005). All of these factors make the time elapsed since 1990 an excellent proxy for a rising level of democratic consolidation, and we use it as such.

Were its foreign policy principled, we would expect Brazil's commitment to democracy to have become progressively stronger, or at least not to weaken significantly over the period examined here. Admittedly, we cannot expect that relationship to be linear. For the sake of survival, new democracies might show a steely commitment to international support for democracy, as they themselves might benefit from it.[4] This is very close to a narrowly defined self-interested approach to foreign policy. To be considered the expression of a profound commitment to democracy as a principle and as a norm, however, a staunch and possibly "interested" early commitment to international democratic norms must be sustained over time and find expression in a principled foreign policy.

As the previous subsection made clear, one does not find much indication of a growing or even sustained commitment to the democratic norm in Brazilian foreign policy. Brazil's behavior, in particular, is not consistent over time, nor does its support for democratic rule become stronger over time: if the government of Fernando Henrique Cardoso, especially in the face of severe challenges, embodied that commitment, it was not sustained over the larger universe of cases, nor was the government's commitment maintained by Cardoso's successor, Lula, irrespective of the severity of the crises examined.

Each administration has its great moments and its bad ones, and one certainly cannot identify a clear movement toward consistent support for norm enforcement. What seems to happen instead is that a dominant attitude of ambivalence and passive support toward enforcement gives way, beginning in the mid-1990s, to both more active support and clearer opposition to democratic norm enforcement. A point of inflection seems to appear around 1995. Before that point, Brazil reacts to most crises by passively supporting international efforts to defend democracy (nine times out of thirteen), while acting decisively in only two cases, Suriname in 1990, where it fought proposals of intervention, and Venezuela in 1992, where it vigorously denounced Chávez's coup against Carlos Andrés Pérez. These proportions are reversed after 1995, where Brazil adopts a passive attitude in five of fourteen cases while acting decisively, again both in favor of and against forceful interventions, in nine out of fourteen cases.

The inflection in the mid-1990s happens to correspond roughly with the beginning of the Cardoso administration, which governed Brazil for eight of the sixteen years examined here. Brazil's reaction is more consistent with democratic norm enforcement under Cardoso than before or after his presidency. Collor de Mello (1990–92) confronted four crises and his government's reaction expressed a range of attitudes, from opposition to enforcement (Suriname, 1990) and resistance to direct intervention (Haiti, September 1991), to clear denunciation and even threat of collective action (Haiti, January 1991, and Argentina, 1990). Itamar Franco, who succeeded Collor after he was impeached following a large-scale corruption scandal, had to deal with nine crises in barely two years. In a manner largely consistent with his domestic behavior, his diplomacy demonstrated a kind of middle ground, limiting itself in most cases to declarations and engaging in active defense of democracy only in the case of the Chávez-led coup in Venezuela—during which Cardoso was minister of foreign affairs. Finally, Cardoso's successor, President Lula da Silva, confronted four crises and went to both extremes, intervening forcefully to ensure a smooth resolution respectful of constitutional rules during the Bolivia crisis in 2003, but also covering what many regard as a Franco-American coup against Aristide in 2004. In sum, none of these three administrations proved as forceful in their defense of democracy as Cardoso had been while in power.

Even Cardoso's case, however, is not straightforward, as one also finds foreign policy decisions under his administration that are more glaring in terms of opposing democratic violations than at any point since Collor's quick papering-over of the coup in Suriname in 1990. This was particularly the case for Peru in 2000, when Brazil forcefully opposed North American efforts to have the OAS denounce the election results.

A look at the severe crises does not dispel the general impression of inconsistency over time. As we saw when we looked at consistency over cases, Brazil's reaction to severe crises has been supremely ambiguous. Moreover, the many cases of highly debatable attitudes toward the defense of democracy span the whole period covered, from 1990 to 2005. As Brazil democratized, in other words, its diplomacy did not become more forceful in its defense of the democracies in the hemisphere.

Question 3: Were Brazil's preferred modalities of intervention in each case really the ones most likely to protect democracy effectively?

Table 6.1 clearly testifies to Brazil's preference for mild pressures—declarations and the sending of envoys, preferably its own diplomats, to the countries in crisis. This is very much in tune with its long tradition of respect for national sovereignty. It is also consistent with Brazil's strong preference for diplomacy, an activity in which it has a distinctive tradition and, for a so-called developing country, a remarkably strong capacity. However, Brazil did not support strong actions even when the seriousness of the crises seemed to call for a firm response (see table 6.2). In only two of the twelve severe crises that we have identified did Brazil support or engage in forceful interventions to defend democracy: in the case of Aristide's overthrow by the military in September 1991, when it backed the imposition of trade sanctions against Haiti; and in the case of General Lino Oviedo's attempted coup against Paraguayan president Juan Carlos Wasmosy in 1996, when it used the privileged access of both its diplomats and generals to convey clear threats of political and economic isolation. Remember, however, that the trade embargo against Haiti was a fallback option promoted by Brazil along with Bolivia and Chile precisely to avoid stronger action, namely a full-fledged military intervention. The strong action advocated by Brazil, in other words, was the weaker of the two options that were on the table.

This general reluctance to intervene has been traced to Brazil's commitment to sovereignty and nonintervention (Santiso 2003). This might imply that Brazilian diplomacy is effectively caught between two norms, democracy on one side and sovereignty on the other. For now, however, we must recognize that Brazil's almost systematic refusal to condone, support, or advocate violations of national sovereignty has led it to defend types of action that sometimes did little to protect democratic regimes.

Question 4: Were the institutional arrangements chosen to deal with the crises best able, in the circumstances, to protect democracy?

Table 6.3 organizes the cases according to the strength of Brazil's support for democratic norm enforcement and identifies Brazil's preferred mode of intervention: bilateral or multilateral (specifying in this case the organizations that were used). Patterns of preference are clear. For the broad universe of cases, bilateral interventions were by far Brazil's preferred instruments, having been used in twelve of the twenty-seven cases we have examined. In terms of acting through multilateral organizations, the Rio Group comes first, with seven instances, followed by the OAS with four, MERCOSUR with two, and the South American Community of Nations with one. UN involvement was supported in two cases, but one of them was the toppling of Aristide in 2004, which can hardly be considered an instance of defense of democracy. In no

Table 6.3. Preferred Institutions (complete universe)

Country	Date	Severe Disruption	Support Strong Action	Brazil's Reaction[a]	Multilateral Organization
Venezuela	April 2002	Y	N	5	Rio Group
Guatemala	February 2001			5	Rio Group
Paraguay	April 1996	Y	Y	5	MERCOSUR
Paraguay	May 2000		Y	5	MERCOSUR
Paraguay	March 1999		Y	5	(Bilateral)
Bolivia	October 2003			4.5	(Bilateral)
Venezuela	November 1992			3	Rio Group
Haiti	January 1991			4	(Bilateral)
Haiti	April 1994	Y	N	3.5	OAS, UN
Haiti	September 1991	Y	Y	3	OAS
Dominican Republic	May 1994			3	OAS
Bolivia	June 2005			3	OAS
Guatemala	May 1992	Y	N	3	Rio Group
Venezuela	February 1992			3	Rio Group
Mexico	March 1994			3	Rio Group
Argentina	December 1990			3	(Bilateral)
Venezuela	May 1993			3	(Bilateral)
Peru	November 2000			3	(Bilateral)
Argentina	December 2001			3	(Bilateral)
Ecuador	January 2000	Y	N	2.5	Rio Group
Peru	April 1992	Y	N	2.5	(Bilateral)
Ecuador	April 2005	Y	N	2	SACN[b]
Nicaragua	December 1992	Y .	N	2	(Bilateral)
Suriname	December 1990	Y	N	1	(Bilateral)
Ecuador	February 1997			1	(Bilateral)
Peru	June 2000			1	(Bilateral)
Haiti	February 2004	Y	N	0	UN

[a]0: Challenges to the norm; 1: Opposition to enforcement; 2: Indifference or ambivalence; 3: Passive support for enforcement; 4: Secondary enforcement; 5: Primary enforcement.
[b]South American Community of Nations.

cases of strong reaction to democratic norm violations on the part of Brazil was either the OAS or the UN involved. In short, for Brazil, active enforcement of democratic rule was a bilateral or subregional affair.

Table 6.4 ranks severe disruptions of democracy according to the strength of Brazil's support for democratic norm enforcement. As should perhaps be expected, bilateral interventions are much less prominent here than in the larger sample: severe crises often call for the kind of pressure that no single country can deliver and in only three of these twelve cases did Brazil prefer bilateral

Table 6.4. Preferred Institutions for Severe Crises

Country	Date	Severe Disruption	Support Strong Action	Brazil's Reaction[a]	Multilateral Organization
Ecuador	April 2005	Y	N	2	SACN[b]
Haiti	February 2004	Y	N	0	UN
Venezuela	April 2002	Y	N	5	Rio Group
Ecuador	January 2000	Y	N	2.5	Rio Group
Paraguay	April 1996	Y	Y	5	MERCOSUR
Haiti	April 1994	Y	N	3.5	OAS, UN
Guatemala	May 1993	Y	Y	3	Rio Group
Nicaragua	December 1992	Y	N	2	(Bilateral)
Peru	April 1992	Y	N	2.5	(Bilateral)
Venezuela	February 1992	Y	N	3	Rio Group
Haiti	September 1991	Y	Y	3	OAS
Suriname	December 1990	Y	N	1	(Bilateral)

[a]0: Challenges to the norm; 1: Opposition to enforcement; 2: Indifference or ambivalence; 3: Passive support for enforcement; 4: Secondary enforcement; 5: Primary enforcement.
[b]South American Community of Nations.

channels. Moreover, its general preference for multilateralism for dealing with serious crises is also not surprising, given the country's postwar diplomatic customs, which have systematically favored multilateral organizations.

The preferred multilateral institution for dealing with severe disruptions of democracy is clearly the Rio Group, which Brazil favored in four cases, followed by the OAS in two cases, and then, in one case each, the South American Community of Nations, MERCOSUR (in the 1996 Paraguayan crisis), and the UN (in Haiti in 1994). The second mention of the UN is once again related to the 2004 toppling of Aristide, in Haiti.

Both tables point to quite a few cases where the choice of institutional arrangements made perfect sense from the standpoint of the defense of democracy. Brazil's use of bilateral channels in smaller countries where it has a great deal of influence, as in Paraguay in 1999 and Bolivia in 2003, was extremely effective. It enabled Brazilian diplomats to use old and multifaceted linkages to convey strong pressures and very credible threats to all actors involved, thus facilitating compromises. For Brazil to articulate its foreign policy through MERCOSUR in the case of Paraguay in 1996 was similarly consistent with an efficient use of the available levers (Valenzuela 1997; Fournier and Burges 2000) as no Paraguayan political player can easily dismiss convergent pressures from Argentina and Brazil.

The larger pattern that emerges from these tables, however, points to Brazil's almost systematic refusal to see the strongest multilateral institutions get involved. Brazil always refused to support UN involvement in the region's democratic crises, even when norm violation was glaring and where alternatives simply did not exist, as was the case of Haiti in 1991 and 1994 (Pessôa de Lima Câmara 1998; Boniface 2002, 371). Support for OAS involvement, which was preferred in only two of the fourteen serious crises, is also somewhat ambiguous. The first of those cases was the September 1991 military coup in Haiti, where, as we saw, OAS involvement and the adoption of strong measures—the trade embargo—was the only alternative to an all-out UN intervention. In the second case, that of Haiti in 1994, when Aristide was put back in power with the support of both the OAS and the UN, Brazil opposed military intervention. Finally, in no case of severe crisis that took place in South America did Brazil support forceful intervention by either the OAS or the UN.

Brazil's choice of institutional arrangements appears not to have been driven by a preoccupation with efficiency. As a rule the stronger the potential sanction that can be brought to bear, which in most cases means the larger and more powerful the institution involved, the better. Of course, Brazil's preference for smaller institutions is not a priori inconsistent with a strong commitment to the defense of democracy. It is in fact generally easier to get a consensus for action in smaller organizations, even if they do not have the legal, political, or military weight of the bigger multilateral institutions. The problem here is that in the cases that we examined it was Brazil itself that prevented the OAS and especially the UN from getting seriously involved.

A degree of indifference toward efficiency is evident, in fact, in Brazil's fondness for the Rio Group and MERCOSUR as levers of democratic intervention. Among the eight instances of severe crises in which it supported some action to defend democracy (see table 6.4), Brazil joined or led multilateral efforts in seven cases, four of them involving the Rio Group and one MERCOSUR. The Rio Group has extremely limited institutional wherewithal. It has no permanent secretariat, no dedicated budget, and thus no administrative capacity beyond what was provided by the most influential of its nineteen members. Beyond condemnations or calls for negotiations, in other words, it can do very little. MERCOSUR is similarly constrained, with a tiny permanent staff and an executive mechanism, the MERCOSUR Group, which is devoid of independent power. Choosing the Rio Group or MERCOSUR over the OAS or the UN implies in most cases that no strong pressure will be brought to bear. This is not true in the case of Bolivia and Paraguay, whose economic and political vulnerability toward Brazil and, to a lesser extent, Argentina makes them more pliable to diplomatic pressure. But in the case of democratic crises in Peru, Venezuela, or Ecuador, to oppose the forceful involvement of the OAS and the UN simply cannot be reconciled with a strong commitment to the defense of democracy.

We can therefore summarize the answers to our four questions as follows: Brazil has not behaved consistently in support of democratic norm enforcement; its own internal democratic consolidation has not been accompanied by increased consistency in the country's response toward democratic crises; Brazil has generally not been supportive of forceful interventions in defense of democracy; and its diplomacy has clearly privileged subregional organizations over the OAS and the UN, even though the first were weak and generally devoid of effective capacity to defend democratic institutions. Our results, in sum, are not consistent with the idea that democratic norm enforcement has become a primary driver of Brazilian policy responses toward political crisis in the Americas. Other factors are clearly at play. From recent discussions of Brazilian foreign policy, we briefly consider two explanations that enable us to make sense of these results.

Alternative Explanations

To explain Brazil's foreign policy behavior, one option is to posit a conflict of norms between democracy and sovereignty. This would suggest that support for the defense of democracy was inconsistent because, in some cases, it would have implied the violation by Brazil of a higher norm, namely, national sovereignty. The other option is to assert the primacy of a traditional realist understanding of national interests within Brazil's foreign policy establishment. From this standpoint, democracy would only be championed when it is compatible with the defense and promotion of the country's economic and security interests. Let us now briefly weigh these alternative explanations on the basis of the material we have just examined.

Conflict of Norms?

One could argue that international involvement in the defense of democracy in a given country clashes with respect for its sovereignty. National independence and sovereignty can indeed be valued as expressions of the collective self-determination of a given society or nation. While many in a given society might value the freedom that is inherent to democracy, others, and sometimes the same people, might also refuse to see their society's political fate being determined by outside intervention. Such an outlook would explain the relatively common banding together of societies behind their leaders, even authoritarian ones, in the face of foreign challenges. One could thus make sense of Brazil's inconsistent defense of democracy on the basis of a strict and principled adherence to the norm of sovereignty, independent of its implications for the country's security or economic interests (Lampreia and Cruz 2005). If this were the case, then the instances where the national sovereignty of the country involved was at stake would be the ones where Brazil condoned the violation of the democratic norm, where it opposed strong foreign interventions in support of democracy, and where it was tepid in its condemnation of violations of the democratic norm.

The primacy of the principle of sovereignty in Brazil's foreign policy would be consistent with the country's systematic preference for diplomatic pressures and for its reluctance to see the UN, under Chapter VII, or the OAS, under Resolution 1080 or the Democratic Charter, become involved in democratic crises. It would neatly explain Brazil's opposition to Venezuela's suggestions of an international intervention after the coup in Suriname in 1990, its reluctance to support the U.S.-led UN intervention in Haiti in 1994, and even Cardoso's refusal to have the June 2000 OAS General Assembly openly denounce the Peruvian elections held the previous April—and shamelessly manipulated by Alberto Fujimori.

The normative primacy of national sovereignty in Brazil's foreign policy, however, does not mesh very well with the country's significant contribution to the proliferation of democratic charters, clauses, and declarations among hemispheric institutions. The latter, as Tom Farer put it, clearly points to a willingness "to redefine [the region's] previous anti-interventionist stance" (1996b, 13). It is also very difficult to reconcile national sovereignty with the openly intrusive way in which Brazil has managed several crises among its small neighbors, particularly the one that shook Paraguay in 1996 and that saw its main instigator, General Lino Oviedo, run to Brazil where he remained in legal exile until returning to Paraguay in 2004. Above all, it is simply impossible to reconcile respect for sovereignty with Brazil's condoning of the U.S.- and France-imposed resignation of Aristide in Haiti.

A Realist Foreign Policy?

A different way to make sense of Brazil's normative inconsistencies, both toward democratic and sovereignty principles, is to assume instead that its foreign policy is guided primarily by a calculus of interest. From that standpoint, the foreign policy of successive democratic governments, not unlike their authoritarian predecessors, would have endeavored to secure the country's sovereignty, to stabilize its neighborhood, to secure its immediate sources of energy, and to gain as much regional and global influence as possible. The pursuit of these objectives, it should be noted, does not always have to conflict with respect for sovereignty or the defense of democracy. When it does, however, the latter are sacrificed.

That outlook is consistent with Brazil's broadly supportive attitude toward democracy since 1990. Given the region's turn to democracy since the 1980s, Brazil's interests, most of the time, could be promoted in unison with the defense of democracy.[5] However, assuming that Brazil's foreign policy is not principled enables one to make sense of the country's many slips in its management of democratic crises, as well as its sometimes cavalier attitude toward national sovereignty. Accordingly, the government's reaction to the 2004 Haiti coup, so problematic from any other perspective, becomes transparent. What was Brazil seeking but the respect of two great powers that were critical to what has openly been described as the country's main foreign policy objective, namely to gain a permanent seat at the UN Security Council (Sader 2004; Saraiva 2005)? Brazil played its part and got good words from the United States in exchange (Estado de São Paulo 2004). Similarly, Brazil's reluctance to see the UN or the OAS get involved too directly in South American political crises, and its preference for smaller and weakly institutionalized multilateral fora in which it has significant or overwhelming weight, is perfectly consistent with the maximization of its relative power in the region. Brazil's strong activism in its immediate vicinity, and its keen interest in the region's stability, particularly in Bolivia and Paraguay, can easily be traced back to the extensive economic interests of a country for which Bolivia is the main source of gas and Paraguay a central partner in the Itaipu dam, its largest hydroelectric facility. The country's indifference to many of the crises taking place in Central America and the Caribbean also makes good sense: where little influence can be waged and where little can be gained, why expend scarce diplomatic and financial resources?

Carlos Santiso (2003) has argued that Brazil in recent years has been redefining its national interest, weaving democratic consolidation into its very fabric. What this study suggests is perhaps less a redefinition than a conjunctural ability to conciliate the national interest with the protection of a democratic norm, most of the time. In a context where the defense and enforcement of that norm would conflict more readily with Brazil's quest for security and influence, the relatively few instances of inconsistency that we have identified would likely multiply. Such inconsistency, it must be noted, is not unique to Brazil. As shown historically by the United States (Shaw in this volume) and as seen in the U.S. attitude toward the coup against Chávez in 2002, opportunistic normativism is very much the standard, even among democratic states and perhaps especially among major powers, or budding ones. This study strongly suggests, in sum, that a realist reading of Brazil's foreign policy remains the most compelling narrative one can construct on the basis of the available evidence.

NOTES

This paper is part of a broader research program comparing Brazilian and Canadian foreign policy since the 1960s. Financial support was provided by a grant from the Social Science and Humanities Research Council of Canada. For their assistance and comments, we would like to thank the editors, the participants to the 2005 Mount Allison workshop, Joanisval Brito Gonçalves, as well as some members of Brazil's foreign policy establishment, who prefer to keep their anonymity.

1. " . . . o Brasil sempre defende a sustentação da ordem democrática" (Cardoso 2006a, 636).

2. Personal interview with Ambassador Antonio Mena Gonçalves (formerly director- general, Department of the Americas, Brazilian foreign ministry), Rio de Janeiro, September 23, 2002.

3. A caveat is in order, however: our ranking of the various levels of enforcement is strictly qualitative. For instance, we do not claim that secondary enforcement (level 4) expresses twice as much consistency with the norm as indifference toward norm enforcement (level 2).

4. This tendency is often referred to as the Moravcsik thesis (2000).

5. This view is strongly suggested in Lampreia (1997) and Barros (1997).

Part II / Election Monitoring

CHAPTER SEVEN

Election Monitoring and the Western Hemisphere Idea

Arturo Santa-Cruz

The scene, or rather its reproduction, was potentially devastating. The video-tape played at Mexico's Federal Electoral Institute by officials opposed to foreign involvement in the 1994 electoral process showed international observers helping Salvadorian voting booth officials to carry out their duties during El Salvador's 1993 elections. A heated debate had been taking place in Mexico about the propriety of allowing foreigners to monitor the 1994 presidential contest. As an advocate of international monitoring admitted in an interview, the video allowed his opponents to make a forceful argument against such international "meddling" in Mexican affairs.[1] Although in the end liberalizers won and observers were present on election day, the Salvadorian images conveyed a message anybody in Mexico could comprehend: allowing foreign election monitors compromises sovereignty.[2]

Asserting national sovereignty over electoral processes was certainly not a uniquely Mexican stance. In fact, elections had long been considered to fall within Article 2(7) of the Charter of the United Nations, which establishes that the organization and its member states cannot intervene "in matters which are essentially within the domestic jurisdiction of any state." As late as

1988 UN secretary-general Javier Pérez de Cuellar noted that the United Nations "does not send observers to elections" in sovereign states (in Stoelting 1992, 372). Since then, however, much has changed. At present elections in sovereign states are regularly monitored by the UN and other intergovernmental organizations (IGOs) including the Organization for Security and Cooperation in Europe and the Organization of American States (OAS), plus a myriad of nongovernmental organizations (NGOs), both domestic and international. International election monitoring has become an established practice worldwide.

This chapter addresses two central issues. First, how did election monitoring emerge and normalize? And, second, what are the effects of international election monitoring on understandings of state sovereignty, which until recently had implied the exclusion of foreigners from electoral processes?

The study of international election monitoring belongs both in the field of international relations and in that of comparative politics. Because it is a systemwide phenomenon that impinges on state sovereignty, one of the ordering principles of international relations, international election monitoring should be studied neither as purely domestic politics nor as purely foreign policy.[3] A transnational politics approach, which is not limited by the two subfields' traditional borders, is useful. Taking a moderate constructivist stance, I argue that sovereignty has been partially transformed by the emergence of international election monitoring.[4] I locate the origins of this change in the Americas and claim that the Western Hemisphere's normative structure, what I call the Western Hemisphere Idea, was particularly conducive to this new understanding of state sovereignty.

I present an overview of the development of international election monitoring, showing how an international norm on this issue emerged. In making sense of this process, I maintain that theoretical approaches matter. As an essentially normative attribute, sovereignty is arguably best studied using socially and historically sensitive approaches, rather than with those focusing on self-interest and material factors. This is underscored by the fact that over the period that international election monitoring became an established practice in the hemisphere, material factors did not substantially change.

In reconstructing the development of international election monitoring, I distinguish three phases: one in which international election monitoring was a states-only affair, dating roughly from 1962 to 1977; a second in which international nongovernmental organizations (INGOs) entered the monitoring scene, from around 1978 to 1989; and a third in which INGOs and IGOs converged, from 1989 onward.

In the first section of this chapter, I briefly discuss transnational politics and network approaches and how these might apply to the study of international election monitoring; here I suggest a mode of norm diffusion that does away with the international relations–comparative politics divide. In the second section I show how the hemispheric understanding of sovereignty was constructed. I maintain that the Western Hemisphere Idea functioned as the constitutional structure of the hemisphere; here I introduce the emergence of international election monitoring within the Organization of American States. In the third section I consider the subsequent appearance of international election monitoring outside the regional body. The convergence of IGOs and INGOs, and the concurrent consolidation of an international election monitoring network are then reviewed in the fourth section. Finally, I present the conclusions and theoretical implications of this piece.

Transnational Politics and Transnational Advocacy Networks

IGO and INGO practices on issues that used to be considered purely domestic form an important component of what is usually referred to as transnational politics, a field of study that challenges the traditional division of labor between international relations and comparative politics. The study of international norms has been particularly relevant in building a bridge between the two disciplines and in understanding the agency (or influence) of IGOs and INGOs. As Hans Peter Schmitz (2004, 408) has noted, "International norms of democratic governance and human rights provide an increasingly dense ideational structure shaping the ideas and interests of transnational and domestic activists. On the agency side, transnational NGOs function as transmission mechanisms for diffusing international norms into a domestic context."

The emergence of what comparativists would call transnational opportunity structures, arenas in which state and nonstate actors engage each other over issues whose compartmentalization in either the international or the domestic sphere is no longer viable, has opened up space for innovative work that draws on both international relations and comparative politics literatures (Finnemore and Sikkink 2001, 411). In this regard, the sovereignty problematic, as a principle that links the "domestic" with the "international," is a good starting point. On the one hand, as James Caporaso (1997, 581) notes, in the Westphalian state system sovereignty has been one requirement to play the game. Within international relations, John Agnew (1994, 92) similarly observes, "state territorial sovereignty is the determining assumption," what he calls the "territorial trap."[5] This foundational—and problematic—international relations notion is pervasive in a different manner in comparative politics. As Patrick Jackson and Daniel Nexon (2002, 91) note, "The maps presupposed by the comparative method derive their plausibility either directly or indirectly from the metageography of the sovereign territorial states system." Both international relations and comparative politics have thus been caught by the same snare.

Even if omnipresent, sovereignty is not immutable. Indeed, the changing notion of this pervasive norm can be fruitfully traced through the lens of what Margaret Keck and Kathryn Sikkink call transnational advocacy networks (TANs). For Keck and Sikkink (1998, 2), TANs include "those relevant actors working internationally on an issue, who are bound together by shared values, a common discourse, and dense exchanges of information and services." Interestingly, TANs are not formed exclusively by nonstate actors, such as NGOs and religious groups; they might also include state agencies and even IGOs. This means that TANs are not necessarily in an external position vis-à-vis the state (or the state system). As Keck and Sikkink (1998, 216) put it, "because part of states and international organizations also participate in these networks, the process of negotiation within the emergent cosmopolitan community is not 'outside' the state."

Activists within TANs focus on communication and information exchange; thus TANs can be thought of as communicative structures (Keck and Sikkink 1998, 3). As such, they create discourses that frame issues in novel ways, bringing them to the international agenda. A TAN is thus both a structure and an agent. As the former, it patterns the interaction of its members and infuses them with identity; as the latter, it puts forward specific policy proposals in the international arena. The key to its dual character lies in its decentralized and horizontal organizational arrangement and in the kind of strategies it employs. The core of the network is a small group of political entrepreneurs and, more fundamentally, the information its members exchange. The social nature of the information gathered (and constructed) becomes the raw material for a new discourse.

The practice of TANs helps redefine not only the role of nonstate actors in the international arena but also the structure of the interstate system. As authors from the English School noted decades ago, and constructivists more recently, the interstate system is not solely characterized by a Hobbesian state of nature in which only material capabilities, as such, matter (Bull 1977; Wendt 1999). At bottom, the modern state system is constituted by institutions and norms that infuse both anarchy and material factors with meaning. The moderate constructivist approach used here maintains that a normative structure underlies the basic components of the state system. Furthermore, it is through the practice of both state and nonstate actors that the state system is reproduced and transformed. That is why it is important to trace the "life history" of international norms and not just to postulate their existence.

How is it that norms that we take for granted in the international arena came to be what they are? What is the origin of norms? It is usually assumed that norms originate in the international system and then trickle down, permeating states (Cortell and Davis 1996, 2000; Legro 2000). But how do norms make it into the international realm in the first place? Risse and Sikkink (1999) argue that the process by which states internalize international norms can be thought of as a process of socialization. However, the spiral model they advance reproduces the previous bias of taking an outside-in approach, in which the focus is the impact of the external environment on specific states. Finnemore and Sikkink (1998), for their part, develop a more inside-out approach: the norm life-cycle model. In it, they describe how norms can reach a "tipping point." However, this approach too is premised on the inside-outside dichotomy.

There is another way in which norms might reach a tipping point. This case is a constitutive one, in which neither sheer numbers nor the consent of "critical" states is essential. In this constitutive model, norms cascade simply by expressing a foundational element of the international *cum* domestic system. Because the element in question in this chapter, state sovereignty, is so deeply embedded into our understanding of what a polity ought to be (from both a domestic and an international point of view), it is very difficult for state leaders to ignore it. State leaders, willingly or not, talk the talk of sovereignty. I suggest that it might be possible for a few, not necessarily "critical" states to embrace and thus promote an emergent norm—making it reach a tipping point. In a sense, it can be said that the emergent norm was always there in a latent state, both on the outside (the international system) and the inside (the domestic structure). The *nature* of the emergent norm, more than the number or the type of states that adopt it, is critical in this model. The constitutive model does not negate the spiral or life-cycle models; it subsumes them. Once a norm is realized in the constitutive path, it spreads out quickly—with or without any of the other paths being present.

The Western Hemisphere Idea and the Emergence of International Election Monitoring

International election monitoring in the Americas started in the early 1960s —but it did not appear out of thin air. It was the result of a thick normative structure underpinning state interaction and transnational practice in the New World, a social tapestry that had been over a hundred years in the making. Significantly, though, it arose in a delimited part of the Americas: Latin America, albeit with North America (and specifically the United States) playing a key role. The interaction between these two regions of the hemisphere helps to explain its emergence. North America and Latin America are two distinguishable regions within the hemisphere, which make the Americas as a whole a unique international subsystem and constitute the *historical* structure that made the emergence of international election monitoring possible.

The idea of the *Americas* as a region is closely related to what has come to be known as the Western Hemisphere Idea. The Western Hemisphere Idea, as defined by Arthur P. Whitaker (1954, 1) refers to "the proposition that the peoples of this Hemisphere stand in a special relationship to one another which sets them apart from the rest of the world." As early as 1813, Thomas Jefferson (cited in Callcott 1968, 14) wrote that the governments to be formed in the nascent states "will be American governments, no longer to be involved in the never-ceasing broils of Europe. The European nations constitute a separate division of the globe; their localities make them a part of a distinct system . . . America has a hemisphere to itself. It must have a separate system of interest which must not be subordinated to those of Europe." According to Whitaker (1954, 29), Jefferson's statement was "the first flowering" of the Western Hemisphere Idea.

Interestingly, the perception of the Americas as being apart from the rest of the world does not necessarily imply the existence of a community of interests *among* the states of the Americas. In effect, implicit in this "special relationship" is the interplay not only of the New World states, but also of its two main subregions—a relationship that most of the time has been contentious. This is important. Some definitions of hemispherism equate it with cooperation. For instance, Javier Corrales and Richard Feinberg (1999, 2) define hemispherism as "the active attempt by nations in the hemisphere to redirect their foreign policies in favor of a closer and coordinated cooperation with one another." Students of hemispherism often focus on formal institutions of cooperation, such as the OAS or the Inter-American Development Bank. But as Whitaker (1954, 5) himself made clear in his seminal text, "the distinction between the idea and its various political expressions . . . should be constantly kept in mind." The Western Hemisphere Idea refers to patterned interaction per se, not to cooperation. In fact, tension-ridden subregional interaction was part and parcel of the Western Hemisphere Idea.

We can therefore clarify the definition of the Western Hemisphere Idea as the normative structure of the Americas as a separate system of interests, with the caveat that it is made of two sharply contrasting regions. By producing and reproducing the fundamental values of representative government, nonintervention, and social order among the member states of the hemisphere, the Western Hemisphere Idea enabled a distinctive idea of state sovereignty to develop. This distinctive understanding of sovereignty would eventually lead to the emergence of international election monitoring in the Americas before any other region of the world (Reus-Smit 1997).

By the third decade of the nineteenth century interaction among the nascent Latin American states and with the United States was producing a regional subsystem, in the sense that a regional identity was experienced not only by its members but also by external actors (Atkins 1977, 10). In this context, Europe was the "relevant other" for the American states. Hence the Monroe Doctrine, which claimed that the system still emerging in the Americas was essentially different from that of Europe, was mostly welcomed by the Latin American states despite its unilateral nature (Davis 1977, 67). Regional identity at this point in time did not go much further than demarcating a territory from which the Europeans were to be excluded. During most of the nineteenth century the United States and Latin America remained distant neighbors.

In the 1880s, after most Latin American states had been consolidated and the United States had endured the Civil War, Pan Americanism gained momentum (Burr 1973, xxi). As Latin American statesmen became increasingly concerned with United States intervention in their internal affairs and a strong anti-Yankee feeling started to spread in intellectual circles in the continent, the United States began a rapprochement with its southern neighbors. It was in this context that the 1889 Washington Conference of American States, widely considered to be the inauguration of the modern inter-American system, took place (Peck 1977, 166). Thereafter, hemispheric conferences at which important regional matters such as nonintervention and the treatment of foreigners were discussed became a feature of state practice in the Americas. During the first half of the twentieth century, there were fifteen conferences or meetings of the inter-American system (Wilson 1989, 477).

The mere existence of these hemispheric fora did not imply a convergence of interests among the participating states. On the contrary, there were deep disagreements among the statesmen of the hemisphere. Perhaps the most salient dispute related to the tutelary aims of the rising hegemon. By the turn of the nineteenth century, not only had the United States become a continental power at the expense of its southern neighbor, but it was also involved in imperial pursuits in other states in the region. Thus, according to the 1905 Roosevelt Corollary to the Monroe Doctrine, "the United States would become the policeman of the western hemisphere. It would interfere in the affairs of any nations unable to handle their own affairs—intervene for the purpose of eliminating conditions which might encourage European intervention" (Burr 1973, xxii). The subordinated states of the hemisphere resented this position, but there was not much they could do. The inter-American subsystem was unquestionably unipolar: no other state in the hemisphere was able to challenge the United States.

Nonintervention became a matter of intrahemispheric division. At the third Pan-American Congress in Rio de Janeiro in 1906, the Latin American states and the United States clashed over this issue, with the United States maintaining its right to intervene (Corrales and Feinberg 1999, 6). Hence, for instance, under the Platt Amendment the United States "legally" intervened in Cuba from 1906 to 1909. But by the 1920s, as Yankee phobia was gaining a second wind in Latin America, the United States began to play a less ostensibly dominant role in the inter-American system (Corrales and Feinberg 1999, 21). The Hoover administration (1929–33) took the first steps toward what under his successor's term would come to be known as the "Good Neighbor" policy. But this did not mean yet a fundamental change in U.S. relations with its hemispheric neighbors. At the 1928 Pan-American Conference in Havana, the United States still opposed the doctrine of nonintervention, so dear to the Latin Americans (Burr 1973, xxiv–xxv).

A few years later, with the arrival of Franklin D. Roosevelt to power, the United States made a veritable about-face in its policy toward Latin America. At the 1936 Inter-American Conference for the Maintenance of Peace, held in

Buenos Aires, the United States accepted the doctrine of nonintervention without reservations. Thus, the Declaration of Principles of Inter-American Solidarity and Cooperation that came out of the Buenos Aires Conference stated that "Intervention by one State in the internal or external affairs of another State is condemned." Significantly, the declaration also noted that the American states "have a common likeness in their democratic form of government and their common ideals of peace and justice, manifested in the several Treaties and Conventions which they have signed for the purpose of constituting a purely American system."[6] Thus, the hemispheric discourse on solidarity based on democratic values, and not only on its severance from the Old World, acquired new salience (Burr 1973, xxvi; Corrales and Feinberg 1999, 7).

The importance of democratic forms of government, that is, of representative government had been the leitmotif of the inter-American system even before the principle of nonintervention became prevalent. For example, the Treaty of Perpetual Union, League, and Confederation adopted at the 1826 Panama Congress called for the suspension or even expulsion of undemocratic governments from the organization (Ball 1969, 491). Similarly, signatories to the 1907 Central American Treaty of Peace committed their countries not to recognize "any other Government which may come into power in any of the five Republics as a consequence of a *coup d'etat,* or of a revolution against the recognized Government, so long as the freely elected representatives of the people thereof have not constitutionally reorganized the country" (Reisman 1990, 868). Although Theodore Roosevelt had warned against basing United States policy "not on the firm ground of national interest but on the treacherous sands of international democratic propagandism" (cited in Hartz 1983, 290), in 1914 President Woodrow Wilson proposed a Pan-American Pact by which, among other things, the signatories would mutually guarantee their republican forms of government (Peck 1977, 173).[7]

It is thus not surprising to find several references to representative democracy as the only legitimate form of government in the 1948 OAS Charter.[8] Its preamble, for instance, states that the "true significance of American solidarity and good neighborliness can only mean the consolidation on this continent, within the framework of democratic institutions, of a system of individual liberty and social justice based on respect for the essential rights of man." More explicitly, Article 5 maintains that "The solidarity of the American States and the high aims which are sought through it require the political organization of those States on the basis of the effective exercise of representative democracy."

At the same time, the OAS Charter equates international order with respect for the independence and sovereignty of states, establishing nonintervention as the hemisphere's other fundamental value. Article 15 of the charter states that "No State or group of States has the right to intervene, directly or indirectly, for any reason whatever, in the internal or external affairs of any other State. The foregoing principle prohibits not only armed force but also any other form of interference or attempted threat against the personality of the State or against its political, economic and cultural elements." Thus, there has long been an inherent tension in the inter-American system: the tension between representative government as a common discourse that unites the states of the Americas as a compact of republican states separated from Europe, and nonintervention as a principle intended to keep the United States out of Latin America.

By the mid-twentieth century, representative government in particular and human rights more broadly had become an integral part of Latin American diplomatic discourse, not only in the hemisphere but in world politics. Latin American diplomats played an active role in the making of the Universal Declaration of Human Rights (Sikkink 1997, 720–21). In what now seems a prophetic statement—since his own country would become an international pariah as a result of Pinochet's 1973 coup—the Chilean representative told the General Assembly that "no one could infringe upon the rights proclaimed in it [the Universal Declaration] without becoming an outcast of the community of states" (Reus-Smit 2001, 532). Latin American diplomats were also instrumental in drafting and passing the American Declaration on the Rights and Duties of Man more than six months before the United Nations passed the Universal Declaration of Human Rights.

Nonetheless, in spite of the importance Latin American states came to attach to representative government and human rights, nonintervention remained their paramount principle. As Wilson and Dent (1995, 27) put it, "the principle of nonintervention is the most important law duty in the [OAS] Charter, and it transcends all the other duties, including that of promoting representative democracy and the protection of human rights." The advent of the Cold War led Latin American states to an increasingly maximalist interpretation of the nonintervention principle.

The fact that the nonintervention principle came to have such legal prominence in the inter-American system was, of course, not reflected in actual practice. Blatant intervention by the United States in Guatemala in the 1950s,

Cuba and the Dominican Republic in the 1960s, Chile in the 1970s, and Grenada and Panama in the 1980s are just a few examples of U.S. breeches of this principle. That is why some scholars see the inter-American principle of nonintervention as a myth and sovereignty as "organized hypocrisy" (Krasner 1999). Similarly, it is argued that the Latin American discourse on human rights and representative government has been little more than empty rhetoric given the dismal historical record of most Latin American states on these issues (Muñoz 1990, 28).

While both remarks are correct insofar as they point to a real gap between lofty statements and practice, they incorrectly dismiss such normative components as trivial. Once the discourse on nonintervention and human rights *cum* representative government was (for whatever reasons) adopted, it was bound to have real effects—intended or otherwise. It produced a particular understanding of sovereignty in the Western Hemisphere and, more specifically, in Latin America. It was a conception of sovereignty informed by the tension enshrined in the Western Hemisphere Idea and grounded on higher-order principles such as human rights and representative government. This constitutional structure shaped state behavior, and it also created states' interests. Its effects were not only regulative but also generative.

In this underlying hemispheric understanding, sovereignty was conceived of as a discursive bundle, containing "clauses" on both nonintervention and representative government. Thus, in the same way that the nonintervention principle constrained and came to inform U.S. behavior and interests in the hemisphere, the emphasis on human rights and representative government affected the identity and foreign relations of Latin American states. That is why, on the one hand, U.S. intervention in the continent has not been more frequent, and, on the other, even the maximalist interpretation of the nonintervention principle made by Latin American governments allowed for external intervention (via foreign observers) in what would otherwise be considered a domestic affair: national elections.

It was this broad understanding of sovereignty that allowed the Western Hemisphere to become the forerunner in international election monitoring. The OAS, in turn, was the concrete institutional arrangement that allowed the states of the Americas to become the pioneer in the field of international election monitoring beginning in 1962. The OAS sent observers to member states on an ad hoc basis through the 1960s, 1970s, and 1980s. With missions to Bolivia, Costa Rica, Dominican Republic, Grenada, Guatemala, and Ecuador, among others, by 1984 OAS missions had observed twenty-two elections in member states.

In a parallel manner, in the United States in the early 1980s the Reagan administration began to make "democracy promotion" a central part of its foreign policy within the hemisphere.[9] In 1982 Reagan gave a speech before the British Parliament, in which he stated his objective "to foster the infrastructure of democracy." One year later, the U.S. National Endowment for Democracy (NED) was created by Congress to "promote United States nongovernmental participation . . . in democratic training programs and democratic institution building abroad" and "to strengthen democratic electoral processes abroad through timely measures in cooperation with indigenous democratic forces" (Jason 1992, 1827).

Initially, the Reagan administration put the democratic seal on regimes that hardly qualified as democratic, such as the Salvadorian one. Nevertheless, having entered the democracy discourse, the Reagan administration had to make its rhetoric more consistent with its deeds. Thus, in 1986 the administration issued a "major policy statement" indicating that it "opposed tyranny in whatever form, whether of the left or of the right" (Pastor 1987, 377). As Carothers (1991a, 244) put it, "having made democracy the stated goal of its policy . . . the Reagan administration soon found that its policy was evaluated in those terms. . . . This opened the way for an evolution toward policies with real pro-democratic substance." The normalization of international election monitoring thus became closely linked to U.S. "democracy promotion" programs.

With the double impetus of the Latin American transitions to democracy of the late 1970s and early 1980s, and the born-again taste for democracy promotion on the part of the regional hegemon, the OAS updated its basic documents (Smith 1994). At a 1985 meeting in Cartagena de Indias, Colombia, the OAS amended its charter, endowing the organization with a new mission, the promotion of democracy. The 1985 Protocol of Amendment, as a later statement from the regional body notes, "provide[d] the general principle for the new kind of election monitoring by the Organization" (OAS 2000b).

Nongovernmental Organizations Start Monitoring Elections

Just as state-sponsored international election monitoring in the Americas was beginning to gather steam, domestic and international nongovernmental organizations entered the scene. The arrival of NGOs to this arena in the late 1970s and early 1980s was an intrinsic component of the development of the democratic discourse in the hemisphere. Those states of the hemisphere with the strongest civil societies were, not surprisingly, the ones with more active NGOs. Here again, the fault line between the United States and the rest of the hemisphere was pronounced. The United States has historically had the most articulated and independent civil society in the Americas, but, in addition, the hegemonic position of the United States put U.S. INGOs in a privileged position vis-à-vis their southern counterparts. As INGOs from the United States that had traditionally worked on conventional human rights issues began to broaden their scope of activities, the convergence with domestic groups in Latin America working on political rights issues came readily. The Washington Office on Latin America (WOLA) started monitoring elections in 1978, sending observers to Bolivia. WOLA observed elections in Guyana in 1980, in Honduras in 1981, and in Argentina in 1983. The International Human Rights Law Group (IHRLG) established its Election Observer Project in 1983, working with domestic activists in target states. In 1984 the group published *Guidelines for International Election Observing,* authored by then project director Larry Garber, a text that became the standard reference for election observing both for NGOs and IGOs (Jason 1992, 1802). In 1984 WOLA and the IHRLG jointly observed the elections in Nicaragua and Uruguay (IHRLG and WOLA 1985a). The IHRLG also observed the 1984 elections in Grenada and 1985 elections in El Salvador and Guatemala. By 1990 it had organized twenty-five election monitoring missions, mostly in Latin America, but also in Asia and Africa.

The National Endowment for Democracy became active shortly after its founding in 1983. Despite its links to the U.S. government, the NED was established as a private nonprofit, bipartisan organization. It is primarily a grant-making institution, and the majority of the democracy promotion programs that it funds are carried out by the National Democratic Institute for International Affairs (NDI) and the International Republican Institute (IRI), both also established in 1983 and affiliated with the Democratic and Republican parties, respectively. These two institutes, but NDI more aggressively, have been very active in monitoring elections worldwide.

Another important NGO player, also with manifest links to the U.S. government, is the Carter Center, established in 1982. Headed by former U.S. president Jimmy Carter, in 1986 it hosted a conference on democracy in the Americas, attended by renowned politicians from throughout the region. As a result of the conference, twelve former and current heads of government established the Council of Freely Elected Heads of Government, based at the Carter Center (Carter Center 1996). The center's staff, and the former president himself, became the core of the council. Among the council's founding goals was "to promote multilateral democratic transitions and to reinforce the consolidation of new and re-emerging democracies in the region" (Carter Center 1996, 7). Its first monitoring mission was to Haiti in 1987, at the request of the Haitian transitional government.

INGOs have been instrumental players in the institutionalization of electoral observation by virtue of their role during specific elections. The Carter Center, for example, played a crucial role in the 1990 Nicaraguan election. President Carter acted as a mediator between the Sandinista government and the opposition in order to solve problems that arose during the electoral process, and he also pushed for the organization of quick counts as a check on official results (Pastor 1990, 18–19). Prominent INGO members, such as the IHRLG's Larry Garber, joined the OAS team in Nicaragua and drafted the guide used by OAS observers for that occasion (Jason 1992, 1817). After using the interstate tapestry to justify their own involvement in election monitoring, INGOs by their practices made it easier for IGOs other than the OAS to monitor elections.[10] Thus, when the proposal to create a specialized electoral unit came before the UN General Assembly in 1990, it was welcomed by INGOs (Jason 1992, 1841).[11]

The constitutional structure created by state practice set the stage for what we can describe as a loosely constituted, INGO-based transnational advocacy network on election monitoring. Because INGOs have very different interests and identities from states or IGOs, the emergence of an INGO-based international election-monitoring TAN in the hemisphere in the 1980s gave rise to a very interesting dynamic. This dynamic involved elections where monitors from IGOs were not present (either because they declined to send a mission, or because they were not invited by the national government), but INGOs were. This happened in Haiti in 1987, in Chile in 1988, and in Panama in 1989 (Jason 1992, 1843). The work of INGOs during this time can thus be considered a second phase in the history of international election monitoring in the continent. In this second phase the monitoring of elections became much more substantial, as the teams sent by INGOs tended to do a more exhaustive job than the token delegations traditionally sent by the OAS. The INGOs, however, were building on the state practice that preceded them within the OAS and, more generally, on the Western Hemisphere Idea as constitutional structure.

The Convergence of IGOs and INGOs

The third phase of international election monitoring started in 1989, when monitoring activities by INGOs, the OAS, and the UN, converged in the lead up to the 1990 Nicaraguan elections. Beginning in August 1989, the UN and the OAS established the largest and most comprehensive electoral observation missions ever in a sovereign country.[12] This was a watershed in the history of international election monitoring. As Pastor has noted, by inviting international monitoring missions, the Nicaraguan government was "crossing [the] Rubicon of sovereignty. . . . Up until that moment, most governments . . . viewed elections as internal matters. . . . With the official invitations [to the OAS, the UN, and the Carter Center], the Nicaraguans transcended conventional definitions of sovereignty" (Pastor 2002, 231).

Before the electoral process in Nicaragua was over, the OAS began to fashion a series of new diplomatic instruments or tools that would support the socialization of the nascent international election monitoring norm. In November 1989 the OAS General Assembly recommended sending observation missions to member states that requested it (AG/RES. 993 [XIX-0/89]). Seven months later, during its Eighth Plenary Session, the OAS General Assembly passed a resolution calling for the creation of the Unit for the Promotion of Democracy in order to "respond promptly and effectively to member states which, in the full exercise of their sovereignty, request advice or assistance to preserve or strengthen their political institutions and democratic procedures." Significantly, the resolution notes "with appreciation" the role the secretary-general and member states had recently played in Nicaragua (AG/RES. 1063 [XX-0/90]). These actions led to the subsequent passage of the Santiago Commitment to Democracy and the Renewal of the Inter-American System (June 4, 1991) and Resolution 1080 (see Boniface and Hawkins and Shaw in this volume).

With the 1991 Santiago Commitment and Resolution 1080, as Domingo Acevedo (1993, 141) has noted, "for the first time, an international organization . . . explicitly ruled that governments should be held internationally accountable to the regional community for the means by which they have taken and secure power." These mechanisms were activated when on April 5, 1992, Peruvian president Alberto Fujimori dissolved Congress, intervened in the judiciary, and suspended some basic civil rights. International pressure forced Fujimori to attend an OAS meeting in Barbados the next month and to accept specific steps to restore democracy in his country (Degregori 2001, 47). These steps included, importantly, electoral supervision. From 1992 on, the OAS became a seemingly permanent fixture in the Peruvian electoral processes (see Santa-Cruz 2005).

Eight years after his self-coup, Fujimori sought reelection in an unfair race. When the head of the OAS mission announced the withdrawal of its observers after the first round of the election, criticizing the software program that Peru's National Office for Electoral Processes was going to use for the vote count in the runoff and calling for the election to be postponed, President Fujimori (ironically) praised the OAS for "respecting the principle of nonintervention."[13]

The transition from the first phase of election monitoring by the OAS, to the second phase of INGO involvement, to the third phase of normalization or institutionalization of election monitoring by IGOs and INGOs alike was neither linear nor smooth; there were no preestablished "stages" nor was there a unidirectional sense of progress leading to a "definitive" condition. The fact that some countries within the hemisphere began to call for international observers did not mean that there was a consensus around this issue. As noted at the beginning of this chapter, for example, Mexico opposed international observers until 1994. The Peruvian case also illustrates that state's effort to reassert the primacy of national sovereignty.

With the emergence of international election monitoring came two important innovations to the constitutional structure represented by the Western Hemisphere Idea. The first came with the involvement of NGOs and, more fundamentally, of INGOs in international election monitoring. For the states of the Americas this development meant two things: the unexpected arrival of a new player in hemispheric relations (nongovernmental organizations), and a change in the nature of international election monitoring itself. Because of the involvement of nonstate actors, it ceased being a symbolic practice (see Lean in this volume). The second innovation to the constitutional structure was state internalization of this renewed, reinvigorated conception of international election monitoring. International election monitoring was not only becoming "the only game in the hemisphere," but states had stopped being the only legitimate players. The normalization of international election monitoring in the 1990s brought with it a veritable change in state identity and interests—and a concomitant partial redefinition of sovereignty.

The fact that international election monitoring appeared first in the Americas was no accident. The region's constitutional structure was conducive to it. In its absence, international election monitoring would likely not have emerged in the Western Hemisphere earlier than anywhere else. This is not to suggest that without the Western Hemisphere Idea, international election monitoring would have never taken place in the Americas. After all, activists, states, and IGOs in other latitudes also began monitoring elections in the late 1980s. In the same way that international election monitoring became an export commodity of the Americas, it could have been imported by the region had it emerged somewhere else. But it did not, and that is the point: the particular constitutional structure that accounts for the emergence of international election monitoring is the Western Hemisphere Idea and not any other. In the Western Hemisphere there was no "ontological gap" between the practice of international election monitoring and the wider normative structure. Once international election monitoring emerged and became normalized in the Americas, it began its worldwide diffusion as an international norm. That is why in 1995 the UN secretary-general Boutros Boutros-Ghali (1995, 3) could assert that "the promotion of democracy is both an end in itself and part of the responsibility of the United Nations to maintain peace and security." It is why the UN Electoral Assistance Division has been actively involved in providing electoral assistance ever since, attending to more than 100 requests from member states around the world.[14] It is why, by the end of the twentieth century, the UN had recognized the right to democratic governance as a human right. The cases mentioned in this chapter are among the building blocks that helped establish such an entitlement in these terms.

In making sense of this process, as noted in the introduction, theoretical approaches matter. We must pay attention to both the historical and normative structure of the international system in order to trace the development of international election monitoring. Among other things, this practice is about state sovereignty—an essentially normative attribute. That is why I argue that a constructivist rendering of its emergence and normalization fares reasonably well. Focusing on self-interest and material factors, as neoliberal and neorealist approaches would, would probably not take us very far in understanding the emergence of international election monitoring. Considering the evolving international normative structure from a constructivist stance does. Similarly, limiting the analysis to the confines of one subfield, be it international relations or comparative politics, will not do. As I hope to have shown, treating international election monitoring as a structural variable that does not pertain to either the international or the domestic realm, but rather to the emerging transnational one, might help us escape the territorial trap. The fact that what happened in El Salvador (in terms of foreign monitoring of electoral processes) later happened, with the necessary changes, in Mexico illustrates the usefulness of a theoretical approach that blurs the artificial distinction between comparative politics and international relations.

NOTES

1. Author's interview with Manuel Carrillo, foreign affairs coordinator at the Mexican Federal Electoral Institute, Mexico City, October 30, 2001.

2. Sovereignty is understood here as the monopoly over claims to legitimate authority within a given territory.

3. International relations scholars who have written on international election monitoring (although focusing on the broader concept of "democracy promotion") tend to treat it as a foreign policy issue. See Carothers (1999); Cox, Ikenberry, and Inoguchi (2000b).

4. Moderate or "conventional" constructivism is an approach to the study of international relations that asks how much structures constrain and enable the actions of actors (Hopf 1998, 172). It is not a critical approach, but rather attempts to do "normal science" while being sensitive to normative and historical matters (Adler 1997).

5. Wimmer and Schiller's (2002) concept of "methodological nationalism" (i.e., "the assumption that the nation/state/society is a natural social and political form of the modern world") conveys a similar idea.

6. The full text, in English, of the Declaration of Principles of Inter-American Solidarity and Cooperation, adopted by the Inter-American Conference for the Maintenance of Peace at Buenos Aires, Argentina on December 21, 1936, can be accessed online at www.yale.edu/lawweb/avalon/intdip/interam/intam07.htm.

7. Fittingly, when Wilson took office, he refused to recognize the government of Victoriano Huerta in Mexico, who had overthrown the democratically elected government of Francisco Madero in 1913. In order to grant its recognition, his administration demanded that a popularly elected government be installed, and that Huerta not be a candidate in the electoral process (Weber 1992, 320).

8. The full text of the 1948 Charter of the Organization of American States, in English, can be found online at http://www.oas.org/juridico/English/charter.html.

9. The kind of democracy to be promoted, of course, was modeled after the system existing in the United States. For critical views, see Carothers (1995, 23) and S. Smith (2000, 73–74).

10. As Larry Garber explained in a personal communication, the monitoring activities of INGOs in the early 1980s were "essential" for international election monitoring's later institutionalization in other fora (e-mail communication, November 15, 2001).

11. The genesis of the proposal is the following: at the Forty-fifth UN General Assembly session in 1990, U.S. president George Bush suggested the creation of a UN electoral commission that would attend to member states' requests for electoral observation and other kinds of electoral assistance. In 1991 the secretary-general designated the under-secretary-general for political affairs as the focal point for electoral assistance activities. The following year, the UN General Assembly approved the establishment of the Electoral Assistance Unit, which in 1994 was upgraded to Division.

12. In all, some 2,578 accredited foreign observers from 279 organizations were present in Nicaragua on election day (Pastor 1990, 18).

13. *Público,* June 8, 2000, 32.

14. www.un.org/Depts/dpa/ead/website5.htm (accessed October 20, 1999, and September 27, 2001).

CHAPTER EIGHT

External Validation and Democratic Accountability

Sharon F. Lean

After four postponements, elections were held in Haiti in February 2006 to replace an interim government that had taken power following former president Jean-Bertrand Aristide's ouster by a rebellion in 2004. Haiti had been immersed in violence ever since, so the elections were held in tense conditions under the supervision of a United Nations peace-keeping force. International nongovernmental organizations provided assistance and support to political parties, the national election authorities, and domestic election observers. Election day proceeded peacefully, to the surprise of many.

René Préval, a candidate with ties to Aristide who had held the presidency once before, was by far the front-runner in a field of more than thirty candidates, but as the votes were tallied, he did not appear to have achieved an absolute majority required to avoid a second-round election.

Préval supporters took to the streets, fearful that their votes were not being properly counted, and the situation threatened to devolve into chaos and renewed violence. The Haitian election council, with encouragement from international observers, interpreted an ambiguity in election law on the matter of how to count blank ballots and decided to distribute the blank votes proportionally among candidates. This gave Préval just over 50 percent of the vote, high enough to avoid the runoff and avert a crisis.

The Haitian case illustrates three trends in democracy assistance in the Americas. First, it embodies the growing trend toward external validation of elections (including an active role for international observers) as a regular part of Latin American politics. Second, it highlights the contemporary idea of democracy as a transnational good, in which states, civic actors, multilateral organizations, and international nongovernmental organizations all have a stake. Third, it exemplifies ongoing questions about both the legitimacy and the efficacy of international organizations in monitoring and mediating election processes: supporters of Préval were concerned during the vote count that international and domestic actors might conspire to prevent a Préval victory particularly if the vote went to a second round; opponents argued that in supporting the eventual outcome, international actors had indeed egregiously meddled. Although the outcome did stabilize the political situation in Haiti, it is an open question whether international actors improved the democratic credentials of Haiti's 2006 election process.[1]

International election monitoring was first practiced in the Americas in 1962, when three delegates of the Organization of American States watched the Costa Rican elections on February 4 of that year. Since that time, election monitoring has become a near-universal component of election processes in the region. Between 1982 and 2002, a total of 146 national elections (including presidential, legislative, and parliamentary elections, as well as constituent assembly elections and national referenda) were held in the twenty-four Latin American and Caribbean countries considered in this chapter; nearly two-thirds of those elections (64%) were observed by one or more international or domestic monitoring missions (Lean 2004, 70). With the exception of Cuba, all countries in the region have invited international observers to be present for elections. In most of these cases, elections were monitored by teams of observers from more than one organization. Furthermore, in recent years international monitors have been present at more than 90 percent of all elections held in the Americas, making election assistance truly a growth industry (Lean 2004, 71).

This chapter investigates the effect of international efforts to promote and support democracy by monitoring elections throughout Latin America and the Caribbean. What is the impact of international election monitoring? Can the international community provide external validation of election processes in a way that is meaningful for the advance of democracy? The evidence presented here shows that initial patterns of international involvement in elections did not meet reasonable criteria for providing credible external validation. However, as a wider range of actors have become involved in monitoring elections, and as monitoring practices have become institutionalized, the ideals of external validation are more frequently met.

The first section of the chapter discusses the idea of external validation and how election monitoring should ideally generate accountability and thus contribute to democracy. A second section of the chapter reviews the history of elections and international involvement in elections in the Americas. The third section presents regionwide data on the election monitoring activities of states, multilateral organizations, and nonstate actors in twenty-four countries and identifies patterns in the practice and its impact over time. A final section summarizes overall trends in election monitoring and draws conclusions about the conditions in which election monitoring provides external validation in a way that helps rather than hinders Latin American democratization processes.

External Validation and Democratic Accountability

In theory, election monitoring is a mechanism that should generate accountability in a domestic political institution seen as necessary for democracy, the institution of elections. International observers monitor the institutional performance of a country's electoral system by evaluating existing electoral law and assessing compliance of domestic political actors with the same using a variety of techniques. Through their presence election monitors seek, ideally, to encourage voter participation by increasing citizen confidence that votes will be cast in secret and counted fairly. They hope to provide a disincentive to violence by promoting elections as a means of resolving power struggles as an alternative to the use of force.[2] However, election monitoring has not been, and is not at present, always successful in achieving these aims.

According to Grant and Keohane (2005, 29), "the idea of accountability implies that some actors have the right to hold other actors to a set of standards . . . it presupposes a relationship . . . where there is a general recognition of the legitimacy of 1) the operative standards for accountability and 2) the authority of the parties to the relationship (one to exercise particular powers and the other to hold them to account)." Thus, for external validation of elections by international monitors to successfully generate accountability, operative standards for accountability must be generally recognized among the competing political parties and candidates, state institutions, citizens, and the international monitors themselves. The authority of the parties to the relationship must also be recognized. On one hand, the authority of election administration boards to run elections and of parties and candidates to campaign must be recognized by the international community. In other words, the international community must respect domestic political forces and political authorities. On the other hand, the domestic community must recognize international monitors as actors with a legitimate auditor role in the electoral process.

As we will see, the degree to which international election monitoring in Latin America has met these standards has changed significantly over time. By examining the evolution of international election monitoring in Latin America, we can better understand current transnational dynamics of democratization in the region. We can also understand the reach and limitations of election monitoring as a means for promoting democracy.

Background

Elections are not new to Latin America. When most countries gained independence in the first decades of the nineteenth century, elections were common and suffrage relatively widespread. Corruption and manipulation of the electorate by *caudillos,* landlords, clergy, and powerful politicians were equally widespread, leading some scholars to characterize Latin America as a region of "elections before democracy" (Posada-Carbó 1996). With some interruptions, corrupt electoral politics continued well into the twentieth century.

By the 1960s and 1970s the region could be more accurately described as one of elections without democracy. Bureaucratic authoritarian regimes, military regimes, and dictators governed most of Latin America. Many authoritarian and dictatorial regimes continued to hold elections, but these were rife with fraud and provided no real choice. Guyana, for example, held farcical elections in both 1968 and 1973 in which more than 100 percent of the eligible voting-aged population supposedly cast votes (International IDEA 2005). Paraguay held regular elections throughout the thirty-five-year tenure of the military dictator General Alfredo Stroessner, who was in power from 1954 to 1989. In Haiti the notorious "Papa Doc" Duvalier "won" office in successive fraudulent elections from 1957 to 1971 (Carey 1998, 142). In the neighboring Dominican

Republic, authoritarian ruler Joaquín Balaguer asserted his claim to rule through fraudulent elections in 1966, 1970, and 1974. Others preserved their power with no institutional nod to democracy. Chile held no national elections between 1973 and 1989; Argentina held no elections between 1973 and 1983; and Uruguayans, similarly, had no opportunity to vote between 1971 and 1984.

In the 1980s, authoritarian regimes throughout the region began to liberalize. Scholars of Latin American politics mark the Dominican Republic election of 1978 that ousted Balaguer as a turning point. Peru followed, holding competitive elections in 1980, and Argentina and Uruguay reinstituted elections in 1983 and 1984, respectively. Haiti scheduled elections for 1987, but these were postponed in progress due to violence at the polling stations and only finally held in 1990. Chile's referendum in 1988 and subsequent election of 1989 gave citizens the means to remove dictator Pinochet. By the early 1990s, with the end of the Cold War and the fall of the Soviet Union, political observers dared to suggest an incipient world consensus on liberal democracy as the preferred (perhaps even inevitable) form of government (e.g., Fukuyama 1992). The Latin American cases appeared to substantiate this trend. Between 1988 and 1991, "an unprecedented record in Latin American electoral history was reached: the celebration, for the first time, of presidential elections in all of the countries of the region, with the single exception of Cuba" (Cerdas-Cruz, Rial, and Zovatto 1992, xviii). Even Cuba's single-party system showed signs of opening, when it institutionalized direct election of members of the National Assembly in 1993 (Prevost 2002, 351).

The Evolution of International Election Monitoring, 1962–1978

Just as the region has a long history of holding elections, it also has a long history of international involvement in elections. The earliest outside involvement in Latin American elections cannot be considered election monitoring, or even election assistance, but merits mention nonetheless. For decades the principal form of international participation in Latin American elections involved bilateral overt and covert support of political actors considered to be strategic allies by the regional hegemon, the United States. This type of intervention did not seek to boost the legitimacy of elections through external validation but rather sought to directly manipulate outcomes. For example, the United States provided $2.6 million in direct support to the campaign of

Table 8.1. OAS Election Observation in Latin America, 1962–1978

Country	Year	No. of Observers
Costa Rica	1962	3
Dominican Republic	1962	36
Nicaragua	1963	3
Honduras	1963	3
Costa Rica	1966	—
Dominican Republic	1966	41
Dominican Republic	1966	—
Bolivia	1966	12
Ecuador	1968	3
Costa Rica	1970	3
Dominican Republic	1970	3
Guatemala	1970	3
Nicaragua	1972	12
Dominican Republic	1978	3
Panama	1978	3
Bolivia	1978	10
Costa Rica	1978	3

Source: OAS 2005c.

the Christian Democratic Party in Chile prior to that country's 1964 elections, a sum complemented by $3 million in covert aid used to produce and disseminate anticommunist propaganda materials (Kornbluh 2003, 3–6). This strategy resulted in the election of the candidate preferred by the United States and typifies the pattern of bilateral U.S. intervention in Latin American elections prevalent during the height of the Cold War.[3]

During the same period, another form of international participation in Latin American elections was developing: the multilateral diplomatic presence of small OAS observer delegations. This is the earliest example of election monitoring in the region. Between 1962 and 1978, representatives of the OAS attended seventeen national-level elections in eight different Latin American states (see table 8.1).

The OAS describes the work of these delegations as "technical assistance" (OAS 2004a). Typically, two or three observers, usually government officials from other OAS member states, would visit the capital city of a given country for a few days around an election.[4] They would call on election officials, incumbents, and challengers and perhaps visit a small number of polling sites on election day. They did not see their role as auditors who might openly challenge the results of the elections, deferring instead to established sovereignty norms. In the words of Robert Pastor (1999, 127), early OAS missions served "less to monitor the electoral process than to show moral support for the elections and the incumbent." They symbolized international support for the principle of holding elections, but the fact that OAS representatives generally did not take a public position on the quality of elections meant that they did not provide any sort of accountability mechanism. In summary, early multilateral involvement in Latin American elections at best provided external validation of the principle of holding elections; at worst it created an impression of international support for questionable election processes.

Moving toward Meaningful External Validation, 1979–1989

The regional return to electoral democracy in the 1980s was accompanied by a trend of increasing international involvement in elections. It was also a time of intense United States involvement in Central America, as the Reagan administration in its two-term tenure (1981 to 1989) aggressively sought to overturn leftist governments in Nicaragua and Grenada and repress leftist movements in Guatemala and El Salvador. The Reagan policy initially emphasized military aid. This aid was justified through anticommunist rhetoric and a public discourse of democracy promotion. Responding to domestic criticism, the Reagan administration began to develop a political component to its bilateral aid to Latin America (Carothers 1991b, 94–95).

Election assistance was a major component of political aid, but in its effects it did not significantly differ from bilateral election intervention in the previous period. Although U.S. political aid for elections was described as a new democracy promotion initiative, it did not serve or even necessarily seek to provide external validation as defined here. For example, the United States provided political aid to El Salvador to enable that nation to hold elections for a Constitutional Assembly in 1982 and then legislative and presidential elections in 1984 and 1985.[5] El Salvador was at the time experiencing the most brutally repressive phase of an extended period of civil war, fueled in part by massive U.S. military assistance to the government. Herman and Brodhead (1984) and others have called the 1982, 1984, and 1985 elections in El Salvador "demonstration elections." These demonstration elections did not try to bring the armed opposition into the system. They were an alternative to a negotiated settlement—not a part of one (Roth 1999, 345–46). Thus, such bilateral political aid for elections did not meet at least one of the criteria for external validation, because it did not recognize all domestic political actors. The United States had, in this case, supplemented direct manipulation of Salvadoran politics via military aid with more "moderate" intervention through political aid, as a means of generating confidence among the American public in Salvadoran politics, that is, external validation for external consumption.

Alongside this more nuanced but still interventionist U.S. role, the nature of multilateral electoral missions by the OAS began to change. In the Dominican Republic elections of 1978, when early returns indicated that the authoritarian incumbent Balaguer was losing, he called on the three-person OAS diplomatic mission to investigate. They did, and finding no evidence of wrongdoing on the part of the opposition, refused to endorse Balaguer's claims of fraud. Following mediation by then U.S. president Jimmy Carter, Balaguer agreed to step down and the opposition took office (Espinal 1998, 95). The changed role of the OAS, in which OAS observers were called on to investigate and pronounce an opinion about the process, set a precedent in which the state legitimized the authority of multilateral observers (an interesting twist given the fact that the invitation to the OAS to expand its role did not have the desired effect from Balaguer's perspective).

Simultaneously, a new type of international actor, international nongovernmental organizations (INGOs) began to monitor Latin American elections. In response to aggressive U.S. foreign policy, small contingents of academics, activists, lawyers, faith-based groups, and others from the United States, Canada, and Europe mobilized grass-roots efforts to observe a series of politically charged elections throughout the region. INGOs in this wave of election observation included academic and advocacy organizations such as the Washington Office on Latin America (WOLA), the International Human Rights Law Group (IHRLG), the Catholic Institute for International Relations (CIIR), and the Latin American Studies Association (LASA). Grass-roots INGOs observed the 1981 and 1985 elections in Honduras, the 1984 election in revolutionary Nicaragua, the 1984 transitional election in Uruguay, the 1985 election in Guatemala, the 1988 referendum and 1989 election in Chile, and the 1989 election in Panama, among other processes (IHRLG and WOLA 1985a, 1985b; Barbieri 1986; *Envio* 1990b). They produced and distributed reports of their observations. Their reports neither reached large audiences nor exercised great power in swaying international policy in the short term; they did not trigger a norm cascade. Significantly, however, they introduced information politics to the practice of election monitoring. Information politics is a tactic in which activists "quickly and credibly generate politically usable information and move it to where it will have the most impact" (Keck and Sikkink 1998, 16). Election monitoring became a form of information politics when grass-roots monitors began to systematically and strategically gather information on election practices and present it in the context of existing election laws and international standards.

The presence of grass-roots observers and their use of information politics encouraged a new set of nongovernmental actors to enter the election monitoring field in the late 1980s: more "mainstream" NGOs, funded primarily through grants from the U.S. Agency for International Development (USAID) and the U.S. National Endowment for Democracy (NED).[6] The entry of INGOs into the election monitoring field was a significant change from past practices of bilateral political aid. The act of subcontracting U.S. political aid to INGOs effectively reduced the direct influence of the U.S. government in how election aid was carried out. As research on bureaucratic politics has long maintained, when multiple organizations are involved in the administration of a policy, the outcome is shaped by the multiple personalities of those organizations (Allison 1971). INGOs, even those reliant on government funding, have goals and constraints that are distinct from those of the U.S. government. Furthermore, their staff have specialized knowledge and experience in the region and in election administration. As Peters (1989) has observed with bureaucrats in general, the specialized knowledge of INGO staff members eventually allowed them to wield considerable influence over design and implementation of election monitoring programs and change the shape of U.S. political aid practices.

The most prominent mainstream INGOs are the National Democratic Institute for International Affairs (NDI), the International Republican Institute (IRI), the Carter Center, and the International Foundation for Election Systems (IFES). NDI and IRI, affiliated with the Democratic and Republican parties, respectively, are core institutes of the NED. With NED support, NDI first observed the Chilean plebiscite of 1988; IRI launched election observation in Haiti in 1990. The Carter Center, founded in 1982 as a nonprofit public policy institute working on issues of peace and health, observed its first election in Panama in 1989.[7] The IFES, based in Washington, D.C., was founded in 1987. It began election work in the Americas in 1989 in Panama and Uruguay, providing technical assistance for election administration. The first election

Table 8.2. International Election Observation in Latin America, 1978–1989

Country	Year	Organizations	Type of Organization
Dominican Republic	1978	OAS	IGO
Bolivia	1978	WOLA	INGO (grass-roots)
Guatemala	1980	OAS	IGO
Guyana	1980	WOLA	INGO (grass-roots)
Honduras	1981	WOLA	INGO (grass-roots)
Costa Rica	1982	OAS	IGO
El Salvador	1982	OAS	IGO
Argentina	1983	WOLA	INGO (grass-roots)
El Salvador	1984	OAS	IGO
Grenada	1984	OAS	IGO
Guatemala	1984	OAS	IGO
		WOLA	INGO (grass-roots)
Nicaragua	1984	WOLA, LASA	INGO (grass-roots)
Uruguay	984	WOLA, IHRLG	INGO (grass-roots)
El Salvador	1985	OAS	IGO
Guatemala	1985	WOLA, IHRLG	INGO (grass-roots)
Haiti	1987	NDI	INGO (mainstream)
		WOLA	INGO (grass-roots)
Honduras	1985	WOLA	INGO (grass-roots)
Suriname	1987	OAS	IGO
Chile	1988	WOLA, LASA, CIIR	INGO (grass-roots)
		NDI	INGO (mainstream)
El Salvador	1988	OAS	IGO
El Salvador	1989	WOLA	INGO
Bolivia	1989	OAS	IGO
Honduras	1989	OAS	IGO
Panama	1989	TCC, NDI, IRI	INGO (mainstream)
Paraguay	1989	NDI, IFES	INGO (mainstream)
		WOLA	INGO (grass-roots)
Uruguay	1989	WOLA	INGO (grass-roots)
		IFES	INGO (mainstream)

Sources: IHRLG and WOLA 1985a, 1985b; Barbieri 1986; Soudriette 1988; NDI and IRI 1989; *Envio* 1990b; Carter Center 1996; Canton and Nevitte 1998; OAS 2005c.

missions by these USAID-supported INGOs were similar to the early OAS missions in size and scope. Table 8.2 summarizes international election observation exercises by this expanded array of actors during the 1980s.

We can see from table 8.2 that by 1989, international participation in Latin American elections, particularly when considered in the aggregate, had changed substantially from the past pattern of bilateral intervention by the U.S.

and multilateral diplomacy through the OAS. More elections were monitored and the field for international election monitoring had diversified. Twenty-five elections in seventeen different countries were observed by the OAS and seven INGOs between 1978 and 1989, and several of these elections had multiple monitoring teams present.

If we define transnational relations as "regular interactions across national boundaries when at least one actor is a nonstate agent or does not operate on behalf of a national government or an intergovernmental organization" (Risse-Kappan 1995, xx), we can assert that international election monitoring became a form of transnational relations in the Americas during the 1980s. However, we should note that in the early 1980s there was little overlap in terms of which elections the different types of international actors attended—some elections drew OAS observers, and others drew grass-roots INGOs. With the entry of mainstream INGOs into the field in the late 1980s, we begin to see some overlap, particularly between the different types of INGO missions.

The transnationalization of the election monitoring field, in turn, was an important step in shifting the dynamic of election monitoring from external intervention toward external validation. The entry of grass-roots INGO observers into election observation helped change the election intervention practices of the United States, encouraging the provision of political aid through state-supported INGOs with varying degrees of independence from U.S. foreign policy prerogatives. The move from political intervention toward political aid began to shift the dynamic of international democracy promotion from coercion toward consensus.[8] Grass-roots election observers also set a precedent of using information politics through public reporting to provide external validation (or external censure) of elections. This precedent would be followed by the OAS and by the mainstream INGOs as they entered the field and set the stage for discussion among election monitoring organizations about what should be recognized internationally as the operative standards for accountability in election monitoring.

External Validation of Latin American Elections in the 1990s

Although the field of election monitoring diversified and began to transnationalize in the 1980s, the Nicaraguan election of February 1990 marked an important turning point in the practice of election monitoring (McCoy 1998; Pastor 1999). The biggest difference was the participation of the United Nations. The UN had observed elections prior to 1989 in countries making a transition from colonial to self-rule but never in an established sovereign state such as Nicaragua (Beigbeder 1994). United Nations involvement in the 1989–90 elections in Nicaragua was a provision of the Esquipulas peace accords that sought to bring an end to civil and guerrilla warfare that had plagued Central America throughout the 1980s. In Nicaragua the UN developed a program of proactive monitoring that was dramatically different from the passive multilateral observation of the past. UN observers began working six months prior to the election. Throughout the campaign period, they took active measures to stimulate dialogue between government and opposition, mediating as conflicts emerged. The UN election mission reported its findings about the state of the campaign to government and opposition leaders and actively encouraged changes in the practice of all parties to encourage compliance with election law. The shift in UN practice created the political opportunity for changes in the practice of election observation by other actors, who increasingly adopted proactive techniques.

The OAS and the nongovernmental Council of Freely Elected Heads of Government (a program of the Carter Center) sent delegations of 433 and 34 observers, respectively, by formal invitation of the Nicaraguan government. During the process a significant degree of collaboration and cooperation emerged between the principal international actors (Santa-Cruz 2004, 201–2). The UN, OAS, and Carter Center pooled resources and information, scheduled regular meetings to update each other on activities and findings, and shared transportation on site visits to remote areas. This level of coordination among multilateral and nonstate actors in an election observation was unprecedented.[9]

Alongside the large multilateral and mainstream NGO delegations, other INGOs and state actors were present. No fewer than twenty-four other grassroots and mainstream international monitoring teams attended, including multiple international nongovernmental organizations from the United States and Canada, and groups representing the embassies of many European States (*Envio* 1990a). In total, nearly 3,000 international observers were present in Nicaragua in February 1990. The U.S. government provided bilateral political aid for holding the election, as well as funding for the campaign of the opposition and a preponderant amount of the financing for the three largest observation missions. The influx of international resources, political observers, activists, journalists, and others into Nicaragua during the 1989–90 election campaign was extraordinary; no other election had been so closely scrutinized by outside observers. The election resulted in the peaceful transfer of power from the revolutionary Sandinista government to an opposition coalition favored by the United States. Although many observers considered the United States to have skillfully manipulated the outcome of the 1990 Nicaraguan elections through increasingly nuanced political aid, scholarship by Anderson and Dodd (2005) suggests that the outcome of the 1990 elections was, despite U.S. involvement, a faithful reflection of citizen preferences. The international election observation effort is considered precedent-setting as a means to encourage the peaceful transfer of power between parties emerging from civil war.

In terms of external validation, the Nicaraguan case had at least one important normative implication: it cemented state recognition of the legitimacy of international monitoring as a practice. We can see this recognition in the institutionalization of election monitoring divisions in multilateral organizations. After the experience of Nicaragua in 1989–90, the member states of the UN voted in the General Assembly to make election assistance a formal area of operations, with the creation of the UN Electoral Assistance Unit in 1991. This unit expanded to become the UN Electoral Assistance Division (UN-EAD) in 1994. The states of the Americas acted in the OAS to formalize electoral assistance as a field of action in 1990, when it established the Unit for the Promotion of Democracy (UPD), now the Department for the Promotion of Democracy. For international election monitoring to improve democratic accountability through external validation, state acceptance and institutionalization of the practice was an important step.

Throughout the 1990s as it became institutionalized, the practice of election monitoring gained momentum in the Americas, but it was problematic. The precedent for international observation was accepted, but the methods and standards of observation were inadequate to the task. The expanded international observer missions of the early 1990s were critiqued in the policy literature for their high cost and lack of efficacy in improving elections. Black (1999, 172), evaluating the heavily observed Paraguayan elections of 1993, decried the narrow focus of international observers on election day technicalities: "swarms of international election monitors and journalists notwithstanding, those elections served to legitimate a presidential election 'show' in which the outcome was never really put at risk." Ottaway and Chung (1999, 102), similarly, questioned the need for eighty different international observer groups at the 1996 Nicaraguan elections, noting also that the cost of those elections reached an astonishing $45 million in a country where annual expenditures for public education reached just over $60 million.

Other shortcomings of election monitoring were amply evident in El Salvador's transitional 1994 election. For that election the UN alone mobilized 900 international observers, while a multiplicity of other organizations from the United States, Canada, and Europe brought in thousands more (Montgomery 1998). In total, nearly 4,000 international observers were present to watch over the country's 355 voting sites. Yet observers were unable to address the serious logistical problems of the 1994 elections. More than 74,000 citizens were disenfranchised before the fact, unable to register to vote without documents that had been destroyed, misplaced, or never issued during the country's civil war; an estimated 350,000 voters never received their voting cards, although their registration applications had been approved; and on election day, tens of thousands of registered voters were turned away due to chaotic and crowded conditions at the voting sites (some sites held more than 300 voting tables, each designed to receive 400 voters) (Spence, Dye, and Vickers 1994, 5–6). The massive international observer presence on election day could not alleviate these problems.

Many international election monitoring organizations recognized these limitations. They developed three responses, which moved the practice of election monitoring closer to the ideal of external validation. First, international efforts to elaborate uniform standards for election observation expanded. The first guide for international election monitoring was written by Larry Garber, director of the International Human Rights Law Group, in 1984 (Garber 1984). By the mid-1990s international organizations were working together to elaborate and endorse criteria for international involvement and codes of conduct for observers (International IDEA 1997; 2000). These efforts culminated in a UN Declaration of Principles for International Election Observation and Code of Conduct for International Election Observers signed on October 27, 2005, and endorsed by a wide range of international actors including the UN Secretariat, the OAS, NDI, IRI, IFES, the Carter Center, the European Commission, and many others.

Second, mainstream INGOs began to specialize, developing strengths in different areas of election assistance. The Carter Center focused on high-level mediation before, during, and after elections, using medium- and short-term observers spread throughout the country to inform mediation. IFES continued with technical assistance to election administration bodies and also mobilized election day supervision. NDI began to concentrate its efforts first on providing assistance to civic organizations for domestic election observation efforts and, later, on supporting political parties.[10] Some grass-roots INGOs also refocused their efforts. The Washington Office on Latin America, for example, shifted from election day observation to documenting and publicizing preelection conditions to provide solid background information for other election observers and the media.

Third, international organizations began to support and encourage the emergence of domestic election monitoring organizations (DMOs). Domestic election monitoring refers to the nonpartisan monitoring of elections by civic associations or networks in their home country. The earliest domestic monitoring experiences in the Americas began in the late 1980s and included Chile's Participa (1988) and Comisión Justicia y Paz in Panama (1989).[11] In Mexico in 1991, midterm elections were monitored by domestic civic actors without the presence of international observers but with international funding. The Electoral Assistance Bureau monitored elections in Guyana (1992) alongside international observers. By the mid-1990s, domestic election monitoring had taken hold as a regionwide trend. This happened with significant international support, particularly from NDI and IFES. Table 8.3 shows the expansion of domestic monitoring in the Americas from 1988 to 2004.

With institutionalization of multilateral election monitoring, specialization among INGOs, and the advent of DMOs, the practice of election monitoring began to encompass what organizations in Latin America refer to as "integral" observation of the entire electoral process. An integral observation begins months before the election and continues until official results are announced and disputes are resolved. The methods developed for integral monitoring made the practice of election monitoring more transparent, more objective, and thus more meaningful as an instrument for external validation. Integral observation, because of its wider scope, also had the potential not only to promote "electoralism" or democracy narrowly defined by a procedural minimum of elections but also to focus domestic and international attention on wider facets of a country's democracy, human rights record, and economic development under the rubric of electoral conditions.

For the preelectoral period, observers developed a variety of techniques to judge conditions for fair competition. These include analysis of the content and implementation of electoral reforms and election law, auditing random

Table 8.3. Domestic Election Monitoring Experiences in the Americas, 1988–2004

Country	Election Year	Domestic Monitoring Organization	No. of Observers[a]
Chile	1988	Participa	n.a.
Chile	1989	Participa	n.a.
Haiti	1990	AHPEL	n.a.
Nicaragua	1990	Via Cívica	n.a.
Mexico	1991	Alianza Cívica predecessors	200
Paraguay	1993	SAKA/Decidamos	5,000
Venezuela	1993	Queremos Eligir	n.a.
Mexico	1994	Alianza Cívica	15,000
Panama	1994	Comisión Justicia y Paz	n.a.
Peru	1995	Transparencia	9,055
Dominican Republic	1996	Participación Ciudadana	1,140
Nicaragua	1996	Etica y Transparencia	4,238
Guyana	1997	Electoral Assistance Bureau	571
Jamaica	1997	Citizen Action for Free and Fair Elections (CAFFE)	965
Mexico	1997	Alianza Cívica	12,700
Dominican Republic	1998	Participación Ciudadana	n.a.
Panama	1998	Comisión Justicia y Paz	1,700
Paraguay	1998	SAKA/Decidamos	600
Venezuela	1998	Queremos Eligir	n.a.
Argentina	1999	Poder Ciudadano	n.a.
Panama	1999	Comisión Justicia y Paz	1,700
Dominican Republic	2000	Participación Ciudadana	7,500
Haiti	2000	Conseil National d'Observatión	7,000
Haiti	2000	CNO/Kozepep	6,000
Mexico	2000	Alianza Cívica	7,400
Peru	2000	Transparencia	19,506
Venezuela	2000	Queremos Eligir	n.a.
Guyana	2001	Electoral Assistance Bureau	1,000
Nicaragua	2001	Etica y Transparencia	9,000
Peru	2001	Transparencia	22,867
Dominican Republic	2002	Participación Ciudadana	n.a.
Ecuador	2002	Participación Ciudadana	n.a.
Jamaica	2002	CAFFE	n.a.
Guatemala	2003	Acción Ciudadana	n.a.
El Salvador	2004	CoCívica	450
Venezuela	2003/2004	Súmate/Momento de la Gente	n.a.
15 countries	37 elections	21 DMOs	6,362 (average)

Sources: Compiled from observation reports and press releases of individual DMOs and reports of DMO activities included in observation reports released by the OAS, Carter Center, IFES, and NDI.

[a]n.a. = not available.

samples of the voter lists for accuracy, observing voter registration, monitoring content and time allotments for different candidates in the media, and surveys to detect vote buying or intimidation of voters in vulnerable areas. On election day, single-site and roving poll watchers began to conduct surveys that captured qualitative aspects of the development of the voting, such as whether polling sites opened in the designated location and on time, whether sufficient voting materials arrived at each site, and whether registered voters had been able to vote in secret and without pressure.

Perhaps the most important technique to be developed was the parallel vote tabulation (PVT), or quick count. In a PVT, observers are deployed to a selected sample of polling sites at the time of the close of voting. They watch the on-site count of ballots and then transmit the results from that site (on a secure phone or data transmission line) to a central data collection point. If the sample is well constructed, the aggregate results of the quick count should closely parallel official results when they are released. Provided there are no problems with the sample, significant discrepancies between a parallel count and official results are a strong indicator of fraud. Parallel vote counts proved to be especially useful in cases where there was a failure (intentional or otherwise) in the official vote count system, such as a computer crash or glitch in the software (e.g., Peru 2000). On more than one occasion, the PVT has served as a proxy for official results until such time as the problem with the official count could be corrected. Where results are contested, as was the case when the Venezuelan opposition contested the recall vote in 2004, a parallel count can provide assurance that official results have not been falsified.[12]

The advent of domestic monitoring was critical to the project of integral monitoring, thus improving external validation of elections in two ways. First, as domestic monitoring contingents grew, the size of international delegations decreased. This improved monitoring efficiency in a number of ways. For example, it relieved the cost of maintaining long-term international observers to conduct preelection activities such as media monitoring. It diminished a sense of "international occupation" around elections in countries like Nicaragua and El Salvador where thousands of international observers had in the past swamped the capital cities. Concurrently, it provided an important exercise of citizenship for the numerous volunteers mobilized in DMOs as citizen-observers.

Second, the presence of domestic monitors improved election day monitoring. Because DMOs could efficiently field larger numbers of observers, they could include larger samples in their quick counts and more easily include remote polling sites in the sample. They were able to provide a visible presence in the field that international monitors alone could not achieve. And they were able to mobilize information that is useful to international observers, about both preelectoral conditions and election day occurrences.

The relationship between domestic and international observers at its best is symbiotic. International organizations provide technical assistance to DMOs in designing a quick count, as well as funding for equipment and infrastructure necessary to carry it out. DMOs in turn provide a broader range of information to international observers than the international organizations could feasibly gather on their own. DMO quick count results are often more robust, statistically speaking, than the quick counts of international organizations. In many elections now, the local DMO and the OAS each conduct a quick count, providing verification of each other's work as well as the official results. Where international and domestic actors cooperate credibly to monitor elections, the authority of international actors as perceived domestically is improved by virtue of their relationship with their domestic counterparts.[13]

However, it is important to note that this symbiosis between international and domestic monitoring organizations is possible only where domestic monitoring organizations are composed of credible nonpartisan domestic actors. When this is the case, it improves general recognition of the authority of all parties to the relationship, including transnational actors. But this condition has not been met by all DMOs in the region. International efforts to create DMOs in both Nicaragua and Haiti in 1990 did not succeed in mobilizing credible domestic civic actors—the groups involved (Via Cívica and AHPEL) were considered partisan. Domestic initiatives to mobilize civic observers in Venezuela by a group called Súmate during the 2003–4 recall process were so closely aligned with the opposition that they did not constitute credible counterparts for international observers (although Súmate did receive support from NED). IRI has been criticized for working with Haitian counterparts with a clear anti-Aristide political agenda (Bogdanich and Nordberg 2006).

Despite these questions, with the expansion of domestic election monitoring in the late 1990s and early 2000s, the field of election monitoring looked significantly different from past experiences: the practice truly transnationalized as it became common to see a mix of state and nonstate, international and domestic actors all working in different ways on the same elections. These actors have developed durable relationships through their repeated interaction in the shared issue area of elections. One example is the South-South network of Latin American civic movements called the Acuerdo de Lima (in which INGOs such as NDI have "observer" status) formed in September 2000.[14]

Conclusion

If election monitoring is to promote democracy, it must generate accountability in the domestic political institution of elections. Latin American and Caribbean states have a long history of holding elections, but also a long history of electoral fraud and election manipulation by both domestic and international actors. For decades elections simply did not provide an opportunity for meaningful participation for the region's citizens. The conceit of election monitoring is that third-party observers can provide external validation of election processes, an accountability mechanism that should be particularly useful in circumstances where elections have been discredited in the past and trust in political institutions is low.

This chapter has suggested that in order for external validation of elections to generate accountability, it must meet some minimal criteria. Relevant actors must reach agreement both about the operative standards of election monitoring and about the authority of those running the elections, where relevant actors can be defined to include the competing political parties and candidates, state election agencies, citizens, and the international monitors themselves. Monitoring experiences in the Americas through the 1960s, 1970s, and 1980s did not meet these criteria. Early multilateral election observation by the OAS reaffirmed the principle of holding elections but did not improve democracy in the country holding elections, because the OAS did not actively use election observation as a tool to improve the quality of elections. Bilateral electoral intervention by the United States subverted Latin American democracy by attempting to manipulate outcomes.

By the 1990s cumulative experiences of election monitoring began to generate changes that improved external validation of elections. Most of these changes can be attributed to the transnationalization of election monitoring. Beginning in the 1970s and 1980s grass-roots INGOs used information politics to change monitoring practices. The United States began to channel election aid through INGOs, which bureaucratized and depoliticized election aid (though not completely). Among other innovations, international monitors began to finance, design, and defend the emergence of domestic election monitors. A wider range of multilateral participation in elections developed, and the practice became institutionalized. These changes together mean that election monitoring now more closely approximates the conditions for effective external validation.

How has transnationalization produced these changes? Each of the actors in the transnational election monitoring field represents different interests and responds to different pressures. Multilateral organizations, INGOs (both grass-roots and mainstream), and DMOs are actors with distinct motivations, resources, strengths, weaknesses, and modes of operation. Their joint (though not always coordinated) participation in election processes has, over time, led to general acceptance of the legitimacy of international actors as election monitors. Increasing complexity in the field drove the need for agreement on the operative standards for holding states and state agencies, parties, and candidates to account for their administration of and participation in elections. Now, more than forty years since the first experience of election observation in the Americas, election monitoring is a transnationalized practice with the potential to provide important external validation. It does not always work—incumbents and challengers may try to manipulate the presence of international monitors to their advantage; domestic election monitors do not always act as nonpartisan democracy advocates and therefore are not always good counterparts; international organizations do not always act impartially; and finally, despite the growth in election monitoring, many elections do not benefit from transnationalized supervision.[15]

During the recall referendum process in Venezuela in 2003 and 2004, Chávez tried to portray international observers as a threat to Venezuelan sovereignty and used the presence of international observers as a nationalist rallying cry to increase his own political support. The Venezuelan domestic election monitoring organization, Súmate, did not simply observe the recall elections; it was directly involved in organizing the recall effort. Because Súmate received support from the U.S. National Endowment for Democracy for its activities, this compromised the perceived impartiality of other international organizations involved in monitoring the recall process. But the Carter Center and OAS persisted, working according to established international monitoring norms and disclosing their methodologies to the press and the public with as much transparency as possible. After the process was complete, the opposition hotly contested the results of the recall election and disparaged the international observers who supported the results. Ultimately, the election stood and Chávez remained in power where his presidency continued to be recognized by the international community, including the U.S. government, which had surely hoped for a different outcome. Even in the Venezuelan case, international observers played an important role in providing validation of the outcome.[16]

In Bolivia, elections held in December 2005 brought Evo Morales, another contentious candidate (and not a U.S. favorite) to office. OAS and domestic civic observers quickly endorsed the elections, providing legitimacy to Morales's win both at home and abroad. In the Haitian case mentioned at the outset of this chapter, elections which had been postponed four times were held in remarkably peaceful conditions. The February 2006 Haitian elections were held with significant international oversight by the UN and CARICOM, along with an array of nongovernmental actors. The role of international actors, particularly the UN and the IRI, was subject to abundant domestic criticism on the grounds of international intervention in domestic affairs, some of it well founded (Lynch 2005; Bogdanich and Nordberg 2006). Nonetheless, international observers provided important external validation, confirming the adequacy of election day conditions and norms of election procedure vis-à-vis international standards. With international support, the Haitian election board averted a potential electoral crisis and confirmed the first-round win of René Préval. In Venezuela, Bolivia, and Haiti, international observers may have ultimately provided an "escape valve," allowing domestic political forces to vent fears about election manipulation and frustration with their opponents, while still serving a validation role due to their adherence to international standards of observation.

By 2006 the practice of election monitoring had evolved to more closely meet ideals for accountability. It was therefore more successful in providing meaningful external validation of elections than in the past, even in cases where domestic and international observers acted in ways that fell short of nonpartisan ideals. The narrow focus of democracy promoters on electoral assistance was decried by some political observers in the 1980s and 1990s for promoting limited, top-down forms of democracy (Robinson 1992; 1996). This practice, however narrow, now appears to have fostered elections that allow broader, previously disenfranchised constituencies to freely express their political preferences. In 2004 and 2005, parties and candidates from the political left began to experience an electoral resurgence throughout the region. The year 2006, with major elections planned in ten countries, promised further change and an opportunity to deepen participatory democracy in the region. International and domestic election observers alike will almost certainly play an important role.

NOTES

The author would like to thank Arturo Santa-Cruz and Dexter Boniface for their detailed feedback. Bruce Bagley also provided constructive comments on an early version of this chapter presented at the International Studies Association–South meeting in Miami, November 3–5, 2005. The research upon which this chapter is based was supported by grants from the University of California Institute on Global Conflict and Cooperation (2001–2), the Pacific Rim Research Program of the University of California (2001–2), University of California MEXUS (2002–3), and the Colgate University Discretionary Grant program (2005).

1. See the chapter by David Goldberg in this volume for a more detailed analysis of the role of international actors in the recent Haitian political crisis.

2. To attribute these motivations to international election monitors does not assume "altruistic" motivation. International actors may seek to promote political participation and provide a disincentive to violence for many reasons: to insure political stability of neighboring nations; to reduce migration flows; to improve conditions for international investment; or to secure access to natural resources, for example. On this topic, see Robinson (1996). Robinson argues that U.S. democracy promotion efforts, including election assistance, promote a limited form of top-down democracy that makes the world safe for global capitalism and does little to advance norms of democracy, such as socioeconomic equality.

3. It is interesting to note that this bilateral electoral intervention was not always effective. Similar U.S. participation in Chile's 1970 elections failed to achieve the same results. Although the United States was determined to prevent the election of socialist candidate Salvador Allende through whatever means necessary, including violence, Allende won the election by a narrow margin and took office in November 1970. He was later overthrown in a military coup supported by the U.S. government. The coup, on September 11, 1973, began the tenure of dictator Pinochet.

4. In the Dominican Republic in 1962 and 1966 the OAS sent larger missions, of thirty-six and forty-one, respectively. The larger size of the 1962 mission was due to a concurrent OAS symposium on representative democracy—all symposium participants were invited to stay for the elections.

5. Political aid to El Salvador included USAID funding for the vote computation system, and cash provided through the Central Intelligence Agency to Duarte, the presidential candidate favored by the U.S. government. See Carothers (1999).

6. The NED, a Reagan initiative, was established in 1984 by an act of Congress and given a mandate to support U.S.-based organizations that work toward the development of democracy abroad. For details on the origins of the NED, see Goldman and Douglas (1998).

7. In 1986 the Americas Program of the Carter Center established a group called the Council of Freely Elected Heads of Government. The Carter Center's election-monitoring work in the Americas originates with the council.

8. For a discussion of control versus consent as different international dimensions of democratization, see Whitehead (1996, 8–22).

9. Author's interview with Dong Nguyen, UNDP elections specialist, Mexico City, Mexico, March 20, 2003.

10. IRI also provided support to domestic civic organizations, particularly special-interest groups aligned with the local business sector, but its activities have been conducted on a smaller scale and with less transparency than those of NDI.

11. USAID funded a civic group called Via Cívica in Nicaragua in 1989–90, which was intended to provide domestic observation of the election, but the organization's work was both limited and partisan. See Robinson (1992). A similar international effort to create a domestic monitoring organization met with limited success in Haiti in 1990.

12. In this case, a quick count conducted by the OAS and the Carter Center provided assurance to the international community. The Venezuelan opposition was not mollified.

13. See Lean (2007) for a detailed analysis of international support for domestic monitoring organizations, their "civic authenticity," and democratic potential.

14. The Acuerdo de Lima, named for the Peruvian capital where civic representatives met to establish the network, has received important support from NDI. The Peruvian DMO, Transparencia, coordinates the collective activities of the Acuerdo de Lima. More information on the Acuerdo de Lima can be found at www.acuer dodelima.org/.

15. In fact, this author's previous research (Lean 2004) shows that elections in countries with the most significant challenges to political and civil rights are less likely to be monitored than those in countries considered to have partly free or free political systems.

16. Legler in this volume provides a detailed treatment of the Venezuelan recall referendum and the role of international actors.

Part III / Crisis Cases

CHAPTER NINE

Haiti 2004

CARICOM's Democracy Promotion Efforts

David M. Goldberg

> Konstitisyon se papye, bayonèt se fè.
> A Constitution is made of paper but the bayonet is made of iron.
>
> KREYOL SAYING

On June 6, 2006, Haiti was readmitted to the Caribbean Community (CARI-COM) after two years of de facto suspension from the organization. The suspension was the result of an ongoing political crisis in Haiti in which incumbent president Jean-Bertrand Aristide left office and Haiti under heavily disputed circumstances on February 29, 2004. The United States claimed that Aristide had resigned from office to avoid bloodshed. Aristide, his supporters, and a number of officials in the region alleged that the president was forced from office at gunpoint in a coup organized by the United States and France.[1] The Organization of American States (OAS) and United Nations, however, did not initially condemn the event. In contrast, CARICOM criticized Aristide's departure as an unconstitutional interruption in democratic governance and removed official recognition of Haiti's interim government.

CARICOM's response is significant given the growing emphasis on democracy promotion efforts by regional and subregional multilateral organizations in the Americas since the end of the Cold War (Bloomfield 1994; Acevedo and Grossman 1996; Cooper and Legler 2001a; Boniface 2002; Goldberg 2003; Anderson 2005). What accounts for the differing responses of CARICOM and the

OAS in the months following the 2004 termination of the Aristide presidency? What do the responses of the UN, OAS, and CARICOM to the crisis of democracy in Haiti in 2004 tell us about the efficacy of multilateral democracy promotion efforts in the early twenty-first century? Is there a distinct role for subregional organizations like CARICOM in the promotion of democracy?

This chapter examines the international response to the Haitian crisis of 2004. My primary argument is that CARICOM's response to the Haitian crisis reflects significant organizational differences from the OAS as well as greater hemispheric currents toward democracy promotion. As OAS efforts at resolving regional crises of constitutional governance encounter new obstacles, CARICOM has taken a more aggressive posture toward preservation of democratic institutions, with mixed results.

The first section of this chapter examines CARICOM's evolution from a trade agreement to an emerging subregional multilateral actor in the promotion of democracy. The next section discusses Haitian politics since 2000 and the events that led up to the political crisis in 2004. Finally, the responses from the UN and OAS and CARICOM are compared with an emphasis on explaining how the reactions differed.

The Growth of CARICOM

While recent years have seen a growing body of scholarship on democracy promotion efforts by the Organization of American States, little attention has been paid to the role of subregional organizations in promoting democracy. Yet subregional organizations are arguably well positioned to play an important role in democracy assistance. CARICOM has worked alongside the OAS to establish and promote democratic norms and constitutional governance among member states. Perhaps most notably CARICOM has taken a lead role in working toward a resolution of the 2004 Haitian political crisis.

CARICOM declared Aristide's February 29, 2004, departure from office to be an interruption in constitutional governance and did not extend diplomatic recognition to the interim government. Since that time CARICOM has worked with Brazil, the OAS, and the United Nations Stabilization Mission in Haiti (MINUSTAH) to promote a resolution of the crisis and create a climate conducive to new legislative and presidential elections. CARICOM's actions in the Haitian crisis highlight the flexibility of smaller regional organizations to evolve responses and address crises in a diverse manner.

Though most of its member states are small in population, the organization has revealed increased diplomatic capacity in recent years. The block of fifteen CARICOM votes is a significant number of member states in the OAS. CARICOM nations played a decisive role in the 2005 election of OAS secretary-general José Miguel Insulza and successfully lobbied to place a representative of a CARICOM member state, Albert Ramdin of Suriname, in the position of OAS assistant secretary-general. CARICOM has also played a vocal role in the debate on expanding the United Nations Security Council.

Historically, CARICOM traces its roots to a four-nation trade promotion accord in 1968 with the enactment of the Caribbean Free Trade Association. The Treaty of Chaguaramas (1973) established the organization and its goal of greater regional economic integration.[2] Parties to the Treaty of Chaguaramas included twelve nations divided into two groups according to level of economic development. The more developed group included Barbados, Jamaica, Trinidad and Tobago, and Guyana, and the less developed group contained Antigua, Belize, Dominica, Grenada, Montserrat, Saint Kitts and Nevis, Saint Lucia, and Saint Vincent. Suriname has since joined in 1995 and Haiti in 2002.

In 2001 CARICOM negotiated a free-trade agreement with the Dominican Republic. The organization has also sought closer trade relations with the European Union, China, and Japan. In 2004 CARICOM made significant progress in replacing the Caribbean Common Market with the CARICOM Single Market and Economy.

Although CARICOM's original goal was to enhance the economic well-being of its member states, the organization has moved toward greater integration on a variety of issues including a regional court system and the revision of its Charter on Civil Society. In addition, there has been progress on the development of a unified foreign policy, such as combating the spread of infectious diseases and preventing use of the Caribbean Sea as a shipment route for drug trafficking and for nuclear weapons and waste (CARICOM 2005). In 2003 a permanent regional judicial body was established among twelve member states. The Caribbean Court of Justice has original jurisdiction over interpretations of the treaty establishing CARICOM and acts as an appeals court on issues of common law among member states.

The majority of CARICOM member states, by virtue of their overlapping membership in the OAS, are committed to the promotion and protection of democracy in accordance with the Summit of the Americas Declaration of Québec City and the Inter-American Democratic Charter.[3] CARICOM itself has separate provisions relevant to the promotion of democracy. The Charter of Civil Society, first developed in 1992, defines the organization's commitment to representative democracy. Article 6 declares "states shall ensure the existence of a fair and open democratic system through the holding of free elections at reasonable intervals" (CARICOM 1997). However, unlike the OAS's Washington Protocol or Inter-American Democratic Charter, neither the revised Treaty of Chaguaramas nor the Charter of Civil Society provides a specific mechanism to suspend member states for violating the provision of democratic governance. Such a mechanism would require amending the treaty and has been the focus of discussion among member states.[4]

The increased commitment to democratic norms among CARICOM member states is a logical outgrowth of the move toward integration. Along these lines, CARICOM has placed great emphasis on free and fair elections among its member states, similar to that developed by the OAS. While the OAS has a longer history of election monitoring, CARICOM has been able to supplement OAS actions for its members. Former CARICOM assistant secretary-general Albert Ramdin has stated a desire to strengthen democracy in the community as the primary justification of a recent increase in election monitoring (Ramdin 2004). Participation in multiple frequently overlapping observation missions also indicates a willingness among member states to accept greater institutional complexity.

The Haitian legislative elections of May 2000 were the first to be formally monitored by the organization.[5] On May 25, 2000, CARICOM sent a second delegation to observe elections for Suriname's National Assembly. Between May 2000 and October 2005, CARICOM sent election observation missions to nine countries. Like the OAS, CARICOM observer missions are invited by the host government but report their findings to the secretary-general. Overall the mission reports reflect a high degree of satisfaction with electoral processes. At no point have the CARICOM missions questioned the overall outcome of any national election that was observed. In the Guyanese elections of March 2001, CARICOM observers criticized the disenfranchisement of some voters and a lack of clarity regarding closing times for polls, but the final report stopped short of stating that the elections were not fair.

CARICOM is headed by the secretary-general, followed by the deputy secretary-general and general counsel. There are directorates for trade, social development and foreign relations. The Counsel for Foreign and Community Relations consists of the states' foreign ministers and is the most significant body in determining foreign relations policy toward member states, the region, and international community. In June 2005 the Counsel for Foreign and Community Relations was instrumental in successfully lobbying for the election of CARICOM's candidate, Albert R. Ramdin, to be the assistant secretary-general of the Organization of American States. In 2005 CARICOM played an important role in debate on reform of the United Nations Security Council.

Haiti's Perpetual Crisis of Governance

In 2002 Haiti was admitted as a voting member to CARICOM. As the fifteenth state to join the organization, Haiti was the most politically unstable and least developed economically.[6] Haitian politics in the twentieth century were dominated by foreign intervention and the repressive Duvalier dictatorship. Prior to his death in 1971, François "Papa Doc" Duvalier lowered the required age to assume the presidency from forty to eighteen, allowing his son to assume power in April 1971. In 1986 Claude "Baby Doc" Duvalier was forced from power and sought refuge in France. In December 1990 reasonably free and fair elections were held in Haiti and populist Catholic priest Jean-Bertrand Aristide was elected president. Military and social elites feared Aristide's populist economic and social statements. On September 30, 1991, Aristide was displaced in a military coup. Most states in the hemisphere were quick to condemn the event. The United States immediately criticized the military's seizure of power and the Organization of American States met under the auspices of Resolution 1080 (see appendix A) to initiate an economic boycott. Over the next two years, the OAS sought to broker talks between Aristide and the Haitian military junta led by Raul Cédras. Cédras informally agreed to allow international human rights observers, but there was no lasting political agreement between the military government and Aristide.

On September 23, 2003, after repeated attempts at mediation and greater provocation by the ruling military forces, the United Nations Security Council passed Resolution 867 authorizing the creation of the United Nations Mission to Haiti (United Nations 1993). On July 31, 2004, it passed Resolution 940 authorizing the use of force to displace the illegitimate military junta by all necessary means. On September 18, 1994, a diplomatic delegation led by former U.S. president Jimmy Carter made a final attempt to reach a nonmilitary solution. Cédras and his military supporters initially balked at the conditions of the agreement but when they realized that an invasion force was literally en route to Haiti, they rescinded power. The following day, the United States led a multinational "intervasion" force that encountered little resistance (P. H. Smith 2000, 315). The military government led by Raul Cédras resigned from office as U.S. paratroopers were mobilized. Eventually, Aristide returned to power in exchange for military amnesty. The predominantly U.S. military presence was replaced by a U.N. peace-keeping mission in March 1995. Aristide served the remaining sixteen months of his term. The Constitution prohibited a president's immediate reelection, at which point a close adviser to Aristide, René Préval, was elected president in 1995. Préval ruled nearly half of his term by decree after a conflict with opposition parties in Congress (Greste 2000).

The 2000 Legislative and Presidential Elections

On May 21, 2000, Haiti held legislative and municipal elections (Miles 2001). According to the Provisional Electoral Council (CEP), voter turnout was approximately 60 percent of the registered electorate.[7] Observers from the OAS, CARICOM, and Francophone nations participated in election monitoring. Election day began with little violence, but as the day unfolded the situation worsened and polling places closed. In some departments armed groups entered polling places and destroyed ballot boxes. The situation worsened due to a delay in the official tallying and reporting of votes between Cap Haïtien and the capital, Port-au-Prince. The reporting delays ranged from hours to days leaving open the possibility of fraud. The OAS Mission reported the arrest and detention of several opposition candidates, resulting in the CEP's call for new elections in two locations on July 1. Disparities between the official tallies and those of the international observers were significant enough to raise additional suspicions about the integrity of the voting process.

In contrast to the experience of international observer missions, nongovernmental organizations under the International Coalition of Independent Observers reached different conclusions about the registration process.[8] The Quixote Center claimed that a significant number of poor neighborhoods were systematically excluded from the registration process. The nongovernmental organization coalition estimates of those unable to register contrasts sharply with the position of the CEP and OAS. Officially more than 93 percent of eligible citizens were registered to vote.

The National Assembly vote for seventeen of thirty-eight Senate seats and all eighty-three seats of the Chamber of Deputies was especially contentious and would ultimately undermine the credibility of the elections nationwide. On June 1 the CEP announced that President Aristide's party Fanmi Lavalas won sixteen seats in the Senate and twenty-three in the Chamber of Deputies. The opposition, led by a multiparty coalition, Democratic Convergence, protested the CEP results and their methodology of calculating votes for the Senate.[9] According to Article 64 of the electoral law, an absolute majority of votes is needed to win a seat. The opposition and the OAS Mission found, however, that the CEP had tabulated vote totals only for the top two to four contenders and did not count votes for the remaining candidates. As a result, it was impossible to determine if the leading candidate had in fact received an absolute majority in the first round of voting. Reducing the number of contenders receiving votes increased the percentage of the leading Lavalas candidates and the likelihood they would receive an outright majority in the first round. Democratic Convergence called for a boycott of the second round of legislative elections and the upcoming presidential election unless a new Senate vote for those contested seats was held. On June 15, in response to growing criticism, three members of the CEP resigned their posts. Among them was the council's president, Leon Manus, who fled to the Dominican Republic, claiming that his life was threatened for refusing to sign off on election results. Shortly after the resignations, the OAS Mission issued a statement criticizing the methodology of counting votes for the Senate. The remaining CEP members defended the Senate elections outcome. On June 20, President Préval made the election results official. The OAS stood by its claims. The mission report to the Permanent Council stated, "The Mission considers that a number of irregularities did compromise the credibility of these elections, particularly with respect to the senatorial race" (OAS 2000a). The United States and the European Union threatened sanctions unless a resolution was negotiated before the second round of legislative elections and the presidential election. The Democratic Convergence called for a boycott of the November elections.

As the crisis unfolded, the OAS and CARICOM launched a joint mission.[10] OAS assistant secretary-general Luigi Einaudi and CARICOM assistant secretary-general Albert R. Ramdin traveled to Port-au-Prince with the hopes of brokering a settlement between the now victorious Fanmi Lavalas and Convergence, the lead opposition coalition.[11] The negotiations were critical for the upcoming elections. If the opposition boycotted, the outcome would be marred.

Convergence took the position that the May election was fraudulent and the vote must be recast. Their second demand was that the CEP be reconstituted with members not involved in the controversy surrounding the May 21 elections (Miles 2001). After several attempts at a negotiated settlement by the two sides, Einaudi declared an end to the efforts. Without a consensus agreement, the United States refused to observe or lend assistance to the November elections. The U.S. position had a cascading effect, leading other states and the United Nations to withhold support for international monitoring efforts. The OAS Electoral Mission issued a formal statement on July 7, calling for the suspension of all observation activity for the second round of legislative elections (OAS 2000a). Only two international actors had a presence. CARICOM sent a team of four monitors and the International Coalition of Independent Observers (ICIO) also sent a team of observers. Without a significant international observer presence, serious questions about the credibility of the legislative runoff elections were raised. A preliminary CARICOM statement released on December 13, 2000, echoed the OAS position that presidential elections had avoided an interruption in constitutional governance but did not address broader issues on participation and Haitian democratic development (Kingsley and Layne 2000). The ICIO observation mission reported largely minor irregularities and voter turnout of around 60 percent in most parts of the country outside of the capital. In Port-au-Prince fear of violence and obstacles to voting led to estimates of voter turnout ranging from 30 to 75 percent (Miles 2001).

In the absence of any significant electoral opposition to Aristide and in the presence of a reduced field of international monitors, the presidential elections proceeded as planned on November 26. President Aristide ran unopposed and won 92 percent of the ballots cast. Both the OAS and CARICOM issued statements criticizing the lack of significant opposition participation but emphasized the significance of proceeding with presidential elections in accordance with the Constitution (OAS 2000a). In light of the opposition party's boycott and the lack of international monitoring, estimates of voter turnout varied considerably. The official turnout estimate of the CEP was 60 percent, while media outlets and CARICOM (which only observed in Port-au-Prince) placed turnout no higher than 10 percent. While the OAS and CARICOM granted some legitimacy to Aristide, other members of the international community took a different approach. The European Union suspended approximately $400 million in development assistance while the Inter-American Development Bank withheld $76 million in aid.[12] As of 2000 European Union aid to Caribbean states is governed by the Cotonou Agreement, which contains respect for human rights and democratic principles as essential elements to continuing relations. According to the European Commission at the time, "The EU considers Haiti as non-complying with the democratic principles of the Cotonou agreement. As of January 2001, suspension of direct budget aid to the government and of further financial measures has taken effect." In addition, the United States suspended most direct aid to Haiti.

Explaining the CARICOM Response

In contrast to financial and diplomatic withdrawal from Haiti by a significant number of countries and multilateral organizations, CARICOM officials remained engaged in the search for a negotiated settlement. This raises the question why CARICOM did not significantly reduce its profile as other international actors had done. The costs of withdrawal for CARICOM were potentially much higher than for the European Union, United Nations, and United States. The continuing nature of the Haitian crisis provided a complicated test for CARICOM. The commitment to representative democracy among member states was under pressure. If CARICOM disengaged from Haiti, other members might view the action as a weakening of the policy. In a broader sense, the United Nations and to a lesser extent the OAS relied on CARICOM to play a larger role in discussions because of its closer ties and credibility as a good-faith negotiating partner. Remaining active in negotiations signaled the real and potentially increasing influence of CARICOM in hemispheric affairs.

In 2000 Haiti was a provisional member of CARICOM. The process of full ascension would not be completed until 2002.[13] CARICOM found itself in the difficult position of participating in the electoral observation of a future member state with a shallow history of democratic governance. The official position as stated to the Permanent Council of the OAS in August 2000 reflected this tension: "It was therefore with much hope that CARICOM looked forward to the successful conduct of the legislative, municipal and local elections in Haiti, the installment of a new parliament and an end to the political crisis and social instability that had gripped that country since 1997. The Community has unfortunately had to acknowledge that the manner in which these events took place did not live up to its expectations" (CARICOM 2000). CARICOM believed that the May 2000 elections had met international standards but agreed with the OAS position on the "questionable interpretation of the electoral law" with respect to the Senate elections. CARICOM sent two additional missions in July to investigate. The organization's offer to look into questions surrounding the first-round victory of Lavalas Senate candidates was rejected. CARICOM proposed a team of experts to participate in interpretation of the electoral law toward resolving the crisis over the Senate elections. This offer was rejected. Unlike the OAS and UN, CARICOM did send a small mission to observe the November presidential election. CARICOM did this in spite of the stated position that elections should not go forward without resolving issues from the Senate election.

If international observers had failed to monitor the presidential election or significantly limited their participation, how could the results rise to the level of acceptable standards? A partial explanation lies in the fact that presidential elections went forward in compliance with the Haitian Constitution's provisions on presidential succession. Article 134-2 requires that presidential elections take place the last Sunday in November of the fifth year of a president's term. Article 134-1 requires that the presidential term end and begin on February 7 following elections.

In addition to the constitutional requirement, CARICOM members had their own reasons for wanting to observe the elections. The position was taken that it would be easier to strengthen Haiti's democratic evolution while a member state of the organization than to condemn the elections and restrict Haiti's ascendancy to full membership. The organization would likely be more successful in influencing Haiti if it was a full member.

The formal CARICOM position was that the presidential election "avoids an interruption in the timetable for presidential succession established by the Constitution of Haiti, but does not alter the need to ensure the broad political representation and citizen participation critical to the development of Haitian democracy" (Kingsley and Layne 2000). The wording stops short of denying the election's legitimacy but admits the context in which it occurred was deeply flawed. CARICOM's position avoided an interruption in constitutional governance in spite of the domestic and international criticisms of the Senate vote count.

Interestingly, the CARICOM position was ultimately adopted by the United States and the OAS. In an unpublished letter, President Bill Clinton addressed Aristide as "President-elect" but stopped short of congratulating him on the election. The result was a tacit recognition of Aristide's victory that by extension imparted an element of legitimacy. The international community ultimately accepted Aristide's election while criticizing the circumstances that contributed to it.

2000–2004: Haitian Deterioration and Collapse

The origins of the 2004 crisis are partially rooted in the absence of a consensus between Lavalas and Convergence following the 2000 legislative elections. The OAS and CARICOM continued to work toward a negotiated solution between the legal opposition and the Aristide administration. The U.S. government was also involved. In December 2000, Clinton administration special envoy Anthony Lake met with President-elect Aristide to mediate a dialogue with the Democratic Convergence. In response, Aristide drafted a letter outlining areas of reform. Among the most significant components were the proposals to allow runoff elections for ten contested Senate seats, the creation of a new Electoral Council, and a semipermanent OAS mediation mission.

On December 17, 2001, a group of former military officials attacked the Haitian National Palace in what appeared to be a failed coup attempt. Aristide supporters responded by attacking Convergence headquarters and launching violent retaliatory strikes against Aristide's opponents. CARICOM reacted by sending a team to meet with government and opposition leaders in an attempt to diffuse tensions. The OAS was also involved. In January the OAS passed Resolution 806 which urged a full investigation of the circumstances surrounding the December violence and the payment of reparations to those political organizations that had suffered property damage (OAS 2002e). The violence on all sides reduced the likelihood that a consensus could be negotiated. After the violence in December, there was retrenchment and deepening polarization among Aristide's supporters, the legal opposition, and a growing number of former military officials who were launching small-scale attacks from the other side of the Dominican border.

For more than three years, the OAS and CARICOM continued to work on an acceptable resolution. Despite the increasingly unstable political context, a tentative accord for new elections in 2003 was reached in June 2002. Both sides agreed to OAS Resolution 822, which emphasized the need for a new Provisional Electoral Council that could be respected by both sides to oversee municipal and legislative elections. The resolution offered an economic incentive for Haiti's compliance, because it included language allowing for the resumption of foreign aid to Haiti. Significant aid from the European Union, United States, France, and international financial institutions had been withheld after the 2000 elections. With unemployment at 75 percent and the economy effectively grinding to a halt, the infusion of new development loans was especially crucial (Sletten and Egset 2004). In July 2003 the Inter-American Development Bank resumed its assistance to Haiti.

However, political tensions could not be easily diffused. By late 2002 a number of former Haitian military officers were in the Dominican Republic receiving arms and training for another coup attempt against Aristide from the other side of the Haitian-Dominican border.[14]

In December 2002 a group of more than 200 civil society groups, in cooperation with members of Convergence, formed the Coalition of 184 Civic Institutions, or Group of 184. The group included peasant organizations, student groups, and a significant number of private-sector business associations. The opposition was divided among extralegal forces, largely criminal gangs, remnants of the army, and the legal opposition led by the Democratic Convergence Party and the Group of 184. Both legal and criminal opposition called for Aristide's resignation and new elections. In response, groups loyal to Aristide and the Haitian National Police (the armed forces had been demobilized after his 1994 return to office) clashed with opposition forces.

Against the backdrop of polarization among the major political factions arose the growing specter of significant corruption. In 2003 Transparency International ranked Haiti the third most corrupt country in the world in its annual survey. The United States alleged that Haiti was becoming a new shipment point for drug trafficking in the hemisphere. Several high-ranking officials, including the former chief of police in Port-au-Prince, have been accused of participating in drug trafficking (Adams 2004). A 2005 report by the Haitian government found that between 2001 and 2004, $120 million was misappropriated by President Aristide and other members of the executive branch.[15]

In January 2004 Haiti commemorated 200 years of independence. On the anniversary of his third year in office, President Aristide resisted calls for his resignation and new elections, insisting he should serve out the remainder of his term as stated in the Constitution. As relations among the legal political factions worsened, rebel leaders seized police stations in the cities of Cap-Haïtien and Gonaïves, cutting off the latter from supplies and contact with the rest of the country.[16] Without a standing army to put down the rebellion or an international peace-keeping force to strengthen his position, Aristide's power weakened and Haiti descended into chaos.[17]

CARICOM foreign ministers, in cooperation with the Organization of American States, the U.S., Canadian, and French governments, and a European Union delegation, attempted to broker a peace deal between the factions. The White House personally encouraged CARICOM leaders to pursue a settlement in the Haitian crisis.[18] On January 31, CARICOM heads of government met in emergency session in Kingston, Jamaica, to discuss the Haitian situation and negotiate a solution. The result was the "Prior Plan of Action." The plan was "aimed at restoring confidence between contending groups and initiating a process of détente which would facilitate dialogue" (CARICOM 2004b). The document contained ten proposals. The most significant dealt with implementation of OAS Resolutions 806, 822, and 1959; the formation of a new government; continued cooperation between the opposition and Lavalas; and a guarantee that Aristide would not seek to extend his term or contest subsequent elections. The plan's components would be overseen and implemented jointly by CARICOM and the OAS. Arguably the most significant concession sought from Aristide was the acceptance of a "neutral and independent person" as prime minister and similar persons in the new government.[19] The agreement was an attempt to hold Aristide accountable to the growing opposition while allowing him to finish his term.

The Plan of Action was approved by Aristide sometime prior to February 9, 2004, and by the OAS on February 19, 2004. But the opposition, both legal and armed, had little incentive to compromise. Rebels approached the capital and violence increased in Port-au-Prince, putting Aristide in an untenable position. On February 23, representatives of the opposition Democratic Convergence held a press conference to announce their rejection of the Plan of Action. Sensing the imminent demise of Aristide, they expressed an unwillingness to support any settlement that allowed Aristide to remain in office. On February 26 Aristide called for the introduction of a UN peace-keeping force to minimize the violence.

Partly as a result of the opposition's unwillingness to sign off on the Plan of Action, the United States and France, representing two significant permanent vetoes on the UN Security Council, signaled the current situation was unsustainable. On February 28, 2004, both the United States and France said they would not support a multilateral force without an existing political agreement, in spite of Aristide's calls for UN intervention. On February 29 Aristide allegedly submitted a letter of resignation to the U.S. Embassy officials, stating he was leaving office to prevent additional bloodshed. He was flown out of the country on an unmarked U.S. military plane that eventually landed in the Central African Republic (Adams 2006). Alexander Boniface, chief justice of the Haitian Supreme Court, was sworn in as the interim president. Article 149 of the Haitian Constitution calls for the chief justice to serve as interim president until a new election can be held subject to approval by the National Assembly. The lower house of parliament had been disbanded in January, and Boniface's presidency was never formally approved.[20] The president serves as head of state under the 1987 Constitution. A new prime minister, Gerard Latortue, was chosen by a "Council of Sages," the result of negotiations among CARICOM, the OAS, United States, and France.[21] Latortue had briefly served as foreign minister under the presidency of Leslie Manigat before a military coup in 1988. During the intervening years he had worked for the United Nations and in private business while living in Florida.

On March 1 Aristide appeared by telephone on U.S. television and flatly rejected the idea that he had voluntarily resigned and claimed he was the victim of a coup d'etat by the United States and France. CARICOM's response was to call for a United Nations or OAS investigation into the circumstances surrounding Aristide's departure from office.[22] That request was opposed by U.S. secretary of state Powell, and no action was taken by the United Nations or the Organization of American States to pursue a formal investigation into the circumstances surrounding Aristide's departure.

On February 29 the United Nations Security Council met in an emergency situation and passed Resolution 1529, authorizing a peace-keeping force that would become the United Nations Stabilization Mission in Haiti (MINUSTAH). CARICOM refused to recognize the interim government or participate in the UN Mission, and Haiti's seat remained vacant. Although all member states supported the denial of recognition to the interim government, there was some disagreement over how states should engage with it. According to published reports, St. Lucia, St. Vincent and the Grenadines and Guyana took the stance that there should be no recognition of the Latortue government, while Barbados, Grenada, Antigua, and Barbuda advocated a more flexible position on engagement (Singh 2004). In taking this position, CARICOM opted to walk a difficult diplomatic tightrope, not recognizing the interim government but pledging support to the Haitian people.

The U.S. and French Responses

As the crisis unfolded in early February 2004, the United States, France, and Canada participated in negotiations in coordination with the OAS and CARICOM. Both the United States and France pledged support for the Prior Plan of Action. On February 25 France withdrew its support for the Aristide government and called for his resignation. The U.S. position became increasingly critical of Aristide's handling of the crisis and alleged Aristide was the source for much of the violence in Port-au-Prince. The United States and France opposed Aristide's call for a UN force to establish stability in the absence of a viable political solution. With U.S. and French opposition, any Security Council action was unlikely to pass.

What factors explain the U.S. and French positions against Aristide's continuation in power? First, the increasing violence that started in Gonaïves quickly spread to Port-au-Prince. The Haitian National Police (HNP) was underequipped and poorly trained to engage the rebel forces. The prospect of a bloodbath in Port-au-Prince was stated as a partial explanation for American and French positions supporting Aristide's removal from office. Even after the fall of Gonaïves, the United States and France continued to oppose the introduction of a UN peace-keeping force. This inaction suggests that U.S. and French policy was more concerned with the removal of Aristide and less with a peaceful resolution to the conflict.

Politically, the opposition had rejected the CARICOM plan to allow Aristide to remain in office. Both the military and the political situation suggested the imminent end of Aristide's presidency through his death, resignation, or removal by coup. The United States and France had little incentive to support any UN action that would stabilize the situation in the short term and allow Aristide to remain in office. The potential for a post-Aristide Haitian political landscape provided greater motivation to the United States and France to avoid a temporary peace-keeping mission. The tacit withdrawal of support for the Plan of Action as the crisis deepened weakened the CARICOM position as lead international organization in resolving the conflict.

The UN's Role in Haiti

Between 1993 and 2005, the United Nations authorized six separate missions to Haiti (Samuels 2005). The missions have dealt with security, professionalization of the armed forces (prior to demobilization) and police, and promoting human rights and free and fair elections. Under the rubric of security, the UN role has focused on creating conditions of stability rather than electoral oversight or resolution of political conflicts. The UN missions that did focus on building institutions and promoting good governance met with mixed success. UN efforts at reforming the Haitian National Police created a poorly equipped, corrupt organization that served the interests of elected officials and criminal elements more than the promotion of respect for law and order. Under Aristide the military was disbanded in April 1995 but little formal effort was made to integrate officers into the police force or civilian politics. The result was a cadre of officers who remained powerful but unaccountable. UN efforts limited to crisis management, such as the restoration of Aristide in 1994 and oversight of elections, were more successful, but these advances were erased by the gradual collapse of the Haitian state between 2000 and 2004.

In the aftermath of Aristide's departure, MINUSTAH was established by UN Security Council Resolution 1529 at the request of the interim government. The UN resolution authorizing an interim force that would be replaced by the MINUSTAH mission was passed the same day as Aristide's departure from Haiti. The UN played a critical role in the lead up to the February 2006 presidential elections. The peace-keeping mandate extended to promote security and law enforcement reform in the face of growing criminal violence.

The UN position in the 2004 crisis was consistent with previous actions it had undertaken and reflects its larger operating principles. The UN role in Haiti has largely been related to security and peace-keeping, not issues of democratic governance. The UN Charter does not contain a commitment to defend democracy or address countries in constitutional crises.

The Role of the OAS

The OAS had a long-established role in efforts to stabilize the Haitian political and economic situation stemming back to Aristide's initial removal from office by coup d'etat in 1991. The OAS response to the coup was one of the earliest examples of a concerted democracy promotion effort by the organization. Resolution 1080 was invoked, economic sanctions imposed, and the Inter-American Human Rights Commission was dispatched. The OAS observed presidential and legislative elections in 1995 as well as the 2000 legislative elections.[23] In March 2003 the OAS (together with CARICOM) participated in a mission to Haiti in anticipation of the upcoming elections to urge compliance from all sides with respect to the OAS resolutions. As the political crisis escalated in January and February 2004, the OAS deferred to the United Nations and CARICOM's leadership role. Permanent Council Resolution 862, passed on February 26, 2004, condemned the escalating violence and called for compliance with the CARICOM Prior Action Plan and immediate action from the United Nation Security Council.

In the aftermath of Aristide's departure, the Permanent Council of the OAS did not issue any resolution, and the General Assembly took no action until the passage of Resolution 2058 in June 2004. The wording of the resolution recognized that an alteration of the constitutional regime had taken place that had begun prior to February 29, 2004. The principles of the Inter-American Democratic Charter were repeatedly invoked but not its formal mechanisms. Article 20, which calls for action by the Permanent Council, was referenced, but Article 21, which allows for suspension of a member state, was not invoked.

The lack of aggressive action by the OAS on Haiti is best explained by the U.S. position. Calls for a formal OAS investigation into the events surrounding Aristide's departure were strongly opposed and dismissed by secretary of state Colin Powell. The United States believed that Aristide had ceased to govern according to democratic principles. The OAS decision not to go forward with an investigation highlighted inherent inconsistencies between the OAS's formalized commitment to democratic governance and its maintenance in practice.

Explaining the CARICOM Response

Aristide's 2004 departure is one in a series of crises that raise questions about the sustainability of the regional multilateral organizations' commitment to representative democracy. The response of virtually all key international actors, including the United States, United Nations, and Organization of American States to Aristide's 2004 undemocratic departure from office was decidedly weaker than responses to similar crises in Venezuela and Peru. The response of the subregional organization CARICOM was the exception. At one level, this difference signals the significant obstacles that continue to impede the institutionalization of democratic norms for the major actors in the hemisphere. At another level it highlights the ability of subregional actors to behave in a more flexible and aggressive manner when threats to constitutional governance arise. The flexibility can be at least partially explained by the absence of a dominant superpower. The powerful role of the United States in the OAS and the UN Security Council is not found in CARICOM.

The Haitian crisis was the first significant test of CARICOM's commitment to representative democracy among its members. In the first official statement after the events of February 29, 2004, the press release issued by CARICOM heads of government was very critical of the response from the UN, United States, and Canada. The statement expresses "disappointment" over the Security Council's unwillingness "to take immediate action in response to appeals for assistance by the Government of Haiti" (CARICOM 2004c). In addition, the statement asserts, "Heads of Government were deeply perturbed at the contradictory reports surrounding the demission from office of the constitutionally elected President," and it goes on to call for a United Nations investigation to clarify the circumstances around the events of February 29, 2004. The tone of these comments contrasts sharply with the language of the OAS and UN, which does not call into question the collapse of support for the Plan of Action by the United States and France or the circumstances surrounding Aristide's departure from office.

In a statement issued after an emergency meeting on March 26, 2004, CARICOM's heads of government affirmed that they viewed Aristide's departure as an interruption in Haitian's constitutional governance. As a result, CARICOM released a statement that "these developments had not made it possible to receive the interim administration in the Councils of the Community" (CARICOM 2004d). Ambiguously, though, the same document goes on to state, "Haiti remains a member of the Caribbean Community." The Charter of Civil Society does not contain a provision to suspend member states, even when they are in violation of the charter.[24] According to the Council for Foreign and Community Relations, Haiti's full standing in the organization would be restored after free and fair elections, in compliance with international standards had taken place. This position highlights a procedural challenge for the community.[25] In order to strengthen the standards of good governnance among members, a state was de facto suspended, although the organization lacked a legal mechanism to do so.

In an advisory legal opinion, the CARICOM Secretariat argued that the Haitian state was distinct from the interim Haitian government. While the former retained its rights and privileges as a full member with participation in the "relevant Organs of the Community," the latter did not. The distinction hinged on the manner in which the interim government took power. Because its constitutionality was at best questionable, the CARICOM Secretariat reserved the right not to recognize and accredit the interim government. The same advisory opinion goes on to recognize that in contrast to Article 19 of the OAS Charter, CARICOM treaty arrangements do not provide measures for addressing interruptions in constitutional governance. In addition, the distinction between a binding treaty and a nonbinding charter is highlighted. "There are relevant provisions in the Charter of Civil Society concerning respect for political rights and good governance but the charter is not formally binding, has not been incorporated into the constituent documents of the Community, and has only general normative value."[26]

Two reasons were initially cited for the decision not to accept the interim Haitian government. The first was Latortue's own withdrawal of recognition of Jamaica's government following Aristide's visit to the island. The second rationale was the potential precedent set by recognizing the new government when the circumstances of Aristide's departure remained unclear. If CARICOM's normative commitment to democratic governance was to be taken seriously, the Haitian case required a strong response, and CARICOM responded accordingly. In comparison to the OAS response to crises in Peru and Venezuela, CARICOM's response was decidedly more assertive.

The impact that CARICOM's lack of recognition of the Haitian interim government may have on future cases remains to be seen, but its action does constitute a significant precedent for a Caribbean commitment to promoting representative democracy. It suggests a number of observations about the role of subregional organizations in democracy promotion. Several characteristics help explain the comparatively strong response from CARICOM. The first is the relative similarity among most member states. With the exception of Haiti and Jamaica, most members are microstates with populations significantly less than 1.5 million. Nearly all members are predominantly English-speaking former British colonies. For the most part, these states rely heavily on tourism as the basis of the economy. Most importantly, with the exception of Haiti, all member states are democratic. CARICOM is, on the whole, more democratic than both the OAS and the UN.[27] As a result, the cost of sanctioning undemocratic behavior among members is lower. Because there is a greater shared sense of what the good governance provisions of CARICOM's Civil Society Charter are, it is easier to determine when they have been violated and to forge collective action among members.[28]

In addition, the Haitian case posed a challenge to CARICOM's commitment to democracy that was qualitatively different from threats to democratic governance among OAS members, such as Peru or Venezuela (see the chapters by Boniface and Legler in this volume). The Haitian case, while complex, provides relatively conventional examples of breaches in democratic governance involving military coups or alleged violations of the Haitian Constitution.[29] In contrast, many hemispheric interruptions in constitutional governance since 1990 have involved authoritarian backsliding among democratic governments (Arnson 2001; Basombrio 2001; Boniface 2002). In these cases, the weakening of institutions frequently was initiated by democratically elected heads of state that centralized political power in the executive branch and reduced the institutional checks and balances on presidential authority (Cameron 2001; 2003).

A final important characteristic of CARICOM is the absence of a hegemonic power among its member states. The United States has played a significant role in the development of the OAS. During the Cold War, the OAS was limited in part because of the conflict between the United States and Soviet Union that played out in various countries in the hemisphere. In the aftermath of the Cold War, the United States has periodically worked to promote OAS mechanisms intended to strengthen democracy. However, other actions of the United States undermine hemispheric democracy promotion. OAS democracy promotion efforts have frequently conflicted with traditional U.S. security and trade promotion goals in the region, including U.S. drug-control operations, free-trade initiatives, and antiterrorism policies.[30] In addition to the United States, Mexico, Brazil, and Argentina are other important regional powers that frequently compete as alternative power blocs. In the aftermath of the 2000 Peruvian presidential elections, as the OAS met in Windsor, Ontario, Mexico opposed discussion of punitive measures against the Fujimori government. In part this position was attributed to the fear that similar actions might be taken against upcoming Mexican elections.[31] The absence of a single overarching political, economic, and military power among CARICOM states has minimized the type of geopolitical conflicts among members that has likely impeded OAS action with regard to threats to democratic governance.

The 2006 Presidential Elections in Haiti

Haiti's presidential elections originally scheduled for November 2005 were rescheduled multiple times with a first round of voting finally taking place on February 7, 2006. Significant logistical and constitutional issues hindered election preparations throughout 2005. Initially anemic voter registration drives were successful in registering nearly 75 percent of the eligible population. Distribution of the necessary voter identification cards was plagued with difficulties (International Crisis Group 2005). The nine-member Provisional Electoral Council (CEP) was chosen in June 2004 without the participation of Aristide's political party, Lavalas.

In spring 2005 the security situation continued to deteriorate. The United Nations Stabilization Mission in Haiti (MINUSTAH) and the Haitian National Police battled with armed drug gangs, former military forces who retain significant power, and forces loyal to former President Aristide. Violent clashes between the Haitian National Police, MINUSTAH forces, and criminal elements throughout Port-au-Prince increased in frequency and intensity. By late 2005 the security situation had improved but was still a significant problem. MINUSTAH worked to disarm various armed groups in Cité Soleil, La Saline, and other slums around Port-au-Prince with mixed success (Lindsay 2005).

On June 7, 2004, a CARICOM delegation met with Haiti's CEP. At that meeting, the CARICOM representative promised to support the electoral process and pledged technical assistance in the attempt to register, fingerprint, and provide national identification cards for nearly 4.5 million Haitian voters. In January 2005 the Organization of American States began voter registration efforts and received $44 million from international donors to support the process. Logistical problems continued during the lead-up to elections, including centralizing the location of polling places for security reasons and problems with the distribution of voter identification cards. The electoral law governing the election was passed in January 2005. The CEP encountered significant problems after many former Aristide loyalists were sacked. The replacement members expressed concerns about the security situation and the lack of communications equipment for groups working in the interior of the country. Tensions between the OAS delegation and the CEP existed over the handling of voter registration.

As election day approached, a total of thirty-three presidential candidates were registered. Observers from the OAS, European Union, Canada, and the United States supplemented the efforts of MINUSTAH and the CEP. Preelection polling showed former president René Préval as the front-runner with former president Leslie Manigat in second place. The field included former officials from the Duvalier regime, Aristide supporters, and a previous chief of police.

On February 7, 2006, voters turned out in massive numbers at more than 800 polling centers with more than 9,000 total polling stations around the country. In spite of the difficulties associated with the voter identification cards and registration efforts, approximately 3.5 million Haitians registered to vote.[32] Early on election day, voters began to complain about polls not opening on time, a lack of ballots, and difficulties with identification cards. These problems were not initially viewed as an attempt to manipulate the process in favor of a particular candidate but the outcome of the chaotic context in which the elections took place. At the close of voting on February 7, the process of tallying the votes began. The preliminary results reported on the CEP Web site on February 11 showed Préval with 50.33 percent of the vote and nearly 75 percent of all votes tallied. If the early projections held, Préval's slim majority would be enough to avoid a second round of voting.

As the count continued, two significant difficulties emerged. The first was the growing number of blank and invalid ballots. According to Article 185 of the electoral law, blank votes would be counted toward the total valid vote. The final count included 80,000 blank votes, roughly 4 percent of the total, which lowered Préval's total below the percent necessary to avoid a second round. Of additional concern were the 7.5 percent of the total, or 125,000 votes, that were declared invalid. The blank votes were counted toward the total, while the invalid ballots were excluded. In both cases, Préval's supporters took to the streets to protest the apparent irregularities and the possibility of a second round of voting. As the vote counting continued over the next several days, tensions and sporadic violence in Port-au-Prince increased. International and domestic observers contended that the irregularities were not systematic and that the overall vote was free and fair. The CEP was confronted with the dilemma of whether to include the blank votes, forcing a second round and increasing the likelihood of widespread violence or, alternatively, adopting some other compromise solution.

The second issue complicating the outcome was the discovery of thousands of partially destroyed ballots in a dump north of Port-au-Prince on February 14 (Thompson and Bracken 2006). It was unclear where the votes came from or who was responsible for their destruction. Many of the ballots were burned or blank, while others failed to indicate a clear candidate preference. The discovery increased tensions and further infuriated Préval's supporters, providing support for their claims of a conspiracy to deny Préval the presidency.

On the evening of February 15, diplomats from the United States, Brazil,

Chile, Canada, France, and the UN met with Préval and the CEP to discuss the situation. According to published accounts, two positions emerged (Mozingo 2006b). The French and Canadian position was to include the blank votes, with the likelihood of a second round of voting, although they recognized the growing problems with the vote count. The second proposal, called "the Belgian Option," would divide the blank votes proportionally among all of the candidates based on their existing vote totals. The adoption of this option gave Préval the necessary votes to win a first-round victory. On February 16 the CEP declared Préval the victor after resolving the blank-vote dilemma. While Préval's supporters and foreign diplomats celebrated both the decision and the peaceful resolution of the crisis, some of the other candidates criticized the outcome as far short of a free and fair election. Rather than ushering in a new era of political stability and compromise, some observers viewed the resulting situation as a continuation of the Haitian political status quo. Human rights advocate Jean-Claude Bajeuxö said, "We are going right back to where we have always been, where the crowds on the street, not elections, have the last say. We are close to losing an historic opportunity" (Thompson and Bracken 2006).

On May 14, 2006, René Préval was inaugurated for his second term as Haiti's president. In early June, CARICOM heads of state officially recognized Préval's government and reinstated Haiti as an active member state in the organization. The active role played by the Caribbean Community in addressing the post-Aristide Haitian crisis is important for hemispheric democracy promotion efforts. CARICOM's actions challenged U.S. dominance of the OAS but at the same time were constrained by the ability of the U.S. to shape the outcome of the crisis and limit investigation into events surrounding Aristide's leaving office. The Haitian crisis was a test case of CARICOM's commitment to democracy promotion. Both the end of Aristide's tenure and the circumstances surrounding the election of René Préval leave significant questions about the future of democracy in Haiti unanswered.

CARICOM and Future Democracy Promotion in Haiti

While the adoption of the Civil Society and Inter-American Democratic Charters by CARICOM member states represents a significant step toward strengthening the commitment to democracy, additional formal mechanisms must be developed to reinforce the role of civil society and the promotion of democratic norms. In February 2006 Prime Minister Kenneth Anthony of St.

Lucia called for the "immediate amendment to the CARICOM Charter of Civil Society . . . to authorize if necessary, expulsion of a member state which repudiates the democratic process by violence and intimidation" (CARICOM 2006). If CARICOM were to adopt such a measure, similar to Article 21 of the Inter-American Democratic Charter, the impact would be far-reaching. The absence of a hegemonic power such as the United States would increase the likelihood that such a measure might be applied on a more even basis. CARICOM could adopt a more assertive stance on member suspensions in the face of violations of constitutional governance.

Among the three relevant international organizations, the United Nations, the Organization of American States, and CARICOM, the latter appears best positioned to accept a forceful position on democracy promotion among member states. The United Nations' primary concerns in the hemisphere are security and peace-keeping, not democracy promotion. The OAS has played a very significant role in institutionalizing democracy promotion norms in the Inter-American Democratic Charter. Nonetheless, the application of those standards in crisis situations has proved more problematic, in part because of U.S. unwillingness to invoke the most demanding standards and in part because of the diversity of circumstances among the cases. With the failure of attempts to strengthen the Democratic Charter at the Fort Lauderdale General Assembly in 2005, OAS efforts appear to have stalled. CARICOM, with momentum from the Haitian crisis leading to a possible revised Civil Society Charter and because of its homogeneous nature, may be the best positioned of the three organizations to push the democracy promotion agenda in Haiti. Most significantly, CARICOM does not have a hegemon able to impose its will on all members and set the agenda.

Since the inauguration of the president and legislative elections in 2006, the immediate political crisis in Haiti has passed. In its place are the chronic problems of institutional underdevelopment, rampant organized criminal violence, and a profound absence of economic development. CARICOM can play an important role in Haitian economic development and the strengthening of its democratic institutions. For instance, many CARICOM member states could lend their experience to Haiti in the restoration of its tourist industry. Most of CARICOM's member states have an inherent advantage over many OAS states. CARICOM's member states, on the whole, enjoy a level of political stability and institutionalization as well as economic prosperity that is superior to many countries in Latin America. The experience of its Caribbean neighbors could be of great value to Haiti in the aftermath of nearly two decades of economic instability and political chaos.

NOTES

1. One regional official and supporter of Aristide's claim, who spoke with him on Friday evening, was surprised by the resignation the following evening.

2. The treaty was substantially revised in 2001.

3. With the exception of Montserrat, all members of CARICOM are also members of the OAS. As a result they all have ratified the Inter-American Democratic Charter of 2001 (see appendix B).

4. Author's interview with Bahamian foreign minister Fred Mitchell, March 7, 2005.

5. Informally, in 1997 a CARICOM observer team undertook an audit of disputed elections in Guyana.

6. Haiti ranked last among members with a per capita gross domestic product of $400.

7. The makeup of the Provisional Electoral Council was itself a subject of controversy. Article 192 of the Haitian Constitution requires that the nine council members be chosen from a list proposed by departmental government assemblies. In 1999 these assemblies had not been elected. As a result, President Préval chose its membership from individuals nominated by the political parties and not civil society or other actors.

8. The coalition consisted of U.S.-based social justice organizations, including the Quixote Center and Global Exchange.

9. Convergence represented a broad range of parties and organizations. With the exception of opposition to Aristide, there was little else on which the organizations' members agreed.

10. This mission represented the first time both the OAS and CARICOM formally joined together to intervene in a democratic crisis among member states.

11. In addition to the OAS, diplomatic overtures from Canada, France, the United States, and United Nations were attempted with little success.

12. As of October 2005 the European Union had partially reinstated some aid in part to support the upcoming elections.

13. Haiti became a provisional member in 1997. Full membership was contingent upon ratification by the newly elected National Assembly.

14. These paramilitary groups included former members of the Front for Advancement and Progress of Haiti and the National Liberation and Reconstruction Front (FLRN), led by former army and police officer Guy Philippe as well as former members of Duvalier's secret police, the Tonton Macoute.

15. On November 3, 2005, the interim government filed a lawsuit in Miami alleging Aristide and officials in his administration embezzled money from the treasury and the state-owned telephone company.

16. The border with the Dominican Republic was used as a staging ground for attacks by armed opposition forces who would cross and return.

17. Aristide had called for the introduction of a UN-led multinational peace-keeping force to limit the spread of violence until a solution could be negotiated.

18. I am grateful to Thomas Legler for this insight from his research.

19. The full plan included additional proposals to negotiate rules for demonstrations; for example, it called for the release of political detainees, the disarmament of gangs, the creation of a broad-based council, and implementation of CARICOM's Civil Society Charter. The section addressing a new prime minister and a greater role for opposition parties was Proposal 3, steps 1 and 2.

20. Article 149 also requires a new presidential election be held no longer than ninety days from the initial vacancy.

21. Negotiations called for the creation of a "Tripartite Council" that would appoint a seven-member "Council of Sages" who would be responsible for appointing a new prime minister in the absence of new elections.

22. CARICOM's call for a UN investigation was supported by the African Union.

23. Permanent Council/Resolution 806 (1303/02) was passed in the aftermath of the violence of December 2001. It called for the creation of an OAS mission to oversee a resolution to the crisis. Permanent Council/Resolution 822 (1331/02) called for the strengthening of democratic institutions and pledged to promote conditions for new national elections. It also expanded the mission created in Resolution 806. General Assembly/Resolution 1959 (6/2003) urged Lavalas and Democratic Convergence forces to work toward a negotiated settlement and an agreement on the makeup of the Provisional Electoral Council.

24. The Revised Treaty of Chaguaramas contains a provision to suspend member states for a budgetary provision. This has not been ratified by all member states and is not binding. Haiti's interim government has paid dues to CARICOM. Bahamian foreign minister and the current head of the Council for Foreign and Community Relations, Fred Mitchell, reiterated that Haiti was not suspended as there was no provision for suspension, but rather "there was no seat at the table for Haiti." Author's interview with Foreign Minister Mitchell, September 9, 2005.

25. At the first Inter-American Forum on Political Parties at Montego Bay, Jamaica, on April 29, 2005, Jamaican prime minister P. J. Patterson (Caribbean Net News 2005) said, "In Québec in Article 20 we said what the OAS would be required to do in cases where it appeared or it was claimed there was an improper interruption of constitutionally elected government. That is the litmus test and it must be applied whether they be governments of the right, of the centre or of the left."

26. I thank Dr. David Berry of the University of the West Indies for highlighting this distinction.

27. While most members of the OAS qualify as democratic, there has been greater variation and a larger number of crises of constitutional governance among its members. Haiti is the first significant test of CARICOM's commitment to democracy among its members.

28. Although there have been irregularities in elections observed by CARICOM, nothing has risen to the level of the Haitian cases. The praises of CARICOM's democracy promotion efforts are tempered by the fact that Haiti is a single case.

29. Here I refer to the 1991 coup against Aristide, the 2000 senatorial elections and their aftermath, and the end of Aristide's presidency in 2004 under questionable cir-

cumstances. Haiti is a member of both organizations, but the first two crises were addressed by the OAS.

30. For an example, see McClintock and Vallas (2003).

31. Author's interview with former Peruvian ambassador to the United States Ricardo V. Luna, August 2000.

32. The final number was 2.2 million voters; approximately 63% of registered voters cast a ballot (www.cep-ht.org/).

CHAPTER TEN

Venezuela 2002–2004

The Chávez Challenge

Thomas Legler

In April 2002 President Hugo Chávez was briefly ousted in a coup, but a combination of popular resistance and international condemnation of the coup helped restore him to power within thirty-six hours. The failed coup, however, did not quell opposition efforts to dislodge Chávez from power. During 2002 and 2003, the opposition, concentrated in an umbrella organization called the Coordinadora Democrática, variously organized a minor military rebellion, a national petition demanding Chávez's resignation, and a sixty-day national strike in the state-run petroleum sector that brought the country to a halt while it lasted. Thereafter, in 2003 and 2004, the Coordinadora Democrática's efforts turned to removing Chávez by constitutional means, via a national recall referendum that took place on August 15, 2004. Chávez won the referendum with 59 percent of the vote, consolidating his hold on power but also ultimately debilitating the Coordinadora Democrática and fragmenting the opposition. A weakened opposition organized a boycott of the December 2005 legislative elections and threatened to boycott the December 2006 presidential elections. Meanwhile, propelled by his referendum victory and by a petroleum export boom, Chávez has accelerated the implementation of his

"Bolivarian Revolution" at home and made efforts to export it abroad. He proposes the Bolivarian Revolution as an alternative to representative democracy and to neoliberal economic practices within the Western Hemisphere.

The Organization of American States (OAS) along with other international actors has actively sought to promote and defend democracy throughout the political crisis that has practically become an "existential struggle" between the Chávez government and its opposition (García-Guadilla, Mallén, and Guillén 2004; McCoy 2005a). Its pro-democracy efforts have included responding to the April 2002 coup against Chávez, facilitating dialogue between the government and opposition, providing technical assistance for and monitoring the August 2004 presidential recall referendum, and observing the subsequent December 2005 legislative elections.

Have the actions of the OAS had a democratizing effect on Venezuela? I argue that the OAS's record defending democracy in Venezuela has been mixed and has even led to some unintended consequences. I begin my analysis by examining the three main phases of OAS involvement in the Venezuelan crisis: the April 2002 coup; the OAS-facilitated democratic dialogue during 2002–3; and, finally, the presidential recall referendum process of 2003–4. In order to understand the OAS's uneven record, I explore the complexities, contradictions, and limits of the OAS's preferred mode of soft intervention. I conclude with a look ahead at the ongoing challenge that Hugo Chávez presents for the OAS.

The Coup of April 11, 2002, and the OAS Response

On April 11, 2002, a coup coalition led by business magnate Pedro Carmona and a group of high-ranking military officers arrested President Hugo Chávez and seized power. The coup can be linked to Chávez's efforts to bury the old Puntofijo political system that had been in force from 1958 to 1998 and replace its established political and economic elites with his supporters. The Puntofijo system had been built on two interconnected pillars: a two-party system in which the social democratic Democratic Action party (AD) shared power and economic wealth and alternated the presidency with the Christian democratic Committee for Independent Political Electoral Organization (COPEI); and an economic base founded on a lucrative state oil monopoly. For forty years, the Puntofijo system underpinned political stability, dynamic economic growth rates, and gradually expanding social inclusion. During the 1960s and 1970s when most Latin American countries found themselves mired in dictatorship, Venezuela was held up as a textbook success story of democracy in the Americas. By the 1980s and 1990s, however, Venezuela's political system had entered into a steady decline, marked by corruption scandals, declining oil prices, alarming rates of poverty, and widespread social exclusion.[1]

In December 1998 Chávez swept to victory on an electoral campaign platform in which he vowed to obliterate the old system in favor of a new pro-poor program of direct democracy, economic redistribution, and nationalism that he called the "Bolivarian Revolution."[2] Chávez systematically excluded former AD and COPEI elites and party faithful from state positions and perks in what Jennifer McCoy (1999) has called the end of Venezuela's "partyarchy."[3] Chávez's break with the traditions of Puntofijo triggered an intense intraelite struggle for survival between the old guard and the new Chávez elites. AD, COPEI, affiliated oil and business elites, and the AD-affiliated Venezuelan Workers' Federation became key actors in the opposition to Hugo Chávez.

At first fragmented, the opposition became united by a series of occurrences during 2001 and early 2002. First, the Bolivarian Revolution failed to deliver many tangible goods during the first few years of the Chávez presidency. Instead, the economy grew worse due to a combination of capital flight and slumping oil prices. Second, in November 2001 Chávez began to use special powers to issue a series of forty-nine far-reaching decrees, a development that incensed many citizens. The perceived "cubanization" of education and health through Chávez's introduction of legions of Cuban teachers and physicians, Chávez's increasingly confrontational stance toward the United States, and the Chávez government's determined efforts to win control over the Venezuelan Workers' Federation also mobilized considerable discontent.

The opposition launched a series of protests that included a one-day general strike on December 10, 2001, and calls by opposition sympathizers in the military for Chávez to step down in early February 2002. Behind the scenes, the growing resistance to Chávez caused a split in the ranks of Chávez supporters between hard-liners and soft-liners on the issue of how to deal with the opposition. Key players defected, such as moderate Luis Miquilena, Chávez's interior minister until January 2001 (Ellner and Rosen 2002). The final blow in a sequence of destabilizing events was Chávez's attempt to wrest control of Venezuela's state oil monopoly from its pro-opposition management and oil workers' union. Petroleos de Venezuela, Sociedad Anónima (PDVSA) was one of the few remaining bastions of power of the old Puntofijo elites. On April 6,

2002, the government announced the firing of seven PDVSA executives who were then replaced by Chávez supporters. In response, on April 9, Carlos Ortega, the leader of the Venezuelan Workers' Federation, and Pedro Carmona Estanga, president of Venezuela's National Federation of Chambers of Commerce, led another general strike to protest the dismissals. On April 11, the third day of the strike, a march of some 200,000 protesters originally destined for PDVSA headquarters was incited by organizers and the media to press onward to the presidential palace of Miraflores to demand Chávez's resignation. In the course of the march toward the palace, opposition protestors encountered throngs of Chávez supporters in the center of the city. Shots broke out from unidentified gunmen located on the bridges in the vicinity of the march, killing at least 10 protestors and wounding nearly 100.

The violence prompted some high-ranking military officials to make televised calls for civil disobedience against the Chávez government. In the early hours of April 12, General Lucas Rincón Romero made a televised announcement that President Chávez had resigned. Subsequent television footage showed Chávez being put under arrest. Pedro Carmona Estanga was sworn in as Venezuela's president, even though the vice president and the head of Congress were next in the constitutionally established line of succession.

The first phase of OAS involvement in the Venezuelan crisis began on April 11, 2002. OAS secretary-general Gaviria issued a statement on the situation in Venezuela, deploring the violence of that day and calling on both protestors and the government to conduct themselves peacefully and with respect for democracy and the rule of law (OAS 2002g).[4] When news filtered in about the coup, Gaviria convened a marathon emergency session of the Permanent Council that began on the evening of Friday, April 12, and lasted until Sunday, April 14. During the first hours following Chávez's ouster, the OAS's response to the coup was delayed, but for good reason. The Rio Group, a regional body established in 1986 that serves as a forum for dialogue between Latin American countries without United States participation, was holding a presidential-level meeting at the time that the coup unfolded.[5] Since the Permanent Representatives of many OAS member states would be taking their cues from their presidents and foreign ministers who were gathered in San José, Costa Rica, for the Rio Group meeting, OAS secretary-general Gaviria thought it prudent to await instructions from the Rio Group. The Rio Group (2002) hastily and unanimously issued the Declaration of the Rio Group on the Situation in Venezuela. The declaration condemned the interruption of the constitutional order in Venezuela and requested that the OAS secretary-general immediately convene a special session of the Permanent Council under Article 20 of the Inter-American Democratic Charter (see appendix B).

The Permanent Council's deliberations yielded Resolution 811, which condemned the coup as an alteration of the constitutional order in Venezuela (OAS 2002f). Resolution 811 authorized an urgent mission led by Secretary-General Gaviria for the purposes of fact-finding and promoting the normalization of Venezuela's democratic order through his position's good offices. The resolution called for a special session of the OAS General Assembly on April 18 at which Gaviria would deliver his mission report and the Assembly would adopt whatever measures it deemed appropriate.

Because of internal divisions within the coup coalition, popular resistance within Venezuela, and a lack of international support, the coup government lasted barely thirty-six hours. President Carmona alienated both domestic and international support on April 12 by issuing a series of antidemocratic decrees characteristic of a classic coup d'etat: suspending the constitution, dissolving the National Assembly, firing Supreme Court judges, and ordering the arrest of key members of the Chávez government. Simultaneously, once the word spread that Chávez had not resigned but instead had been forcefully ousted, thousands of Chávez supporters from the poorer areas of Caracas mobilized in front of Miraflores Palace demanding his restoration. Key military units declared their support for Chávez. Faced with the prospect of defending an unpopular interim president, military officers who had hitherto supported Carmona called for his resignation. Chávez militants and loyal paratroopers were able to reestablish control over the presidential palace during the afternoon and evening of April 13, prompting Carmona to flee. At 3:00 a.m. on April 14, Chávez returned by helicopter from a naval base on the island of Orchila where he had been held captive.

The coup episode highlights some of the persistent challenges faced by the OAS in mounting effective responses to threats to democracy. First, despite provisions in the new Inter-American Democratic Charter (OAS 2001b) to help prevent political crises from occurring,[6] the OAS failed to act in a proactive fashion to prevent Venezuela's descent into full-blown political crisis. No special Permanent Council or General Assembly sessions were held to consider the deteriorating situation in Venezuela. An expression of concern by Secretary-General Gaviria criticizing Colonel Pedro Soto for attempting to incite military rebellion in February 2002 was the only OAS action during the tide of events in Venezuela that led up to the coup (OAS 2002b). As in so many previous cases, such as the crises in Peru (1992, 2000), Haiti (1991), and Paraguay (1996, 1999), the OAS again found itself in "firefighting" mode (Acevedo and Grossman 1996, 148). In fairness, however, there was little the OAS could do in the months prior to the coup without a formal request from the Chávez government for assistance. Such an invitation was never issued.

The coup episode also underscores the necessity of reliable information for effective OAS action. As the Permanent Council deliberated a course of action, its ability to respond decisively and rapidly was hampered by conflicting reports of what was happening as well as a fluid situation in Venezuela. One source of confusion was the question of whether Chávez had formally resigned or been forced from office. The confusion convinced the Permanent Council of the need to gather more information before making any dramatic decisions, such as suspending Venezuela's membership in the OAS. This, of course, delayed the passage of Resolution 811, such that Chávez was already on his way back to power before the OAS had defined its course of action.

In the immediate aftermath of the coup, the OAS confronted another recurring problem with pro-democracy interventions: the question of how to sustain its engagement on the ground in order to strengthen democracy and encourage national reconciliation. Pursuant to Resolution 811, Secretary-General Gaviria made a fact-finding mission to Venezuela on April 15–17. The subsequent special General Assembly held on April 18 produced Resolution 1 (OAS 2002h), which established a certain degree of oversight via a previously scheduled site visit by the Inter-American Commission on Human Rights. As this visit had been planned prior to the coup in response to an official invitation from the Venezuelan government in September 1999, the Venezuelan government was not in a position to refuse. Nonetheless, newly restored in office, President Chávez at first refused other OAS offers of support. It would take a further deterioration of the political situation before Chávez endorsed a renewed role for the OAS in Venezuela.

Even so, there were some positive developments for the OAS. With the exception of the United States and its allies Colombia and El Salvador, the vast majority of OAS member states condemned the coup. Even Mexico, a perennial defender in the OAS of the rights of self-determination and non-intervention, strongly criticized Carmona's illegal seizure of power. In stark contrast, the United States appeared to support the overthrow of Chávez.[7] Latin American and Caribbean consensus helped convincingly strengthen one of the Americas' new regional democracy norms: classic coups d'etat were unacceptable as a means of changing governments. The acceptance of this norm was illustrated by the fact that the U.S. government found itself compelled to backpedal on the earlier statements it had made that seemed to endorse the coup. By extension, the incident also underlined that the collective leadership by OAS member states on the democracy issue was powerful enough to (re)shape the U.S. agenda on Venezuela.

After the Coup: OAS Dialogue Facilitation

The second phase of OAS pro-democracy activity in Venezuela developed after the coup. It involved promotion and facilitation of dialogue between government and opposition. By June 2002, it was clear that the Chávez government's efforts to promote dialogue with the opposition had failed and that the political situation in the country had once again begun to deteriorate. Thousands of opposition supporters took repeatedly to the streets to demand Chávez's resignation. Chávez turned to former U.S. president Jimmy Carter, requesting his help to foster dialogue between government and opposition. At that point in time, however, opposition leaders perceived Carter as an ally of Chávez and refused to endorse his efforts to initiate talks. Finally, in August the Venezuelan foreign minister extended an invitation to the OAS to foster dialogue, but with a catch: the Carter Center and the United Nations Development Program (UNDP) were also invited to collaborate in the effort.

While a tripartite mission comprised of the OAS, Carter Center, and the UNDP seemingly added an unnecessary layer of complexity that could have conceivably hindered attempts to get the two sides talking, in hindsight the three actors operated with surprising complementarities. Secretary-General Gaviria as chief facilitator and mission leader had to be extra sensitive in respecting Venezuela's sovereignty and in avoiding any actions that might be construed as partial, but President Carter and the Carter Center faced no such restraints. Carter enjoyed the benefit of an amicable relationship with Chávez and, unlike Gaviria, had the ability to make proposals without worrying so much what the Permanent Council might think. The UNDP provided welcome technical and logistical support for the mission.

Chávez's decision to have the OAS, Carter Center, and UNDP participate jointly in the mission had the unintended consequence of expanding diplomatic efforts beyond traditional inter-American multilateralism (Cooper and

Legler 2006). The inclusion of the Carter Center added an important nonstate component to regional multilateralism that was normally the exclusive domain of states and their leaders. This provides an interesting illustration of how democracy promotion is a constitutive process in which the arrows of influence point in both directions: not only did international intervention have an impact on Venezuela, but the demands of problem solving on the ground in Venezuela resulted in the modification of multilateralism.

As in the cases of Peru (2000) and Haiti (2001–4), the centerpiece of the mission's effort was the creation of the Roundtable for Negotiation and Agreements or Mesa de Negociación y Acuerdos, facilitated by Secretary-General Gaviria himself.[8] After several months of groundwork by OAS, Carter Center, and UNDP officials, the *mesa* was formally launched on November 8, 2002. It comprised an impartial facilitator (Gaviria) and six representatives each from the Venezuelan government and the opposition. Each side was also allowed one adviser. In the beginning, the tripartite mission attempted to get the two sides to agree to a common, twelve-point agenda. When this proved impossible, the mission refocused efforts on getting the government and opposition representatives to endorse a more limited agenda and set of rules. As laid out in the *Declaración de principios por la paz y la democracia en Venezuela* (OAS 2002a, 2002c) and the *Síntesis operativa* (OAS 2002d), the dialogue participants agreed to focus their discussions on three key issues: the strengthening of the electoral system, the establishment of a truth commission to investigate the violence of April 11–13, and civilian disarmament.

Progress in dialogue negotiations was painfully slow. Neither the government nor the opposition originally channeled its full energies into the *mesa* process. For the Chávez government, the international presence enhanced its legitimacy and dissuaded any would-be coup conspirators. Chávez's allies possessed a majority in Congress so the *mesa* had no particular use as a parallel congress.[9] The opposition participated in the OAS-facilitated dialogue process but treated it as but one of several tracks in a multitrack strategy to oust the Chávez government. The opposition continued to pressure the government through highly confrontational means including mass demonstrations, an attempted rebellion by anti-Chávez military officers, a "consultative referendum" that purportedly gathered more than 2 million signatures to demand Chávez's resignation, and a two-month general strike led by petroleum workers that paralyzed the country during December 2002 and January 2003.[10]

It took the strike as a "detonator" event to focus government and opposition energies on dialogue (Cooper and Legler 2005; 2006). The two-month general strike led by the Coordinadora Democrática not only hurt the economy but also seriously crippled opposition ranks. Many business supporters were bankrupted by the action, while thousands of opposition sympathizers lost their jobs or valuable income because of the work stoppages. While the government managed to weather the strike, the opposition was severely weakened. Forced to put major street tactics on hold, the opposition turned its efforts toward finding a negotiated solution to the crisis, favoring a proposal made in January 2003 by Jimmy Carter advocating either early elections or a presidential recall referendum as the means to escape the current political deadlock (Carter 2003).

In the end, the two sides agreed to an avenue proposed by President Chávez from the beginning: a presidential recall referendum as stipulated in Article 72 of the Venezuelan Constitution. The formal outcome of the Table of Negotiation and Agreements was the May 23 Agreement (OAS 2003a). It endorsed the recall referendum as a democratic, constitutional solution to the crisis and also created an important follow-up role for the OAS as the referendum's guarantor. Concretely, the OAS would continue to facilitate communications between government and opposition via a Comisión de Enlace or Linkage Commission.

The *mesa* in Venezuela has been described as an example of an emerging OAS mode of action: intervention without intervening (Cooper and Legler 2006). That is, the OAS (together with the Carter Center and the UNDP) inserted itself into Venezuelan domestic politics with minimal intrusion into its political decisions. The OAS effectively moved inside the political life of a member state while treading softly. At the same time, the OAS left the details of political change to the Venezuelan elites themselves. Secretary-General Gaviria took great pains to serve as a neutral, impartial dialogue facilitator rather than a decision maker.

This soft mode of intervention did not mean that the OAS was powerless (Cooper and Legler 2006). Although Gaviria's role was restrained, he enjoyed certain subtle but powerful soft-power resources to influence the dialogue process without participating in the actual decision making.[11] First, Gaviria and his team played a pivotal role in establishing the agenda for discussion as well as the rules for participation at the *mesa*. Second, the OAS facilitation process helped prompt the fragmented opposition forces to unite and articulate the Coordinadora Democrática as the single legitimate interlocutor before the Chávez government.[12] Third, because Gaviria as facilitator also served as the *mesa*'s official spokesperson, his public announcements could be used as a tool to keep both sides committed to agreements made at the table. Finally, as the concrete local embodiment of an inter-American commitment to defend democracy, Gaviria and his team were a constant reminder to domestic elites that undemocratic means of resolving the crisis were unacceptable in the eyes of the international community.

Paradoxically, then, intervention without intervening meant both treading softly and leaving lasting imprints. Ultimately, OAS dialogue facilitation enabled nationals to address their own political crisis, something they would not likely have been willing or able to do without an external helping hand, given the highly polarized context of Venezuelan politics. While the process of dialogue at the *mesa* was initially very slow, during its existence from October 2002 through May 2003, it provided a vital link for communication between Venezuela's polarized elites. The fact that the *mesa* provided a venue for communications during the tensest moments of the opposition-led general strike and that both sides at the *mesa* had pledged not to resort to violence undoubtedly helped prevent an explosion of violence in Venezuela. In this way, the OAS was able to intervene in defense of democracy within a member state without violating the sovereignty rights held so sacred by its member states.

The Presidential Recall Referendum of August 15, 2004

The third phase of OAS's involvement in the Venezuela crisis came during the August 15, 2004, presidential recall referendum.[13] The Chávez government and the opposition had formally committed themselves through the May 23 agreement to pursue the referendum as the means to resolve their conflict. As stipulated in Article 72 of the Venezuelan Constitution, any elected official in the country could be subject to a recall referendum provided those in favor of such a measure raised the required number of supporting signatures, a number equivalent to a minimum of 20 percent of registered voters. In the case of President Chávez, Article 72 meant that the opposition had to collect 2,436,083 signatures in order to trigger a recall referendum. This was the first time such a referendum had been attempted. Accordingly, the lack of precedent meant that the Venezuelan National Electoral Council (CNE) found itself inventing a plethora of procedures and regulations as the process unfolded. The referendum process took nearly a year from start to finish, far exceeding constitutional time limits. The OAS and its partners, the Carter Center and the UNDP, were invited to provide technical assistance, facilitate negotiations between government and opposition, and monitor all phases of the referendum.

There were four phases to the referendum. First, the CNE formally issued the dates of November 28 to December 1, 2003, as the period in which the opposition would be permitted to undertake a formal signature collection. This process was monitored closely by both Chávez supporters and international observers from the OAS and the Carter Center. On December 19, the opposition delivered approximately 3.4 million signatures gathered during the formal collection period to the CNE.

The second phase was a formal count and verification of the signatures by the CNE. This process formally began on January 13, 2004. Despite a thirty-day time limit stipulated in the Constitution, the CNE took until March 7 to make an *initial* announcement about the results of its verification process. The delay raised suspicions of wrongdoing by the CNE. The preliminary CNE result heightened the opposition's concerns: the CNE had invalidated more than 900,000 signatures on the grounds of "similar handwriting" on the signature forms.[14] The Coordinadora Democrática argued that on numerous occasions opposition signature collection officials had filled in the personal information required for those who signed, but that this in no way invalidated the signatories' distinct signatures and fingerprints. Chávez supporters accused the opposition of attempting to perpetrate fraud. The CNE's preliminary announcement nullifying so many signatures triggered mass protests by the opposition, leading to violent clashes with police. At this point the OAS and the Carter Center issued public statements that strongly criticized the CNE for not respecting the will of the 900,000 signatories whose signatures had not been honored. They watched with concern as violence in Venezuela's streets mounted.

On April 23, 2004, more than four months after the opposition had originally submitted the signatures, the CNE announced its final verification results. The CNE declared 1,910,965 signatures valid and 375,241 completely invalid. Under pressure both domestically and from abroad, the CNE declared that an additional 1,192,914 signatures were considered invalid due to "similar handwriting," but that a third phase of the recall referendum would take place in which opposition supporters whose signatures had been rejected would be given a chance to "repair" them (Carter Center 2005, 28).

Because no provisions existed in the Constitution for such a signature repair process, the CNE accepted an offer from the OAS and the Carter Center to help it facilitate negotiations between the Chávez administration and the opposition in order to agree upon a set of procedures for this third phase of the recall referendum. Following intense negotiations and lengthy preparations, the signature repair process took place from May 28–31, 2004. According to an agreement between the two sides, "repair" meant that signatories would have the right either to confirm a signature or to retract it. As a precondition for supporting the repair process, the Chávez government insisted on the option for citizens to withdraw their signatures, alleging that employees who were pro-Chávez had been intimidated by their pro-opposition employers into signing. This briefly raised the concern among the opposition that a flood of citizens would remove their signatures under pressure from pro-government forces and defeat their bid for a referendum. On June 3, the CNE announced that through the repair process the opposition had indeed raised the number of signatures required for a recall referendum against President Chávez.

The fourth and final phase of the process was the referendum itself. On August 15, 2004, an impressive 70 percent of the electorate turned out to vote. In the early hours of August 16, the CNE announced that President Chávez had defeated the opposition bid to oust him via referendum by a vote of 5,800,629 to 3,989,008; 59 percent of voters had declared their support for Chávez, while 41 percent had cast their vote for his recall. Based on their own observation and a secret quick count of referendum votes, the OAS and Carter Center rapidly issued public statements confirming the CNE's official result.

Key elements of the opposition refused to accept the result and accused the OAS and the Carter Center of complicity in a massive fraud orchestrated by the government-controlled CNE. The OAS and the Carter Center responded by encouraging the CNE to conduct a post-referendum audit. Chávez supporters, the opposition, the OAS, the Carter Center, and other international observers were all invited to monitor the CNE audit. The opposition opted to boycott it. The audit reaffirmed Chávez's victory in the referendum but failed to convince the opposition. Once regarded as heroes who had successfully pressured the CNE to hold a signature repair process, the OAS and the Carter Center became vilified by the opposition.

In the end the referendum did not prove to be the solution to Venezuela's political crisis. It did not lead to national reconciliation as the opposition refused to accept its result. While Chávez won the referendum, more than 40 percent of the electorate had voted against him. Such a plebiscite in a highly polarized context was bound to be divisive (McCoy 2005a). Nonetheless, the referendum did help to improve democratic governability in the sense that Chávez's landslide victory furnished him with a renewed popular mandate and at the same time sealed the fate of the Coordinadora Democrática. Within months, the sting of defeat and bitter infighting led to its eventual dissolution. Following the referendum, Chávez no longer faced a serious challenge from the opposition and for the first time could govern without serious resistance. With the demise of the Coordinadora Democrática following the referendum, the OAS's principal tool for continued engagement in Venezuela, the Comisión de Enlace (Linkage Commission), also became defunct.

Assessing the OAS Record in Venezuela

Did the OAS's efforts to defend and promote democracy during Venezuela's crisis have a democratizing effect? On the positive side, widespread condemnation by OAS member states of the April 2002 coup helped to delegitimize the short-lived coup government and defend an elected head of state, thus helping to restore Chávez to power. OAS and Carter Center efforts helped steer the Venezuelan government and opposition energies and rivalry into a constitutional and democratic route provided through the presidential recall referendum mechanism found in Article 72 of the Venezuelan Constitution. Ongoing OAS facilitation of intraelite dialogue also helped maintain vital channels of communication between government and opposition and in all likelihood helped prevent Venezuela from erupting in political violence and civil war. The presidential recall referendum that the OAS promoted and observed also awarded Chávez with renewed democratic legitimacy. Ultimately, the OAS presence in Venezuela during 2003 and 2004 helped Chávez to consolidate his power with a renewed popular mandate.

On a less positive note, as in previous political crises in the region in which the OAS had intervened, we encounter the recurrence of two problems for which the Inter-American Democratic Charter was supposed to provide the necessary countermeasures: crisis prevention and sustained engagement. Despite clear signs of the deterioration of the political situation in Venezuela, the OAS was not able to prevent the April 2002 coup. It also encountered ongoing difficulty in staying engaged in Venezuela following the coup and after the August 2004 recall referendum, although the political crisis had not fully abated.

In December 2005, despite a previous pledge to the OAS electoral observation mission, the five main opposition political parties boycotted the legislative elections, ostensibly out of concern that the CNE was under the partisan control of Chávez sympathizers. The uncontested elections allowed Chávez's own political party, Movimiento Quinta República, and its political allies to gain complete control over Congress. The absence of opposition legislators in Congress eliminated the one remaining forum for dialogue between Chávez supporters and opposition. As Venezuelans approached the contentious December 2006 presidential election, there were no major mechanisms in place to promote dialogue and communication between the two sides, and the OAS no longer had an on-the-ground presence.

Furthermore, the Chávez government has been guilty of a series of undemocratic measures that add up to incremental authoritarian backsliding, yet this provoked little response from the OAS. First, Chávez undertook what arguably constitutes authoritarian backsliding at the same time that the OAS and its partners, the Carter Center and the UNDP, were present in Venezuela. In early 2004, at the height of the referendum process, Chávez initiated legislation to increase the size of the Supreme Court by twelve new justices and stack it with his loyalists. The OAS secretary-general and the Permanent Council did not officially protest this action, although it clearly undermined the separation of powers in Venezuela. They were surely concerned not to jeopardize the OAS presence on the ground during the crucial referendum process, because their presence relied on the consent of the Venezuelan government. However, OAS silence on this issue had a high price: permitting the undermining of judicial independence.

As noted, thanks in part to the OAS's efforts to defend democracy, Chávez emerged from the referendum more powerful than ever. Disturbingly, in the aftermath of the referendum, he has used his democratically elected position to continue to chip away at Venezuelan democracy.[15] Press releases from the Inter-American Commission on Human Rights have painted a worrisome picture. A new International Cooperation Law passed by the pro-Chávez Congress severely constrains the ability of Venezuelan nongovernmental organizations (NGOs) to obtain external funding. It requires them to be included in a government NGO registry and provide full accounting of all foreign funding they receive at the request of the government or any individual (CIDH 2006b). A Social Responsibility Law threatens media freedom and violates the American Convention on Human Rights by subjecting journalists to the threat of criminal sanctions for criticizing public authorities (CIDH 2004). Similarly, despite the fact that Chávez himself has used undiplomatic language to verbally insult such heads of state as George W. Bush of the United States, Alejandro Toledo of Peru, and Vicente Fox of Mexico, Article 147 of the Venezuelan Criminal Code now states that anyone who fails to respect the Venezuelan president may be subject to a prison term ranging from three to thirty months.[16]

The 2005 annual report of the Inter-American Commission on Human Rights (CIDH 2006a) criticizes the Venezuelan government on a disturbing number of counts: for the persistence of provisional judges appointed by the president and a largely transitional justice system; the use of military courts against civilians; the maintenance and misuse by authorities of a list containing the names and personal information of those who signed the referendum against Chávez;[17] and hostility and threats against human rights activists in Venezuela. The OAS has been either unwilling or unable to challenge this additional incremental erosion of democracy by the Chávez government.

International efforts to support Chávez as an elected leader inadvertently helped strengthen a leader intent on challenging both representative democracy and the defense-of-democracy regime in the Americas. Despite the fact that Chávez was a personal beneficiary of the OAS's collective defense of democracy in April 2002, his government's foreign policy (with its emphasis on sovereignty, nonintervention, and self-determination) has become an obstacle to OAS efforts to mount other pro-democracy interventions, particularly because the OAS is an organization that arrives at decisions by consensus. Ostensibly Chávez is promoting an alternative vision of participatory democracy and social justice. He is critical of what he considers the elitist bent of representative democracy as well as what he sees as the perversion of democracy through the poverty and inequality created by neoliberal economic policies.[18] His regional project includes the negotiation of a Social Charter, alongside the existing Inter-American Democratic Charter, that would enshrine social justice and popular participation as regional norms. Some observers, such as the Friends of the Democratic Charter, worry that his proposed Social Charter would contradict the existing Democratic Charter rather than bolster it.[19]

Chávez's rising influence in the region since the 2004 referendum, together with the exacerbation of conflict with the United States, has had the effect of "geopoliticizing" ongoing efforts by the OAS to promote and protect democracy. For example, Chávez has quite vocally and justifiably called into question the intentions of U.S. government statements and actions with respect to democracy. By raising the specter of U.S. imperialism, Chávez has resurrected

Latin American concerns about defending sovereignty at a time when OAS secretary-general Insulza and others long to strengthen the OAS's ability to intervene in member countries to defend democracy.

Ironically, Chávez himself has not respected the norms of self-determination and nonintervention he defends. He has, for example, sought to influence the outcome of various presidential elections in the region. His government allegedly provided financial backing for the populist candidates Evo Morales during the December 2005 Bolivian elections and for Ollanta Humala during the Peruvian April and June 2006 elections. In the latter case, then-president Toledo and presidential candidate Alan Garcia lodged official diplomatic protests against Chávez's intrusions in Peruvian affairs. Despite these protests and the strong criticism by the chief of the OAS election monitoring mission in Peru, Lloyd Axworthy, neither the OAS secretary-general nor the Permanent Council censured Chávez for his conduct.

In sum, OAS attempts to protect and promote democracy in Venezuela have had decidedly mixed and even contradictory results. These contradictory outcomes can be explained by examining the OAS's preferred mode of soft intervention. As distinct from hard forms of intervention such as the use of military force or economic sanctions,[20] in Venezuela and other crisis cases, the OAS has utilized and honed diplomatic tools of soft intervention such as fact-finding missions, site visits by the Inter-American Commission on Human Rights, the facilitation of intraelite dialogue, and election observation.

For a variety of reasons, the OAS with only a few exceptions has found itself restricted to employing soft forms of intervention in order to defend and promote democracy.[21] There have been two main constraints on OAS soft intervention. First, in developing the regional defense-of-democracy regime, OAS member states put a crucial limit on collective interventions in defense of democracy: they could only be launched at the express invitation of the host government under threat. The proviso that OAS pro-democracy interventions require the consent of the host government reflects ongoing tension between newer regional democracy norms and more established sovereignty norms. This tension is apparent in Article 2(b) of the OAS Charter, which sets out the following potentially contradictory purpose of the OAS: "To promote and consolidate representative democracy, with due respect for the principle of nonintervention" (OAS 1997). This article is reiterated in the opening preamble clause of the Democratic Charter (OAS 2001b). A strong tradition of upholding the sovereign rights of nonintervention, self-determination, and territorial inviolability in the Americas, enshrined in Articles 3(e) and 19 of the OAS Charter, has constrained the ability of the OAS to launch actions to defend democracy.

The juxtaposition of democracy and sovereignty norms also affects what kind of democracy multilateral agents can defend and promote. This explains why we find OAS activity concentrated in soft forms of intervention that are consistent with member states' interests, such as OAS election observation missions, which help governments achieve an external stamp of approval on their election processes, or OAS dialogue facilitation, which helps governments project a positive image to the international community without necessarily committing to concrete reforms. It also explains why OAS intervention is more likely, as in Paraguay in 1996 or Nicaragua in 2005, when the incumbent government finds itself in imminent danger of being ousted undemocratically.

By contrast, the OAS has found it most difficult to mount efforts to defend democracy when incumbent elected leaders, such as Chávez in Venezuela or Fujimori in Peru, undertake measures that undermine democracy in their own countries. In these instances, the sovereignty-democracy norm nexus can lead to a perverse situation in which the OAS must obtain permission from a potential pariah government in order to intervene to defend democracy. As has been elaborated elsewhere (Jackson 1990; Philpott 2001), governments that are members of intergovernmental organizations such as the OAS can invoke sovereignty rights to prevent international efforts to hold them accountable for their abuses of democracy and human rights.

Second, the regional normative context overlaps with an important geopolitical dimension to OAS efforts to defend democracy, that of U.S.-Latin American relations. During the 1990s, unprecedented excellent relations between U.S. and Latin American political and economic elites underpinned the expansion of the fledgling OAS collective-defense-of-democracy regime. In stark contrast, in the new millennium regional geopolitics has taken a dramatically negative turn (Hakim 2006; Shifter and Jawahar 2006). Actions by the Bush administration have resurrected a collective Latin American memory of past unilateral and undemocratic U.S. intervention. In addition to its much criticized conduct during the April 2002 coup against Chávez, for example, the U.S. government has sparked controversy for some of its actions in Haiti, Ecuador, Bolivia, and Nicaragua. During January and February 2004, the United States raised suspicions about its commitment to representative democracy when it refused to invoke the Inter-American Democratic Charter in defense of elected president Jean-Bertrand Aristide against an armed rebellion in Haiti. U.S. forces subsequently transported Aristide by airplane into exile in the Central African Republic. In Ecuador, the U.S. government triggered widespread popular Ecuadorian resentment for supporting the government of Lucio Gutiérrez, despite clear signs of authoritarian backsliding prior to his fall in April 2005. During Bolivia's presidential election in 2005, U.S. officials were outspoken critics of leftist presidential candidate Evo Morales. Similarly, during the run-up to the November 2006 Nicaraguan elections, U.S. embassy personnel and other officials appeared to campaign against presidential candidate Daniel Ortega and, accordingly, interfere in Nicaraguan affairs. These types of actions have made many OAS member states reluctant to support new interventions that could be manipulated by the United States for ends other than democracy.

There is little doubt that prospects for future OAS efforts to defend democracy have been complicated by the present state of geopolitics in the region. As evidence, Latin American and Caribbean member states resoundingly rejected a United States proposal to strengthen the Inter-American Democratic Charter at the OAS General Assembly in Fort Lauderdale in June 2005 (see Hawkins and Shaw and Levitt in this volume). They perceived the U.S. proposal for a mechanism to monitor member state compliance with the Inter-American Democratic Charter as a thinly veiled attempt to find the means to attack its enemy, Venezuela, and not as a genuine effort to strengthen the OAS's capacity for defending democracy. In short, the worsening of United States–Latin American relations has put a damper on the inter-American cooperation necessary for the collective-defense-of-democracy regime both to work and to be strengthened.

Venezuelan Democracy's Death by a Thousand Cuts?

On December 3, 2006, President Hugo Chávez was reelected by landslide, winning almost 63 percent of the vote, with runner-up Manuel Rosales polling approximately 37 percent. Although the election observation missions of the OAS and the European Union identified persistent problems of ample use of public resources for Chávez's election campaign (and, to a much lesser extent, for Rosales'), widespread institutional propaganda in favor of the incumbent, voter coercion against public employees, and unbalanced media coverage, both claimed that the election was peaceful and transparent and complied with international standards (European Union 2006a, 2006b; OAS 2006c).

Even though some positive gains were made, OAS efforts to defend democracy in Venezuela between 2002 and 2004 revealed serious ongoing limits to its preferred mode of soft intervention. Following the 2006 presidential election, the situation in Venezuela underlined the pressing need to address and resolve such limitations. Although Rosales and his electoral coalition officially recognized Chávez's victory and their own defeat, the Venezuelan government and opposition still lack formal institutional channels for communication or dialogue. Despite the fact that the OAS identified an urgent need for resuming national dialogue following the December 2005 legislative elections, which the opposition boycotted,[22] it has not been invited to lend international assistance.

Meanwhile, Chávez made no secret of his intention to remain in power indefinitely. On September 1, 2006, he vowed to supporters at a political rally in Caracas that he would organize a referendum in 2010 to change his own Constitution in order to remove any limit on the number of terms he could serve as president. As noted, Chávez since 2004 has undertaken a series of highly criticized measures that have incrementally eroded Venezuelan democracy. Barely after the votes were counted, Chávez announced publicly on December 29, 2006, that his government would not renew the broadcasting license of Radio Caracas Television (RCTV), one of two remaining pro-opposition mass media companies. A few days later, OAS secretary general Insulza (OAS 2007) expressed his concern in a press conference about Chávez's intention to close down RCTV. Chávez responded by publicly demanding Insulza's resignation, calling him a "viceroy" of the (U.S.) empire, and describing him with one of the worst expletives in the Spanish language. On January 31, 2007, the national legislature approved legislation in a special session that authorized Chávez to rule by decree in eleven key sectors of the economy for the following 18 months.

Apparently none of Chávez's individual actions on their own seems to constitute a serious enough authoritarian transgression to merit attention and action by the OAS Permanent Council. Accordingly, Venezuelan democracy may well suffer a "death by a thousand cuts," reverting to full-scale authoritarianism before the OAS can mount an effective response. Furthermore, even if the OAS were to find a way to take action within the bounds of sovereign limits on regional collective defense of democracy, the OAS and the broader international community have little leverage with which to compel oil-rich Venezuela to stay true to representative democracy (Gunson 2006, 63). Venezuela in the coming years may prove to be the battleground that determines whether the OAS's collective-defense-of-democracy regime becomes a fixture in inter-American affairs or an ephemeral phenomenon.

NOTES

1. For details of the crisis and demise of the Puntofijo system, see Crisp and Levine (1998); Levine and Crisp (1999); Ellner and Hellinger (2003); and McCoy and Myers (2004).

2. On the Bolivarian Revolution, see the collection of essays in Ellner and Hellinger (2003).

3. The term *partyarchy* was originally coined by Michael Coppedge (1996).

4. For detailed accounts of the OAS response to the April 11 coup, see Cooper and Legler (2006); Levitt (2006b); and Parish and Peceny (2006).

5. The Rio Group was established in 1986 from the merging of the Contadora Group (Venezuela, Mexico, Panama, and Colombia) and its support group (Argentina, Brazil, Peru, and Uruguay), and today counts the majority of Latin American countries as members. Much of the catalyst for its formation was the widespread perception that the OAS was a U.S.-dominated body. In a similar manner to the OAS, the Rio Group has set democracy as a criterion of membership with its membership facing suspension for any interruption in democratic rule, as in the cases of Panama in 1989 and Peru in 1992. In accordance with its antihegemonic origins, the Rio Group opposes the use of military force and/or unilateral interventions to restore overthrown governments. Its preferred option has been persuasion through political dialogue and negotiation, not coercion (Frohmann 1994).

6. For the text of the Inter-American Democratic Charter, see the appendix in this volume. For analysis on the Democratic Charter, see the special issue of *Canadian Foreign Policy* 10 (3) (2003), edited by Max Cameron. See also Legler (2007) and Ayala Coroa and Nikken Bellshaw-Hógg (2006).

7. Senior Bush administration officials met several times with key opposition figures in the months prior to the coup. In the immediate aftermath of the coup, White House spokesman Ari Fleischer and National Security Adviser Condoleezza Rice remarked that Chávez had provoked his own downfall and that his government had suppressed a peaceful demonstration. On the U.S. role in the coup, see Hakim (2002); Kay (2002); Shifter (2002a); Valenzuela (2002); Slevin (2002); DeYoung (2002); Krugman (2002); Marquis (2002).

8. For detailed analyses of OAS dialogue facilitation in Venezuela, see Cooper and Legler (2005; 2006) and Parish and Peceny (2006).

9. During the Peruvian crisis that culminated in the resignation of President Alberto Fujimori in November 2000, a similar *mesa de diálogo* (dialogue roundtable) facilitated by the OAS served for a time as a parallel congress, arriving at a series of important

negotiated reforms that would not easily have passed in Peru's real Congress. See Cooper and Legler (2005; 2006).

10. In the context of the general strike, another supporting multilateral grouping was created alongside the tripartite mission. Brazil and the United States took the initiative to form a consortium of six countries, called the Group of Friends of the Secretary-General, to lend their weight to Secretary-General Gaviria's efforts to find a negotiated solution to Venezuela's crisis. In addition to the United States and Brazil, the group included Chile, Mexico, Portugal, and Spain. On the Group of Friends, see OAS (2003b; 2003c).

11. On soft power, see Joseph Nye (1990).

12. The formation of the *mesa* was an important catalyst behind the August 2002 creation of the opposition umbrella organization, the Coordinadora Democrática. For the *mesa,* the Coordinadora had the difficult challenge of selecting six participants plus an adviser from among a fractious, heterogeneous group of affiliate organizations that included nineteen political parties, seventy-nine civil society organizations, and a sixteen-member executive.

13. For an in-depth look at OAS involvement in the recall referendum, see Cooper and Legler (2006) and Parish and Peceny (2006).

14. Forms with such similar handwriting became known as *planillas planas.*

15. For additional analysis of authoritarian backsliding under Chávez, see Corrales (2006).

16. This observation was made by Eduardo Bertoni (2006), former OAS special rapporteur for freedom of expression.

17. Popularly referred to as the "Lista Tascón," the claim is that this list has been used punitively, resulting in job dismissals and the prevention of access to public services for some who signed to support Chávez's removal.

18. For a sample of the Venezuelan government's views on democracy, see Valero (2005) and Government of Venezuela (2001).

19. The Friends of the Democratic Charter is a transnational advocacy network comprised of former presidents, prime ministers, high-ranking government officials, and their academic advisers whose prime objective is to strengthen the Inter-American Democratic Charter so that it can be implemented in a more timely and effective manner to protect and promote democracy in the Americas. For more on the Friends, see McCoy's contribution in this volume.

20. On the distinction between hard and soft intervention, see Tesón (1996).

21. Economic sanctions were imposed against the military junta that ousted Haiti's democratically elected president Jean-Bertrand Aristide in 1991; military intervention was used in Haiti in 1994 and again in 2004 through the United Nations Security Council under the rubric of threats to international security.

22. See the report prepared by Rubén M. Perina (2006), chief of the OAS Electoral Observation Mission to the Parliamentary Elections of December 4, 2005.

CHAPTER ELEVEN

Ecuador 2004–2005

Democratic Crisis Redux

Barry S. Levitt

In Latin America, the "biggest leadership problem used to be strongmen who overstayed their welcome," a newspaper article has noted with more than a hint of irony. "These days, leaders are just as likely to be tossed from the presidential palace before their time is up" (Chauvin 2003). Remarkable as it might seem to foreigners, the last time a president of Ecuador finished a full term of office was more than a decade ago. In the four years that Sixto Durán Ballén governed (1992–96), the country was paralyzed by dozens of strikes and hundreds of protests, and the president declared states of emergency an average of once every four months, but at least he could claim that constitutional order had been maintained. The presidency of Durán Ballén, though stable in comparison to those who followed him, nonetheless foreshadowed precisely the sort of political fragmentation, civil society mobilization, and weak levels of support for institutions that would bring down each of his elected successors. This chapter examines recent episodes of crisis in Ecuador, and the role of the hemisphere's main international organization, the Organization of American States (OAS), in responding to such crises.

The chapter begins with an overview of OAS mechanisms for defending democracy in the Americas. It goes on to recap the past decade of Ecuador's democratic instability before delving deeper into the latest (2004–5) episode of political crisis in that country, one that led the OAS to invoke the Inter-American Democratic Charter (IADC; see appendix B) and culminated in the ouster of President Lucio Gutiérrez in April 2005. The chapter also briefly touches on subsequent discussions at the June 2005 OAS General Assembly in Fort Lauderdale, Florida, regarding the creation of new mechanisms for enforcing the Democratic Charter. As we will see, the performance of the OAS defense-of-democracy mechanisms in Ecuador in 2004 and 2005 was, for a variety of reasons, rather lackluster.

What is more, this analysis of crisis in Ecuador indicates that transnationalism is still trumped by national interests, at least on the issue of the defense and promotion of democracy. Compelling explanations for foreign policy decision making on questions of hemispheric democracy can be found largely within the domestic politics of OAS member states. While new methodological approaches to international relations emphasize ideas, networks, and nonstate actors, the simple self-interests of state actors still explain a great deal about who does—or does not—defend democracy in the region.

The OAS and the Defense-of-Democracy Regime

Although the OAS has always paid lip service to democratic governance in its member states, with the end of the Cold War the organization took a more active role in democracy promotion (see OAS 1948). As depicted in earlier chapters of this volume, key milestones in this process included the passage of Resolution 1080 (OAS 1991; see appendix A) and the Inter-American Democratic Charter (OAS 2001b). Some scholars have gone so far as to call these new mechanisms an "OAS defense-of-democracy regime" (Bloomfield 1994; see also Acevedo and Grossman 1996; Steves 2001; Parish and Peceny 2002). A regime is, in this usage, an agreed-upon system of rules and procedures governing a certain issue area in the international arena (see Krasner 1983).

International regimes often raise the classic social science problem of collective action: how to get different actors to cooperate for their mutual benefit, when there is a risk of losing out if some actors cooperate and others do not. Regimes exist because they are thought to provide some sort of positive outcome, though the benefits are not always distributed evenly. In the case of the defense-of-democracy regime, even if democracy in the region is good for everyone in the long run—a big "if"—individual member states may be wary about the costs of defending democracy. The downsides to collective action might include increased interstate tension or conflict, the interruption of trade or aid, or the backlash of domestic actors at home (expressed in street protests or at the ballot box). Perhaps most pressing on the minds of the foreign policy makers of a member state is the potential threat that the defense-of-democracy regime could be applied against *them* next (see Cooper and Legler 2001a; Levitt 2006a).

As Oran Young (1999) points out, international regimes also require some basic level of shared understanding of the issues covered by the regime. Within a defense-of-democracy regime, member states need to more or less agree on what constitutes democracy, how to measure its presence or absence, what methods should be used to protect it, and how to define and remedy violations. Yet the language used to set these standards in the IADC is rather vague (McCoy 2001; Cameron 2001, 2003). What is more, in the case of the 2004–5 Ecuador crisis, as in many other recent crises, the OAS has been stymied by threats to democracy that deviate from what we might call the textbook military coup. These new threats include *autogolpes* (executive branch coups against other branches of government), illegal or questionable impeachment processes, and the erosion of the rule of law. Perhaps most problematic—and increasingly common—are cases in which mobilization and protest on the part of civilian, nongovernmental forces play a role in deposing or forcing the resignation of elected officials. It is often unclear to member states what the role of the OAS should be in preventing, averting, or responding to "civil society coups" and other challenges to democracy posed by unarmed nonstate actors (see McCoy 2006).

Ecuador has experienced several different outbreaks of this new form of democratic crisis. In the ouster of President Lucio Gutiérrez in 2005, however, the tactics used by those who deposed him are not new to Ecuadorian politics. Gutiérrez was himself catapulted into political life by a ploy strikingly similar to the one that ultimately toppled him. As we shall see, the ability of the OAS to respond to or avert such crises has not improved much over the past decade.

Ecuador: A Legacy of Democratic Crises

Ecuador's political system is highly fragmented along regional and ethnic lines. It has endured multiple waves of instability in rapid succession over the past decade. As Shelley McConnell (2001, 74) writes, "public disenchantment with democratic institutions has given a green light to protest politics and thinly veiled military recalibration of unbalanced presidencies."

The first contemporary episode took place in the mid-1990s. A flamboyant former mayor of Guayaquil, Abdalá Bucaram—nicknamed "El Loco," the crazy one—was elected president in 1996 on a strongly populist platform. His highly theatrical style was no substitute for good governance or political savvy. Bucaram's turn to neoliberal reforms, coupled with his flagrantly corrupt political practices, alienated elite and popular sectors of Ecuadorian society alike. Social movements such as the Confederation of Indigenous Nationalities of Ecuador (CONAIE), Ecuador's largest national indigenous organization, began protesting Bucaram's austerity policies in late 1996. In early February 1997 the group organized a two-day general strike against the government, blocking roads and effectively paralyzing most of the country. CONAIE enjoyed the support of a wide range of labor unions, student groups, and religious associations. Even the nation's Chamber of Commerce allied with the protesters, having felt the economic pinch of the new president's graft and seen the entire economy suffer as a result of his poor stewardship and corrupt practices (Selverston 1997).

On February 6, 1997, Ecuador's national legislature voted to remove "El Loco" Bucaram from office, due to his supposed "mental incapacity." The military then quietly but clearly withdrew its support for the president, more or less sealing his fate. Though the grounds for Bucaram's impeachment were —notwithstanding his nickname—somewhat dubious, he had woefully little public support just six months into his term of office.

While few Ecuadorians were sad to see him go, the procedures for filling the vacated presidency were not clear. On the days following Bucaram's removal, three different people claimed to be the legitimate head of state: Bucaram himself, as he did not recognize the legitimacy of the impeachment and tried to rally the military to renew its support for him; Vice President Rosalia Arteaga, who had the strongest legal case for assuming the presidency; and the president of Congress and that institution's majority pick to assume the presidency of the nation, Fabian Alarcón. A compromise brokered by the military and political parties put Arteaga in power for a brief period while the Constitution was amended by Congress to allow Alarcón to take power (Schemo 1997). Alarcón ultimately served as interim president until 1998.

The OAS Permanent Council expressed concern regarding these events, and sent a mission (including then-secretary-general César Gaviria) at the request of the Bucaram government to investigate and, it hoped, defuse the conflict before it exploded. But as Gaviria (2004, 13) recalls in his memoirs: "Upon our arrival in Guayaquil, we warned that the Organization would not accept a rupture of democracy. Nevertheless, the resistance and repudiation of the Government were undeniable, making it impossible to facilitate mediation." What is more, while the OAS tried to be proactive in its response to the crisis, it did not invoke Resolution 1080, even though both the president's removal and the presidential succession process were suspect.

The ouster was legitimized, or at least politically validated, several months later when Interim President Alarcón held a national plebiscite. This May 1997 referendum asked voters whether they approved of the removal of Bucaram, his replacement with Alarcón, and the convoking of a new Constituent Assembly to redraft the Constitution (Barczak 2001). All three items were indeed approved, thus polishing, post facto, the constitutional luster of the resolution to this crisis. But it would not be the last crisis of democracy that Ecuador would face.

New elections were held in two rounds in May and June of 1998. Quito mayor Jamil Mahuad's victory in the presidential elections appeared, at the time, to promise a measure of stability for the nation. Mahuad was elected on a platform of ending the deep economic crisis in which Ecuador was mired. Yet just a few months into his mandate, four of the country's major banks had failed and were being bailed out by the government. In a period of shrinking budgets and reduced public services, this fed the perception that the state served only the country's elite. The value of the sucre against the dollar dropped precipitously, as did most Ecuadorians' real wages. Although Mahuad's popularity increased in 1999 with the signing of a peace treaty with Peru, by the end of that year his approval ratings were in single digits. As a last-ditch effort to turn the economy around, Mahuad proposed *dolarización:* phasing out the sucre as the national currency and replacing it with the U.S. dollar.

Ecuador's vibrant civil society reacted very negatively to this gambit. The indigenous people's association CONAIE again deployed strategies such as strikes, road blockages, and other acts of civil disobedience. On January 11, 2000, CONAIE and other social movements formed a "Parliament of Peoples" and called for national protest and uprising. These civil society groups were aided by midlevel military officers who, although under orders to stop the demonstrations, instead transported large numbers of protesters to the capital and even helped breach the security perimeters of government buildings. On January 21 the lead officer in charge of Carondelet Palace, the seat of the executive branch, informed Mahuad that he could no longer guarantee his safety and requested that the president abandon the palace. A triumvirate consisting of a military officer, the leader of CONAIE, and a former Supreme Court justice declared themselves the Junta of National Salvation and celebrated what they thought to be a "revolution without blood," overthrowing the political elites in the name of the Ecuadorian people (see Lucero 2001).

Although the junta would last only a few hours and remain in flux the entire time, it did succeed in removing Mahuad from office. General Carlos Mendoza, the head of the military's Joint Command, joined the junta while the coup was underway and displaced Colonel Lucio Gutiérrez, the representative of the midlevel officers. Perhaps bowing to economic pressure from the United States, Mendoza decided (without consulting with the other junta members) to strike a deal. Mahuad would leave office, and the presidency would be assumed by Vice President Gustavo Noboa. On January 22, the day after his ouster, Mahuad publicly recognized the Noboa presidency and fled the country. He did not officially resign so as not to lend an air of legitimacy to his unconstitutional ouster.

At a meeting of the OAS Permanent Council held while the crisis was underway, member countries expressed their support for Jamil Mahuad and for Ecuador's Constitution. As in the previous crisis, states disagreed about the applicability of Resolution 1080 and the potential involvement of the OAS. The representative of Ecuador argued that Resolution 1080 could be applied but urged the council to wait and see how the crisis would develop. Chile, Costa Rica, Argentina, Paraguay, and the United States felt that the OAS should act immediately, preferably under the auspices of Resolution 1080. Brazil, hemispheric rival of the United States in many policy areas, was more cautious about OAS involvement. Peru, then under the less-than-democratic rule of President Alberto Fujimori, lamented the toppling of Mahuad but made no mention at all of Resolution 1080. And other questionably democratic countries such as Mexico and Venezuela took an even stronger stand against intervention, arguing that this was a matter to be decided by the Ecuadorian people, not the OAS. By the end of its January 21 session, the council passed Resolution 763 condemning the coup, expressing support for democratic institutions in Ecuador, and instructing the secretary-general to stay informed. But the Permanent Council did not set in motion a concerted response to the crisis as stipulated in Resolution 1080. Once the Noboa presidency was in place, the OAS readily accepted its legitimacy.

Although the irregular termination of executives in Ecuador reflects a broader trend across Latin America, the revolving door to Quito's presidential palace represents a particularly acute problem. Since the mid-1990s, Ecuadorian public opinion has turned even more viscerally against political parties and representative institutions, and citizens have become increasingly drawn toward extrainstitutional solutions to the nation's political and economic problems.[1]

The 2004–2005 Crisis

One of the key military figures in the 2000 coup was Colonel Lucio Gutiérrez, whose participation in the uprising garnered him a great deal of popularity among Ecuador's lower-class and indigenous citizens. Gutiérrez went on to form his own personalistic political party, the January 21 Patriotic Society, whose name commemorates the date of the 2000 uprising. With the support of the Pachakutik indigenous party—which is in turn linked to CONAIE—Gutiérrez won the 2002 presidential election and took office in January 2003.

By August 2003, however, Gutiérrez had shifted away from his leftist campaign platform. He lost Pachakutik as a coalition partner and consequently lost control of Congress. By November 2004 he had so alienated his former supporters that they joined with the more conservative Social Christian Party in proposing to impeach Gutiérrez for spending improprieties. Though the impeachment motion did not move forward, it did prompt Gutiérrez to seek a new alliance with two of his erstwhile adversaries: Alvaro Noboa of the Institutional Renewal Party of National Action, whom he defeated in the second round of the 2002 elections, and exiled former president Bucaram of the Roldosista Party. Claiming that political bias in the judicial branch was jeopardizing democracy, in November and December 2004 a congressional alliance between members of Gutiérrez's, Noboa's, and Bucaram's parties voted to purge most of the justices of the Supreme Electoral Council, the Constitutional Tribunal, and, most egregiously, the Supreme Court itself (Shifter 2004). This was carried out despite the fact that, under Ecuador's Constitution, Congress has no role in the hiring and firing of Supreme Court justices (Edwards 2005).

Newly appointed members of the Supreme Court then took it upon themselves to drop charges against several of the president's new allies, including "El
Loco" Bucaram himself.

Civil society responded negatively to these machinations. According to a
report by the Washington Office on Latin America, "professional legal organizations, the national association of mayors, national and local chambers of
commerce, national leaders of the Catholic Church and major national media"
all publicly criticized the move (Edwards 2005, 5). Internationally, both the
Inter-American Commission on Human Rights of the OAS and UN High
Commissioner for Human Rights were petitioned on behalf of the aggrieved
judges. Beginning in mid-February 2005, public demonstrations became commonplace in Quito, increasingly disrupting daily life in that city.

Various OAS member states within the Permanent Council, as well as the
acting secretary-general,[2] made overtures to Gutiérrez, offering to intervene
diplomatically to stave off the gathering political storm. However, the president balked at the offers. Because Article 18 of the IADC is understood to
require the consent of the member state in question prior to sending diplomatic missions, Gutiérrez's rebuff prevented the OAS from potentially helping
to alleviate the crisis from the outside (*Miami Herald* 2005b). Yet such restrictions apparently did not hobble the United Nations. The UN Human Rights
Commission sent Dr. Leandro Despouy to conduct an in situ investigation in
March 2005 and produced a strongly worded report outlining how the independence of the judicial branch—and democracy itself—was in jeopardy in
Ecuador (Edwards 2005).

In early April 2005 former president Bucaram took advantage of his acquit-
tal and returned to Ecuador. By April 15 the sustained public outcry over both
the assault on institutions and the return of the exiled ex-president led Gutiérrez to declare a state of emergency in Quito. The state of emergency was lifted
the following day, and large-scale protests continued—with the encouragement of Gutiérrez's political foes in the Social Christian Party. Even more
curious was the president's dismissal of the same Supreme Court justices
with whom he had recently packed the court. The congressional alliance that
Gutiérrez had cobbled together began to fall apart. On April 20, sixty-two
members of Congress, all opponents of the president, met in a special session.
This session was held without the presence of thirty-eight members perceived
to be Gutiérrez allies and did not even take place in the Congress building itself. This improvised legislative body voted to declare that the presi-

dent had vacated his position by neglecting his constitutional duties, and appointed Vice President Alfredo Palacio—who had broken with Gutiérrez several months prior—in his stead. By this time the Quito chief of police had resigned rather than attempt to quell the crowds calling for Gutiérrez to leave the presidential palace. The leadership of the military also withdrew its support for Gutiérrez and decided to back Palacio. It may also have briefly considered forming a civil-military junta (as was also attempted in the 2000 removal of President Mahuad). According to one analyst of civil-military relations, "During at least five hours Palacios [*sic*] was without military protection, and was threatened by an unruly mob. There was considerable give and take on [the prospect of a civil-military junta], and according to well-placed observers, it was resolved only when foreign governments made it clear that this would be unacceptable in view of the commitment to democracy by important allies and the OAS" (Bruneau 2006). Meanwhile, the nation's acting attorney general issued an arrest warrant for Gutiérrez, who was escorted out of the presidential palace and took refuge in the Brazilian embassy. He and his family were eventually airlifted to exile in Brasilia.

The OAS Response to Ecuador's 2004–2005 Crisis

The OAS Permanent Council had been informally following the growing crisis in Ecuador since the judicial purges began in late 2004 but had not taken any action pursuant to the IADC. The ambassadors were in a regularly scheduled meeting on April 20, 2005, when news reached them that the crisis had become more acute. The representative for Ecuador, acting on behalf of the still-standing Gutiérrez government, spoke at length.[3] He depicted the crisis as a product of the economic and political chaos that Gutiérrez had inherited upon taking office. The terminated judges, he explained, had exceeded their periods in office. President Gutiérrez, in this view, was merely attempting to depoliticize the judiciary and reform the Constitution with the input of civil society. Ecuador's ambassador to the OAS depicted the violence in the streets and rumors of a coup as merely an intense political debate, one that was healthy for a democracy.

The U.S. representative then spoke. Since 2003 the Bush administration had viewed Gutiérrez as an important ally in the region, and consequently U.S. foreign policy makers were not quick to condemn his increasingly authoritarian moves.[4] An analyst for the Heritage Foundation, a conservative think tank, contended that "while the United States did a good job encouraging Gutiérrez to back free trade, abstain from joining the International Criminal Court (ICC), and consent to United States use of Ecuadorian military facilities for drug interdiction, promoting responsible governance and effective institutions was a secondary goal" (Johnson 2005). Now, in the face of an overt crisis, the U.S. representative did not openly contradict the version of events recounted by his Ecuadorian colleague, though he did urge all OAS member states to engage with this issue and "firmly support Ecuador's democracy, which includes *all of its institutions*" (OAS 2005g; emphasis added).

While the Permanent Council did not yet have a draft resolution of its own to debate, the foreign ministers of the southern continent were meeting in Brazil that week under the auspices of the newly created South American Community of Nations and had already produced a communiqué expressing their concern and calling on Ecuador's state and civil society to reconcile peacefully. The Permanent Council decided to adopt this communiqué but did not activate the IADC mechanisms per se.

The Permanent Council met again in an extraordinary session the next morning, April 21. Even earlier that day, the OAS ambassadors of members of the Latin American Integration Association (ALADI), a regional trade organization including most of South America plus Mexico and Cuba, also met. This delayed the scheduled start of the Permanent Council meeting and aggravated Caribbean Community (CARICOM) countries and other OAS member states not included in ALADI.

By the time the full Permanent Council meeting took place, Ecuador was already speaking through an alternate representative, reflecting the change in presidents that had occurred the day before while the Permanent Council was out of session. When interim representative Jaime Barberis explained Gutiérrez's ouster to the Permanent Council on April 21, he depicted it as wholly within the bounds of the nation's Constitution. It represented, he claimed, the consolidation rather than the violation of the rule of law. Consequently, he saw no need to invoke the IADC, though he did mention that Ecuador would welcome the OAS's support to continue this process of "democratic consolidation."

Several member states then spoke out on the need for more information about the president's ouster. Panama wondered how Ecuador's Congress could determine that the president had vacated his post, since Gutiérrez's behavior suggested that he was in fact trying desperately to hang on to it.[5] Peru's representative went even further, interpreting the ouster as unconstitutional and insisting that terminating a government in this way contravened the IADC. Though the Peruvian delegate understood that the crisis had, in a narrow sense, been resolved institutionally (i.e., by the vice president succeeding to the presidency), he noted with consternation how the OAS appeared averse to intervening in crises of separation of powers such as this one, even when there was an irrefutable alteration of constitutional order—an event which should have triggered the IADC.

Venezuela, on the other hand, thanked Ecuador for the information it had offered and noted that Venezuela's foreign minister was working with his counterparts from Chile and Brazil to activate South American regional mechanisms—ALADI or the South American Community of Nations instead of, or perhaps in addition to, the OAS itself—to address this crisis.

Virtually all representatives then agreed to call a recess, in order to gather more information and consult with their respective foreign ministries. The ambassador from Grenada hinted that IADC mechanisms could be applied in this case and called for OAS agencies themselves to advise and inform the Permanent Council, so that the body would not have to rely solely on the statements of Ecuadorian representatives. This sentiment was echoed by St. Kitts and Nevis. As another Permanent Council representative said, "most of what we know [about this crisis] comes from watching CNN" (OAS 2005g)! So the council agreed to reconvene the following day, and this time scheduled the next session to allow time for ALADI and other regional and subregional groups to meet prior to reconvening as the Permanent Council.

By the morning of April 22, Palacio had dispatched a larger delegation to the OAS, including Ecuador's former ambassador to the OAS, Blasco Peñaherrera, and the future permanent ambassador, Mario Alemán. This delegation was charged with thwarting any potential efforts to demand Gutiérrez's restoration or delay recognition of the new government.[6] On the floor of the Permanent Council, they retraced the origins of this crisis to Gutiérrez's unconstitutional uses of Congress to purge the courts and asked for an OAS resolution in support of the new government. A representative of the OAS Department of Democratic and Political Affairs then presented a report on the trajectory of the crisis, in which he too highlighted arguments suggesting that Gutiérrez's removal might not have been unconstitutional.

The Panamanian representative (who was president of the Permanent Council during the initial months of this crisis) spoke in defense of the OAS's earlier inaction, noting that the organization cannot really take sides in these interinstitutional standoffs. He further opined that, while there certainly were irregularities in the way that the crisis was resolved, it would do the OAS no good to pore over the details of the past. The Venezuelan representative took an even more extreme position, arguing that a spontaneous popular movement had taken action in Ecuador and that the OAS must respect this. Although he defended the role of the OAS as an arbiter of democratic standards, he also viewed the events in Ecuador as a legitimate rejection of established forms of political representation and the birth of a new, inclusive, popular political system. (This stance was consistent with Venezuela's previous positions on breaches of democracy and with its reluctance to sign on to the IADC itself.)

Two different versions of a draft resolution were circulating that day, but both seemed to include the widely supported idea of immediately sending an OAS mission to Ecuador to assess the situation and report back to the Permanent Council. It is noteworthy that several member states were quite concerned that the assessment mission reflect the diversity of subregions within the OAS. Member states also seemed very aware that the organization was being criticized for not being able to act expeditiously and put out a resolution while the crisis was reaching a fever pitch. Yet, at the same time, there was much confusion and disagreement about how to proceed with the drafting and discussion of these resolutions.

By the end of the April 22 session, the council approved Resolution 880, in which it pledged:

> In accordance with Article 18 of the Inter-American Democratic Charter, and in keeping with the invitation issued by the delegation of Ecuador at this Permanent Council meeting, to send to that Republic a Mission, as soon as possible, comprising the Chair of the Permanent Council, the Acting Secretary General, and representatives of subregional groups, to work with officials of that country and with all sectors of Ecuadorian society in their effort to strengthen democracy. (OAS 2005d)

In discussions subsequent to passing the resolution, several member states again noted, with differing degrees of understanding and consternation, that the Permanent Council simply does not have the capacity to make decisions in "real time" as acute episodes of crisis are underway. However, most seemed to agree that this postcrisis use of the IADC was nonetheless a milestone in the inter-American defense of democracy, as it represented the first formal application of this particular clause (Article 18) of the Democratic Charter.

The mission proposed in Resolution 880 took place April 26–30, 2005. Participants included Interim Secretary-General Luigi Einaudi; Permanent Council President Alberto Borea of Peru; the ambassador of Canada to Ecuador; and Permanent Council ambassadors or other representatives from Chile, the United States, Guyana, Honduras, Mexico, and Venezuela. The mission met with government officials, opposition politicians, legal scholars, and civil society groups and subsequently drafted a report, sometimes referred to as preliminary, sometimes as final, dated May 9. The report provided a summary of the prolonged crisis and its aftermath that was as politically neutral as possible. But the report went further, proposing a series of reforms, including the creation of a process of national dialogue in Ecuador to foster peace and institution building across political lines. The document also recommended that agencies of the OAS could offer technical support on legal and political matters as Ecuador attempted to rebuild its democratic institutions.

This report caused significant response from the country it was meant to assist. Even before the Ecuadorian representative to the Permanent Council saw the document, Palacio's government had been irked by side proposals, from both the United States and Brazil, that he cut short his term of office and hold new elections (*Economist* 2005a). Then, when the report itself was presented to the rest of the Permanent Council representatives and discussed on May 11, it was initially taken as an offense to Ecuador's sovereignty. That country's newest representative to the Permanent Council passionately expressed the opinion that Ecuador was not the only country in the hemisphere with problems of democracy, that it was not "disabled" nor could it be subjected to "tutelary democracy" as a "guinea pig" for the OAS's democracy-building efforts (OAS 2005h; see also *Agencia Bolivariana de Noticias* 2005). He also depicted the OAS as "nothing more than a large family," but a family of adults, none of whom should be treated like children and "have their ears pulled" (OAS 2005h). More concretely, Ecuador maintained that only the Permanent Council, not the mission per se, had the power to make specific recommendations, and that the report should have been submitted to the Palacio government for approval prior to presenting it to the Permanent Council.

In the debate that followed in the Permanent Council, member states expressed both satisfaction with this first application of Article 18 of the IADC and, on the other hand, a growing concern that the IADC was ineffective at preventing or even responding to crises of this sort. Panama reminded Ecuador that national sovereignty, as well as the defense of democracy, is supported by the IADC, but that the role of the OAS in responding to this crisis was legitimate. Nicaragua, too, viewed the report as an act of support requested by Ecuador itself, not an affront to it. Guatemala, Honduras, and Colombia also expressed their backing for the mission and its performance.

In addition to their support, Chile and Barbados both expressed concern regarding the usefulness of the IADC as it is currently designed. For Chile, the potential sanctions of the IADC are its least important functions. Instead, the charter should be applied primarily in preventing rather than responding to crises, not just in one or two trouble spots but in all member states. The Chilean ambassador to the Permanent Council, who had participated in the mission, noted that virtually everyone they interviewed in Ecuador asked why the OAS did not get involved earlier. (The idea that the OAS did not get involved earlier because Ecuador did not invite it to do so was apparently not, for this diplomat, an adequate answer.) The representative from Barbados similarly noted that the IADC is most effective as a strategic rather than a tactical instrument—that is, as a long-term, proactive mechanism for strengthening democracies rather than a tool for responding to imminent crises. This was an idea echoed by numerous other delegates. Furthermore, the fact that, amid multiple unconstitutional alterations of power in the region, the punitive clauses of the IADC have not once been invoked since 2001 suggested to Barbados that the OAS might need to rethink its defense-of-democracy regime.

Venezuela, too, held that the IADC was best interpreted as preventative rather than punitive and strongly emphasized that sovereignty and democratic development are complementary and not contradictory. The Venezuelan representative also took this opportunity to critique, not for the first time, the "reductionist" view of democracy—representative, rather than popular or participatory—enshrined in the Democratic Charter. Though this criticism was nothing new, in a final remark the representative added that Venezuela would strongly oppose any efforts to create OAS mechanisms for monitoring member states' democracy on an ongoing basis. This foreshadowed the conflict over deepening the IADC, which would erupt a few weeks later at the 2005 OAS General Assembly meeting in Fort Lauderdale, Florida.

In the wake of the Ecuador crisis, the United States proposed that the OAS significantly strengthen and institutionalize the IADC. But the United States, which was the host delegation of the General Assembly, circulated a draft of its proposed "Declaration of Florida" just a few days prior to the Assembly's June 5 start date. This declaration attempted to clarify some of the provisions in the IADC, suggesting for example that democratically elected leaders who then went on to breach democratic practices could face the sanctions of the charter (see Abelson 2005). What is more, it called for the OAS to "develop a process to assess, as appropriate, situations that may affect the development of a Member State's democratic political institutional process" (cited in Zacharia 2005). However, it was not made clear whether the body that would perform this monitoring function would be the entire existing OAS Permanent Council, a subset of member states, or a consultative group made up of experts and civil society representatives. Although many scholars and nongovernmental organizations throughout the hemisphere had been calling for clarification and institutional deepening since the charter was adopted in 2001, the proposal was roundly rejected by a large majority of member states at the General Assembly. By some accounts only six out of thirty-four supported the U.S. draft, while alternate drafts were put forth by ALADI and by CARICOM (see Gindin 2005). While member states may have differed somewhat in their rationales for opposing the U.S. draft, the fact that it was proposed at the last minute and perceived as just another U.S. attempt at isolating Venezuela from the inter-American community doomed it to failure (Oppenheimer 2005).

Notwithstanding this failure to further entrench the mechanisms of the IADC, and the particularly staunch pro-sovereignty views held by Ecuador, Venezuela, and several other member states, the OAS did in fact keep one foot in Ecuadorian politics on a sustained basis. Resolution 883, adopted by the Permanent Council on May 20, 2005, instructed the secretary-general, "with the consent of the government of Ecuador, to make available the resources and experience of the OAS, and such assistance as Ecuador may request, in order to support the strengthening of democracy in that country" (OAS 2005e). Ecuador indeed set up a national dialogue, called the Citizen's Coordination System, though it is not clear how active or effective this system really was. What is more, in a July 2005 follow-up visit by the new secretary-general José Miguel Insulza, the organization pledged continued technical support for judicial reforms. A few weeks later the OAS named two legal scholars, one Chilean and one Costa Rican, to officially observe the recomposition of the Supreme Court.

In late November 2005 the Supreme Court was finally reestablished. The OAS (along with a host of other international actors such as the UN, the Andean Community, and the Government of Spain) could rightfully take credit for overcoming the institutional paralysis of Ecuador's judiciary—a task that Ecuador's political elites were seemingly not able to accomplish without a neutral arbiter.[7] Yet, as of the end of 2005, Ecuador still lacked a comptroller general, a prosecutor general, and a working constitutional tribunal (U.S. Department of State 2005b). And although in February 2006 the OAS would offer technical support to make Ecuador's Electoral Tribunal functional in time for elections in October and November of that year, in general the country's key democratic institutions remained weak and in disarray (OAS 2006b).[8]

In an ironic twist that is becoming all too common in the region, Palacio himself increasingly became the object of mass protest. In an even more eerie moment of déjà vu, Lucio Gutiérrez returned to Ecuador in October 2005 and was arrested, but in early March 2006 a Quito court dropped all charges against the ex-president and ordered his immediate release. In statements made soon thereafter, Gutiérrez pledged "to regain the presidency" in the near future (Prensa Latina 2006).

Conclusions

What can be learned from this case study of democratic crisis? Initially, the story of recent politics in Ecuador could be read as a lesson on how useful an early warning system and a set of established, graduated responses to democratic breakdown might be.[9] Another reading, however, suggests that early warnings may not be enough. In Ecuador the warning signs were manifest, and they were certainly noticed by anyone paying attention in late 2004, but they did not spur effective action within the hemisphere. As long as the Gutiérrez government maintained that it did not need the help of the hemispheric organization, no response was deemed possible by OAS member states. This inaction was exacerbated by the fact that the OAS had no sitting secretary-general between October 2004 and May 2005 and that member states' attention was consumed by the ongoing campaign to elect a new secretary-general during much of this period. The OAS, which holds a specific mandate to defend democracy in the region, responded even later than the United Nations.

When the 2004–5 crisis in Ecuador came to a head, the effectiveness of the defense-of-democracy regime was middling at best. It is possible that the existence of democratic norms in the hemisphere deterred Ecuador's military from deciding to hold power on its own. What is more, the crisis in Ecuador did elicit an OAS response, arguably the first such response, based on Article 18 of the IADC. The OAS successfully sent a mission, albeit after the fact and with some reluctance on the part of its "host" government. The OAS also played a (modest) part in supervising the reconstruction of the judicial system, though this process has been slow and incomplete.

But, overall, the way that the Ecuador crisis was handled within the Permanent Council, and the subsequent failure of the United States version of the "Declaration of Florida" at the 2005 General Assembly, suggest that problems of authoritative interpretation and collective action continue to plague the IADC. The nature of Ecuador's 2004–5 crisis, one spurred on by civil society movements and an ostensibly democratic legislature fomenting instability, made it particularly challenging for the OAS to respond early and forcefully. Yet this type of crisis is becoming more and more commonplace in the Americas. In addition to Ecuador's own legacy of instability, variations on this type of crisis have occurred in Paraguay (1999), Peru (2000), Bolivia (2003 and 2005), and Nicaragua (2004–5).[10]

The case of Ecuador also amply illustrates how debates within the Permanent Council are consistently hampered by a lack of information about crises in progress and by the limitations of relying on the member states in question for such information. Yet the scarcity of timely information is merely a symptom of the weak institutionalization of the defense-of-democracy regime. At the same time, most member states have expressed ambivalence about deepening the institutional development of the regime and moving it beyond belated, ad hoc responses to crises. Increasingly, member states seem to interpret the function of the IADC as supporting democracy rather than punishing states that breach it. But given that the OAS's finances are perennially unstable, it seems difficult to imagine it sustaining an adequate, hemisphere-wide supply of incentives in the form of institutional support for democracy building. The IADC is thus in danger of dissolving into yet another set of empty platitudes about democracy in the Americas.

The OAS member states that are strongest in responding to crises and defending democracy in the hemisphere tend, perhaps not surprisingly, to be those that are themselves more democratic. Incentives for cooperation and enforcement in the "inter-American defense-of-democracy regime" seem to stem in large part from the democratic character (or lack thereof) of member states' domestic politics (see Levitt 2006a). While both Canada and the United States have been supporters of the defense-of-democracy regime, the United States has a greater range of competing geopolitical interests (trade negotiations, drug interdiction, ideological rivalries, etc.), and—as the case of Ecuador's crisis might suggest—these other interests sometimes take priority. Among newer democracies, those that exhibit a higher quality of democracy, such as Chile and Costa Rica (see Altman and Pérez-Liñán 2002), tend to support the defense of democracy elsewhere. So do countries that have recently transitioned from a more authoritarian period of domestic politics. For example, Peru under the rather autocratic President Fujimori (1990–2000) was loath to apply Resolution 1080 but has been at the forefront of developing and applying the IADC since then, and its ambassador to the OAS in 2005 was among the most vocal critics of the manner in which Gutiérrez was removed.

Even when geopolitical incentives might lead a member state to oppose the defense-of-democracy regime, democratic domestic politics can sometimes mitigate this realpolitik. Brazil opposed the heavy-handed attempts by the United States to strengthen the IADC, and the two are generally considered to be hemispheric rivals on international trade and other issues; yet democratic Brazil actually worked closely with the United States in promoting an institutional, civilian solution to Ecuador's political impasse. On the other hand, member states with more dubious records of democracy at home are understandably wary of imposing standards of democratic governance abroad. For example, Venezuela's strong aversion to the OAS judging the quality of democracy in Ecuador and in other countries in crisis is clearly motivated by concerns that such judgments not be passed against its own current Chávez government. Despite the imperative of this volume to move beyond "methodological nationalism," the case of Ecuador's 2004–5 crisis suggests that nation-states and the domestic sources of those states' foreign policy still matter a great deal.

Furthermore, domestic politics within the country in crisis also seem to have an impact on how the inter-American system responds. In the most recent crisis in Ecuador, for example, the unpopularity of Gutiérrez at the time he was removed, and the sense that at least some part of the demonstrations that toppled him was an authentic expression of mass public opinion, made it even less likely that the OAS would prop him up. As McCoy (2006, 768) has noted, in such circumstances the proclivity of the OAS is instead to "accept the fait accompli of the forced removal of a president, but ensure that his replacement would have some semblance of constitutionality."

In the 2004–5 Ecuadorian crisis and its aftermath, we might also be witnessing the strengthening of an unexpected new international dynamic. Decision making and organization within the Americas seems increasingly to be based on subregional, in addition to hemispheric, cooperation. MERCOSUR already has a track record of attempting diplomatic action to resolve crises, as evidenced in its swift response to the 1999 assassination of Paraguay's vice president. Bodies such as ALADI and the new South American Community of Nations are now more visible, too. This new dynamic may be driven by geopolitical change, as some Latin American and Caribbean state actors have grown wary of a perceived increase in U.S. unilateralism since the turn of the twenty-first century. Future research should examine which countries most benefit from an increased reliance on these subregional organizations, and how.

More perniciously, we might even be witnessing a new pro– versus anti– United States divide. A great deal of the limited attention that U.S. foreign policy makers pay to Latin America seems to be directed at undermining the current government of Venezuela—one of the OAS member states most reluctant to allow the defense-of-democracy regime to develop teeth. The obtuse manner in which the United States has dealt with problems of democracy in Venezuela since President Hugo Chávez was elected has generated ill will in the hemisphere. This was clearly visible in the failure of U.S. leadership on developing and institutionalizing the IADC mechanisms in 2005. Although such efforts were supported by new OAS secretary-general José Miguel Insulza, they were thwarted by the perception of an anti-Chávez political agenda behind what could have been a huge step forward for the defense of democracy in the Americas.

The opening chapter of this edited volume posed three central questions: How effective have international and transnational actors been at promoting and defending democracy in the Americas? What type of democracy is being promoted by international and transnational actors? And how transnational are contemporary democratization processes in Latin America? In answer to the first question, the 2004–5 crisis in Ecuador did elicit the first formal application of the IADC's Article 18, permitting a site visit and some ongoing technical assistance from the OAS. Yet this chapter has demonstrated that the

IADC and, indeed, the "inter-American defense-of-democracy regime" more broadly, remains badly in need of institutional development in order to solve problems of authoritative interpretation (what constitutes a breach of democracy, and what are appropriate responses) and of collective action. Second, the sort of democracy being promoted is a rather modest vision of elections and representative institutions. Yet even this minimal standard cannot always be fully and effectively safeguarded, it seems. At least in the ambit of formal multilateral diplomacy, efforts to defend and promote democracy are hampered by the very framework created by the IADC: vague, ad hoc, and poorly institutionalized. Finally, in terms of the role of transnational forces in bolstering democracy in the Americas, it appears that national interests and domestic politics still strongly condition state behavior within the OAS. While international and transnational forces surely matter, the OAS has not yet brought the promise of defending and promoting democracy into full fruition. This has been made devastatingly clear in the case of Ecuador.

NOTES

A version of this chapter was presented at the XXVI Congress of the Latin American Studies Association, San Juan, Puerto Rico, March 15–18, 2006. The author wishes to thank his co-panelists from that conference, as well as the editors of this volume, for their invaluable feedback.

1. The results of the 2005 Latinobarometer survey indicate that, among Latin American societies, Ecuador has some of the lowest levels of confidence in democracy and its central institutions (congress, the presidency, political parties, etc.). See also McConnell 2001.

2. At the time of the 2004–5 Ecuador crisis, the OAS was engaged in a prolonged and, at times, paralyzing process of choosing a new secretary-general.

3. The overview presented here, of the debates within the Permanent Council on April 20, 21, and 22, are based on the author's analysis of video recordings of these sessions. Written transcripts should be available in 2007 or 2008.

4. I am grateful to Tom Legler for bringing this to my attention.

5. As late as mid-June 2005, Gutiérrez would insist that he was Ecuador's legitimate head of state and ask to address the OAS Permanent Council in this capacity (see *Hoy* 2005).

6. The United States might have supported a Permanent Council demand for Gutiérrez's return; more moderate critics, such as Peru's ambassador Albert Borrea, then president of the Permanent Council, preferred formally delaying recognition of the Palacio government until the OAS could investigate.

7. I am grateful to Tom Legler for bringing this to my attention. See also U.S. Department of State (2005b); UNDP (2005b).

8. In a personal communication, Tom Legler indicated that Ecuador's political elites perceive themselves to be the beneficiaries of this disorganized, underinstitutionalized status quo.

9. This is an idea that the Carter Center and its "Friends of the Democratic Charter" group have been floating for several years (see *Miami Herald* 2005b). The OAS itself may have been heeding the call for more proactive strategies with the 2004 reorganization of its Secretariat for Political Affairs and its democracy-promotion activities, as well as the creation of an Office for the Prevention and Resolution of Conflicts.

10. See McCoy (2006) for further comparative analysis.

Part IV / Critical Reflections

CHAPTER TWELVE

The International Political Economy of Democracy Promotion

Lessons from Haiti and Guatemala

Yasmine Shamsie

Since the early 1990s, Western governments and multilateral organizations, such as the Organization of American States (OAS) and the Inter-American Development Bank (IDB), have been supporting democratic transitions across the Caribbean Basin. They have directed millions of dollars each year to fostering and strengthening fledgling democratic institutions, electoral processes, human rights, and independent media. Yet some have argued that the global economic policy environment has never been more hostile to such a project (Oxhorn and Ducatenzeiler 1998; Cornia 1999; Isaacs 2000; Whitehead 2004). Economic processes linked to globalization have undermined the capacity of national governments to develop and implement democratic reforms, making advancing democracy an especially challenging exercise. The dual principles of sovereignty and majority rule have been increasingly challenged by what has come to be called the new global economy (Held 1996). In short, globalization has clear implications for the meaning and development of democracy.

The purpose of this chapter is to consider two cases of democratization, Haiti and Guatemala, in order to explore how aspects of economic globalization can influence the course of democratic transitions. More specifically, the chapter illustrates how certain aspects of the current economic order—aid and loan conditionality and trade and investment accords—can affect democratization by challenging basic notions of political authority and legitimacy. The case of Haiti is used to explore how international donors and lenders influence democratization through the conditionality they attach to aid, and the case of Guatemala illustrates how transnational capital influences local democratization processes through its ability to shape trade and investment agreements.

There have been important economic and political developments in Haiti and Guatemala in recent times. Haiti, considered by some to be the region's most turbulent country, seems to be finally moving toward peace and democracy since the election of President René Préval on February 7, 2006.[1] International actors have been heavily involved in this transition. Nine thousand peace-keepers ensured stability for the presidential elections; the OAS helped the country's electoral council organize and carry out the elections; and Canada, Haiti's second most important bilateral donor, funded a special mission to observe the process. The role of outside actors in Haiti is likely to deepen over the coming years. The fact that directly following his election, President Préval traveled to numerous countries (the Dominican Republic, Brazil, Chile, Argentina, Cuba, Venezuela, Canada, and the United States), called for the United Nations peace-keeping mission to remain in the country, and made requests before the Security Council and the OAS for long-term development aid speaks to Haiti's acute dependence on foreign assistance and the concomitant influence that international donors can exert on Haiti's democratic transition (International Crisis Group 2006).

Guatemala has seen a lessening of authoritarian tactics since the return of civilian rule in 1986 and the signing of the peace accords in 1996. Still, recently it has been plagued by a wave of dissent that has descended on the Central American region as a whole, led by citizens opposed to the Dominican Republic–Central American Free Trade Agreement (DR-CAFTA). Even though the Guatemalan parliament ratified and implemented the agreement, it remains controversial and deeply contested. Debates surrounding its potential effects on public policy and numerous demands by the U.S. Trade Representative for the Guatemalan government to make changes to laws that did not comply with the trade pact delayed implementation from January to July 2006.

Why choose to examine the cases of Haiti and Guatemala? What can we learn from these two experiences? Although some might argue that these countries should be excluded from inquiry given their less-than-propitious conditions for democratic development, I believe they deserve consideration precisely because of their status as "fragile" states. The donor community is increasingly engaging in countries in which conditions for building democracy are unfavorable—Afghanistan, East Timor, Uganda, Sierra Leone—thus underscoring the need to understand and analyze these interventions (de Zeeuw and Kumar 2006). Moreover, academic work on democratization has tended to privilege those countries perceived as having the necessary conditions for democracy, leaving a gap in the literature on democratic development in countries that have been weakened by conflict and in failed states. Haiti and Guatemala also share a number of political and social characteristics that make them good candidates for comparative study: high levels of inequality, elite sectors that have used violence to politically exclude the majority of the population, serious environmental and landownership problems, and a legacy of colonial and postcolonial exploitation. Furthermore, both countries have garnered intense attention from international donors, have had to deal with decades of domestic conflict and human rights abuses, and must address high levels of social marginalization while strengthening weak political institutions. Finally, I would add that both countries will require more than advances on the formal political terrain in order to experience meaningful democratic transitions (Kumar and Lodge 2002).

This chapter begins with a discussion of neoliberal globalization and how it is helping shape the variant of democracy that is emerging in the region's dependent postconflict nations. This is followed by a discussion of how the pressure to implement free-market reforms, the enhanced role of international lending institutions, and the exigencies associated with trade and investment accords are influencing democratic development in Haiti and Guatemala.

Democracy Building in the Neoliberal Era

To begin, I suggest that we need to consider current democratization processes (including the ubiquitous democracy promotion activities of foreign donors) as firmly embedded within the dynamics of globalization and deeply connected to its current economic project, neoliberalism.[2] In other words, we cannot properly investigate the development of democracy or the democracy-promotion activities of outside actors without considering the socioeconomic restructuring that developing countries are undergoing. Following from this, I argue that the form of democracy being advanced by donors complements these processes of economic restructuring. This form of democracy, labeled "polyarchy" by William Robinson (1996) and "low-intensity" democracy by Gills, Rocamora, and Wilson (1993), is a political system in which elite minority rule and socioeconomic inequalities exist alongside formal political freedom and elections. This notion of democracy privileges civil and political rights over social and economic rights and focuses on order and stability, the two prerequisites for capitalist growth.[3] Initially, it tends to legitimize the status quo, preserving existing economic and social arrangements as well as maintaining the existing distribution of power. Accordingly, the terms of the democratic transition tend to be set by internationalized ruling elites, rather than those popular sectors that suffered so egregiously in the era of dictatorships. Gills, Rocamora, and Wilson (1993) have noted that one difference between prior dictatorships and these newer "low-intensity" democracies lies in the redistribution of power *among traditional elite factions*, with the military fading in the background and conservative politicians taking the lead, supported by the business community. The allure of this political arrangement is that it allows a country to address the exigencies of the global economy while maintaining a satisfactory level of stability and garnering a high degree of international legitimacy through its adherence to electoral processes.

Much of the conventional wisdom on democratization suggests that in order to consolidate and deepen democracy in Latin America, political structures must be improved or redesigned to provide greater "accountability, transparency, participation, and responsiveness" (Diamond 1996, 94). At the same time, recent theorizing on political economy has argued that the far-reaching power of capital under the current phase of globalization is exerting considerable power both directly and indirectly on governments today. The former is evident in the power of transnational corporations and the growth of international networks, while the latter (structural power) is exercised more passively, but no less effectively, through the international business climate, interstate competition, and the international mobility of capital (Gill and Law 1988), posing effective challenges to the goals of democratic accountability and responsiveness.

While some scholars go so far as to argue that capital has overtaken the nation-state, thereby challenging its ability to shape national policy, others have suggested that the state has become a "mediator" between the policies formulated by external forces and their domestic constituencies (Panitch 1994). Robert Cox (1987) argues that states are internalizing a notion of international obligation to the world economy, referring to this process as the "internationalization of the state." He suggests that the central feature in this process is the conversion of the state into an organ that aligns national economic policies with the perceived exigencies of the global economy (Cox 1992). At the same time, governments have been affected by the internationalization of authority: the process by which international organizations are not only assuming a greater role in the management of the global economy but in the management of individual nation-states as well.

This process became particularly evident in the Americas during the 1980s when the region's economies descended into the debt crisis, with the Caribbean Basin experiencing its most serious economic recession of the twentieth century (Deere et al. 1990). Indebted governments had to introduce structural adjustment programs, collectively known in some circles as Washington Consensus policies, in order to qualify for further aid and loans. These policies, advanced by the International Monetary Fund (IMF) and the World Bank as well as a legion of academics and business leaders, consisted of trade liberalization, financial deregulation, and privatization. This neoliberal body of public policy remained preeminent until the mid-1990s, when many of its deficiencies began to surface and some of its elements began to be questioned, particularly its antistate orientation. The response was the emergence of a post–Washington Consensus, which emphasized the need for an active state and the consent of civil society (Martin 2000). This is not an insignificant modification because it reasserts the importance of the political realm to a successful integration into global markets. Indeed, it is this shift in thinking that has made democracy promotion programs—with their institution-building and civil-society-strengthening components—both attractive and ubiquitous. In short, developments in the political realm (the drive to promote a particular variant of democracy) are tightly linked to those in the economic sphere (post–Washington Consensus prescriptions).

Democratization in Haiti: The Conditionality Lever

Haiti's democratization path after 1990 offers a valuable window into how the autonomy of elected officials can be undermined by the economic prescriptions and exigencies of international donors. Haiti is the poorest country in Latin America. The United Nations Development Program's (UNDP) 2005 Human Development Report ranks it 153 out of 177 countries based on achievements in life expectancy, educational attainment, and adjusted real income. According to the World Bank (2006, iii), 54 percent of the population live below the US$1-a-day line, and 78 percent below the US$2-a-day line. Moreover, the country "suffers from substantial inequality, with nearly half of the national income going to those in the richest 10 percent of the population" (World Bank 2006, iii). Haiti's rural areas and its peasant farmers are the most destitute. The rural poor account for three-quarters of the country's poor, with only one-quarter of these having access to safe water and one in six to adequate sanitation (Erikson 2004, 4). The adult literacy rate is 51.9 percent and health expenditure per capita is US$83 (UNDP 2005a).

Since the fall of the twenty-nine-year-long Duvalier dictatorship in 1986, international actors have played a central role in the country's slow and tumultuous journey toward democracy. There have been some decisive interventions. For instance, international actors organized and monitored the elections that swept Jean-Bertrand Aristide to power in 1990.[4] Indeed, some Haiti experts have suggested that the international presence "neutralized customary intervention in the process by the army, oligarchy, and foreign powers" (Castor 1994). Similarly, when the president was ousted by the military seven months later, the OAS, the UN, and Washington helped negotiate the army's withdrawal and his return, but not until three years later, in 1994. The OAS and the UN also established a joint civilian mission to monitor human rights conditions during the three years of military rule and later assisted in institution-building efforts (Shamsie 2004; 2005). These efforts constituted important steps toward advancing democratic governance in Haiti. In the end, however, processes related to globalization (the internationalization of the state and the internationalization of authority) have worked against the political and economic enfranchisement of Haiti's people. Democracy in Haiti after 1994 has been shaped in a number of ways by the economic prescriptions and the development orientation of major donors. In other words, the economic dimension of intervention has had clear political consequences.

The trajectory of Haiti's economic recovery was determined by a host of bilateral and multilateral donors including the World Bank, the Inter-American Development Bank, the United States Agency for International Development (USAID), the UNDP, and the OAS. These actors met with the Haitian government in Paris, just prior to the landing of U.S.-led forces, and developed an economic and financial framework, which was called the Emergency Economic Recovery Plan (EERP). According to one observer, "submitting to structural adjustment conditionality was the quid pro quo for U.S. support for Aristide's return to Haiti in 1994" (McGowan 1997, 9). The plan was essentially a structural adjustment program designed by the IMF and the World Bank to establish a stable macroeconomic environment and to provide an incentive framework for private-sector investment. The Donors Consultative Group pledged a total of US$1.2 billion over five years to the plan.[5] Most of that sum was provided by four agencies: the World Bank, the IMF, the IDB, and USAID (Inter-American Development Bank 1995).[6]

The lack of attention to economic structures of power was evident from the fact that the economic plan slated distributional equity far below other goals, in particular, the broader objective of creating an enabling environment for transnational capital.[7] For instance, it focused almost exclusively on the export-manufacturing sector, devoting little attention to rural Haiti. In a country where close to 65 percent of the population is engaged in some form of agricultural production, assisting peasant farmers would have been the most direct way of alleviating poverty (donors contended poverty alleviation was their overall objective) and addressing the vast imbalance between rich and poor, thereby fostering political equality. Yet international donors directed less than 1 percent of the US$550 million in donor aid and loans distributed in fiscal year 1994–95 to peasant agriculture (McGowan 1997, 22). In fact, the IMF, in collaboration with the World Bank and Haiti's Ministry of Finance, was very specific in its instructions to the Haitian government regarding credit. The state was allowed to establish policies enabling others to set up credit funds but not to provide funds for agricultural research, extension, and productive credit to the poor (McGowan 1997, 19). The agricultural financing that was made available was aimed at road and irrigation system repair and at promoting export crops such as coffee and mangoes. The provision and transformation of productive inputs—seeds, tools, fertilizer, credit, marketing cooperatives, land tenure reform—would have been of greater benefit to the masses in the countryside (Inter-American Development Bank 1995).

Although a good number of democratization scholars have forcefully argued that the persistence of wide socioeconomic disparities does constitute an obstacle to political equality, which in turn has implications for the prospects of democracy (Macpherson 1977; Shivji 1990; Vilas 1997; Rueschemeyer 2004), donors have failed to place equity issues at the forefront of the economic packages they impose on countries. This is due in part to the fact that the solutions to the profound problems of a country like Haiti (including the lack of democracy) are believed to lie in the realm of governance rather than in that of socioeconomic organization.

The lack of attention to class structure is of no small consequence, although it is to be expected when "low-intensity" democracy is the objective. Analyses of Haitian history suggest that the lack of democracy has been intimately linked to how the country's elites have historically enriched themselves and maintained their life-style (Trouillot 1990; Fatton 2002). Haiti scholar Michel-Rolph Trouillot (1994, 122) argues that the unwillingness to view history and class as serious explanations for Haiti's political dilemma have prevented Washington and other international donors from truly understanding the country: "class remains the capital taboo of U.S. political analysis, a divide not to be mentioned—except as a measure of income. Yet class structure, rather than income, and history, rather than the immediate past, are at the roots of the current Haitian crisis." The distinguished Caribbean scholar Sidney Mintz concurs. He noted, soon after Aristide's return to power in 1994, that if policy was geared "to sustain . . . the present distribution of economic power in Haiti, hardly anything can be done that could have long-range beneficial *political* consequences" (Mintz 1995, 86; emphasis added).

Not only did the EERP fail to address the distribution of economic power in the island nation, it actually placed the burden of balance-of-payments adjustment on those who could least shoulder it, thus further shoring up the country's prevailing inegalitarian structure. Moreover, the popular forces in Haiti that had consistently mobilized for a more expansive vision of democracy (those social movements that had brought down the Duvalier dictatorship and sought radical structural changes) were greatly debilitated by the EERP's economic reform policies, while elite sectors linked to international capital—the same elites who have historically shown only a superficial commitment to political change—were advantaged by economic reforms.

It is also important to note that international actors explicitly chose to support those actors in civil society linked to the ancien regime (i.e., the prior era of authoritarian rule). The bulk of assistance went to those organizations that favored careful incremental change through the institutions and processes associated with representative democracy (Maguire et al. 1996). The consequences of these interventions by outside actors were substantial. By advancing an economic project that explicitly favored and strengthened certain sectors of civil society over others, donors influenced the terms and direction of the democratic transition. In short, the EERP systematically weakened those social forces that pushed for broader socioeconomic change and social justice as part of the democratization process and in doing so undermined their political project.

As noted earlier, simultaneously supporting economic restructuring and political liberalization (or "democracy promotion") has become accepted wisdom among aid officials. Still, the link between democracy and free markets, and whether the two are mutually reinforcing, despite ample scholarship on the subject, remains to be proved. Several misgivings have been noted regarding this proposition, especially if economic restructuring is being driven by external forces and planned and implemented without popular input or consent, as it has been (and continues to be) in the case in Haiti. Anita Isaacs (2000, 278–79) has argued that democratic development has been made more difficult by the imposition of the neoliberal economic model for the following reasons: privatization has led to corruption; reductions in public spending have increased levels of poverty and inequality; public participation in politics has become less likely as people struggle merely to survive; and, finally, such development has contributed to "declining institutional legitimacy and capacities."

Adam Przeworski (1992, 56) has made similar observations, suggesting that neoliberal reforms can weaken representative institutions due to the top-down fashion in which they are conceived and implemented. The debates that took place in Haiti over privatization support these views. Aristide had agreed to privatize nine state-owned enterprises upon signing structural adjustment agreements in August 1994 and January 1995, in return for $1.8 billion in much-needed loans and grants. The companies included the country's telecommunications and electricity companies, the ports, the airports, the cement factory, the flour factory, the National Bank of Credit, the Haitian Popular Bank, and a vegetable oil plant. Although President Aristide promised to privatize the public utilities and reduce the public payroll by half in the first eighteen months of his tenure, he ended up reneging on that pledge due to strong domestic opposition. The Haitian people feared privatization would simply transfer a series of private monopolies to the very Haitian elites that had supported the military coup. As Maguire et al.'s (1996, 74) study notes, "divestment of state enterprises was problematic. . . . True, the enterprises generally were inefficient and had never served the Haitian people. But large segments of the newly empowered population wanted such entities to serve them, not foreigners or discredited elites. They wanted to make the state accountable, not to give away its assets."

The international financial institutions (IFIs) responded by freezing the credits they had pledged.[8] The clear contradiction inherent in advancing democratic governance while simultaneously dictating economic policy from above was not lost on observers. As Andrew Reding (1996, 23) noted, "Ironically, Aristide's change of mind came about precisely because of the democratic process that was a prime goal of foreign intervention in the first place." The implications for democracy in Haiti are plain and were poignantly alluded to by the secretary-general of the Platform of Haitian Human Rights Organizations, when he commented on the extremely low turnout for Senate and local elections in April 1997 (three years after the return to constitutional rule):

> The people of Haiti waited a long time for a government that would take into consideration its demands. It did not expect the government would deliver magic solutions, but it did expect it to listen and respond even in a minimal way to its demands. One has to remember after all that this government is here today because it promised that henceforth the smallest peasant would be considered and treated like a citizen and that "the people" would be "an actor." So the people placed their demands before the government, and they continue to do this today, but they have the deep-seated sentiment of having been betrayed by their political leaders. That is the principal reason behind the low electoral turnout.[9]

It is worth noting that, as time went on, a widespread disillusionment with the political process developed among Haitians. A survey of the Haitian press following the president's return reveals a pervasive sense of disappointment with organized politics, especially among Aristide's constituency, the country's popular organizations (Shamsie 2001). By way of illustration, one need only remember that Aristide won the 1990 elections with close to 70 percent of the vote, with 85 percent of the registered electorate voting. But, according to the OAS, legislative elections in June and August 1995, following the return to constitutional government, drew approximately 50 percent of registered voters to the polls, while presidential elections in December 1995 drew less than 25 percent. International observers estimated the turnout for the controversial Senate and local elections of 1997 to be between 5 and 15 percent (Carey 1998).[10] This growing political apathy was arguably generated by the perception that, despite regime change, the Haitian state remained accountable only to the country's small elite and its partners abroad, rather than to the vast majority of Haitians. Decreasing interest in politics in the formal arena was accompanied by public unrest in the streets, as popular sectors repeatedly took part in demonstrations and rallies to protest their lack of input into the policy-making process and their opposition to neoliberal reforms. These events serve to highlight why political instability is often a trait of low-intensity democracy. It is worth noting that, despite the myriad of logistical problems associated with the recent 2006 presidential elections, 59.3 percent of registered voters did manage to cast their ballots, signaling a profound desire for stability, security, and political change (IFES Election Guide 2006). The second round of parliamentary elections on April 21, 2006, attracted only 30 percent of the 3.5 million registered voters to cast ballots for the 127 available parliamentary seats (COHA 2006).

In summary, the form of democracy that slowly emerged after 1994 (only to recede again) was not the result of domestic legitimacy; it was not based on consent or local authenticity. Rather, it entailed an internationally sponsored institutional arrangement that failed to address economic structures of power, legitimized the structural adjustment efforts of foreign governments and international financial institutions (through elections), and demobilized popular forces (by weakening them through economic attrition).

The Guatemala Case Study

The case of Guatemala highlights how a country's further incorporation into the world economy through trade and investment regimes inevitably shapes its domestic politics, with implications for its democratization process. The Guatemalan Congress ratified the Dominican Republic–Central America Free Trade Agreement (DR-CAFTA) in March 2005 and it entered into force on July 1, 2006.[11] This analysis of the trade accord's influence on Guatemalan politics and its potential impact on the country's National Peace Accords suggests that simultaneously supporting economic liberalization and democratization is not a straightforward proposition. Laurence Whitehead (2004, 144–45) has observed that, while the benefactors of economic liberalization, transnational corporations, have the potential to act as agents of modernization that support the foundations of democracy, they also constitute "concentrations of economic power beyond the reach of democratic accountability" that can exert a durable influence on emerging democracies. As we shall see, Whitehead's point deserves strong consideration in cases like Guatemala's, where an egalitarian economy and participatory polity are still absent.

Guatemala, the most populous country in Central America with 12.7 million people, struggles with some of the most dismal social indicators in the hemisphere. Although it is considered a lower-middle-income group country, with a per capita gross income of US$1,740 per year, poverty levels are high with about 80 percent of the population living in poverty and two-thirds of that number in extreme poverty. The rate of infant mortality is among the worst in the region (39 per 1,000 live births) and chronic malnutrition remains a serious problem for 49 percent of the population (U.S. Department of State 2005a). Like Haiti, it is the rural people of Guatemala who are the most disadvantaged. More than 2 million children do not attend school, most of them indigenous girls in rural areas and, according to UNICEF (2005), some 67 percent of indigenous children suffer from chronic malnutrition. The distribution of income and wealth is highly skewed. The wealthiest 10 percent of the population receives almost one-half of all income, while the top 20 percent receives two-thirds of all income (U.S. Department of State 2005a). Finally, the concentration of landownership is among the highest in the hemisphere, according to the United Nations (MINUGUA 1995, 1–2).

While international donors (such as USAID, the IDB, and the World Bank) have supported the implementation of the country's historic 1996 National Peace Accords and broader democratization reforms, they have also promoted regional trade and investment agreements. The relationship between DR-CAFTA, democratization in Guatemala, and the peace accords therefore warrants attention. The basic argument presented here is that DR-CAFTA's investment provisions are likely to hamper the government's ability to carry out the will of its voters as well as the full implementation of the country's historic peace accords. The peace accords, which were negotiated between the Guatemalan government and the insurgent National Revolutionary Unity (Unidad Revolucionaria Nacional Guatemalteca), ended an armed conflict that began in 1960, and continued throughout the Cold War, varying in intensity over thirty-six years. It is commonly accepted that the country's long-standing conflict stemmed from three factors: high levels of political violence; an exclusionary state, which systematically excluded the Mayan ethnic majority; and a highly skewed distribution of land. Consequently, observers have divided the peace accords into two categories: those which address the effects of the war (the Human Rights Accord, the Judicial Reform Accord, and the Accord on the Establishment of a Commission on Historical Clarification) and those which deal with the causes of the conflict (the Socio-Economic Accord, the Indigenous Rights Accord, and the Accord on Demilitarization). The accords were an impressive achievement, not only because they succeeded in putting an end to the conflict but also because their provisions sought to address its causes. However, according to the United Nations Verification Mission in Guatemala and a Norwegian study that assessed the implementation of the peace accords, those accords associated with the causes of the conflict have been "implemented to the least degree" (Salvesen 2002, 15).

In order to capture the significance of Guatemala's peace accords to democratic development, they must be situated within a broader historical context. North and Simmons (1999) view the accords as an attempt to recapture the advances Guatemalans secured during the country's brief "democratic spring," from 1945 to 1954, when political liberalization, social reforms, progressive labor legislation, and land reform were finally addressed. It was the prospect of agrarian reform, more than any other single issue, however, that led to the overthrow of the Arbenz presidency in 1954, ending Guatemala's fleeting experience with democracy and societal reforms. In sum, the causes of Guatemala's long civil conflict (1960–96) were the very issues that reformers attempted to resolve in the political arena during the country's democratic spring, and which remain unresolved today.

The prospects for consolidating peace and democracy in Guatemala will, therefore, depend on the successful reform of political, legal, and military institutions; the implementation of redistributive reforms; and the renegotiation of political participation, in particular equal participation for historically marginalized indigenous groups. Whether the Guatemalan government challenges the inequitable status quo, especially regarding land, will be critical. According to Paragraph 28 of the Socio-Economic Accord, "Historic events . . . have left deep traces in ethnic, social, and economic relations concerning property and land use. . . . It is essential to redress and overcome this legacy and promote more efficient and equitable farming" (cited in Palma Murga 1997, 5). It is important to note that the Agreement on Social and Economic Aspects and the Agrarian Situation does not envision a structural transformation in this area; this type of change would have entailed a state-led redistribution of land, a land tax discouraging unproductive usage, and measures to improve labor conditions and basic services in rural areas. Still, the accord does set out measures that, if implemented, could alter the model of economic development and the pattern of landholding in the country.

Many Western governments, such as the Group of Friends of the Guatemala Peace Process—Colombia, Mexico, Norway, Spain, the United States, and Venezuela—as well as Germany and Japan, and multilateral actors such as the UN, the OAS, and the IDB have supported Guatemala's democratization process and the implementation of the peace accords. The majority of these donors, particularly the United States and the development banks, have also supported a market-based approach to economic development in Guatemala, which includes a commitment to liberal international trade. This has meant unqualified support for DR-CAFTA, and the still-to-be-realized Free Trade Area of the Americas (FTAA). Indeed, it has been argued that the highest profile U.S. foreign policy initiative in Guatemala during 2004 and 2005 was DR-CAFTA (Camilleri 2005). While the project of Central American integration emerged in the 1960s, the captivation with the notion of hemispheric integration began in the 1990s when the U.S. government launched the proposal for a hemispheric-wide trade pact, the Enterprise for the Americas Initiative. The plan, which was enthusiastically embraced by the region's governments, subsequently evolved into the proposal for an FTAA. This event signaled the consolidation of a new hemispheric consensus based on transitions to representative democracy in the political sphere and trade liberalization and deregulation in the economic sphere. The region's political and economic institutions (the OAS and the IDB) have supported the establishment of DR-CAFTA, viewing it as an important step toward regional integration and an impetus toward establishing the FTAA.

The principal objective of DR-CAFTA is to attract foreign investment in order to spur economic growth. One way the trade pact seeks to accomplish this is by bolstering the position of investors, ensuring they are protected from discriminatory regulation of investment and uncompensated expropriation of property. This was the purpose of the investment chapter (Chapter 11) of the North American Free Trade Agreement (NAFTA). DR-CAFTA's investment chapter (Chapter 10) is modeled after NAFTA's Chapter 11. Since NAFTA entered into force in 1994, investors (corporations) in Mexico, Canada, and the United States have taken advantage of their rights under the accord's investment chapter to challenge an important number of public policies and regulations in all three countries in areas such as health and environmental protection (Mann 2001).[12] The fact that NAFTA's Chapter 11 has prevented or dissuaded the three governments from achieving important public policy objectives has obvious implications for democratic governance. It would be worrisome if this experience were carried over to DR-CAFTA countries. The NAFTA experience has already led some scholars who have studied Guatemala's peace accords to suggest that higher standards of investor protection could prevent the Guatemalan government from fulfilling a number of its commitments under both the Socio-Economic Accord and the Indigenous Accord. Gus Van Harten's (2000) assessment relies on an anticipatory analysis of the arguments that investors might use to challenge various policies stemming from the accords. For instance, an investor could challenge government land policies, demanding compensation losses, "as violations of broad notions of national treatment, prohibitions on performance requirements, and protections from expropriations" (Van Harten 2000, 26–28). In fact, the establishment, in 1994, of the National Land Trust Fund, expressly intended to benefit poor *campesinos* without land or with insufficient land, could have been challenged had DR-CAFTA been in effect in 1994, on the basis that it constitutes a violation of national treatment by limiting eligibility for the fund to Guatemalans. Van Harten goes on to show how investors could challenge policies related to the redistribution of undeveloped land, the establishment of a land tax, communal land ownership, compensation for usurped land, as well as a number of policies aimed at promoting and protecting the land rights of the Maya peoples. In sum, investors such as agribusiness and resource development companies could challenge a number of prospective reforms by strategically resorting to an investor-to-state-claim (Van Harten 2000, 26–32). Finally, it is important to note that regardless of whether corporate claims are actually upheld, the threat of a multibillion-dollar lawsuit is often enough to persuade the poorest developing countries to back down from enacting or repealing laws.

While it may be true that the Guatemalan government could have exempted laws and regulations expressly aimed at fulfilling the peace accords from the high standards of investor protection provided by DR-CAFTA, it chose not to do so. Guatemala's elites have always cultivated and benefited from strong ties with foreign interests. Moreover, the transnational faction of the elite, while admittedly weaker than the traditional agro-export oligarchy, has been an enthusiastic supporter of DR-CAFTA and of greater integration of Guatemala into global markets in general. The transnational faction became more important in the 1980s with the "introduction and expansion of new economic activities . . . including a powerful new financial sector tied to international banking, incipient export-oriented industry such as maquila textile production, nontraditional agricultural exports promoted by the IFIs, and new commercial groups" (Robinson 2001, 198).

Given these circumstances, it is not surprising that the Guatemalan government failed to push for special exemptions through side agreements. By making it possible for investors such as landowners, agribusiness companies, and resource development firms to challenge land-related reforms recommended in both the Socio-Economic Accord and the Indigenous Accord, Guatemala's elites would be further bolstering their own social-economic status and power. In fact, the trade agreement could accomplish what these elites were unable to ensure once the peace accords were signed—guaranteeing that the country's social structure remains unchanged. This point highlights that, while a country's integration into the global economic system may be on unequal and dependent terms, these conditions should not deny its agency. In the past elites used the colonial system to strengthen their position vis-à-vis other social groups in society; today they continue to "derive much of their income and status from their relationship with the international system" (Abrahamsen 2000, 7). One can therefore argue that the transnational faction of the Guatemalan elite is eagerly shaping its destiny (reinforcing and consolidating its position) through its interaction with external actors (transnational corporations, foreign governments, and international organizations).

Exploring the potential impact of DR-CAFTA on domestic politics and on Guatemala's democratic transition suggests that trade regimes can affect democratization processes in two ways. First, the agreement can benefit, and therefore strengthen, certain social sectors over others (for instance, modernized capitalist farmers, often linked to agro-industrial and international capital over local peasant producers). Rueschemeyer, Stephens, and Stephens (1992) argue that democracy occurs when subordinated social groups are able to attain enough access to the state so as to transform it. According to these authors, democracy must be imposed on a capitalist state, which makes the power balance within civil society important. While trade and investment pacts may increase economic growth in certain sectors, they also affect the correlation of forces in civil society, strengthening and benefiting specific groups in society while disadvantaging others. In the case of Guatemala, the winners are likely to be the sectors that have traditionally failed to embrace democracy with either enthusiasm or commitment.

The second way trade agreements can influence the trajectory of fledgling democracies is by significantly reducing the ability of elected officials to carry out the will of citizens. This is particularly true in the Global South. Grinspun and Kreklewich (1994, 36–40) have shown that trade and investment agreements have two long-term effects: they constitute a "conditioning framework" regarding the policy options open to governments and they serve to "lock in" neoliberal reforms. Both processes have important implications for democratic practice.

Recent decisions on health policy in Guatemala reveal how DR-CAFTA has already allowed foreign pharmaceutical manufacturers, which have vigorously pressed for enhanced patent protection, to trump Guatemalan law, diluting the influence of the Guatemalan electorate. Just prior to the implementation of the trade accord, the U.S. Trade Representative and the U.S. Embassy in Guatemala successfully pressured the Guatemalan Congress into repealing an Intellectual Property Law (Decree 34-2004) that was designed to improve access to affordable generic medicines by expediting the registration and marketing approval of generic equivalents of new medicines so they could be rapidly made available. The law, which had been overwhelmingly passed by the Guatemalan Congress, would have also prevented companies manufacturing brand name pharmaceuticals from extending their twenty years of market exclusivity by a further five years, starting from the drug's date of registration in Guatemala. Even though the law was fully compliant with the World Trade Organization Agreement on Trade-Related Aspects of Intellectual Property Rights,[13] which allows countries to "take measures to protect public health . . . and to promote access to medicines for all," the U.S. Trade Representative insisted it did not comply with DR-CAFTA's provisions (Russell and Baker 2005).[14] Despite protests from Guatemalans, the government repealed the law. Drug companies can now keep their test data under seal for five years. Because generic drug makers need these data to receive marketing approval for their drugs, it will now take longer and be more difficult for generic drugs to become commercially available in Guatemala (Médecins Sans Frontières 2005). The trade representative also insisted on a number of other changes to Guatemalan legislation. These demands were met by passing a new law, the "Law of Implementation," which made adjustments "to 16 laws related to telecommunications, state employment law, intellectual property, commerce, services, the penal system, and the environment, among others"; and by ratifying three international treaties dealing with intellectual property: the International Union for the Protection of New Varieties of Plants, the Budapest Treaty on the International Recognition of the Deposit of Microorganisms for the Purposes of Patent Procedure, and the Washington Patent Cooperation Treaty (Barreda 2006, 20). Following this flurry of legislation, Guatemala became the fourth Central American country to join DR-CAFTA.

The ties between citizens and the state (the internal legitimacy of regimes) in "low-intensity" democracies are already fragile because the economic and political transition is often crafted by outsiders (foreign aid donors and international financial institutions) and the very elites who were engaged in predatory class rule, rather than the poor majorities who struggled for change. Limiting the ability of a government to control and protect key areas of public policy, such as health care and access to medicines (as the intellectual property provisions of many trade and investment agreements do), further erodes those fragile bonds, making democratic consolidation all the more challenging.

Democratization and the Constraining Nature of International Economic Arrangements

This chapter has explored the relationship between democratic development and changes in the global economy. I have argued that broad processes of internationalization (the internationalization of the state and of authority) can work against the development of substantive democracy in fragile and dependent postconflict societies. External international actors (global and regional organizations, financial institutions, and major donors) believe that building democracy and economic liberalization are mutually reinforcing objectives. Their faith in this proposition is sustained by pointing to the slow emergence of democratic governance across the hemisphere, including in more intractable cases such as Haiti and Guatemala. However, the case studies presented in this chapter suggest that the requirements of economic liberalization favor a particular variant of democracy—"low-intensity" democracy. In other words, successfully twinning democracy and neoliberal free-market reforms through conditionality requires artful maneuvering: democratization is not a given, and the form of democracy that emerges is wanting. Only if low-intensity democracy is the political intent does the symbiotic relationship hold true.

The current political and global economic context allows for the emergence of a fragile form of democracy that displays the chief markers of procedural democracy but does not accommodate popular aspirations for inclusion and social justice. Low-intensity democracy tends to be extremely fragile and unstable for three reasons. First, the bonds of accountability tend to be directed outward rather than inward. Second, the pursuit of justice is frequently postponed or abandoned, permitting the cycle of impunity to continue. Third, political power and wealth remain concentrated in the hands of a small minority, and the social arena (health, education, water, etc.) is often neglected in order to deal with economic exigencies, such as deficits and loan arrears. There is little in this model for citizens to embrace and strive to protect. Haiti is a case in point.

In conclusion, the chapter offers two observations. First, it supports those scholars who suggest that the neoliberal economic prescriptions of donors must be viewed critically with regard to their compatibility with democratic development. The Haiti case study shows that conforming to the prescriptions of donors and capital markets can often run counter to clear popular electoral mandates. President Préval has set out his objectives for the country during his election campaign—get every child in school, create a functioning health care system, reform the judicial system, and assist the peasantry (Mozingo 2006a). At the same time, Haiti's profound economic dependence on external sources will necessarily inform the contours of the country's development plan, as it has in the past. Préval's government will be expected to develop, in consultation with major donors (including the World Bank, the IDB, and the UNDP) and Haiti's stakeholders, a medium-term Poverty Reduction Strategy Paper to move development and democracy forward. It remains to be seen whether the new medium-term development strategy covering the period 2006–9 will incorporate the stated objectives of the Préval leadership. Paul Cammack's (2002) work has suggested that Poverty Reduction Strategy Papers constitute a vehicle by which individual countries, rather than the World Bank and the International Monetary Fund, become responsible for organizing support for an externally determined policy package through local consultations with civil society organizations. This is an exercise that Haiti knows all too well—an exercise that genuinely turns the democratic process on its head.

The second related observation that this chapter advances concerns the expanded reach of trade and investment agreements. Because these accords extend across an increasingly diverse range of domestic matters—removing important public policy goals from democratic consideration—it is important to weigh their alleged benefits against the risks to democratic governance associated with unaccountable global, technical, or private authority. This is particularly true in the case of weak democracies emerging from conflict, where the bonds between the state and citizens are considerably frayed and particularly fragile. Most of the Central American nations have adopted the necessary regulatory and legislative frameworks to bring them into line with DR-CAFTA. At the same time, the region's citizens have mounted considerable protests and parliamentarians have expressed grave misgivings about the legislation required to implement the trade pact. Clearly, trade and investment agreements, which sit at the junction between domestic politics and the international order, are proving to be critical in shaping the politics of democratization. One can expect popular mobilizations and legal challenges[15] to continue as Central Americans strive to strengthen national processes of democratization—ideals of accountability, transparency, participation, and responsiveness—in the context of pressures generated by a global political economy that is intensifying patterns of inequality and further reducing the autonomy of countries in the Global South.

NOTES

1. René Préval is a former president of Haiti (1996–2001) and prior to this, was prime minister of Haiti under the first government of President Jean-Bertrand Aristide, which was overthrown by a military coup d'état in 1991.

2. Neoliberalism refers to a body of thought and an economic project that is directed at increasing and assuring the mobility of capital on a global scale. Consequently, neoliberal restructuring aims at eliminating barriers to trade, ensuring macroeconomic stability, and harmonizing fiscal and monetary policies, because these are essential to increased transnational capital investment.

3. See Gills, Rocamora, and Wilson (1993); Robinson (1996); and, on Haiti, Fatton (2002).

4. The Organization of American States sent numerous preliminary missions to the country between March and May 1990 to observe electoral preparations. More than 200 observers and advisers from twenty-six OAS member states took part. The high level of commitment accorded by the OAS to the December 16, 1990, elections—elections that ultimately culminated in the election of Aristide—was made evident by the secretary-general's presence as head of the final observation mission. These elections were monitored as well by the UN, a number of national governments, and numerous nongovernmental organizations.

5. Along with the international financial institutions others in the group included

the United Nations, the European Union, the OAS, and several governments such as Canada, France, Japan, and Taiwan among others.

6. The Government of Haiti officially adopted the structural adjustment program on October 18, 1996. For details see Inter-American Development Bank (1995); International Monetary Fund (1996).

7. To be sure, the IDB and other donors supported the strengthening of tax enforcement among wealthy Haitians. But even this policy would not assist poor Haitians if the tax code continued to be regressive in nature (see McGowan 1997, 14).

8. More than US$100 million was withheld by the IMF and the World Bank and US$4.6 million by USAID. Given that the country's entire budget was only US$350 million, this sum represented a substantial loss in revenue.

9. Interview with Chenet Jean Baptiste, Secretary-General, Platform of Haitian Human Rights Organizations, Port-au-Prince, 16 February 1998.

10. In 2000 Haiti held legislative elections on May 21 (first round) and July 9 (second round), as well as presidential elections on November 26. But due to the controversial nature of these elections, no official turnout results were posted by sources such as the International Foundation for Election Systems or the International Institute for Democracy and Electoral Assistance. The main opposition group, the Democratic Convergence, boycotted the presidential vote in protest of alleged irregularities in the earlier May elections. The Lavalas Family Party, to which Jean-Bertrand Aristide belongs, won 80 percent of the available seats in the legislative elections and 91 percent of the votes in the presidential elections.

11. In order to obtain the votes necessary for ratification, the government committed itself to approving sixteen laws aimed at mitigating the treaty's most harmful effects. To date, a majority of these laws has not been approved.

12. Howard Mann (2001) provides examples of numerous NAFTA investment claims.

13. The intellectual property agreement was established during the Uruguay Round (1986–94) of trade negotiations and entered into operation in 1994. It covers protection of trademarks, copyrights, industrial designs, data secrets, and patents (on drugs, electronic, and mechanical devices, etc.).

14. Eleven members of the U.S. Congress called on the U.S. Trade Representative to cease pressure on Guatemala to repeal its law, given charges that CAFTA violates the Doha Declaration establishing the rights of countries to prioritize public health over private patent rights.

15. In Nicaragua, the National Worker's Front has challenged CAFTA implementation before the country's Supreme Court. It found that fifteen of CAFTA's requirements contravene the country's Constitution, including the provision granting foreign corporations special legal rights to seek monetary damages in response to regulatory efforts. Court battles are also pending in El Salvador.

CHAPTER THIRTEEN

Transnational Response to Democratic Crisis in the Americas, 1990–2005

Jennifer L. McCoy

The premature removal of more than a dozen presidents since 1990 amid perceptions of growing fragility in the third wave of Latin American democracy makes it timely to analyze the international response to democratic crises in the hemisphere. The establishment of a clear regional democratic norm in the Organization of American States (OAS) protocols and subregional organization democracy clauses has gone a long way toward overcoming the historic sovereignty defense against international intervention. The more specific practice of international election monitoring has made this form of "intervention" in the supremely domestic affair of choosing a country's leaders an accepted expectation.

Yet, democracies remain fragile in the face of weak institutions and inability to meet citizen demands for improved living standards and expanded rights. Hemispheric actors are repeatedly stymied in the wake of constitutional crises and social turmoil, and national interests may collide with efforts to collectively defend democracy. The lack of conceptual specificity of democracy and its violations and the requirement in the Inter-American Democratic Charter (appendix B) for invitation from the affected government create a gap between the expectation for democratic government and the ability of international actors to enforce it. The result is a strong hemispheric democracy norm demanding democratic forms of governance to participate in regional affairs, but weaker tools available to collectively defend democracy or help prevent democratic crises and erosion.

Scholars have recently shown increased interest in the OAS response to democratic crisis and collective democracy defense in the hemisphere (see Cooper and Legler 2001a, 2006; Shaw 2003; Arceneaux and Pion-Berlin 2005; Levitt 2006a; Hawkins and Shaw, Boniface, Legler, and Levitt in this volume), but there has been much less attention paid to other actors, from the United Nations to international nongovernmental organizations (INGOs).[1] This volume points out the importance of the transnational dimension of democratization, and this chapter emphasizes the responses (and nonresponses) of additional intergovernmental organizations (IGOs) and INGOs to democratic crisis. It focuses on old and new forms of democratic crisis and draws lessons from international and transnational efforts to prevent or contain such crises in the Americas between 1990 and 2005.

Understanding the Changing Threats to Democracy

In order to assess international capacity to respond to and avert democratic crises, we need to understand the nature of the threats to democracy.[2] As Legler, Lean, and Boniface note in chapter 1, there is a growing disconnect between the procedural conceptualization of democracy in the inter-American system, its definition in the democratization literature, and the meaning of democracy on the ground in impoverished Latin American countries. This disconnect has produced new forms of democratic crisis that are particularly problematic for international actors, especially IGOs, to address.

Many scholars have noted the persistence of democratic deficits in the region, with some focusing on the illiberal nature of regional democracies (Zakaria 2003; P. Smith 2005), and others on hybrid democracies (Diamond 2002) and even electoral authoritarianism (Levitsky and Way 2002; Schedler 2006).[3] The normal range of scholarly complaints about Latin American democracy includes institutional weakness, party systems collapsing in a crisis of representation, corruption and lack of transparency, and emaciated states unable to provide basic services, security, and justice.[4]

The grass-roots understanding of democracy, on the other hand, is rooted in citizenship demands. O'Donnell (2004) and UNDP (2004) discuss citizenship as having political, civil, and social dimensions. Latin America has achieved political rights for the vast majority of its citizens, while civil rights (freedoms and access to justice) are incomplete and inconsistent, and social rights (providing basic capabilities to citizens to make free choices) are dramatically underprovided. Citizens across the board, but especially in the volatile Andean subregion, have lost patience with the promise of improved living standards to follow democratization and market opening. Those excluded for decades or even centuries, are more and more willing to take to the streets, sometimes with harmful roadblocks, to demand change. In some countries, they have learned that this is the most effective way to extract concessions from beleaguered governments.[5]

Neopopulism and delegative democracy describe two of the more worrisome results of these trends (see Di Tella 1997; O'Donnell 1994; Roberts 2000; Peeler 2004, ch. 5; Legler 2006). These political modalities share a style of governing without mediation between a leader and the people, denigrating representative institutions and the separation of powers. They are emblematic of what is commonly referred to today as "backsliding" democracies. The antiestablishment and antiparty discourse of contemporary populist leaders tears down the old institutions without providing new ones, and in this way is dangerous for representative democracy. Neopopulism does not espouse a particular ideology, but utilizes continuous movement politics, mobilizing the marginalized to follow a charismatic leader who is often a political "outsider," without necessarily organizing the poor with sustainable institutions or mechanisms of representation and inclusive decision making.

The current "wave" of neopopulist elected leaders (first Peru's Fujimori and in some ways Argentina's Menem, and more recently Venezuela's Chávez, Ecuador's Gutiérrez, Bolivia's Morales, and perhaps Argentina's Kirchner) may reflect a deeper social transformation with political implications. If the earlier wave of classical populism in the first half of the twentieth century organized workers and incorporated them into the political system, the contemporary wave of neopopulism reflects a demand for full citizenship by the unorganized urban poor and indigenous peoples. With existing political institutions failing to include these groups in political and socioeconomic terms, they are finding their voice through street politics and increasingly the ballot box. These forms of political participation often result in early removal of presidents through "civil society coups" (Encarnación 2002) or "impeachment coups" (Boniface in this volume).

Some see the active participation of citizens in voicing their demands as a welcome sign of more truly democratic societies. Others see it as a threatening sign of mob rule. I see it as a test of whether democratic institutions are capable of redrawing the basic national bargain required for democracies to function in a globalized world. The demand for expanded citizenship will require a redistribution of resources and political power in this region with the most unequal distribution of income in the world. This may be seen as a new stage of democratization that creates inherent conflicts as the privileged resist the encroachment of the marginalized. O'Donnell (2004, 25) notes that the very process of expanding political rights has historically often resulted in violence, as elite interests resist the incorporation of new sectors. The challenge today is for existing democratic institutions to manage the negotiation of a reformulated democratic bargain that expands citizenship in the political, civil, and social realms.

Past attempts at such a transformation through democratic institutions have run into foreign intervention or domestic resistance ending in violence (Guatemala in the 1950s, the Dominican Republic in the 1960s, Chile in the 1970s, Central America in the 1980s). Although the post–Cold War era provides a more propitious environment, with international norms and existing democratic experience to allow a reformulation of the social compact *within* the democratic framework, experience to date is mixed. Chile, Uruguay, and Brazil have found means to provide some social benefits and reduce poverty within a market economy under social democratic governments.

On the other hand, Fujimori destroyed Peruvian democratic institutions with popular approval. Aristide ruled in the name of the Haitian poor while alienating elites and failing to negotiate new rules (particularly electoral) and was twice removed by force. Chávez viewed his mandate for change as requiring the elimination of establishment parties and institutions in Venezuela, while his opponents believed that nothing less than his removal from power would save the country. Neither side was willing to negotiate a new bargain, and the country remains in an uneasy truce masking a deep polarization. Evo Morales took office with high expectations from his majority indigenous supporters and the threat of secession of oil- and gas-rich Santa Cruz. His government (with a strong electoral mandate and no extraordinary resources to buoy him) may be the best test of whether democratic institutions and significant international attention can forge a new social contract in a peaceful way.

The stakes are high. The alternative to a new democratic bargain in the twenty-first century may well be electoral authoritarianism. While the earlier incorporation of workers under classical populism contributed to the rise of bureaucratic-authoritarian reactions, the current demand for inclusion by the urban poor and indigenous may result in electoral authoritarianism, with governments forced by international and domestic democratic norms to maintain the semblance of electoral competition while closing political space and manipulating electoral conditions sufficiently to ensure their survival in power.[6]

A neopopulist or charismatic outsider variant of electoral democracy or electoral authoritarianism becomes more likely where three factors are present: perceived citizen exclusion is high; traditional party systems are fractured or break down; and major parties, but social democratic partisan alternatives in particular, have disappeared or have failed to meet demands.[7] The degree of exclusion is important because it gives rise to demands for expanded citizenship. The deinstitutionalization or breakdown of party systems hinders the ability of a democratic framework to handle a peaceful reformulation of the democratic bargain. The availability of a social democratic or center-left partisan alternative, in particular, is relevant in that it has traditionally (though not exclusively) led to an inclusionary expansion of citizenship rights. As examples, consider the failure of Acción Democrática in Venezuela and the Radicals and their center-left allies in Argentina, as well as the absence of strong center-left parties in Bolivia, Peru, and perhaps Colombia, all leading to social protests and outsider or neopopulist governments. In contrast, Chile and Brazil under strong center-left governments (and to some extent Mexico under the PAN) have tentatively begun to address the demands for expanded citizenship within their democratic and existing party frameworks and are also the only countries in the region making a dent in poverty.

Sources of Democratic Crisis

As the chapters by Legler, Lean, and Boniface and by Boniface note, the nature of the threat to democratic governability has been changing following the Cold War. One way to analyze those threats is to examine the actors who have generated democratic crises. Focusing on the sources of democratic crises (the actors and their behaviors) rather than the functional threats themselves allows us to determine whether international actors respond differently to threats by different actors. It is my contention that in terms of both political will (motivation) and capacity, international actors respond differently not only to different types of democratic crisis but also to different originators.[8] I consider five sets of domestic actors: military actors, incumbent elected leaders, intragovernmental conflict, armed nonstate actors, and unarmed nonstate actors.

Traditional military force refers to coups attempted by high-ranking military officers with support from the armed forces. Even if the coup fails, I distinguish here between coups attempted primarily by military forces acting alone and/or involving high-ranking officers and coups attempted by lower-ranking officers acting alone or in conjunction with other actors, but put down by the high command. (The latter are included under armed nonstate actors.) As the chapters by Legler, Lean, and Boniface, Hawkins and Shaw, and Boniface demonstrate, the inter-American system has developed a well-codified set of rules to respond to and proscribe traditional coups and coup attempts. When military action is combined with congressional action or societal protest, the response becomes less clear.

Incumbent elected leaders are a source of democratic crisis when they abuse executive power in ways that close political space for citizens or their representative institutions, such as curtailing freedoms, manipulating elections, packing the courts, overriding the legislature, or carrying out *autogolpes*. The difficulty in identifying and assessing international response to democratic threats posed by these leaders is that often this type of behavior results in "illiberal democracy" or ongoing democratic deficits that span a number of years. International organizations are more apt to respond to specific grievous episodes, and "nonaction," which can be just as significant (and damning), is difficult to measure. Boniface (in this volume) uses change in Freedom House scores and the Electoral Democracy Index of the UN Development Program as possible indicators of democratic crisis, without necessarily identifying the source of crisis. Careful examination of these data could provide a useful indicator of incumbent leaders closing political space.[9]

Intragovernmental conflict refers to constitutional crises arising from clashes between branches of civilian government in which one branch may usurp prerogatives of another, such as congressional attempts to impeach the president or reduce his or her powers in questionable constitutional maneuvers, court intervention in legislative purviews, or electoral branch disputes with (or in collusion with) the judicial branch. As legislatures have become more asser-tive in the third wave of democracy, challenging the traditional presidentialist systems in Latin America, we see more legislative-executive gridlock and even impeachment attempts. Here we should not include "normal" legislative-executive gridlock in divided governments, but only those actions where the legislature attempts to usurp presidential powers in maneuvers with question-able constitutional underpinnings. That is, constitutionally sound impeach-ment procedures should not be included as a threat to democracy.

We should also take into account the other branches of state, which in many countries now include a fourth branch, an autonomous electoral authority, and in Venezuela at least, a fifth branch, the citizen's branch consisting of comptroller general, attorney general, and ombudsman, charged with provid-ing for accountability and fighting corruption. In some instances, we have seen collusion between the Supreme Court and the Electoral Authority, for in-stance, to privilege certain candidacies and restrict others. In other cases, there may be conflict among various judicial tribunals, such as a constitutional court and a supreme court, or among various *salas* of a supreme court.

Armed nonstate actors can threaten democratic functioning in the form of criminal factions (mafias, drug lords), rebellious military factions (generally below the top brass), and illegal armed groups, such as gangs, guerrillas, paramilitaries, and private militias. Although this is a serious threat to democ-racy, these actors (with the exception of rebellious military factions acting with unarmed actors) merit a different class of intervention and are addressed here only cursorily.

Unarmed nonstate actors include societal mass protests. (The media, both public and private, sometimes convert into political actors when they control information and use it for political purposes. They may constitute another actor contributing to democratic crises that warrants further analysis.) Soci-etal protests are particularly difficult to assess in terms of democratic threat. Certainly the right to peaceful protest and political dissent is a fundamental liberty we strive to protect within liberal or what the OAS calls representative democracy. Even when protests turn violent, we must assess whether the vio-lence originates in overreaction from (usually untrained) police or national guards or from the protestors themselves. So, for example, when mass protests in which several citizens were killed led Argentine president Fernando de la Rúa to resign, the democratic threat here would not be the protest or the resignation itself but the ability of the system to handle a transition under constitutional rules.

On the other hand, when societal protests utilize methods such as road blockades, small bombs at night when buildings are supposedly empty, or burning tires in the street, these can threaten the health and well-being of fellow citizens, raising the question of constitutional rights of protest versus the state's obligation to provide security. Aside from legal issues, such actions are certainly disruptive to the normal functioning of the economy and polity. Our analytical dilemma arises not only from legal issues but also from the political reality that many groups feel forced to resort to such behavior when excluded from existing channels of decision making. Many also learn that such behavior is the most efficient tool to elicit concessions from a beleaguered government. If governments react only when there is the threat of violence or economic disruption, then can we blame citizens who cross the line from peaceful protest?

Table 13.1 shows the sources of democratic crises over time from 1990 to 2005.[10] Note that some crises are posed by a combination of actors, and these may evolve rapidly as the crisis episode plays itself out. For example, the Ecuadorian coup against Jamil Mahuad in 2000 began as a threat from non-state actors as popular indigenous groups protested outside the presidential palace and were then joined by mid-ranking military officers and finally by a high-ranking officer, all of whom physically removed the president and installed a three-person military-civilian junta. Shortly thereafter, the high command intervened again and installed the vice president as president.

Some surprising results emerge from table 13.1. First, traditional military threats (in the form of coups and coup attempts), though decreasing, are not completely a thing of the past, and occurred as recently as 2002 in Venezuela. If we add to these the participation of rebellious military units in challenging civilian leaders (included under nonstate actors), as in the case of Haiti in 2004, Paraguay 1999 and 2000, Ecuador 2000, and Venezuela 1992, we see a continued challenge for democratic governance from security forces in new guises. Second, intragovernmental clashes resulting in constitutional crises are a recent phenomenon, most starkly illustrated in the 2004 and 2005 crises in Ecuador and Nicaragua. This reflects in part the growing strength and independence of other branches of government relative to the traditional presidentialism of Latin American politics. We note their appearance in this analysis in

Table 13.1. *Evolving Internal Sources of Democratic Crisis in Latin America and Caribbean,*
1990–2005

Years	Nonstate	Intragovernmental	Incumbent	Traditional Military
1990				Suriname
1991	Nicaragua			Haiti
1992	Venezuela	Brazil	Peru	
1993			Guatemala	
1994			Dominican Republic	
			Colombia	
1995			Haiti	
			Peru	
1996				Paraguay
1997	Guatemala	Ecuador	Guatemala	
1998	Colombia			
1999		Paraguay		
		Venezuela		
2000	Ecuador	Peru	Peru	
	Bolivia	Paraguay	Haiti	
	Paraguay			
2001	Haiti	Peru	Haiti	
	Argentina	Trinidad and Tobago		
2002	Colombia	Peru	Colombia	Venezuela
	Venezuela	Nicaragua	Haiti	
	Haiti			
2003	Bolivia	Bolivia	Haiti	
	Haiti	Nicaragua		
2004	Haiti	Ecuador	Ecuador	
	Venezuela		Venezuela	
2005	Bolivia	Ecuador	Colombia	
	Haiti	Nicaragua		
		Haiti		
		Bolivia		

1997 with the Ecuadorian congressional removal of Bucaram on grounds of mental incompetence, followed by the 2000 removal of Mahuad and the 2005 removal of Gutiérrez for vacating their posts. Other examples include the 1999 Venezuelan replacement of the Congress and intervention in the Supreme Court by the Constituent Assembly, the 2001 constitutional crisis in Trinidad and Tobago, and repeated intragovernmental clashes in Peru and Nicaragua.

Third, threats from armed and unarmed nonstate actors mushroomed after 1997, particularly as demands for expanded citizenship and high expectations of democratic governments were unmet, leading to mass protests, at times resulting in violence. Armed gangs and mafia forces (including those in the illicit drug trade) may reflect growing globalization as well. Finally, threats from incumbents are persistent over the entire time period and, as noted earlier but not shown in table 13.1, may be long-lasting. These include authoritarian backsliding that may be quite gradual. Here we note only specific episodes that trigger (or should trigger) international responses.

International and Transnational Responses to Democratic Crisis: What Have We Learned?

Elsewhere I analyze the international response to specific democratic crises, focusing on diplomatic statements, proactive assistance (incentives), sanctions (disincentives), and military force (McCoy 2006).[11] Multiple types of international responses often are used for a single crisis, and these also may evolve as the crisis plays out. In the Ecuadorian example, the international community reacted swiftly as protestors surrounded the presidential palace, with diplomatic statements to convey support for Mahuad and threats by the United States to cut aid and block loans. After the president had been removed, however, the international community shifted gears to focus on a constitutional transition, still condemning the coup but not demanding that Mahuad be restored.

Likewise, not only multiple international but also transnational actors may be involved. Just as Santa Cruz (in this volume) and Lean (in this volume) describe the growing role of INGOs and IGOs in election monitoring, so too do we observe the multiplication of actors responding to democratic crises. These include the Tripartite Working Group formed by the UN, OAS, and Carter Center (two IGOs and one INGO) to mediate the Venezuelan political crisis 2002–4 (see Legler in this volume); the nongovernmental Friends of the Democratic Charter missions to Nicaragua in 2005;[12] CARICOM's mediation role in Haiti in 2004 (see Goldberg in this volume); the United Nations Human Rights Commission in Ecuador in 2004; the Rio Group, MERCOSUR, Andean Community, and South American Community diplomatic responses and behind-the-scenes efforts in crises in Bolivia, Paraguay, Ecuador, and Venezuela (see Burges and Daudelin in this volume); and many INGOs offering democracy assistance and conflict resolution services.

Drawing on the analysis in this volume and McCoy (2006), I present six basic conclusions and identify potential actions that could be taken by transnational and international actors to strengthen their role in hemispheric democracy protection and promotion.

1. *The set of hemispheric democracy norms is strong and has become legalized to a greater extent than in any other regional grouping outside of Europe.*

As Hawkins and Shaw note (in this volume), the Western Hemisphere has the most well-developed set of regional democracy norms in the world outside of Europe. These norms have been codified in a range of instruments within the inter-American system. The resulting legalization obligates states to abide by their commitments and provides for oversight mechanisms to interpret and implement those rules and commitments. Legalization gained momentum in the 1990s, pushed by the experiences of specific states coming out of authoritarianism and attempting to "lock-in" democracy, U.S. democracy promotion after the Cold War and before 9/11, and the prior development of democratic norms. These commitments are frequently, if inconsistently, referenced in international responses to democratic threats, from MERCOSUR or the Rio Group threatening suspension of membership due to their democracy clauses, to the frequent references in OAS resolutions to the Inter-American Democratic Charter (even while infrequently actually invoking Articles 18–21 as a basis for action).

2. *The specification of democracy and particularly what actions constitute a violation sufficient to warrant international intervention remain vague, hindering consistent action.*

Despite the progress in establishing norms and legalizing them, the analysis in this volume and elsewhere demonstrates that the international community has a mixed record in response to incumbents who close political space or usurp the authority of other branches of government. The strongest reactions have come, not surprisingly, to the *autogolpes* of Fujimori in 1992 and Serrano in 1993, with not only diplomatic and proactive measures, but also threat of sanctions. Nevertheless, once Fujimori bowed to pressures to hold elections following his *autogolpe* in 1992, the OAS accepted his continued rule, even though the elections were not for his replacement but rather for a constituent assembly. They were held in such poor conditions that some major opposition parties refused to participate. INGOs monitored elections and condemned unfair conditions and possible fraud in 1995 (the Latin American Studies

Association), and in 2000 (National Democratic Institute and Carter Center joint mission), as did the OAS mission in 2000, but the OAS member states refused to condemn the elections or to comment when Fujimori's stacked Constitutional Court approved an illegal run for a third term in 2000.

While the UN Declaration on Human Rights and the OAS Charter both reference representative democracy as a fundamental human right and commitment of member states, these were rarely enforced during the Cold War period. The recent accomplishment of the Inter-American Democratic Charter spells out the essential elements of representative democracy in Article 3. Yet, in reality a debate continues in the region, and in the world, over the operationalization of these commitments.

One of the glaring omissions of the Inter-American Democratic Charter is an explicit definition of what would constitute a violation. Although the addition of the criterion of an "alteration" to the democratic order (beyond the "interruption" specified in Resolution 1080 and the Washington Protocol) was meant to include new kinds of threats beyond the traditional military coup, there is no further specification of what constitutes an "alteration" and therefore merits intervention of the organization. Without such a specification, many factors can lead to inertia or lack of effective response: sovereignty norms and fear of reciprocal intervention when flaws in one's own state are identified by outsiders; fear of offending an important neighbor or trade partner; and "veto" power of the affected state or another member state in an organization that practices consensus decision making and in which the Democratic Charter itself requires the consent of the affected state for intervention. The result, as Boniface (in this volume) notes, is that the charter has never been invoked against a sitting president, reflecting the difficulty of deterring or curtailing abuses of power by incumbents.

Hawkins and Shaw (in this volume) explain the relative lack of further legalization after 9/11 in terms of a renewed fear by Latin and Caribbean states of U.S. unilateral intervention, especially following the failure of the United States to condemn the Venezuelan coup and the invasion of Iraq. We should also note the growing competition between the United States and Venezuela for political influence in multilateral fora, and the perception by Venezuela's neighbors that the U.S. efforts to strengthen democracy-defense legal instruments are thinly disguised attempts to target Venezuela, thus provoking a counterreaction.[13]

One proposal to address the lack of specificity in the charter is a set of basic conditions identified by the Carter Center's Friends of the Inter-American Democratic Charter, to help alert the OAS and other international actors to the emergence of a democratic crisis and a potential violation of the charter:

1. Violation of the integrity of central institutions, including constitutional checks and balances providing for the separation of powers
2. Holding of elections that do not meet minimal international standards
3. Failure to hold periodic elections or to respect electoral outcomes
4. Systematic violation of basic freedoms, including freedom of expression, freedom of association, or respect for minority rights
5. Unconstitutional termination of the tenure in office of any legally elected official by any other elected or nonelected actor
6. Arbitrary or illegal removal or interference in the appointment or deliberations of members of the judiciary or electoral bodies
7. Interference by nonelected officials, such as military officers, in the jurisdiction of elected officials
8. Systematic use of public office to silence, harass, or disrupt the normal and legal activities of members of the political opposition, the press, or civil society
9. Unjustified and repeated use of states of emergency[14]

3. The newest threats involving intragovernmental disputes and crises emanating from nonstate actors are particularly difficult for international actors to evaluate and judge.

The newest types of threats are especially challenging for outsiders. The Inter-American Democratic Charter in particular fails to address societal sources of crisis and lacks clear guidelines to address intragovernmental disputes.

Intragovernmental conflicts and constitutional crises. Disputes between branches of government often involve constitutional interpretations that other governments believe are outside their authority to judge. When those disputes involve various national juridical bodies competing among themselves (such as a constitutional court and a supreme court, or various *salas* of a supreme court), this becomes particularly difficult for international actors. The extreme measure of the abolition of a supreme court in the case of Ecuador in 2004, however, did generate an immediate response from the UN Human Rights Commission and an eventual international effort to help that country restore a branch of government when there were no constitutional procedures to guide them. That international response was led, however, by the United Nations, as the OAS languished between secretary-generals and not even the United States took the crisis seriously.[15] (See also Levitt in this volume.)

Likewise, in Venezuela, there was little international reaction when the 1999 Constituent Assembly under Hugo Chávez declared itself to have "originating" powers and reduced the powers of the elected Congress,[16] as well as intervened in the courts to remove judges. Paraguay's constitutional crisis in 1999, following the assassination of the vice president in an apparent attempt to eliminate rivals within the ruling party, did lead to strong international reaction. Nevertheless, when the United States attempted to invoke Resolution 1080, Mexico and Paraguay resisted, leading to a three-month stalemate in the OAS. Once again, in the face of OAS paralysis, other actors stepped in. The United States, Brazil, and the Papal Nuncio mediated and put pressure on President Cubas (allegedly the puppet of the general behind the assassination) to resign.

The only time the Inter-American Democratic Charter (or the previous Resolution 1080) has been invoked in an intragovernmental conflict is by Nicaragua in 2005. As Boniface (in this volume) notes, this is also the first time the charter was invoked in a preventative manner, *before* a coup, though in this case it was still at the invitation of the government.[17]

Unarmed nonstate actors. Mobilized citizen protests also pose challenges for international actors. As discussed earlier, we encounter normative, analytical, and empirical dilemmas in defining this type of threat. The protection of the rights to dissent, speak freely, and assemble are enshrined in our concept of liberal democracy and in most of the constitutions of the hemisphere. Yet the enforcement of these rights presents dilemmas to governments charged also with protecting the public peace and providing basic services, not to mention trying to maintain a tenuous hold on power when approval ratings dip exceedingly low and fractious legislatures make policy making difficult. International actors routinely condemn violence and call for dialogue, but rarely move beyond that.

International actors could help societies develop more effective representation and participation mechanisms so that excluded groups do not feel forced to resort to disruptive forms of protest and pressure. The UNDP has focused on democratic dialogue to open political space, the OAS has recognized the need for political party strengthening, and many INGOs offer assistance in participatory law making, political party development, and the like. Nevertheless, more attention needs to be paid to the nexus of political and economic factors, and to the imbalance among political, civil, and social citizenship rights as a cause of democratic crisis and weakening. Much more innovative assistance needs to be developed to spur the reformulation of the democratic social contract that will allow for the development of fuller citizenship in all of its components.

4. International actors favor reaction to crisis, rather than preventative action, and they prefer to preserve the semblance of constitutional succession rather than press for restoration of ousted elected leaders.

Faced with the premature removal of a president in the face of mass protests combined with questionable congressional action or militarized force, the international community tends to switch from support for the beleaguered leader before his ouster, to accepting the change of government and focusing on a constitutional transition once the ouster is a fact.

Three cases involved mass protests combined with military force: the forced removals of Ecuadorian president Mahuad in 2000, Venezuelan president Chávez in 2002, and Haitian president Aristide in 2004. In each case, the OAS, foreign governments, and international NGOs condemned violence, provided initial support to the beleaguered government, and lamented an alteration in the constitutional order, but eventually accepted the removal of the president after a reported resignation and worked toward a constitutional succession.

There was international dissension in two of the cases: those of Chávez and Aristide. The coup against Chávez was condemned by the Rio Group, but initially accepted and even applauded by the United States, Spain, El Salvador, and Colombia. None of the governments asked for Chávez's restoration, but rather accepted the report of his resignation and called for an immediate constitutional succession. In the case of Aristide's removal in 2004, mediation by CARICOM was cut short when the United States removed its protection of Aristide and escorted him out of the country in the face of armed gangs and implacable opposition resistance to a negotiated compromise (with that resistance reportedly supported by France and factions of the U.S. government). CARICOM protested the U.S. action and refused to recognize the interim government, but the OAS and UN provided technical assistance leading to new elections, a multinational force led by Brazil strove to provide security, and most governments recognized the interim president. With the removal of

Mahuad and the installation of a civic-military junta in Ecuador in 2000, international pressure went into overdrive to convince the high command to intervene and ensure a constitutional succession. That international pressure was successful in averting a military government but failed to restore Mahuad to power. (See chapters in this volume by Levitt, Legler, Goldberg, and Burges and Daudelin for more details on these cases.)

In all three of these cases, then, the international community was faced with an ambiguous resignation reported by the interveners (and denied by the presidents) and mass societal protests joining with armed factions of the military or militias. The response was to satisfice—accept the fait accompli of the forced removal of a president but ensure that his replacement would have some semblance of constitutionality that could be cemented with early elections.

In the five cases of societal protests combined with congressional action to prematurely remove a president (Paraguay's Cubas, Peru's Fujimori, Bolivia's Sánchez de Lozada and also Mesa, and Ecuador's Gutiérrez), we see a repeat of the pattern in that the departure of the president was accepted as a fait accompli and the emphasis was placed on how to move forward. The cases of Cubas's and Fujimori's resignations merit special caveats, however. Cubas was forced out under heavy domestic and international pressure following the assassination of his own vice president on the alleged order of the former general perceived to be the "sponsor" of Cubas. Fujimori's resignation followed dramatic videotaped revelations of an intricate network of bribery and blackmail orchestrated by Fujimori's intelligence chief and confidante, Vladimir Montesinos. The scandals surrounding these two resignations allowed the international community to offer extensive support to the succeeding governments.

The cases of Sánchez de Lozada in Bolivia and Gutiérrez in Ecuador were similar in that both presidents resisted resigning and stepped down only after Congress removed its support (Sánchez de Lozada) or declared the post vacant (Gutiérrez), in the face of widespread protests turned violent and congressional divisions. Both Sánchez de Lozada and Gutiérrez also sought to clear their names and faced criminal trials in their countries. Bolivian interim president Mesa, on the other hand, threatened to resign once in the face of massive protests and an intransigent Congress, solicited a political compromise that in the end went unfulfilled, and six months later resigned without asking for international help.[18]

The pattern of international response identified here reflects the inability and/or unwillingness of international actors to intercede early on in a pro-active sense. Instead they wait and react to full-blown crises. In the reactive phase, the tendency is to solve the immediate crisis by accepting citizen dis-satisfaction and the ouster of the unpopular leader, but to satisfy the demo-cratic norm by insisting on a constitutional succession. Even this is not always accomplished. In Ecuador in 2000, the military unconstitutionally recognized the vice president as the new president before the Congress acted. In Venezuela in 2002, the line of succession was not followed after the alleged presidential resignation was reported to include his firing of his vice president and entire cabinet.

An early warning system, along with clear criteria and tools for action, could help to alleviate this reactive nature of the international community. The Comisión Andina de Juristas conducts an early warning analysis, monitoring six Andean countries daily and sending out alerts when a democratic erosion occurs. Such an independent assessment would be helpful on a hemisphere-wide basis.

5. Transnational actors are increasingly important.

Several chapters in this volume focus on limits and progress of the OAS's response, while others also note the importance of transnational actors in promoting and defending democracy. McCoy (2006) identifies the strong set of positive assistance (incentive) measures taken by a range of international and transnational actors to assist countries with a variety of democratic crises. Once we include a broader range of actors—not only the OAS, but also the United Nations, subregional groups like CARICOM, MERCOSUR, and the Rio Group, individual governments, and international NGOs—we see a much more comprehensive set of tools brought to bear to address democratic crises.

In particular, countries in chronic crisis have received abundant inter-national attention. Ecuador and Bolivia illustrate the range of sometimes in-novative international responses, as well as the limitations. With the unenvi-able status of having four presidents in four years, being the poorest country in South America, and a major source of coca, Bolivia has received unusual international attention, again primarily in the proactive sense. The United Nations has assisted with social and economic dialogues as early as 2000 and more recently with political dialogue; the OAS monitors elections; and the Club of Madrid has offered the services of former presidents to advise Bo-livia's interim presidents and now newly elected Evo Morales on executive-legislative relations, organizing a presidential office and formats for writing a new constitution.

We should recognize and utilize the comparative advantage of international IGOs and NGOs. This includes different sources of leverage (material incentives and disincentives versus moral authority, for example) as well as constraints (IGOs must respond to member governments; NGOs may have more flexibility but also may have political agendas that should be recognized). As Legler notes in this volume, the Tripartite Working Group (UN, OAS, Carter Center) in Venezuela made very effective use of its members' varying relationships with the different domestic actors as well as the comparative resources they brought to the table, while also presenting a unified international voice to the Venezuelans.

Nevertheless, competition and overlapping jurisdictions of international actors constitute a significant problem to be addressed in more effectively responding to democratic crises and helping countries strengthen democratic commitment. International actors often compete over their jurisdictional or political authority and give conflicting messages to a country in crisis. (For example, the UN and OAS election observation missions in Nicaragua in 1990 organized large, expensive parallel missions rather than joining forces. The OAS and CARICOM have held conflicting views over Haiti. INGOs compete for democracy assistance funds. Multiple actors in a given country, such as during an election monitoring, can give different messages to the populace as they compete for international attention or emphasize different facets of a process.)

This competition can damage their efforts to help strengthen democracy in a country by causing confusion among the domestic actors and by allowing domestic actors to play the international actors off each other and to "use" their perceived international allies in their conflict with their domestic counterparts. (Two further examples highlight this problem: the Haiti political stalemate 2000–2004 when Haitian actors relied on their respective Democratic and Republican allies within the U.S. government to support their own positions and resisted a negotiated compromise, and Venezuela in 2002 when the domestic actors initially divided between the OAS and the Carter Center to be the key international facilitator.)

I do note improvement on this score, however, as the UN has increasingly recognized the role of regional actors like the OAS and encouraged them to take the lead in resolving political crisis in their region, even while competition and recrimination can still occur in the field during joint missions. In addition, many international and transnational actors now make a more concerted effort to agree on a unified voice and to coordinate efforts. (Witness the joint OAS–Carter Center observation mission during the Venezuelan recall, and the UN-OAS cooperation in Haiti after the removal of Aristide in 2004.)

6. Regional powers can play an important role.

The United States as hegemon is not the only power defending the democratic norm. Regional powers, such as Canada and Brazil, have made important contributions. Canada has played a strong role in strengthening the OAS's democracy norm and legalizing democracy after Canada joined the OAS in 1990. Nevertheless, as Major (in this volume) notes, Canada, like other powers, has shown inconsistencies in its policy, reflecting its bias in favor of procedural democracy over socioeconomic rights, its lack of participation in the Inter-American Human Rights Convention and Court, and its attempt to distinguish itself from the United States.

Likewise, Brazil has played a significant role in some democratic crises, either preventing coups or urging constitutional restoration. Burges and Daudelin (in this volume) find, however, that Brazil's responses, like those of Canada and the United States, are inconsistent. They argue that national interests outweigh principled democratic norm commitments to explain Brazil's tendency to intervene directly and defend democracy only in neighboring states with strong commercial ties (Bolivia and Paraguay), while preferring multilateral declarations of support through groups such as the South American Community or the Rio Group in most other democratic crises. Being careful to protect its own sovereignty and foreign policy autonomy, Brazil actually opposed norm enforcement in some notable cases, including Peru in 2000 and Ecuador in 1997.

The growing independence of Latin America and the Caribbean from U.S. political positions reflects both a maturing of the relationship and a changing U.S. image within Latin America. Concomitantly, there is greater political space, and a willingness to take it, for actors and organizations that do not include the United States to act in the defense of democracy. Whether it is MERCOSUR in Paraguay, Brazil in Bolivia, the Rio Group in Venezuela, or various INGOs, the proliferation of groups able and willing to respond to democratic threats allows the flexibility for comparative advantages of different actors to be utilized.

In sum, then, the era following the Cold War has witnessed an important strengthening of democratic norms and widening range of actors prepared to assist in democracy promotion and protection. Progress in democratic institutions (such as more independent legislatures and courts) and in giving a political voice to previously excluded citizens has developed simultaneously with democratic deficits and a stagnation in expanding citizenship rights to produce frustrated expectations and new types of democratic crises. The result is a need for clearer criteria for international involvement and a new set of responses from international and transnational actors, some of which have been suggested in this chapter.

NOTES

1. Exceptions to this generalization include chapters by Santa-Cruz, Lean, Goldberg and Shamsie in this volume.

2. This and the next section draw from and update the discussion in McCoy (2006).

3. P. Smith and Zeigler (2006) argue that illiberal democracies are now the dominant regime type in Latin America. For attempts to conceptualize and measure variants of semidemocracies and semiauthoritarianism, see Carothers and his respondents in the special issue of *Journal of Democracy* 13, no. 3 (2002); and Schedler (2006).

4. See useful attempts to conceptualize and measure the quality of democracy in the special of issue of *Democratization* 11, no. 5 (December 2004) and O'Donnell, Vargas Cullell, and Iazzetta (2004).

5. This was especially the case with the Confederation of Indigenous Nationalities of Ecuador in the late 1990s and early 2000s, and various groups in Bolivia in the early 2000s.

6. For definitions of electoral or competitive authoritarianism, and analysis of their dynamics, see the discussions in Levitsky and Way (2002); Schedler (2002; 2006).

7. I appreciate the insights gained from conversations with Thomas Legler, Jorge Dominguez, and Jonathan Hartlyn, which helped to formulate these arguments.

8. Note that I am not analyzing structural (national or international) threats to democracy but focusing on conscious behaviors of domestic actors. We could add a fifth source of behaviors originating in foreign interventions that would include such behaviors as foreign financing or veto of a particular candidate for office, supplying arms to an armed group, deliberate destabilization of a sitting government, or armed intervention.

9. Changes in Freedom House and Electoral Democracy Index scores identified by Boniface as democratic crises are generated not only by clear incumbent threats such as *autogolpes*, but also such diverse sources as traditional military coups and coup threats, the Chilean crisis of Pinochet's detention in London in 1998, the Argentine societal protests resulting in the presidential resignation of 2001, and election irregularities.

10. An appendix detailing the cases, and the international responses to them, is available from the author.

11. *Diplomatic* responses refer to unilateral government declarations, multilateral organization resolutions, extraordinary sessions of the governing council of IGOs, fact-finding missions, and general peer pressure. *Proactive assistance (incentives)* includes good offices, democratic dialogues, mediation, technical assistance and democracy promotion efforts (election monitoring, civil society capacity building, demining, etc.), oversight, and monitoring. *Sanctions (disincentives)* refer to revoking personal visas and freezing assets; conditioning or suspending economic aid and loans; and curtailing trade privileges. They may also include a country's membership suspension from a multilateral organization. *Military force* includes multilateral peace-keeping forces and armed intervention by a foreign military.

12. A group of former elected officials, ministers, and human rights officers formed to promote the effective and constructive use of the Inter-American Democratic Charter.

13. Several authors in this volume describe the failed U.S. attempt to strengthen democracy tools at the 2005 OAS General Assembly as one example of this dynamic.

14. For further discussion of the charter and reference to these points, see McCoy (2005b); Carter (2005); Ayala Coroa and Nikken Bellshaw-Hógg (2006).

15. Personal conversations of the author with U.S. diplomats in the spring of 2005.

16. The Assembly actually took over the meeting space of the Congress and adopted legislative powers, in addition to constitution-writing responsibilities.

17. The OAS Permanent Council invoked Article 18 for the first time immediately *after* Gutiérrez was removed in Ecuador in order to send a fact-finding mission and at the invitation of the replacement government. The OAS never declared whether the removal was unconstitutional. In the Nicaraguan case, it was the first time a beleaguered government itself had invoked the Democratic Charter to seek help in the face of a democratic threat.

18. The OAS and the Carter Center, among others, offered to help in the days before his final resignation, but Mesa refused the offers, perhaps viewing his presidency as unviable in light of the extremely strenuous circumstances.

Appendix A

OAS Resolution 1080

AG/RES. 1080 (XXI-O/91) Representative Democracy
(Resolution adopted at the fifth plenary session, held on June 5, 1991)

WHEREAS:

The Preamble of the Charter of the OAS establishes that representative democracy is an indispensable condition for the stability, peace, and development of the region;

Under the provisions of the Charter, one of the basic purposes of the OAS is to promote and consolidate representative democracy, with due respect for the principle of non-intervention;

Due respect must be accorded to the policies of each member country in regard to the recognition of states and governments;

In view of the widespread existence of democratic governments in the Hemisphere, the principle, enshrined in the Charter, that the solidarity of the American states and the high aims which it pursues require the political organization of those states to be based on effective exercise of representative democracy, must be made operative; and

The region still faces serious political, social, and economic problems that may threaten the stability of democratic governments,

THE GENERAL ASSEMBLY

RESOLVES:

To instruct the Secretary General to call for the immediate convocation of a meeting of the Permanent Council in the event of any occurrences giving rise to the sudden or irregular interruption of the democratic political institutional process or of the legitimate exercise of power by the democratically elected government in any of the Organization's member states, in order, within the framework of the Charter, to examine the situation, decide on and convene an ad hoc meeting of the Ministers of Foreign Affairs, or a special session of the General Assembly, all of which must take place within a ten-day period.

To state that the purpose of the ad hoc meeting of Ministers of Foreign Affairs or the special session of the General Assembly shall be to look into the events collectively and adopt any decisions deemed appropriate, in accordance with the Charter and international law.

To instruct the Permanent Council to devise a set of proposals that will serve as incentives to preserve and strengthen democratic systems, based on international solidarity and cooperation, and to apprise the General Assembly thereof at its twenty-second regular session.

Appendix B

The Inter-American Democratic Charter

(Adopted by the OAS General Assembly at its special session held in Lima, September 11, 2001)

THE GENERAL ASSEMBLY,

CONSIDERING that the Charter of the Organization of American States recognizes that representative democracy is indispensable for the stability, peace, and development of the region, and that one of the purposes of the OAS is to promote and consolidate representative democracy, with due respect for the principle of nonintervention;

RECOGNIZING the contributions of the OAS and other regional and sub-regional mechanisms to the promotion and consolidation of democracy in the Americas;

RECALLING that the Heads of State and Government of the Americas, gathered at the Third Summit of the Americas, held from April 20 to 22, 2001, in Québec City, adopted a democracy clause which establishes that any unconstitutional alteration or interruption of the democratic order in a state of the Hemisphere constitutes an insurmountable obstacle to the participation of that state's government in the Summits of the Americas process;

BEARING IN MIND that existing democratic provisions in regional and subregional mechanisms express the same objectives as the democracy clause adopted by the Heads of State and Government in Québec City;

REAFFIRMING that the participatory nature of democracy in our countries in different aspects of public life contributes to the consolidation of democratic values and to freedom and solidarity in the Hemisphere;

CONSIDERING that solidarity among and cooperation between American states require the political organization of those states based on the effective exercise of representative democracy, and that economic growth and social development based on justice and equity, and democracy are interdependent and mutually reinforcing;

REAFFIRMING that the fight against poverty, and especially the elimination of extreme poverty, is essential to the promotion and consolidation of democracy and constitutes a common and shared responsibility of the American states;

BEARING IN MIND that the American Declaration on the Rights and Duties of Man and the American Convention on Human Rights contain the values and principles of liberty, equality, and social justice that are intrinsic to democracy;

REAFFIRMING that the promotion and protection of human rights is a basic prerequisite for the existence of a democratic society, and recognizing the importance of the continuous development and strengthening of the inter-American human rights system for the consolidation of democracy;

CONSIDERING that education is an effective way to promote citizens' awareness concerning their own countries and thereby achieve meaningful participation in the decision-making process, and reaffirming the importance of human resource development for a sound democratic system;

RECOGNIZING that a safe environment is essential to the integral development of the human being, which contributes to democracy and political stability;

BEARING IN MIND that the Protocol of San Salvador on Economic, Social, and Cultural Rights emphasizes the great importance of the reaffirmation, development, improvement, and protection of those rights in order to consolidate the system of representative democratic government;

RECOGNIZING that the right of workers to associate themselves freely for the defense and promotion of their interests is fundamental to the fulfillment of democratic ideals;

TAKING INTO ACCOUNT that, in the Santiago Commitment to Democracy and the Renewal of the Inter-American System, the ministers of foreign affairs expressed their determination to adopt a series of effective, timely, and expeditious procedures to ensure the promotion and defense of representative democracy, with due respect for the principle of nonintervention; and that resolution AG/RES. 1080 (XXI-O/91) therefore established a mechanism for collective action in the case of a sudden or irregular interruption of the democratic political institutional process or of the legitimate exercise of power by the democratically-elected government in any of the Organization's member states, thereby fulfilling a long-standing aspiration of the Hemisphere to be able to respond rapidly and collectively in defense of democracy;

RECALLING that, in the Declaration of Nassau [AG/DEC. 1 (XXII-O/92)], it was agreed to develop mechanisms to provide assistance, when requested by a member state, to promote, preserve, and strengthen representative democracy, in order to complement and give effect to the provisions of resolution AG/RES. 1080 (XXI-O/91);

BEARING IN MIND that, in the Declaration of Managua for the Promotion of Democracy and Development [AG/DEC. 4 (XXIII-O/93)], the member states expressed their firm belief that democracy, peace, and development are inseparable and indivisible parts of a renewed and integral vision of solidarity in the Americas; and that the ability of the Organization to help preserve and strengthen democratic structures in the region will depend on the implementation of a strategy based on the interdependence and complementarity of those values;

CONSIDERING that, in the Declaration of Managua for the Promotion of Democracy and Development, the member states expressed their conviction that the Organization's mission is not limited to the defense of democracy wherever its fundamental values and principles have collapsed, but also calls for ongoing and creative work to consolidate democracy as well as a continuing effort to prevent and anticipate the very causes of the problems that affect the democratic system of government;

BEARING IN MIND that the Ministers of Foreign Affairs of the Americas, at the thirty-first regular session of the General Assembly, held in San Jose, Costa Rica, in keeping with express instructions from the Heads of State and Government gathered at the Third Summit of the Americas, in Québec City, accepted the base document of the Inter-American Democratic Charter and entrusted the Permanent Council of the Organization with strengthening and expanding the document, in accordance with the OAS Charter, for final adoption at a special session of the General Assembly in Lima, Peru;

RECOGNIZING that all the rights and obligations of member states under the OAS Charter represent the foundation on which democratic principles in the Hemisphere are built; and

BEARING IN MIND the progressive development of international law and the advisability of clarifying the provisions set forth in the OAS Charter and related basic instruments on the preservation and defense of democratic institutions, according to established practice,

RESOLVES:
To adopt the following:

INTER-AMERICAN DEMOCRATIC CHARTER

I

Democracy and the Inter-American System

ARTICLE 1

The peoples of the Americas have a right to democracy and their governments have an obligation to promote and defend it.
Democracy is essential for the social, political, and economic development of the peoples of the Americas.

ARTICLE 2

The effective exercise of representative democracy is the basis for the rule of law and of the constitutional regimes of the member states of the Organization of American States. Representative democracy is strengthened and deepened by permanent, ethical, and responsible participation of the citizenry within a legal framework conforming to the respective constitutional order.

ARTICLE 3

Essential elements of representative democracy include, *inter alia,* respect for human rights and fundamental freedoms, access to and the exercise of power in accordance with the rule of law, the holding of periodic, free, and fair elections based on secret balloting and universal suffrage as an expression of the sovereignty of the people, the pluralistic system of political parties and organizations, and the separation of powers and independence of the branches of government.

ARTICLE 4

Transparency in government activities, probity, responsible public administration on the part of governments, respect for social rights, and freedom of expression and of the press are essential components of the exercise of democracy.
The constitutional subordination of all state institutions to the legally constituted civilian authority and respect for the rule of law on the part of all institutions and sectors of society are equally essential to democracy.

ARTICLE 5

The strengthening of political parties and other political organizations is a priority for democracy. Special attention will be paid to the problems associated with the high cost of election campaigns and the establishment of a balanced and transparent system for their financing.

ARTICLE 6

It is the right and responsibility of all citizens to participate in decisions relating to their own development. This is also a necessary condition for the full and effective exercise of democracy. Promoting and fostering diverse forms of participation strengthens democracy.

II

Democracy and Human Rights

ARTICLE 7

Democracy is indispensable for the effective exercise of fundamental freedoms and human rights in their universality, indivisibility and interdependence, embodied in the respective constitutions of states and in inter-American and international human rights instruments.

ARTICLE 8

Any person or group of persons who consider that their human rights have been violated may present claims or petitions to the inter-American system for the promotion and protection of human rights in accordance with its established procedures. Member states reaffirm their intention to strengthen the inter-American system for the protection of human rights for the consolidation of democracy in the Hemisphere.

ARTICLE 9

The elimination of all forms of discrimination, especially gender, ethnic and race discrimination, as well as diverse forms of intolerance, the promotion and protection of human rights of indigenous peoples and migrants, and respect for ethnic, cultural and religious diversity in the Americas contribute to strengthening democracy and citizen participation.

ARTICLE 10

The promotion and strengthening of democracy requires the full and effective exercise of workers' rights and the application of core labor standards, as recognized in the International Labour Organization (ILO) Declaration on Fundamental Principles and Rights at Work, and its Follow-up, adopted in 1998, as well as other related fundamental ILO conventions. Democracy is strengthened by improving standards in the workplace and enhancing the quality of life for workers in the Hemisphere.

III

Democracy, Integral Development, and Combating Poverty

ARTICLE 11

Democracy and social and economic development are interdependent and are mutually reinforcing.

ARTICLE 12

Poverty, illiteracy, and low levels of human development are factors that adversely affect the consolidation of democracy. The OAS member states are committed to adopting and implementing all those actions required to generate productive employment, reduce poverty, and eradicate extreme poverty, taking into account the different economic realities and conditions of the countries of the Hemisphere. This shared commitment regarding the problems associated with development and poverty also underscores the importance of maintaining macroeconomic equilibria and the obligation to strengthen social cohesion and democracy.

ARTICLE 13

The promotion and observance of economic, social, and cultural rights are inherently linked to integral development, equitable economic growth, and to the consolidation of democracy in the states of the Hemisphere.

ARTICLE 14

Member states agree to review periodically the actions adopted and carried out by the Organization to promote dialogue, cooperation for integral development, and the fight against poverty in the Hemisphere, and to take the appropriate measures to further these objectives.

ARTICLE 15

The exercise of democracy promotes the preservation and good stewardship of the environment. It is essential that the states of the Hemisphere implement policies and strategies to protect the environment, including application of various treaties and conventions, to achieve sustainable development for the benefit of future generations.

ARTICLE 16

Education is key to strengthening democratic institutions, promoting the development of human potential, and alleviating poverty and fostering greater understanding among our peoples. To achieve these ends, it is essential that a quality education be available to all, including girls and women, rural inhabitants, and minorities.

IV

Strengthening and Preservation of
Democratic Institutions

ARTICLE 17

When the government of a member state considers that its democratic political institutional process or its legitimate exercise of power is at risk, it may request assistance from the Secretary General or the Permanent Council for the strengthening and preservation of its democratic system.

ARTICLE 18

When situations arise in a member state that may affect the development of its democratic political institutional process or the legitimate exercise of power, the Secretary General or the Permanent Council may, with prior consent of the government concerned, arrange for visits or other actions in order to analyze the situation. The Secretary General will submit a report to the Permanent Council, which will undertake a collective assessment of the situation and, where necessary, may adopt decisions for the preservation of the democratic system and its strengthening.

ARTICLE 19

Based on the principles of the Charter of the OAS and subject to its norms, and in accordance with the democracy clause contained in the Declaration of Québec City, an unconstitutional interruption of the democratic order or an unconstitutional alteration of the constitutional regime that seriously impairs the democratic order in a member state, constitutes, while it persists, an insurmountable obstacle to its government's participation in sessions of the General Assembly, the Meeting of Consultation, the Councils of the Organization, the specialized conferences, the commissions, working groups, and other bodies of the Organization.

ARTICLE 20

In the event of an unconstitutional alteration of the constitutional regime that seriously impairs the democratic order in a member state, any member state or the Secretary General may request the immediate convocation of the Permanent Council to undertake a collective assessment of the situation and to take such decisions as it deems appropriate. The Permanent Council, depending on the situation, may undertake the necessary diplomatic initiatives, including good offices, to foster the restoration of democracy. If such diplomatic initiatives prove unsuccessful, or if the urgency of the situation so warrants, the Permanent Council shall immediately convene a special session of the General Assembly. The General Assembly will adopt the decisions it deems appropriate, including the undertaking of diplomatic initiatives, in accordance with the Charter of the Organization, international law, and the provisions of this Democratic Charter. The necessary diplomatic initiatives, including good offices, to foster the restoration of democracy, will continue during the process.

ARTICLE 21

When the special session of the General Assembly determines that there has been an unconstitutional interruption of the democratic order of a member state, and that diplomatic initiatives have failed, the special session shall take the decision to suspend said member state from the exercise of its right to participate in the OAS by an affirmative vote of two thirds of the member states in accordance with the Charter of the OAS. The suspension shall take effect immediately. The suspended member state shall continue to fulfill its obligations to the Organization, in particular its human rights obligations. Notwithstanding the suspension of the member state, the Organization will maintain diplomatic initiatives to restore democracy in that state.

ARTICLE 22

Once the situation that led to suspension has been resolved, any member state or the Secretary General may propose to the General Assembly that suspension be lifted. This decision shall require the vote of two thirds of the member states in accordance with the OAS Charter.

V

Democracy and Electoral Observation Missions

ARTICLE 23

Member states are responsible for organizing, conducting, and ensuring free and fair electoral processes. Member states, in the exercise of their sovereignty, may request that the Organization of American States provide advisory services or assistance for strengthening and developing their electoral institutions and processes, including sending preliminary missions for that purpose.

ARTICLE 24

The electoral observation missions shall be carried out at the request of the member state concerned. To that end, the government of that state and the Secretary General shall enter into an agreement establishing the scope and coverage of the electoral observation mission in question. The member state shall guarantee conditions of security, free access to information, and full cooperation with the electoral observation mission. Electoral observation missions shall be carried out in accordance with the principles and norms of the OAS. The Organization shall ensure that these missions are effective and independent and shall provide them with the necessary resources for that purpose. They shall be conducted in an objective, impartial, and transparent manner and with the appropriate technical expertise. Electoral observation missions shall present a report on their activities in a timely manner to the Permanent Council, through the General Secretariat.

ARTICLE 25

The electoral observation missions shall advise the Permanent Council, through the General Secretariat, if the necessary conditions for free and fair elections do not exist. The Organization may, with the consent of the state concerned, send special missions with a view to creating or improving said conditions.

VI

Promotion of a Democratic Culture

ARTICLE 26

The OAS will continue to carry out programs and activities designed to promote democratic principles and practices and strengthen a democratic culture in the Hemisphere, bearing in mind that democracy is a way of life based on liberty and enhancement of economic, social, and cultural conditions for the peoples of the Americas. The OAS will consult and cooperate on an ongoing basis with member states and take into account the contributions of civil society organizations working in those fields.

ARTICLE 27

The objectives of the programs and activities will be to promote good governance, sound administration, democratic values, and the strengthening of political institutions and civil society organizations. Special attention shall be given to the development of programs and activities for the education of children and youth as a means of ensuring the continuance of democratic values, including liberty and social justice.

ARTICLE 28

States shall promote the full and equal participation of women in the political structures of their countries as a fundamental element in the promotion and exercise of a democratic culture.

References

Abbott, Kenneth W., Robert O. Keohane, Andrew Moravcsik, Anne-Marie Slaughter, and Duncan Snidal. 2000. The concept of legalization. *International Organization* 54 (3): 401–20.

Abelson, Adam. 2005. OAS 2005: The democracy debate. *Observatorio* (FLACSO Chile) 12 (December). www.flacso.cl/flacso/biblos.php?code=1528.

Abrahamsen, Rita. 2000. *Disciplining democracy: Development discourse and good governance in Africa*. London: Zed Books.

Acevedo, Domingo E. 1993. The Haitian crisis and the OAS response: A test of effectiveness in protecting democracy. In *Enforcing restraint: Collective intervention in internal conflicts*, ed. L. F. Damrosch, 119–55. New York: Council on Foreign Relations.

Acevedo, Domingo E., and Claudio Grossman. 1996. The OAS and the protection of democracy. In *Beyond sovereignty: Collectively defending democracy in the Americas*, ed. Tom J. Farer, 132–49. Baltimore: Johns Hopkins Univ. Press.

Adams, David. 2004. Taint of drugs reaching Haiti's upper-echelons. *St. Petersburg Times*. April 3.

——. 2006. Aristide's last days. *St. Petersburg Times*. February 26.

Adler, Emanuel. 1997. Seizing the middle ground: Constructivism in world politics. *European Journal of International Relations* 3 (3): 319–63.

Agence France-Presse. 1992. Le gouvernement démet le bureau du Parlement et nomme un collège provisoire. December 31.

——. 2005a. Comunidade Sul-American de Nações enviarrá missão a Quito. April 24.

——. 2005b. Ecuador-Crisis/Argentina: Gobierno argentino molesto con Brasil por intermediary en Ecuador. April 24.

Agencia Bolivariana de Noticias (Venezuela). 2005. Ecuador rechaza informe de la OEA. May 11. www.aporrea.org/dameverbo.php?docid=60257.

Agnew, John. 1994. Timeless space and state-centrism: The geographical assumptions of international relations theory. In *The global economy as political space*, ed. S. Rosow, N. Inayatullah, and M. Rupert, 87–106. Boulder, CO: Lynne Rienner.

Allison, Graham. 1971. *The essence of decision: Explaining the Cuban Missile Crisis*. Boston: Little Brown.

Altman, David, and Aníbal Pérez-Liñán. 2002. Assessing the quality of democracy: Freedom, competitiveness and participation in eighteen Latin American countries. *Democratization* 9 (2): 85–100.

Anderson, Leslie E. 2005. Idealism, impatience and pessimism: Recent studies of democratization in Latin America. *Latin American Research Review* 40 (3): 390–402.

Anderson, Leslie E., and Lawrence C. Dodd. 2005. *Learning democracy: Citizen engagement and electoral choice in Nicaragua, 1990–2001.* Chicago: University of Chicago Press.

Arceneaux, Craig, and David Pion-Berlin. 2005. *Transforming Latin America: The international and domestic origins of change.* Pittsburgh: Univ. of Pittsburgh Press.

Armijo, Leslie Elliot, Philippe Faucher, and Magdalena Dembinska. 2006. Compared to what? Assessing Brazil's political institutions. *Comparative Political Studies* 39 (6): 759–86.

Arnson, Cynthia, ed. 2001. *The crisis of democratic governance in the Andes.* Wilson Center Reports on the Americas 2. Washington, DC: Woodrow Wilson International Center for Scholars, Latin America Program.

Associated Press. 1990. OAS calls meeting on Suriname coup. December 27.

Atkins, G. Pope. 1977. *Latin America in the international political system.* New York: Free Press.

——. 1997. *Encyclopedia of the inter-American system.* Westport, CT: Greenwood.

Axworthy, Thomas S., and Leslie Campbell. 2005. The Democracy Canada Institute: A blueprint. Concept paper. IRPP Working Paper Series 2005-02b, Institute for Research on Public Policy, Montreal, Québec.

Axworthy, Thomas S., Leslie Campbell, and David Donovan. 2005a. The Democracy Canada Institute: A blueprint. Executive summary. IRPP Working Paper Series 2005-02a, Institute for Research on Public Policy, Montreal, Québec.

——. 2005b. The Democracy Canada Institute: A blueprint. Canadian experience and expertise. IRPP Working Paper Series 2005-02c, Institute for Research on Public Policy, Montreal, Québec.

Ayala Coroa, Carlos, and Pedro Nikken Bellshaw-Hógg. 2006. Collective defense of democracy: Concepts and procedures. Diffusion of the Inter-American Democratic Charter 5 (January). Lima: Andean Commission of Jurists/Carter Center.

Ball, Margaret M. 1969. *The OAS in transition.* Durham, NC: Duke Univ. Press.

Barbieri, Leyda. 1986. *Honduran elections and democracy: Withered by Washington.* Washington, DC: Washington Office on Latin America.

Barczak, Monica. 2001. Representation by consultation? The rise of direct democracy in Latin America. *Latin American Politics & Society* 43 (3): 37–60.

Barreda, Carlos. 2006. DR-CAFTA imposition and poverty in Guatemala. Trans. Network in Solidarity with the People of Guatemala (NISGUA). In *Monitoring report: DR-CAFTA in year one,* 19–22. Stop CAFTA Coalition. www.cispes.org/cafta/CAFTA_Monitoring.pdf.

Barros, Sebastião do Rego. 1997. A política externa e a defensa nacional-XXXII Curso de Aperfeiçoamento de Diplomatas. March 31.

Basombrio, Carlos. 2001. Peru: The collapse of Fujimorismo. In *The crisis of democratic governance in the Andes,* ed. Cynthia Arnson, 11–32. Wilson Center Reports on the Americas 2. Washington, DC: Woodrow Wilson International Center for Scholars, Latin America Program.

BBC. 1993. Summary of World Broadcasts. Nicaragua: Vice-President Godoy comments on the political situation. ME/1583/D. January 11.

——. 2004. Aristide: US forced me to leave. March 2. http://news.bbc.co.uk/2/hi/americas/3524273.stm/.

Beigbeder, Yves. 1994. *International monitoring of plebiscites, referenda and national elections.* Dordrecht, Netherlands: Martinus Nijhoff.

Bertoni, Eduardo. 2006. Venezuelans harshly punished if they insult Chávez. *Miami Herald,* international edition, September 27.

Black, Jan Knippers. 1999. *Inequality in the global village: Recycled rhetoric and disposable people.* West Hartford, CT: Kumarian Press.

Bloomfield, Richard J. 1994. Making the Western Hemisphere safe for democracy? The OAS defense-of-democracy regime. *Washington Quarterly* 17 (2): 157–69.

Bogdanich, Walt, and Jenny Nordberg. 2006. Mixed U.S. signals helped tilt Haiti toward chaos. *New York Times,* January 29.

Boniface, Dexter S. 2002. Is there a democratic norm in the Americas? An analysis of the Organization of American States. *Global Governance* 8 (3): 365–81.

Boutros-Ghali, Boutros. 1995. Democracy: A newly recognized imperative. *Global Governance* 1 (1): 3–11.

Bruneau, Thomas C. 2006. Ecuador: The continuing challenge of democratic consolidation and civil-military relations. *Strategic Insights* 5 (2). www.ccc.nps.navy.mil/si/2006/Feb/bruneauFeb06.asp.

Bull, Hedley. 1977. *The anarchical society.* New York: Columbia Univ. Press.

Burr, Robert. 1973. United States Latin American policy 1945–1973: Introduction. In *The dynamics of world power: A documentary history of United States foreign policy, 1945–1973,* ed. A. M. J. Schlesinger, 3:xix–li. New York: Chelsea.

Callcott, Wilfrid Hardy. 1968. *The Western Hemisphere: Its influence on United States policies to the end of World War II.* Austin: Univ. of Texas Press.

Cameron, Maxwell A. 1998. Self-coups: Peru, Guatemala, and Russia. *Journal of Democracy* 9 (1): 125–39.

——. 2001. Re: Draft Inter-American Democratic Charter. Unpublished memorandum to civil society groups, May 23.

——. 2003. Strengthening checks and balances: Democracy defence and promotion in the Americas. *Canadian Foreign Policy* 10 (3): 101–16.

——. 2004. We're failing elected leaders. *Globe and Mail,* March 9.

Cameron, Maxwell A., and Maureen Appel Molot. 1995. Does democracy make a difference? In *Canada among nations, 1995: Democracy and foreign policy,* ed. Maxwell A. Cameron and Maureen Appel Molot, 1–25. Ottawa: Carleton Univ. Press.

Camilleri, Michael J. 2005. Age of Enlightenment? Contemporary US policy in Guatemala. *Revista: Harvard Review of Latin America* 4 (2) (Spring): 25–27.

Cammack, Paul. 2002. The mother of all governments: The World Bank's matrix for global governance. In *Global governance: Critical perspectives,* ed. R. Wilkinson and S. Hugues, 36–55. London: Routledge.

Canada. 2006. Speech from the throne: Turning a new leaf. Canada's new government, 1st sess., 39th parliament. April 4. www.sft-ddt.gc.ca/sft-ddt_e.pdf.

Canton, Santiago A., and Neil Nevitte. 1998. Domestic electoral observation: The practical lessons. In *Electoral observation and democratic transitions in Latin America,* ed. K. J. Middlebrook, 33–52. La Jolla, CA: Center for U.S.-Mexican Studies, Univ. of California, San Diego.

Caporaso, James. 1997. Across the great divide: Integrating comparative and international relations. *International Studies Quarterly* 41: 563–92.

Cardoso, Fernando. 2001. *Charting a new course: The politics of globalization and social reform.* Lanham, MD: Rowman & Littlefield.

——. 2006a. *A arte da política: A história que vivi.* Rio de Janeiro: Civilização Brasileira.

Cardoso, Fernando, with Brian Winters. 2006b. *The accidental president of Brazil: A memoir.* New York: Public Affairs.

Carey, Henry F. 1998. Electoral observation and democratization in Haiti. In *Electoral observation and democratic transitions in Latin America,* ed. Kevin J. Middlebrook, 141–66. La Jolla, CA: Center for U.S.-Mexican Studies, Univ. of California, San Diego.

Caribbean Net News. 2005. CARICOM continues to provide support for the people of Haiti, says Jamaican PM. May 4. www.caribbeannetnews.com/2005/05/04/provide .shtml.

CARICOM. 1997. *Charter of Civil Society for the Caribbean Community.*

——. 2000. Statement to the Special Session of the Permanent Council of the Organization of American States on Haiti, Washington, DC, August 4, 2000. News release 104/2000, August 8.

——. 2004a. Entitlement of interim administration in Haiti to participate in the organs of the community. Advisory Legal Opinion.

——. 2004b. Statement issued by the Caribbean Community on the situation in Haiti. News release 15/2004, February 9.

——. 2004c. Statement issued by CARICOM heads of government at the conclusion of an emergency session on the situation in Haiti, Kingston, Jamaica, March 2–3. News release 22/2004, March 3.

——. 2004d. Statement on Haiti issued by the fifteenth inter-sessional meeting of the Conference of Heads of Government of the Caribbean Community, Basseterre, St. Kitts and Nevis, March 25–26. News release 49/2004, March 29.

——. 2005. Communiqué issued at the conclusion of the sixteenth inter-sessional meeting of the Conference of Heads of Government of Caribbean Community, Paramaribo, Suriname, February 16–17. News release 46/2005, February 18.

——. 2006. St. Lucia prime minister urges colleagues to amend Charter of Civil Society. News release 33/2006, February 10.

Carothers, Thomas. 1991a. *In the name of democracy: U. S. policy toward Latin America in the Reagan years.* Berkeley: Univ. of California Press.

——. 1991b. The Reagan years: The 1980s. In *Exporting democracy: The United States and Latin America,* ed. A. F. Lowenthal, 90–122. Baltimore: Johns Hopkins Univ. Press.

——. 1995. Democracy promotion under Clinton. *Washington Quarterly* 18 (4): 13–28.

——. 1999. *Aiding democracy abroad: The learning curve.* Washington, DC: Carnegie Endowment for International Peace.

——. 2002. The end of the transition paradigm. *Journal of Democracy* 13 (1): 5–21.

Carter Center. 1996. *The journey to democracy: 1986–1996.* January. Atlanta: Carter Center.

——. 2005. *Observing the Venezuela presidential recall referendum: Comprehensive report.* February. Atlanta: Carter Center.

Carter, Jimmy. 2003. *A proposal to restore peace and harmony in Venezuela.* President Carter's Trip Report: Venezuela, January 22. Atlanta: Carter Center. www.cartercenter.org/printdoc.asp?docID=1157&submenu=news.

———. 2005. The promise and perils of democracy. Keynote speech to the OAS lecture series of the Americas. January 25. www.cartercenter.org/news/documents/doc1995.html.

Castor, Suzy. 1994. Democracy and society in Haiti: Structures of domination and resistance to change. In *Latin America faces the twentieth century: Reconstructing a social justice agenda*, ed. S. Jonas and E. McCaughan, 158–69. Boulder, CO: Westview.

Cerdas-Cruz, Rodolfo, Juan Rial, and Daniel Zovatto. 1992. Introducción. In *Una tarea inconclusa: Elecciones y democracia en América Latina 1988–1991*, ed. Cerdas-Cruz, Rial, and Zovatto, xvi–xxii. San José, Costa Rica: Instituto Interamericano de Derechos Humanos, Centro de Asesoría y Promoción Electoral.

Chauvin, Lucien. 2003. People power rules in S. America. *Christian Science Monitor*, October 21. www.csmonitor.com/2003/1021/p06s01-woam.html.

Checkel, Jeffrey T. 1998. The constructivist turn in international relations theory. *World Politics* 50 (January): 324–48.

CIDA. 2006. Government of Canada shows support for rebuilding Haiti. News release, July 25. www.acdi-cida.gc.ca/cidaweb/acdicida.nsf/En/MIC-72594751-J7H#1.

CIDH. 2004. *CIDH manifiesta preocupación por la aprobación del "Proyecto de Ley sobre Responsibilidad Social en Radio y Televisión" en la República Bolivariana de Venezuela*. News release 25/04, November 30. Washington, DC: Inter-American Commission on Human Rights.

———. 2006a. *CIDH expresa preocupación por la situación de los derechos humanos en Venezuela*. News release 15/06, May 2. Washington, DC: Inter-American Commission on Human Rights.

———. 2006b. *Comisión Interamericana de Derechos Humanos preocupada por Proyecto de Ley de Cooperación Internacional de Venezuela*. News release 26/06, July 19. Guatemala City: Inter-American Commission on Human Rights.

CNN.com. 2000. Clinton urges Aristide to resolve Haiti's electoral impasse. December 7. http://archives.cnn.com/2000/WORLD/americas/12/07/haiti.clinton.ap.

———. 2004. Aristide says U.S. deposed him in "coup d'etat." March 1. http://edition.cnn.com/2004/WORLD/americas/03/01/aristide.claim/index.html.

COHA. 2006. René Préval: Haiti may get one last chance in spite of Washington's best efforts. *COHA Report*, May 13.

Cohen, Andrew. 2002. Canadian-American relations: Does Canada matter in Washington? Does it matter if Canada doesn't matter? In *A fading power*, ed. Norman Hillmer and Maureen Appel Molot, 34–48. Canada among Nations. Don Mills, ON: Oxford Univ. Press.

Conaway, Janelle. 2002. Responding with the Democratic Charter. *Americas*, no. 4 (July–August): 54.

Cooper, Andrew F. 2001. The Québec City democracy summit. *Washington Quarterly* 24 (2): 159–71.

———. 2004. The Making of the Inter-American Democratic Charter: A Case of Complex Multilateralism. *International Studies Perspectives* 5 (1): 92–113.

Cooper, Andrew F., and Thomas Legler. 2001a. The OAS democratic solidarity paradigm: Questions of collective and national leadership. *Latin American Politics and Society* 43 (1): 103–26.

———. 2001b. The OAS in Peru. A model for the future? *Journal of Democracy* 12 (4): 123–36.

——. 2005. A tale of two mesas: The OAS defense of democracy in Peru and Venezuela. *Global Governance* 11: 425–44.

——. 2006. *Intervention without intervening: The OAS defense and promotion of democracy in the Americas.* New York: Palgrave Macmillan.

Cooper, Andrew F., and Jean-Philippe Thérien. 2004. The inter-American regime of citizenship: Bridging the institutional gap between democracy and human rights. *Third World Quarterly* 25 (4): 731–46.

Coppedge, Michael. 1996. Venezuela: The rise and fall of partyarchy. In *Constructing democratic governance: South America in the 1990s,* ed. Jorge I. Domínguez and Abraham F. Lowenthal, 3–19. Baltimore: Johns Hopkins Univ. Press.

Cornia, Giovanni Andrea. 1999. Liberalization, globalization and income distribution. Working paper 157. United Nations University and World Institute for Development Economics Research (WIDER), Helsinki, Finland.

Corrales, Javier. 2006. Hugo Boss. *Foreign Policy* 152 (January–February): 32–40.

Corrales, Javier, and Richard E. Feinberg. 1999. Regimes of cooperation in the Western Hemisphere: Power, interests, and intellectual traditions. *International Studies Quarterly* 43: 1–36.

Cortell, Andrew P., and James Davis. 1996. How do international institutions matter? The domestic impact of international norms and rules. *International Studies Quarterly* 40: 451–78.

——. 2000. Understanding the domestic impact of international norms: A research agenda. *International Studies Review* 2 (1): 65–87.

Cox, Michael G., John Ikenberry, and Takashi Inoguchi, eds. 2000a. *American democracy promotion: Impulses, strategies and impacts.* Oxford: Oxford Univ. Press.

——. 2000b. Introduction to *American democracy promotion: Impulses, strategies, and impacts,* ed. Michael Cox, G. John Ikenberry, and Takashi Inoguchi, 1–20. Oxford: Oxford Univ. Press.

Cox, Robert W. 1987. *Production, power and world order: Social forces in the making of history.* New York: Columbia Univ. Press.

——. 1992. Global perestroika. In *New world order? The socialist register, 1992,* ed. R. Milliband and L. Panitch, 26–43. London: Merlin.

Crisp, Brian F., and Daniel H. Levine. 1998. Democratizing the democracy? Crisis and reform in Venezuela. *Journal of Inter-American Studies and World Affairs* 40 (2): 28–61.

Dade, Carlo. 2004. Rebuilding Haiti: The test for Canada. *FOCAL Point* 3 (3): 9–10. www.focal.ca/pdf/focalpoint_mar04.pdf.

Daudelin, Jean. 2005. Brazil: The good news scandal. *FOCAL Point* 4 (8): 1–2.

Davis, Harold. 1977. Relations during the times of troubles, 1825–1860. In *Latin American diplomatic history: An introduction,* ed H. E. Davis, J. J. Finan, and F. T. Peck, 65–106. Baton Rouge: Louisiana State Univ. Press.

Deere, Carmen Diana, Peggy Antrobus, Lynn Bolles, Edwin Melendez, Peter Phillips, Marcia Rivera, and Helen Safa. 1990. *In the shadow of the sun: Caribbean development alternatives and U.S. policy.* Boulder, CO: Westview.

Degregori, Carlos Iván. 2001. *La década de la antipolítica: Auge y huida de Alberto Fujimori y Vladimiro Montesinos.* Lima: Instituto de Estudios Peruanos.

Deibert, Michael. 2005. *Notes from the last testament: The struggle for Haiti.* New York: Seven Stories.

DeYoung, Karen. 2002. U.S. seen as weak patron of Latin democracy. *Washington Post,* April 16.

de Zeeuw, Jeroen, and Krishna Kumar, eds. 2006. *Promoting democracy in postconflict societies.* Boulder, CO: Lynne Rienner.

DFAIT. 1995. Canadian Foreign Policy Review. Canada in the world. www.dfait-maeci .gc.ca/foreign_policy/cnd-world/menu-en.asp.

———. 2006a. Minister MacKay announces funding for Haiti. News release 2006: 62. June 3. http://w01.international.gc.ca/minpub/Publication.aspx?isRedirect=True& publication_i=384061&Language=E&docnumber=62.

———. 2006b. Notes for an address by the Honourable Peter MacKay, Minister of Foreign Affairs and Minister of the Atlantic Canada Opportunities Agency, at the plenary session of the 36th general assembly of the Organization of American States. Media Room. June 5. www.dfait-maeci.gc.ca.

Diamond, Larry. 1996. Democracy in Latin America: Degrees, illusions, and direction for consolidation. In *Beyond sovereignty: Collectively defending democracy in the Americas,* ed. Tom Farer, 52–106. Baltimore: Johns Hopkins Univ. Press.

———. 2002. Thinking about hybrid regimes. *Journal of Democracy* 13 (2): 21-35.

Diamond, Larry, and Leonardo Morlino. 2004. The quality of democracy: An overview. *Journal of Democracy* 15 (4): 20–31.

Di Tella, Torcuato. 1997. Populism into the twenty-first century. *Government and Opposition* 32 (2): 187–200.

Drake, Paul W. 1991. From good men to good neighbors: 1912–1932. In *Exporting democracy: The United States and Latin America,* ed. Abraham F. Lowenthal, 3–40. Baltimore: Johns Hopkins Univ. Press.

Economist. 2000. Ecuador's post-coup reckoning. January 27.

———. 2003. Zimbabwe and the Commonwealth. December 13.

———. 2004. Whose coup in Haiti? March 6.

———. 2005a. After the Palacio coup: Now let's spend! May 5.

———. 2005b. How to protect Latin American democracy. June 9.

Edwards, Sandra. 2005. Outside the rule of law: Ecuador's courts in crisis. *Special Update: Ecuador* (April). Washington, DC: Washington Office on Latin America.

Ellner, Steve, and Daniel Hellinger, eds. 2003. *Venezuelan politics in the Chávez era: Class, polarization, and conflict.* Boulder, CO: Lynne Rienner.

Ellner, Steve, and Fred Rosen. 2002. Chavismo at the crossroads: Hardliners, moderates and a regime under attack. *NACLA Report on the Americas* 35 (6): 8–14.

Encarnación, Omar G. 2002. Venezuela's "Civil Society Coup." *World Policy Journal* 19 (2): 38–48.

Envio. 1990a. International election observers: Nicaragua under a microscope. No. 103 (February): 20–31.

———. 1990b. Nicaragua's 1984 elections: A history worth the retelling. No. 102 (January): 22–35.

Erikson, Daniel P. 2004. Haiti: Challenges in poverty reduction. Conference Report, Inter-American Dialogue workshop, December 7–8, 2003. Washington, DC: Inter-American Dialogue. www.thedialogue.org/publications/country_studies/haiti_ poverty.pdf.

———. 2005. Haiti after Aristide: Still on the brink. *Current History* 104 (679): 83–90.

Espinal, Rosario. 1998. Electoral observation and democratization in the Dominican Republic. In *Electoral observation and democratic transitions in Latin America,* ed. K. J. Middlebrook, 93–113. La Jolla, CA: Center for U.S.-Mexican Studies, Univ. of California, San Diego.

Estado de São Paulo. 2004. Powell detalha política externa de Bush e faz elogio ao Brasil. November 10.

European Union. 2006a. Declaration by the Presidency on behalf of the European Union on the presidential elections in Venezuela. Press release 520/2006, December 7.

———. 2006b. Preliminary statement: European Union election observation mission, presidential elections Venezuela 2006. Caracas, December 5.

FAC. 2005. *A role of pride and influence in the world. Canada's International Policy Statement.* http://geo.international.gc.ca/cip-pic/current_discussions/ips-archive-en.asp.

Farer, Tom J., ed. 1996a. *Beyond sovereignty: Collectively defending democracy in the Americas.* Baltimore: Johns Hopkins Univ. Press.

———. 1996b. Collectively defending democracy in the Western Hemisphere: Introduction and overview. In *Beyond sovereignty: Collectively defending democracy in the Americas,* ed. Tom J. Farer, 1–29. Baltimore: Johns Hopkins Univ. Press.

Fatton, Robert, Jr. 2002. *Haiti's predatory republic: The unending transition to democracy.* Boulder, CO: Lynne Rienner.

———. 2006. Haiti: Hope for a fragile state. In *The fall of Aristide and Haiti's current predicament,* ed. Yasmine Shamsie and Andrew S. Thompson, 15–24. Waterloo, ON: Wilfrid Laurier University Press.

Finnemore, Martha. 1996. *National interests in international society.* Ithaca, NY: Cornell Univ. Press.

Finnemore, Martha, and Kathryn Sikkink. 1998. International norm dynamics and political change. *International Organization* 52 (4): 887–917.

———. 2001. Taking stock: The constructivist research program in international relations and comparative politics. *Annual Review of Political Science* 4: 391–416.

Font, Mauricio A. 2003. *Transforming Brazil: A reform era in perspective.* Lanham, MD: Rowman & Littlefield.

———, ed. 2004. *Reforming Brazil.* Lanham, MD: Rowman & Littlefield.

Fournier, Dominique, and Sean W. Burges. 2000. Form before function: Democratization in Paraguay. *Canadian Journal of Latin American and Caribbean Studies* 25 (49): 5–32.

Franck, Thomas. 1992. The emerging right to democratic governance. *American Journal of International Law* 86 (1): 46–91.

Freedom House. 2003a. Freedom in the world 2004: Global freedom gains amid terror, uncertainty. www.freedomhouse.org/research/survey2004.htm.

———. 2003b. Freedom in the world country ratings, 1972 through 2003. www.freedomhouse.org/ratings/allscore04.xls.

———. 2004. Freedom in the world 2005: Civic power and electoral politics. www.freedomhouse.org/research/survey2005.htm.

Frohmann, Alicia. 1994. Regional initiatives for peace and democracy: The collective diplomacy of the Rio Group. In *Collective responses to regional problems: The case of*

Latin America and the Caribbean, ed. Carl Kaysen, Robert A. Pastor, and Laura W. Reed, 129–41. Cambridge, MA: American Academy of Arts and Sciences.

Fukuyama, Francis. 1992. *The end of history and the last man.* New York: Free Press.

Garber, Larry. 1984. *Guidelines for international election observing.* Washington, DC: International Human Rights Law Group.

García-Guadilla, María Pilar, Ana Mallén, and Maryluz Guillén. 2004. The multiple faces of Venezuelan civil society: Politicization and its impact on democratization. Paper presented at the 2004 congress of the Latin American Studies Association, Las Vegas, October 7–9.

Gardini, Gian Luca. 2005. Two critical passages on the road to MERCOSUR. *Cambridge Review of International Affairs* 18 (3): 405–20.

Gaviria, César. 2004. *The OAS in transition: 1994–2004.* Washington, DC: Organization of American States.

Gill, Stephen, and David Law. 1988. *The global political economy: Perspectives, problems, and policies.* Baltimore: Johns Hopkins Univ. Press.

Gills, Barry J., Joel Rocamora, and Richard Wilson. 1993. *Low intensity democracy: Political power in the new world order.* London: Pluto.

Gindin, Jonah. 2005. Whose democracy? Venezuela stymies U.S. (again). *Venezuelanalyis,* June 8. www.venezuelanalysis.com/articles.php?artno=1473.

Globe and Mail. 2006. Harper tells US audience "Canada is back." September 20.

Goldberg, David. 2003. Evaluating the emergence of a democratic regime of the Americas: Evolving norms and changing standards. Ph.D. diss., Northern Illinois Univ., DeKalb.

Goldman, Ralph, and William A. Douglas, eds. 1998. *Promoting democracy: Opportunities and issues.* New York: Praeger.

Goldstein, Judith, Miles Kahler, Robert O. Keohane, and Anne-Marie Slaughter. 2000. Introduction: Legalization and world politics. Special issue, *International Organization* 54 (3): 385–400.

Government of Venezuela. 2001. *Propuesta de Venezuela al proyecto de Carta Democrática Interamericana.* www.venezuela-oas.org/Doc%20Propuestas.htm.

Graham, John W. 2002. A Magna Carta for the Americas: The Inter-American Democratic Charter: Genesis, challenges and Canadian connections. FOCAL Policy Paper, Ottawa. www.focal.ca/pdf/iad_charter.pdf.

———. 2005. La OEA se hunde: ¿Merece ser salvada? *Foreign Affairs en Español* 5 (2): 93–98.

Grant, Ruth W., and Robert O. Keohane. 2005. Accountability and abuses of power in world politics. *American Political Science Review* 99 (1): 29–43.

Greste, Peter. 2000. Haiti goes to the polls. *BBC News,* May 9. http://news.bbc.co.uk/2/hi/americas/737270.stm.

Grinspun, Ricardo, and Robert Kreklewich. 1994. Consolidating neoliberal reform: "Free trade" as a conditioning framework. *Studies in Political Economy* 43: 33–61.

Grugel, Jean. 1999a. Conclusion: Toward an understanding of transnational and non-state actors in global democratization. In *Democracy without borders: Transnationalization and conditionality in new democracies,* ed. Jean Grugel, 157–63. London: Routledge.

———, ed. 1999b. *Democracy without borders: Transnationalization and conditionality in new democracies.* London: Routledge.

Guimarães Reis, Fernando. 1991. Suriname: Missão brasileira para a retomada da co-operação bilateral: Memorandum para o Sr. Secretário-Geral de Política Exterior. Secretaria de Estado das Relações Exteriores, Brasil. October 14.

Gunson, Phil. 2006. Chávez's Venezuela. *Current History* 105 (688): 58–63.

Hakim, Peter. 1993. The OAS: Putting principles into practice. *Journal of Democracy* 4 (3): 39–49.

———. 2002. The world, democracy, and U.S. credibility. *New York Times,* April 21.

———. 2006. Is Washington losing Latin America? *Foreign Affairs* 85 (1): 39–53.

Halperin, Morton H., and Mirna Galic, eds. 2005. *Protecting democracy: International responses.* Lanham, MD: Lexington Books.

Halperin, Morton H., and Kristen Lomasney. 1998. Guaranteeing democracy: A review of the record. *Journal of Democracy* 9 (2): 134–47.

Hartlyn, Jonathan, and Jennifer McCoy. 2001. Elections with "adjectives" in contemporary Latin America: A comparative analysis. Paper presented at the annual meeting of the Latin American Studies Association, Washington, DC, September 6–8.

Hartz, Louis. 1983. *The liberal tradition in America.* San Diego: Harvest/HBJ Book.

Hawkins, Darren G. 2002. *International human rights and authoritarian rule in Chile.* Lincoln: Univ. of Nebraska Press.

Held, David. 1996. *Models of democracy.* 2nd ed. Stanford, CA: Stanford Univ. Press.

Herman, E., and F. Brodhead. 1984. *Demonstration elections: US-staged elections in the Dominican Republic, Vietnam and El Salvador.* Boston: South End Press.

Hopf, Ted. 1998. The promise of constructivism in international relations theory. *International Security* 23 (1): 171–200.

Hoy (Quito). 2005. Gutiérrez y Peñaherrera, en cruce verbal en los EEUU. June 16. www.hoy.com.ec/NoticiaNue.asp?row_id=207221.

IFES Election Guide. 2006. Country Profile: Haiti. www.electionguide.org/country-events.php?ID=94.

IHRLG and WOLA. 1985a. From shadow into sunlight: A report on the 1984 Uruguayan electoral process. Washington, DC: International Human Rights Law Group/Washington Office on Latin America.

———. 1985b. 1985 Guatemalan election: Will the military relinquish power? A Delegation Report. Washington, DC: International Human Rights Law Group/Washington Office on Latin America.

Inter-American Conference for the Maintenance of Peace. 1936. *Declaration of principles of inter-American solidarity and cooperation.* Buenos Aires, December 1–23. Avalon Project, 1988. www.yale.edu/lawweb/avalon/intdip/interam/intam07.htm.

Inter-American Development Bank. 1995. *Emergency economic recovery program: Haiti: A report of the joint mission (7–30 Nov 1994).* Washington, DC: Inter-American Development Bank.

International Crisis Group. 2005. *Haiti's elections: The case for a short delay.* Latin America/Caribbean Briefing 9. November 25. Port-au-Prince and Brussels: International Crisis Group. www.crisisgroup.org/home/index.cfm?id=3806&l=1.

———. 2006. *Haiti after the elections: Challenges for Préval's first 100 days.* Latin America/Caribbean Briefing 10. May 11. Port-au-Prince and Brussels: International Crisis Group. www.crisisgroup.org/home/index.cfm?id=4104&l=1.

International IDEA. 1997. *Code of conduct: Ethical and professional observation of elections.* Stockholm: International Institute for Democracy and Electoral Assistance.

——. 2000. *Guidelines for determining involvement in international election observation.* Stockholm: International Institute for Democracy and Electoral Assistance.

——. 2005. Voter turnout: Guyana. www.idea.int/vt/country_view.cfm?Country Code=GY.

International Monetary Fund. 1996. IMF approves three-year ESAF loan for Haiti. News release 96/53, October 18. Washington, DC: IMF.

Isaacs, Anita. 1996. International support for democratization. In *Beyond sovereignty: Collectively defending democracy in the Americas,* ed. Tom J. Farer, 277–86. Baltimore: Johns Hopkins Univ. Press.

——. 2000. International assistance for democracy: A cautionary tale. In *The future of inter-American relations,* ed. J. Dominguez, 259–86. New York: Routledge.

Jackson, Patrick, and Daniel Nexon. 2002. Globalization, the comparative method, and comparing constructions. In *Constructivism and comparative politics,* ed. Daniel Green, 88–120. Armonk, NY: M. E. Sharpe.

Jackson, Robert. 1990. *Quasi-states: Sovereignty, international relations and the third world.* Cambridge: Cambridge Univ. Press.

Jason, Karen J. 1992. The role of non-governmental organizations in international election observing. *International Law and Politics* 24: 1795–1843.

Jentleson, Bruce W. 2004. *American foreign policy.* New York: Norton.

Johnson, Stephen. 2005. Ecuador's no. 1 problem. WebMemo 732. Heritage Foundation. April 26. http://www.heritage.org/Research/LatinAmerica/wm732.cfm.

Kacowicz, Arie M. 2005. *The impact of norms in international society: The Latin American experience, 1881–2001.* Notre Dame, IN: Univ. of Notre Dame Press.

Karl, Terry Lynn. 1990. Dilemmas of democratization in Latin America. *Comparative Politics* 23: 1–21.

Katzenstein, Peter J., ed. 1996. *The culture of national security: Norms and identity in world politics.* New York: Columbia Univ. Press.

Kay, Katty. 2002. Bush team met Chávez coup leaders. *Times,* April 17.

Keck, Margaret, and Kathryn Sikkink. 1998. *Activists beyond borders: Advocacy networks in international politics.* Ithaca, NY: Cornell Univ. Press.

Kennan, George. 1999. Latin America as a problem in United States foreign policy. In *Neighborly adversaries,* ed. Michael LaRosa and Frank O. Mora, 177–203. Boulder, CO: Rowman & Littlefield.

Keohane, Robert O., and Josph E. Nye. 1971. Transnational relations and world politics: An introduction. In *Transnational relations and world politics,* ed. Robert O. Keohane and Joseph E. Nye, ix–xxix. Cambridge, MA: Harvard Univ. Press.

Khagram, Sanjeev, James V. Riker, and Kathryn Sikkink, eds. 2002. *Restructuring world politics: Transnational social movements, networks, and norms.* Minneapolis: Univ. of Minnesota Press.

Kingsley, H. E., and C. A. Layne. 2000. Statement on behalf of the Caribbean Community on the presidential and senatorial elections of November 26, 2000, in Haiti, by the ambassador and permanent representative of St. Vincent and the Grenadines. Official news release 154/2000.

Klotz, Audie. 1995. *Norms in international relations: The struggle against apartheid.* Ithaca, NY: Cornell Univ. Press.

Kornbluh, Peter. 2003. *The Pinochet files: A declassified dossier on atrocity and accountability.* New York: New Press.

Krasner, Stephen, ed. 1983. *International regimes*. Ithaca, NY: Cornell Univ. Press.
———. 1999. *Organized hypocrisy*. Princeton, NJ: Princeton Univ. Press.
Krugman, Paul. 2002. Losing Latin America. *New York Times,* April 16.
Kryzanek, Michael J. 1996. *U.S.-Latin American relations*. 3rd ed. Westport, CT: Praeger.
Kumar, Chetan, and Sara Lodge. 2002. *Sustainable peace through democratization: The experiences of Haiti and Guatemala*. New York: International Peace Academy.
LaFeber, Walter. 1999. Inevitable revolutions. In *Neighborly adversaries,* ed. Michael LaRosa and Frank O. Mora, 113–25. Boulder, CO: Rowman & Littlefield.
Lagos, Enrique, and Timothy D. Rudy. 2002. The third Summit of the Americas and the thirty-first session of the OAS General Assembly. *American Journal of International Law* 96 (1): 173–81.
Lagos, Marta. 2003. A road with no return? *Journal of Democracy* 14 (2): 163–73.
Lampreia, Luiz Felipe. 1997. A política externa brasileira frenta à democracia e à integração. Lecture, Consejo Argentino de Relaciones Internacionales (CARI). March 6.
Lampreia, Luiz Felipe, and Ademar Seabra da Cruz Jr. 2005. Brazil: Successfully coping with structural constraints. In *Diplomacy and developing nations: Post–cold war foreign policy-making structures and processes,* ed. Justin Robertson and Maurice A. East, 97–113. New York: Routledge.
Latinobarometer. 2005. *Latinobarómetro Report 2005*. Democracy. www.latinobaro metro.org/uploads/media/2005_02.pdf.
Lean, Sharon F. 2004. The transnational politics of democracy promotion. Ph.D. diss., University of California, Irvine.
———. 2007. Democracy assistance to domestic election monitoring organizations: Conditóns for success. *Democratization* 14(2): 289–312.
Legler, Thomas. 2003. Peru then and now: The Inter-American Charter and Peruvian democratization. *Canadian Foreign Policy* 10 (3): 61–73.
———. 2006. Bridging divides, Breaking impasses: Civil society in the promotion and protection of democracy. Paper presented to the conference on "Civil Society and Democracy Promotion" in the Americas, FOCAL, Ottawa. March 1–2.
———. 2007. Empty pieces of paper or a living document? The Inter-American Democratic Charter. In *Governing the Americas: Assessing multilateral institutions,* ed. Gordon Mace, Jean-Philippe Thérien, and Paul Haslam. Boulder, CO: Lynne Rienner.
Legro, Jeffrey. 2000. Whence American internationalism. *International Organization* 54 (2): 253–89.
Levine, Daniel H., and Brian F. Crisp. 1999. Venezuela: The character, crisis, and possible future of democracy. *World Affairs* 161 (3): 123–65.
Levitsky, Steven, and Lucan Way. 2002. The rise of competitive authoritarianism. *Journal of Democracy* 13 (2): 51–65.
———. 2005. International linkage and democratization. *Journal of Democracy* 16 (3): 20–34.
Levitt, Barry S. 2006a. A desultory defense of democracy: The Organization of American States, Resolution 1080 and the Inter-American Democratic Charter. *Latin American Politics and Society* 48 (3): 93–124.
———. 2006b. Promise and peril: Assessing the Inter-American Democratic Charter. Paper presented to the XXVI International Congress of the Latin American Studies Association. San Juan, Puerto Rico, March 15–18.

Lindsay, Reed. 2005. Civilians caught in deadly cross fire in Haiti: As U.N. peacekeepers take on gangs, human rights groups question death toll. *San Francisco Chronicle*, May 16. www.sfgate.com/cgibin/article.cgi?f=/c/a/2005/05/16/MNGGVCPO3N1.TL.

Linz, Juan, and Alfred Stepan. 1996. *Problems of democratic transition and consolidation.* Baltimore: Johns Hopkins Univ. Press.

Lowenthal, Abraham F., ed. 1991. *Exporting democracy: The United States and Latin America.* Baltimore: Johns Hopkins Univ. Press.

Lucero, José Antonio. 2001. Crisis and contention in Ecuador. *Journal of Democracy* 12 (2): 59–73.

Lutz, Ellen L., and Kathryn Sikkink. 2001. The international dimension of democratization and human rights in Latin America. In *Democracy in Latin America: (Re)Constructing political society,* ed. Manuel Antonio Garretón M. and Edward Newman, 278–300. Tokyo: United Nations Univ. Press.

Lynch, Colum. 2005. UN peacekeeping more assertive, creating risk for civilians. *Washington Post,* August 15.

Macpherson, C. B. 1977. *The life and times of liberal democracy.* Oxford: Oxford Univ. Press.

Maguire, Robert, Edwige Balutansky, Jacques Fomerand, Larry Minear, William G. O'Neill, Thomas G. Weiss, and Sarah Zaidi. 1996. *Haiti held hostage: International responses to the quest for nationhood, 1986–1996.* Providence, RI: Thomas J. Watson Jr. Institute for International Studies, Brown Univ.

Mainwaring, Scott. 2006. The crisis of representation in the Andes. *Journal of Democracy* 17 (3): 13–27.

Mainwaring, Scott, Daniel Brinks, and Aníbal Pérez-Liñán. 2001. Classifying political regimes in Latin America, 1945–1999. *Studies in Comparative International Development* 36 (1): 37–65.

Mann, Howard. 2001. *Private rights, public problems: A guide to NAFTA's controversial chapter on investor rights.* Winnipeg, MB: International Institute for Sustainable Development/World Wildlife Fund.

Marquis, Christopher. 2002. Bush officials met with Venezuelans who ousted leader. *New York Times,* April 16.

———. 2004. Aristide flees after a shove from the U.S. *New York Times,* March 1.

Marshall, Monty G., and Keith Jaggers. 2002. Polity IV Dataset. [Computer file; version p4v2002]. College Park: Center for International Development and Conflict Management, Univ. of Maryland.

Martin, Brendan. 2000. *New leaf or fig leaf? The challenge of the New Washington Consensus.* London: Bretton Woods Project/Public Services International.

McClintock, Cynthia. 2001. The OAS in Peru: Room for improvement. *Journal of Democracy* 12 (4): 137–40.

McClintock, Cynthia, and Fabian Vallas. 2003. *The United States and Peru: Cooperation at a cost.* New York: Routledge.

McConnell, Shelley. 2001. Ecuador's centrifugal politics. *Current History* 110 (643): 73–79.

McCoy, Jennifer L. 1998. Monitoring and mediating elections during Latin American democratization. In *Electoral observation and democratic transitions in Latin America,* ed. K. J. Middlebrook, 53–90. La Jolla, CA: Center for US-Mexican Studies, Univ. of California, San Diego.

——. 1999. Chávez and the end of "partyarchy" in Venezuela. *Journal of Democracy* 10 (3): 64–77.

——. 2001. Comments on the Inter-American Democratic Charter. *Summits of the Americas Bulletin* 1 (1): 3–4.

——. 2005a. The referendum in Venezuela: One act in an unfinished drama. *Journal of Democracy* 16 (1): 109–23.

——. 2005b. The vulnerabilities of democracy and the Inter-American Democratic Charter. *FOCAL Point* 4 (3): 7–9. www.focal.ca/pdf/focalpoint_march05.pdf.

——. 2006. International response to democratic crisis in the Americas: 1990–2005. *Democratization* 13 (5): 756–75.

McCoy, Jennifer, and David J. Myers, eds. 2004. *The unraveling of representative democracy in Venezuela.* Baltimore: Johns Hopkins Univ. Press.

McGowan, Lisa. 1997. *Democracy undermined, economic justice denied: Structural adjustment and the aid juggernaut in Haiti.* Washington, DC: Development GAP.

McKenna, Peter. 1995. *Canada and the OAS: From dilettante to full partner.* Ottawa: Carleton Univ. Press.

McKenna, Peter, and John M. Kirk. 2002. Canadian-Cuban relations: Is the honeymoon over? *Canadian Foreign Policy* 9 (3): 49–64.

Mearsheimer, John J. 1994–95. The false promise of international institutions. *International Security* 19 (3): 5–49.

Médecins Sans Frontières. 2005. Data exclusivity and access to medicines in Guatemala. Briefing document, Campaign for Access to Essential Medicines, February 15. www.doctorswithoutborders.org/news/2005/access_guatemala_briefingdoc.pdf.

Merrill, Tim. 1994. *Nicaragua: A country study.* 3rd ed. Washington, DC: Federal Research Division of the Library of Congress. http://lcweb2.loc.gov/cgi-bin/query/r?frd/cstdy:ffeld(DOCID+ni0011).

Miami Herald. 2005a. Bush touts trade, but U.S. bid to empower OAS stalls. June 7.

——. 2005b. Erosion of democracy a challenge for OAS. Editorial, May 8.

Middlebrook, Kevin J., ed. 1998. *Electoral observation and democratic transitions in Latin America.* La Jolla, CA: Center for U.S.-Mexican Studies, Univ. of California, San Diego.

Miles, Melinda. 2001. Elections 2000: Participatory democracy in Haiti. Executive summary. Haiti Reborn. www.quixote.org/hr/election-2000/.

Ministério das Relações Exteriores do Brasil. 1990. Golpe no Suriname: Nota a Imprensa 27 Dez 1990. *Resenha de Política Exterior do Brasil* 16 (67): 91.

Mintz, Sidney W. 1995. Can Haiti change? *Foreign Affairs* 74 (1): 73–87.

MINUGUA. 1995. *La problemática de la tierra en Guatemala.* Guatemala: Unidad de Análisis y Documentación, MINUGUA.

Montgomery, Tommie Sue. 1998. International missions, observing elections and the democratic transition in El Salvador. In *Electoral observation and democratic transitions in Latin America*, ed. Kevin J. Middlebrook, 115–40. La Jolla, CA: Center for U.S.-Mexican Studies, Univ. of California, San Diego.

Moravcsik, Andrew. 2000. The origins of human rights regimes: Democratic delegation in postwar Europe. *International Organization* 54 (2): 217–52.

Mozingo, Joe. 2006a. Préval's return to the ballot shakes Haitian establishment. *Miami Herald,* January 31.

——. 2006b. Preval's victory eases week of tension. *Miami Herald,* February 16.

Munck, Gerardo L., and Jay Verkuilen. 2002. Conceptualizing and measuring democracy: Evaluating alternative indices. *Comparative Political Studies* 35 (1): 5–34.

Muñoz, Heraldo. 1990. The rise and decline of the inter-American system: A Latin American view. In *Alternative to intervention: A new U.S.-Latin American security relationship,* ed. R. J. Bloomfield and G. F. Treverton, 27–37. Boulder, CO: Lynne Rienner.

———. 1993. The OAS and democratic governance. *Journal of Democracy* 4 (3): 29–38.

———. 1996. Collective action for democracy in the Americas. In *Latin American nations in world politics,* ed. Heraldo Muñoz and Joseph S. Tulchin, 17–34. Boulder, CO: Westview.

———. 1998. The right to democracy in the Americas. Trans. Mary D'Leon. *Journal of Interamerican Studies and World Affairs* 40 (1): 1–18.

NDI and IRI. 1989. *The May 7, 1989 Panamanian elections: International delegation report.* Washington, DC: National Democratic Institute for International Affairs/ National Republication Institute for International Affairs.

New York Times. 2005a. Latin states shun US plan to watch over democracy. June 9.

———. 2005b. US proposal in the OAS draws fire as an attack on Venezuela. May 22.

North, Liisa L., and Alan B. Simmons, eds. 1999. *Journeys of fear: Refugee return and national transformation in Guatemala.* Montreal, QC, and Kingston, ON: McGill-Queen's Univ. Press.

Nye, Joseph. 1990. Soft power. *Foreign Policy* 80 (Fall): 153–71.

OAS. 1948. *Charter of the Organization of American States.* N.p.

———. 1965. *Documents of the council of the Organization of American States on the draft convention on the Effective Exercise of Representative Democracy.* Doc. 8, March 1. Second special Inter-American Conference, Rio de Janeiro.

———. 1969. *Convención Americana sobre Derechos Humanos "Pacto de San José."* San José, Costa Rica, November 7–22.

———. 1985. *Protocol of amendment to the charter of the Organization of American States "Protocol of Cartagena de Indias."* Office of International Law. Washington, DC: OAS. www.oas.org/juridico/english/treaties/a-50.htm.

———. 1990. *Unit for the Promotion of Democracy.* AG/RES. 1063 (XX-0/90). June 8.

———. 1991. *Representative democracy* (Santiago Accords). AG/RES. 1080 (XXI-O/91). June 5. Santiago, Chile. www.oas.org/juridico/english/agres1080.htm.

———. 1992a. Actas y Documentos. OEA/Ser.P/XVI-E. December 14.

———. 1992b. Comisión General, Acta de la Cuarta Sesión. AG/CG/ACTA 169/92. May 20.

———. 1992c. *Report of the Special Committee on Amendments to the Charter.* OEA/Ser.P, AG/doc.6 (XVI-E/92) and addenda. November 23.

———. 1992d. Washington Protocol. December 14.

———. 1997. *Charter of the Organization of American States.* Signed in Bogotá in 1948 and amended by the Protocol of Buenos Aires in 1967, by the Protocol of Cartagena de Indias in 1985, by the Protocol of Washington in 1992, and by the Protocol of Managua in 1993. Washington, DC: General Secretariat of the Organization of American States.

———. 1999. *Antecedentes sobre la participación de la sociedad civil en la OEA.* OEA/ Ser.G/CP/CSC-3/99/26.

———. 2000a. Electoral Observation Mission in Haiti: Chief of Mission Report to the OAS Permanent Council. July 13.

——. 2000b. *Manual para la organización de misiones de observación electoral.* Washington, DC: OAS.

——. 2000c. *Mission of the chair of the General Assembly and the OAS Secretary General to Peru.* AG/RES. 1753 (XXX-0/00).

——. 2001a. Comentarios y propuestas de los estados miembros al Proyecto de Carta Democrática Interamericana: Canadá. OEA/Ser.G, GT/CDI-2/01 add.1(1). July 17.

——. 2001b. *Inter-American Democratic Charter.* OEA/Ser.D/XX SG/UPD/III. September 11. Lima, Peru. www.oas.org/OASpage/eng/Documents/Democratic_ Charter.htm.

——. 2002a. *Declaración de principios por la paz y la democracia en Venezuela.* September 13, 2002. Washington, DC: Organization of American States. www.oas.org/ library/mant_press/press_release.asp?sCodigo=VEN.

——. 2002b. OAS Secretary General calls on Venezuelans to defend democracy. News release E027/02, February 8. oas.org/OASpage/press2002/en/Press2002/february 2002/027020802.htm.

——. 2002c. Secretario General de la OEA informa sobre Declaración de Principios por la Paz en Venezuela. News release C-203/02, October 16. www.oas.org/library/ mant_press/press_release.asp?sCodigo=C-203/02.

——. 2002d. *Síntesis operativa de la Mesa de Negociación y Acuerdos.* November 7. Caracas: Organization of American States. www.oas.org/OASpage/eng/Venezuela 2002_Negocia.htm.

——. 2002e. *The situation in Haiti.* CP/RES 806 (1303/02). January 16.

——. 2002f. *Situation in Venezuela.* OEA/Ser.G CP/RES 811 (1315/02). April 13.

——. 2002g. Statement of the OAS Secretary General on the situation in Venezuela. News release E-078–02, April 11. www.oas.org/OASpage/press2002/en/Press2002/ april2002/078—041102.htm.

——. 2002h. *Support for democracy in Venezuela.* OEA/Ser.P AG/RES. 1 (XXIX-E/02). April 18.

——. 2002i. *Support for strengthening democracy in Haiti.* CP/RES. 822 (1331/02). September 4.

——. 2003a. *Agreement between the government of the Bolivarian Republic of Venezuela and the political and social groups supporting it, and the Coordinadora Democrática and the political and civil society organizations supporting it.* May 23. Caracas: Organization of American States.

——. 2003b. Group of Friends to support Secretary General in his facilitation efforts in Venezuela. News release, January 16. www.oas.org/OASpage/eng/Venezuela/ News_01602.htm.

——. 2003c. Group of Friends of the OAS Secretary General for Venezuela. News release, E-020/03, January 31. www.oas.org/library/mant_press/press_release.asp ?sCodigo=E-020/03.

——. 2003d. *Support for strengthening democracy in Haiti.* AG/RES. 1959 (XXXIII O/03). June 10.

——. 2004a. Electoral Observation Missions. www.upd.oas.org/lab/special/eom.html.

——. 2004b. Report on OAS activities involving Haiti from November 11, 2003, to March 10, 2004.

——. 2005a. Declaration of Florida: Delivering the benefits of democracy. AG/DEC. 41 (XXXV-O/05). Adopted at the fourth plenary session, held on June 7.

———. 2005b. Declaration of Florida: Delivering the benefits of democracy. US draft proposal. OEA/Ser.P AG/doc.4476/05. June 1. www.oas.org.

———. 2005c. OAS Electoral Missions, 1962–1989. www.upd.oas.org/lab/special/eoms 62_89.html.

———. 2005d. OEA/Ser.G CP/Res. 880 (1478/05). April 22.

———. 2005e. OEA/Ser.G CP/Res. 883 (1484/05). May 20.

———. 2005f. Opening of the Organization of American States General Assembly. June 6. www.oas.org/speeches/speech.asp?sCodigo=05–0113.

———. 2005g. Organization of American States Permanent Council sessions, April 20, 21, 22. Video recordings. Videos on Demand. www.oas.org/main/main.asp?sLang =E&sLink=http://www.oas.org/OASpage/videosondemand/home_eng/videos.asp.

———. 2005h. Organization of American States Permanent Council sessions, May 11. Video recordings. Videos on Demand. www.oas.org/main/main.asp?sLang=E&s Link=http://www.oas.org/OASpage/videosondemand/home_eng/videos.asp.

———. 2005i. Remarks by Secretary of State Condoleezza Rice. June 5. www.oas.org/ speech/speech.asp?sCodigo=05–0110.

———. 2006a. OAS Electoral Observation Missions (list). Secretariat for Political Affairs. www.sap.oas.org/opd/electoral/default.htm.

———. 2006b. OAS signs agreement with Supreme Electoral Tribunal of Ecuador. News release C-022/06, February 10. www.oas.org/OASpage/press_release.asp?sCodigo =C-02206.

———. 2006c. Informe verbal del jefe de la misión de observación electoral en Vene-zuela—elecciones presidenciales celebradas el 3 de diciembre 2006. Speech, Decem-ber 16. Washington, DC.

———. 2007. OAS Secretary General expresses concern over decision not to renew broad-casting license of Venezuelan television station. Press release E-001/07, January 5. Washington, DC.

O'Brien, Robert, Anne Marie Goetz, Jan Aart Scholte, and Marc Williams. 2000. *Con-testing global governance: Multilateral economic institutions and global social move-ments.* Cambridge: Cambridge Univ. Press.

O'Donnell, Guillermo. 1994. Delegative democracy. *Journal of Democracy* 5 (1): 55–69.

———. 1996. Illusions about consolidation. *Journal of Democracy* 7 (2): 34–51.

———. 2004. Human development, human rights, and democracy. In *The quality of democracy: Theory and applications,* ed. Guillermo O'Donnell, Jorge Vargas Cullell, and Osvaldo Iazzetta, 9–92. Notre Dame, IN: Univ. of Notre Dame Press.

O'Donnell, Guillermo, Jorge Vargas Cullell, and Osvaldo Iazzetta, eds. 2004. *The qual-ity of democracy: Theory and applications.* Notre Dame, IN: Univ. of Notre Dame Press.

O'Donnell, Guillermo, and Philippe C. Schmitter. 1986. *Tentative conclusions about uncertain democracies.* Vol. 4 of *Transitions from authoritarian rule.* Baltimore: Johns Hopkins Univ. Press.

O'Donnell, Guillermo, Philippe C. Schmitter, and Laurence Whitehead, eds. 1986. *Transitions from authoritarian rule.* 4 vols. Baltimore: Johns Hopkins Univ. Press.

Office of Summit Follow-Up. 2002. Official documents from the Summits of the Amer-icas process from Miami to Québec City. Washington, DC: OAS.

Olesen, Thomas. 2005. *International Zapatismo: The construction of solidarity in the age of globalization.* London: Zed Books.

O'Neill, Daniel P. 2004. When to intervene: The Haitian dilemma. *SAIS Review* 24 (2): 163–74.

Oppenheimer, Andrés. 2005. U.S. proposal: Great idea, bad strategy. *Miami Herald*, June 6.

Ottaway, Marina. 2003. *Democracy challenged: The rise of semi-authoritarianism.* Washington, DC: Carnegie Endowment for International Peace.

Ottaway, Marina, and Teresa Chung. 1999. Toward a new paradigm. *Journal of Democracy* 10 (4): 99–133.

Oxfam America. 2005. Oxfam condemns US pressure on Guatemala: USTR pushes for law limiting public health protection. News release, February 2. http://tula.ca/health/Oxfam%20Condemns%20US%20Pressure% 20on%20Guatemala.pd.

Oxhorn, Philip, and Graciela Ducatenzeiler. 1998. *What kind of democracy? What kind of market? Latin America in the age of neoliberalism.* University Park: Pennsylvania State Univ. Press.

Palma Murga, Gustavo. 1997. Promised the earth: Agrarian reform in the socio-economic agreement. In *Negotiating rights: The Guatemalan peace process.* Accord: An International Review of Peace Initiatives, no. 2. London: Conciliation Resources.

Panitch, Leo. 1994. Globalisation and the state. *Socialist Register* 30: 60–93.

Parish, Randall, Jr., and Mark Peceny. 2002. Kantian liberalism and the collective defense of democracy in Latin America. *Journal of Peace Research* 39 (2): 229–50.

———. 2006. Venezuela and the collective defense of democracy regime in the Americas. Paper presented at the XXVI International Congress of the Latin American Studies Association, San Juan, Puerto Rico, March 15–18.

Pastor, Robert A. 1987. The Reagan administration and Latin America: Eagle insurgent. In *Eagle resurgent? The Reagan era in American foreign policy,* ed. K. A. Oye, R. J. Lieber, and D. Rothchild. Boston: Little, Brown.

———. 1990. Nicaragua's choice: The making of a free election. *Journal of Democracy* 1 (3): 13–25.

———. 1999. The third dimension of accountability: The international community in national elections. In *The self-restraining state: Power and accountability in new democracies,* ed. A. Schedler, L. Diamond, and M. Plattner, 123–42. Boulder, CO: Lynne Rienner.

———. 2002. *Not condemned to repetition: The United States and Nicaragua.* 2nd ed. Boulder, CO: Westview.

———. 2003. A community of democracies in the Americas: Instilling substance into a wondrous phrase. *Canadian Foreign Policy* 10 (3): 15–29.

Peck, Taylor. 1977. Latin America enters the world scene, 1900–1930. In *Latin American diplomatic history: An introduction,* ed. H. E. Davis, J. J. Finan, and F. T. Peck, 146–90. Baton Rouge: Louisiana State Univ. Press.

Peeler, John A. 2004. *Building democracy in Latin America.* Boulder, CO: Lynne Rienner.

Perina, Rubén. 2006. Informe verbal preliminar: Misión de observación electoral de la Secretaría General de la OEA. Elecciones parlamentarias del 4 de diciembre de 2005 en la República Bolivariana de Venezuela. Presented to the Permanent Council of the OAS, February 1. Washington, DC.

Pessôa de Lima Câmara. 1998. *Em nome da democracia: A OEA e a crise Haitiana, 1991–1995.* Brasília: Instituto Rio Branco/FUNAG/Centro de Estudos Estratégicos.

Peters, Guy B. 1989. *The politics of bureaucracy: A comparative perspective.* White Plains, NY: Longman.

Pevehouse, Jon C. 2002a. Democracy from the outside-in? International organizations and democratization. *International Organization* 56 (3): 515–49.

———. 2002b. With a little help from my friends? Regional organizations and the consolidation of democracy. *American Journal of Political Science* 46 (3): 611–26.

———. 2005. *Democracy from above: Regional organizations and democratization.* Cambridge: Cambridge Univ. Press.

Philpott, Daniel. 2001. *Revolutions in sovereignty: How ideas shaped modern international relations.* Princeton, NJ: Princeton Univ. Press.

Pollard, Duke E. 2003. *The CARICOM system: Basic instruments.* Kingston, Jamaica: Caribbean Law Publishing Company.

Posada-Carbó, Eduardo, ed. 1996. *Elections before democracy: The history of elections in Europe and Latin America.* Institute of Latin American Studies Series. London: Macmillan Press.

Prensa Latina. 2006. Jailbird seeks Ecuador presidency again. March 3. www.plenglish.com/.

Prevost, Gary. 2002. Cuba. In *Politics of Latin America: The power game,* ed. H. Vanden and G. Prevost, 325–56. New York: Oxford Univ. Press.

Pridham, Geoffrey, ed. 1991. *Encouraging democracy: The international context of regime transition in Southern Europe.* New York: St. Martin's.

Przeworski, Adam. 1992. The neoliberal fallacy. *Journal of Democracy* 3 (3): 45–59.

Przeworski, Adam, Michael Alvarez, José Antonio Cheibub, and Fernando Limongi. 1996. What makes democracies endure? *Journal of Democracy* 7 (1): 39–55.

Przeworski, Adam, and Fernando Limongi. 1997. Modernization: Theories and facts. *World Politics* 49 (2): 155–83.

Ramdin, Albert. 2004. CARICOM in Action. Speech delivered at the Inter-American Dialogue, Washington, DC, May 5.

Randall, Stephen J. 2002. In search of a hemispheric role: Canada and the Americas. In *A fading power,* ed. Norman Hillmer and Maureen Appel Molot, 235–55. Canada among nations. Don Mills, ON: Oxford Univ. Press.

Reding, Andrew. 1996. Exorcising Haiti's ghosts. *World Policy Journal* 13 (1): 15–26.

Reis, Fernando Guimarães. 1991. Suriname: Missão brasileira para a retomada da cooperação bilateral: Memorandum para o Sr. Secretário-General de Política Exterior. Secretaria de Estado das Relações Exteriores, Brasil. October 14.

Reisman, Michael. 1990. Sovereignty and human rights in contemporary international law. *American Journal of International Law* 84 (4): 866–76.

Remmer, Karen. 1996. External pressures and domestic constraints: The lessons of the four case studies. In *Beyond sovereignty: Collectively defending democracy in the Americas,* ed. Tom Farer, 286–93. Baltimore: Johns Hopkins Univ. Press.

Reus-Smit, Christian. 1997. The constitutional structure of international society and the nature of fundamental institutions. *International Organization* 51(4): 555–89.

———. 2001. Human rights and the social construction of sovereignty. *Review of International Studies* 27: 519–38.

Rio Group. 2002. *Declaración del Grupo de Rio sobre la situación en Venezuela.* April 12. San José, Costa Rica.

Risse, Thomas. 2002. Transnational actors and world politics. In *Handbook of international relations,* ed. Walter Carlsnaes, Thomas Risse, and Beth A. Simmons, 254–74. London: Sage.

Risse, Thomas, and Kathryn Sikkink. 1999. The socialization of international human rights norms into domestic practices: Introduction. In *The Power of Human Rights: International norms and domestic change,* ed. Thomas Risse, Stephen C. Ropp, and Kathryn Sikkink, 1–38. Cambridge: Cambridge University Press.

Risse-Kappen, Thomas, ed. 1995. *Bringing transnational relations back in: Non-state actors, domestic structures, and international institutions.* Cambridge: Cambridge Univ. Press.

Roberts, Kenneth. 2000. Populism and democracy in Latin America. Paper presented at the conference "Challenges to Democracy in the Americas," the Carter Center, Atlanta, October.

Robinson, William I. 1992. *A Faustian bargain: U.S. intervention in the Nicaraguan elections and American foreign policy in the post–cold war era.* Cambridge: Cambridge Univ. Press.

——. 1996. *Promoting polyarchy: Globalization, US intervention and hegemony.* Cambridge: Cambridge Univ. Press.

——. 2001. Neoliberalism, the global elite, and the Guatemalan transition: A critical macrosocial analysis. In *Globalization on the ground: Postbellum Guatemalan democracy and development,* ed. Christopher Chase-Dunn, Susanne Jonas, and Nelson Amaro, 189–205. Lanham, MD: Rowman & Littlefield.

Rochlin, James. 1994. *Discovering the Americas: The evolution of Canadian foreign policy towards Latin America.* Vancouver: UBC Univ. Press.

Roth, Brad. 1999. *Governmental illegitimacy in international law.* Oxford: Clarendon.

Rueschemeyer, Dietrich. 2004. Addressing inequality. *Journal of Democracy* 15 (4): 76–90.

Rueschemeyer, Dietrich, Evelyne Huber Stephens, and John D. Stephens. 1992. *Capitalist development and democracy.* Chicago: Univ. of Chicago Press.

Russell, Asia, and Brook K. Baker. 2005. Response to USTR fact sheet on CAFTA and access to medicines. Myths and realities: US pressure on Guatemala regarding data exclusivity, CAFTA and access to medicines. Health Gap Report, February 10. http://tula.ca/health/021005_HGAP_BP_CAFTA_guatemala.pdf.

Sader, Emir. 2004. What is Brazil doing in Haiti? ZNet, July 6. www.zmag.org/content/showarticle.cfm?ItemID=5838.

Salvesen, Hilde. 2002. *Guatemala: Five years after the peace accords; The challenges of implementing peace.* Oslo: International Peace Research Institute, Norwegian Ministry of Foreign Affairs.

Samuels, Kirsti. 2005. Sustainability and peace building: A key challenge. *Development in Practice* 15 (6): 728–36.

San Francisco Chronicle. 1999. Latin America shoots down U.S. proposal. June 18.

Santa-Cruz, Arturo. 2004. Redefining sovereignty, consolidating a network: Monitoring the 1990 Nicaraguan elections. *Revista de Ciencia Política* 24 (1): 189–208.

——. 2005. Constitutional structures, sovereignty, and the emergence of norms: The case of international election monitoring. *International Organization* 59 (Summer): 663–93.

Santiso, Carlos. 2003. The Gordian knot of Brazilian foreign policy: Promoting democracy while respecting sovereignty. *Cambridge Review of International Affairs* 16 (2): 343–58.

Saraiva, José Flávio S. 2005. O Brasil e o Conselho de Segurança das Nações Unidas. *Colunas de Relnet,* no. 11, month 1–6.

Schedler, Andreas. 2002. Elections without democracy: The menu of manipulation. *Journal of Democracy* 13 (2): 36–50.

———, ed. 2006. *Electoral authoritarianism: The dynamics of unfree competition.* Boulder, CO: Lynne Rienner.

Scheman, L. Ronald. 2003. *Greater America.* New York: New York Univ. Press.

Schemo, Diana Jean. 1997. Ecuador's crisis over presidency ends peacefully. *New York Times,* February 10.

Schlesinger, Stephen, and Stephen Kinzer. 1999. Bitter fruit: The untold story of the American coup in Guatemala. In *Neighborly adversaries,* ed. Michael LaRosa and Frank O. Mora, 145–55. Boulder, CO: Rowman & Littlefield.

Schmitter, Philippe C. 2001. The influence of the international context upon the choice of national institutions and policies in neo-democracies. In *The international dimensions of democratization: Europe and the Americas,* ed. Laurence Whitehead, 26–54. Oxford: Oxford Univ. Press.

Schmitter, Philippe C., and Terry Lynn Karl. 1996. What democracy is . . . and is not. In *The global resurgence of democracy,* ed. Larry Diamond and Marc F. Plattner, 49–62. Baltimore: Johns Hopkins Univ. Press.

Schmitz, Gerald J. 2004. The role of international democracy promotion in Canada's foreign policy. *IRPP Policy Matters* 5 (10): 1–52.

Schmitz, Hans Peter. 2004. Domestic and transnational perspectives on democratization. *International Studies Review* 6 (3): 403–26.

Schoultz, Lars. 2002. Evolving concepts of intervention: Promoting democracy. In *The globalization of US-Latin American relations,* ed. Virginia M. Bouvier, 27–46. Westport, CT: Praeger.

Selverston, Melina. 1997. The unraveling of a presidency. *NACLA Report on the Americas* 30 (6): 11.

Shamsie, Yasmine. 2000. Un compromiso con la sociedad civil: Lecciones de la OEA, el ALCA, y las Cumbres de las Américas, 1–26. Ottawa: North-South Institute.

———. 2001. The politics of building democracy: Efforts by the Organization of American States to promote democracy in Haiti, 1990–1998. Toronto: York Univ.

———. 2004. Building "low intensity" democracy in Haiti: The OAS contribution. *Third World Quarterly* 25 (6): 1097–1115.

———. 2005. How the Organization of American States tackled impunity in Haiti. *Journal of Haitian Studies* 10 (1): 165–80.

Shaw, Carolyn M. 2003. Limits to hegemonic influence in the Organization of American States. *Latin American Politics and Society* 45 (3): 59–92.

———. 2004. *Cooperation, conflict and consensus in the Organization of American States.* New York: Palgrave Macmillan.

Shifter, Michael. 2002a. Democracy in Venezuela, unsettling as ever. *Washington Post,* April 21.

———. 2002b. The United States, the Organization of American States, and the origins of the inter-American system. In *The globalization of US-Latin American relations,* ed. Virginia M. Bouvier, 85–104. Westport, CT: Praeger.

——. 2003. Breakdown in the Andes. *Foreign Affairs* 83 (5): 126–38.

——. 2004. Looking away as a democracy dies. *Los Angeles Times,* December 28.

Shifter, Michael, and Vinay Jawahar. 2006. The divided states of the Americas. *Current History* 105 (688): 51–57.

Shivji, Issa. 1990. The pitfalls in the debate on democracy. *CODESRIA Bulletin* 1 (12): 17–29.

Sikkink, Kathryn. 1997. Reconceptualizing sovereignty in the Americas: Historical precursors and current practices. *Houston Journal of International Law* 19 (3): 705–29.

Simpson, Jeffrey. 2004a. Desperately seeking ideas for governing. *Globe and Mail,* March 10.

——. 2004b. Foreign Policy: One down, one to go. *Globe and Mail,* May 14.

Singh, Rickey. 2004. CARICOM to release consensus statement on Haiti. *Jamaica Observer* (Kingston), November 11.

Sletten, Pal, and Egset Willy. 2004. *Poverty in Haiti.* Oslo: Fafo (Institute for Applied Social Science).

Slevin, Peter. 2002. Chávez provoked his removal, U.S. officials say. *Washington Post,* April 13.

Smith, Peter H. 2000. *Talons of the eagle: Dynamics of US-Latin American relations.* 2nd ed. New York: Oxford Univ. Press.

——. 2005. *Democracy in Latin America: Political change in comparative perspective.* Oxford: Oxford Univ. Press.

Smith, Peter H., and Melissa Zeigler. 2006. Liberal and illiberal democracy in Latin America. Paper presented at the International Congress of the Latin American Studies Association, San Juan, Puerto Rico, March 15–18.

Smith, Steve. 2000. US democracy promotion: Critical questions. In *American democracy promotion: Impulses, strategies and issues,* ed. M. Cox, G. J. Ikenberry, and T. Inoguchi, 63–82. Oxford: Oxford Univ. Press.

Smith, Tony. 1994. *America's mission: The United States and the worldwide struggle for democracy in the twentieth century.* Princeton, NJ: Princeton Univ. Press.

Soudriette, Richard. 1988. *Report of the 1988 Paraguayan general elections.* Washington, DC: IFES.

Spence, Jack, David R. Dye, and George Vickers. 1994. *El Salvador: Elections of the century.* Cambridge, MA, and San Salvador, El Salvador: Hemispheric Initiatives.

Stepan, Alfred, ed. 1989. *Democratizing Brazil: Problems of transition and consolidation.* Oxford: Oxford Univ. Press.

Stevenson, Brian J. R. 2000. *Canada, Latin America, and the new internationalism.* Montreal, QC, and Kingston, ON: McGill-Queen's Univ. Press.

Steves, Franklin. 2001. Regional integration and democratic consolidation in the Southern Cone of Latin America. *Democratization* 8 (3): 75–100.

Stoelting, David. 1992. The challenge of UN-monitored elections in independent nations. *Stanford Journal of International Law* 28: 371–424.

Sundstrom, Lisa McIntosh. 2005. Hard choices, good causes: Exploring options for Canada's overseas democracy assistance. *IRPP Policy Matters* 6 (4): 1–40.

Tarrow, Sidney. 2001. Transnational politics: Contention and institutions in international politics. *Annual Review of Political Science* 4: 1–20.

——. 2005. *The new transnational activism.* Cambridge: Cambridge Univ. Press.

Tesón, Fernando. 1996. Changing perceptions of domestic jurisdiction and intervention. In *Beyond sovereignty: Collectively defending democracy in the Americas,* ed. Tom J. Farer, 29–51. Baltimore: Johns Hopkins Univ. Press.

Thede, Nancy. 2005. Human rights and democracy: Issues for Canadian policy in democracy promotion. *IRPP Policy Matters* 6 (3): 1–40.

Thérien, Jean-Philippe et al. 2004. Le Canada et les Amériques: La difficile construction d'une identité régionale. *Canadian Foreign Policy* 11 (3): 17–37.

Thompson, Ginger, and Amy Bracken. 2006. Deal reached to name victor in Haiti's vote. *New York Times,* February 16.

Trouillot, Michel-Rolph. 1990. *Haiti: State against nation.* New York: Monthly Review.

——. 1994. Haiti's nightmare and the lessons of history. In Haiti: Dangerous crossroads. *NACLA Report on the Americas* 27 (4): 121–32.

UNDP. 2004. *Democracy in Latin America: Towards a citizens' democracy.* New York: United Nations Development Programme. Also available in Spanish as *La Democracia en América Latina: Hacia una democracia de ciudadanas y cuidadanos.*

——. 2005a. *Human Development Report.* http://hdr.undp.org/statistics/data/country _fact_sheets/cty_fs_HTI.html.

——. 2005b. Supreme Court of Justice of Ecuador reinstated with support of UNDP and the international community. News release, November 29. http://content.undp .org/ go/newsroom/undp-ecuador29112005.en?categoryID=349435&lang=en.

UNICEF. 2005. *Excluded and invisible: The state of the world's children, 2006.* New York: UNICEF.

United Nations. 1993. Security Council Resolution 867 (1993). September 23.

U.S. Department of State. 2005a. Background note: Guatemala. Bureau of Western Hemispheric Affairs. www.state.gov/r/pa/ei/bgn/2045.htm.

——. 2005b. Ecuador's Supreme Court of Justice. News release, November 30. Washington, DC.

Valenzuela, Arturo. 1997. Paraguay: The coup that didn't happen. *Journal of Democracy* 8 (1): 45–55.

——. 2002. Bush's betrayal of democracy. *Washington Post,* April 16.

——. 2004. Latin American presidencies interrupted. *Journal of Democracy* 15 (4): 5–19.

Valero, Jorge. 2005. Democracia, cultura y civilizaciones. Speech delivered in Washington, DC, May 3. www.venezuela-oas.org.

Valor Econômico (São Paolo). 2005. Brasil tenta intermediary solução para o Equador. April 22.

Van Harten, Gus. 2000. *Guatemala's peace accords in a Free Trade Area of the Americas.* Toronto: Centre for Research on Latin America and the Caribbean (CERLAC), York Univ.

Vilas, Carlos M. 1997. Participation, inequality, and the whereabouts of democracy. In *The new politics of inequality in Latin America: Rethinking participation and representation,* ed. D. Chalmers, C. M. Vilas, K. Hite, and S. Martin, 3–42. Oxford: Oxford Univ. Press.

Walsh, Catherine E. 2001. The Ecuadorian political irruption: Uprising, coups, rebellions, and democracy. *Nepantla: Views from South* 2 (1): 173–205.

Warren, Cristina. 2003. Canada's policy of constructive engagement with Cuba: Past, present, and future. Background briefing, from the FOCAL Research Forum on Cuba. Ottawa: FOCAL. www.cubasource.org/pdf/cuba_canada.pdf.

Weber, Cynthia. 1992. Writing sovereign identities: Wilson administration intervention in the Mexican Revolution. *Alternatives* 17: 313–37.

Wendt, Alexander. 1999. *Social theory of international politics.* Cambridge: Cambridge University Press.

Whitaker, Arthur P. 1954. *The Western Hemisphere idea: Its rise and decline.* Ithaca NY: Cornell Univ. Press.

Whitehead, Laurence. 1996. Three international dimensions of democratization. In *The international dimensions of democratization: Europe and the Americas,* ed. Laurence Whitehead, 3–25. Oxford: Oxford Univ. Press.

———. 2004. Democratization with the benefit of hindsight: The changing international components. In *The UN role in promoting democracy: Between ideals and reality,* ed. E. Newman and R. Rich, 135–66. Tokyo: United Nations Univ. Press.

Wilson, Larman C. 1989. The OAS and promoting democracy and resolving disputes: Reactivation in the 1990s? *Revista Interamericana de Bibliografía* 39 (4): 477–99.

Wilson, Larman C., and David W. Dent. 1995. The United States and the OAS. In *U.S.-Latin American policymaking: A reference handbook,* ed. D. W. Dent, 24–44. Westport, CT: Greenwood.

Wimmer, Andreas, and Nina Glick Schiller. 2002. Methodological nationalism and beyond: Nation-state building, migration, and the social sciences. *Global Networks* 2 (4): 301–34.

Wood, Bryce. 1999. The making of the Good Neighbor policy. In *Neighborly adversaries,* ed. Michael LaRosa and Frank O. Mora, 105–12. Boulder, CO: Rowman & Littlefield.

World Bank. 2002. World development indicators. Washington, DC: World Bank.

———. 2004. World Bank list of economies. July. www.worldbank.org/data/databytopic/CLASS.XLS.

———. 2006. *Haiti: Options and opportunities for inclusive growth.* Country Economic Memorandum. Washington, DC: World Bank.

Wucker, Michele. 2004. Haiti: So many missteps. *World Policy Journal* 21 (1): 41–49.

Young, Oran. 1999. *Governance in world affairs.* Ithaca: Cornell University Press.

Zacharia, Janine. 2005. Venezuela, Brazil rebuff U.S. on monitoring democracy. Bloomberg.com, June 6, www.bloomberg.com/apps/news?pid=10000103&sid=aTv.lb_B5ws8.

Zakaria, Fareed. 2003. *The future of freedom: Illiberal democracy at home and abroad.* New York: Norton.

Contributors

Dexter S. Boniface is an assistant professor in the Department of Political Science at Rollins College, where he teaches courses in comparative politics and international relations, with a specialization in Latin American politics. He received his Ph.D. in political science from the University of Illinois at Urbana-Champaign. His research interests include the political economy of contemporary Brazil and democracy promotion efforts in Latin America. His published work appears in journals such as *Comparative Politics, Global Governance,* and *Latin American Politics and Society.*

Sean Burges holds a Ph.D. from the University of Warwick and has taught at the University of Wales at Aberystwyth, Carleton University, and the University of Ottawa. He has also held a Canadian Social Science and Humanities Research Council Postdoctoral Fellowship at the Norman Paterson School of International Affairs at Carleton University in Ottawa and was the 2006–7 Cadieux-Léger Fellow in the Government of Canada's Department of Foreign Affairs and International Trade. He has published in the *Cambridge Review of International Affairs,* the *Bulletin of Latin American Research, International Journal,* and *Canadian Foreign Policy.*

Jean Daudelin is an associate professor at the Norman Paterson School of International Affairs, where he teaches on development and conflict. He is primarily a Latin Americanist with expertise on Nicaragua and Brazil. His current research touches on Brazilian and Canadian trade and security policies; on tenure regimes, property rights, and resource conflicts; and on humanitarian intervention. He is the guest editor of a forthcoming special issue on Brazil of the *Canadian Journal of Latin American and Caribbean Studies* and, in addition to various book chapters, he has published in *International Peacekeeping, Third World Quarterly,* the *Journal of Church and State, International Journal,* and the *Canadian Journal of Development Studies.*

David M. Goldberg is an assistant professor of political science at College of DuPage in Glen Ellyn, Illinois. He has held positions at Beloit College and Northern Illinois University. His research interests include democracy promotion efforts by international organizations and their theoretical implications. His current work focuses on the role of CARICOM in Haiti. He received his Ph.D. in political science from Northern Illinois University in May 2003.

Darren Hawkins is an associate professor of political science at Brigham Young University, where he is also director of the international relations program. His research focuses on international norms and institutions that promote democracy and human rights. He has published *International Human Rights and Authoritarian Rule in Chile* with the University of Nebraska Press (2002) and articles in the *Journal of Politics, International Studies Quarterly, Global Governance, Comparative Politics,* and *Political Science Quarterly,* among others. A coedited volume, *Delegation and Agency in International Organizations* was recently published by Cambridge University Press (2006).

Sharon F. Lean is an assistant professor in the Political Science Department at Wayne State University. She received her Ph.D. in political science from the University of California, Irvine, and her Masters in social science from the Latin American Faculty of Social Science (FLACSO) in Mexico City. Her work has been published in *Democratization, Latin American Politics and Society* and the Mexican journal *Sociedad Civil.* Since 1996 she has monitored numerous Latin American elections with groups including the Carter Center, the National Democratic Institute for International Affairs, and the Mexican civic association Alianza Cívica.

Thomas Legler is a professor of international relations at the Universidad Iberoamericana in Mexico City. Previously he taught at Mount Allison University, the University of Victoria, and the University of Toronto. A specialist on Latin American politics and development, he holds a doctorate in political science from York University. Dr. Legler has an ongoing research interest in the international promotion and defense of democracy in the Americas, for which he has received major funding from the Social Sciences and Humanities Research Council of Canada. He is the coauthor with Andrew F. Cooper of *Intervention without Intervening? The OAS Defense and Promotion of Democracy in the Americas* (Palgrave Macmillan, 2006). His publications have appeared in *Global Governance, Journal of Democracy, Latin American Politics and Society, Canadian Foreign Policy,* and *Hemisphere.* Dr. Legler has observed elections in the Dominican Republic, Mexico, Nicaragua, Peru, and Venezuela, including missions for the Carter Center and the OAS.

Barry S. Levitt recently joined the faculty of Florida International University as an assistant professor of political science. He previously held appointments at Reed College and Emory University. Dr. Levitt's research to date has focused on political parties and presidentialism, public trust in institutions, the management and observation of elections, and democracy promotion in the inter-American system. He has published articles in the *Latin American Research Review* and *Latin American Politics and Society* and is currently completing a book manuscript entitled *Echo Chamber: Presidents, Parties, and Legislative Institutions in Peru and Beyond, 1985–2006.*

Flavie Major is a policy analyst at the Department of Foreign Affairs and International Trade in Canada and a Ph.D. candidate in political science at Université Laval in Québec City. Her research interests include the design of the Inter-American Democratic Charter, the role of multilateral organizations in the collective defense of democracy in the Americas and Canada's foreign policy in the region. She previously obtained a B.A. in political science and Spanish from the University of Ottawa (1999) and an M.A. in political science from the University of British Columbia (2000). She is an inaugural member of the Action Canada Fellowship (2003–4).

Jennifer L. McCoy is a professor of political science at Georgia State University, and director of the Americas Program at the Carter Center in Atlanta. Specializing in international and comparative politics, Dr. McCoy's research focuses on democratization in Latin America, the role of international actors in mediating processes of democratization, and elections. Dr. McCoy is editor of and contributor to *The Unraveling of Representative Democracy in Venezuela* (Johns Hopkins University Press, 2004) and *Political Learning and Redemocratization in Latin America: Do Political Leaders Learn from Political Crises?* (North-South Center/Lynne Rienner Press, 2000), and has authored articles in such journals as *World Politics, International Politics, Latin American Research Review,* and *Journal of Democracy.* She was the Carter Center's representative to the International Tripartite Working Group on Venezuela (OAS, UNDP, Carter Center), working to promote dialogue and reconciliation in that country. She has directed the center's election observer projects to Venezuela, Nicaragua, Panama, Mexico, Peru, and Jamaica.

Arturo Santa-Cruz is an associate professor at the Department of Pacific Studies, Universidad de Guadalajara. He received his Ph.D. from the Government Department, Cornell University. He has published in specialized journals including *International Organization* and the *Journal of Latin American Studies*. He is the author of *International Election Monitoring, Sovereignty, and the Western Hemisphere Idea: The Emergence of an International Norm* (Routledge, 2005), *Un debate teórico empíricamente ilustrado: La construcción de la soberanía japonesa, 1853–1902* (University of Guadalajara Press, 2000), editor of *What's in a Name? Globalization, Regionalization, and APEC* (University of Guadalajara Press, 2003), and coeditor of *Globalization, Regionalization, and Domestic Trajectories in the Pacific Rim: The Economic Impact* (University of Guadalajara and University of Technology–Sydney Presses, 2004).

Yasmine Shamsie is an assistant professor in the Department of Political Science at Wilfrid Laurier University where she teaches Latin American politics and international relations. She specializes in the political economy of democracy promotion and civil society engagement in the inter-American system. Her research has focused on the OAS's peace-building efforts in Haiti and its conflict prevention work in Guatemala. She is a Fellow at the Centre for Research on Latin America and the Caribbean (CERLAC) at York University. She has published in *Third World Quarterly* and is the coeditor of a forthcoming volume entitled *Whose Canada? Continental Integration, Fortress North America, and the Corporate Agenda* (McGill-Queen's University Press, 2007).

Carolyn M. Shaw is currently an associate professor at Wichita State University. Her research interests include human rights, peace-keeping, and international organizations. She has published in *Latin American Politics and Society, International Studies Perspectives,* the *International Journal on World Peace,* the *Journal of Human Rights,* and *Africa Quarterly.* Her book *Cooperation, Conflict and Consensus in the Organization of American States* was published with Palgrave Macmillan in 2004.

Index